CONRAD KAIN

CONRAD KAIN

Letters from a Wandering Mountain Guide, 1906–1933

Edited with an Introduction by ZAC ROBINSON

Translated by MARIA AND JOHN KOCH

THE UNIVERSITY OF ALBERTA PRESS

Published by

The University of Alberta Press
Ring House 2
Edmonton, Alberta, Canada T6G 2E1
www.uap.ualberta.ca

Introduction and annotations copyright © 2014,
Zac Robinson.

LIBRARY AND ARCHIVES CANADA
CATALOGUING IN PUBLICATION

Kain, Conrad, 1883–1934
[Correspondence. Selections. English]
    Conrad Kain : letters from a wandering
mountain guide, 1906–1933 / edited with an
introduction by Zac Robinson ; translated by
Maria and John Koch.

(Mountain cairns)
Includes bibliographical references and index.
Issued in print and electronic formats.
Letters translated from the German.
ISBN 978-1-77212-004-2 (pbk.).—
ISBN 978-1-77212-016-5 (epub).—
ISBN 978-1-77212-017-2 (Amazon kindle).—
ISBN 978-1-77212-018-9 (pdf)

    1. Kain, Conrad, 1883–1934—Correspondence.
2. Mountaineering guides (Persons)—Rocky
Mountains, Canadian (B.C. and Alta.)—
Correspondence. 3. Mountaineers—Rocky
Mountains, Canadian (B.C. and Alta.)—
Correspondence. 4. Mountaineering—Rocky
Mountains, Canadian (B.C. and Alta.). I. Koch,
W. John, translator II. Koch, Maria, translator
III. Robinson, Zac, 1975–, editor IV. Title.
V. Title: Correspondence. Selections. English
VI. Series: Mountain cairns

GV199.92.K34A3 2014   796.522092   C2014-905576-5
                                   C2014-905577-3

Index available in print and PDF editions.

First edition, first printing, 2014.
Printed and bound in Canada by Houghton
Boston Printers, Saskatoon, Saskatchewan.
Copyediting and proofreading by
Brendan Wild.
Maps by Wendy Johnson.
Indexing by Judy Dunlop.

The University of Alberta Press is committed
to protecting our natural environment. As part
of our efforts, this book is printed on Enviro
Paper: it contains 100% post-consumer recy-
cled fibres and is acid- and chlorine-free.

The University of Alberta Press gratefully
acknowledges the support received for its
publishing program from The Canada Council
for the Arts. The University of Alberta Press
also gratefully acknowledges the financial
support of the Government of Canada
through the Canada Book Fund (CBF) and the
Government of Alberta through the Alberta
Media Fund (AMF) for its publishing activities.

This book has been published with the help
of a grant from the Canadian Federation for
the Humanities and Social Sciences, through
the Awards to Scholarly Publications Program,
using funds provided by the Social Sciences
and Humanities Research Council of Canada.

For the campfire, and the carefree life

...

and for Elizabeth, who still writes letters

CONTENTS

FOREWORD

Conrad Kain, Guide and Mountaineer

CHIC SCOTT

Conrad Kain was one of the world's greatest guides in the early decades of the twentieth century, and one of its greatest mountaineers. Unlike those of his contemporaries, Kain's exploits ranged across the globe, from the European Alps to the Rocky and Purcell Mountains of Canada, and on to the Southern Alps of New Zealand. He was a master of rock and a master of ice. Despite his short stature, he was of prodigious strength. He loved to build cairns and linger on summits. He was also a master storyteller.

Kain's climbing achievements in Canada are fairly well known to the climbing community, but most people do not realize that he was already a star when he came to Canada in 1909. Kain began his guiding career in 1904. Although he had almost no instruction in the mountain arts, within a year he was leading clients on some of Europe's most challenging climbs. In 1905, for example, he twice led the Delago Tower, one of the breathtakingly spectacular Vajolet Towers in the Dolomites. The following year, in the Mont Blanc Range, high above Chamonix, France, he led the Aiguille du Grépon, twice. First climbed in 1881, the Grépon had a reputation as the hardest climb in the world at that time. In Switzerland, he twice led ascents of the Matterhorn, still a very notable climb in those days; the complex and difficult Weisshorn; and the ice-covered Lyskamm. In 1907, in the Dolomites, he led the spectacular Guglia di Brenta, an impressive spire that sticks up like a pencil from the surrounding meadows and screes. Kain was only the seventh guide to lead the climb. "To this day," he wrote, "I have never done another bit so exposed." Finally, in the Dauphiné region of France, Kain led the complex and difficult traverse of Le Meije on several occasions, the Barre des Écrins, and the Pelvoux. It must be remembered that he guided these routes being unable to speak the local language and without the benefit of the detailed guidebooks that we take for granted today. Ropes were made of hemp, there was very little in the way of climbing hardware to protect one's progress, and the dulfersitz rappel technique, which allowed climbers to slide back down the rope with relative ease, had not yet been developed. And, of course, always behind him were demanding clients who expected to be led without hesitation to their summits.

Kain was such a good guide, and so charming, that he had troubles with the local guides wherever he went. Kain made them look second rate. In the Dolomites, he got into a fight with them; in Chamonix, the French guides chased him back to his hotel room threatening to beat him. In Canada, the Swiss guides felt threatened and challenged his credentials. In New Zealand, local guides had him imprisoned during the First World War, ostensibly because he was of Austrian birth and therefore a potential threat to national security, but in actual fact it was because he had showed them up as guides and was damaging their businesses and reputations. On the other hand, some of the best guides in the world—men like Italian Joseph Petigax, Mattias Zurbriggen from Switzerland, Sepp Innerkofler in the Tyrol, Tita Piaz in the Dolomites, and Peter Graham of New Zealand—treated him with courtesy and respect and welcomed him as one of their own.

Kain had a most adventurous spirit and loved to travel. His appetite for foreign lands was whetted on his 1906 excursion to Corsica with Albert Gerngross, and his departure for Canada in 1909 was one of the high points of his life. But his travels of 1912–1913 are the most remarkable. In May of 1912, he left from Banff and took the train to Quebec City, where he caught a boat for England. Dr. Tom Longstaff, one of the most prominent mountaineers of the day, hosted him briefly in London, after which he travelled by train to St. Petersburg. Then, with Ned Hollister from the Smithsonian Institute in Washington, DC, he continued to the furthest reaches of Siberia, where he trapped animals for scientific research. His return trip took him back to St. Petersburg, then to Vienna by train, where he visited long-time friends and family. From there, he travelled via Paris to London, then by boat through the Mediterranean and the Suez Canal to Australia and on to New Zealand, where he spent four months working like a slave in the bush. After all this, he boarded a ship in Wellington that took him to San Francisco via Tahiti, and from there to Vancouver where he boarded a train back to Banff. Not bad for the self-proclaimed "breaker of stones" in the first years of the twentieth century.

But Kain's reputation rests primarily upon his achievements in Canada and, to a lesser extent, New Zealand. His ascents of Mount Robson, Mount Louis, Bugaboo Spire, Howser Spire, and Farnham Tower were all outstanding climbs with complex route finding, difficult rock and ice work, cold bivouacs, and unknown descents. And he made all these ascents with clients. They always had confidence in him, and he always brought them back safely.

In fact, it is worth noting the calibre of Kain's clients. Men and women like Dr. Erich Pistor, director of the Vienna Chamber of Commerce, who was fluent in twelve languages; Albert Gerngross, also a prominent Viennese businessman; and the Malek sisters, who were among Vienna's upper crust. In Canada, he was the right-hand man of A.O. Wheeler (one of the founders of the Alpine Club of Canada (ACC)) on both the Alberta–BC boundary survey and at the ACC camps. His most loyal client in Canada was Albert MacCarthy, a banker and naval captain from Summit, New Jersey, with whom he made most of his great ascents. On the Mount Robson climb, Kain and MacCarthy were joined by W.W. "Billy" Foster, who was deputy minister of public works and a member of the British Columbia legislature. These were all people who expected the very best, and, from Kain, they got it.

His solo ascent of Mount Whitehorn is a bit of an anomaly in his career. But what an anomaly! Climbing alone all day to the remote, yet-unclimbed summit, then descending in rain and storm across a crevassed glacier, his path lit only by the flash of lightning strikes.

In New Zealand, his first ascents are a testament to his skill, as well. But his most notable climb is the traverse of Mount Cook that he led in 1916: "A marvelous feat unequalled for daring in the annals of the Southern Alps." Fifty-nine-year-old Jane Thomson was his client, and he was the lone guide. This traverse had been done before, but there had been two guides—and a much younger client. The crux was the descent, during which one guide would have to cut steps down the mountain and the other would have safeguarded the team from above. But Kain led the way down, confident that his client would not slip. Perhaps it was this particular ascent that so distressed the local guides.

At the ACC's 1924 camp at Mount Robson, Kain led ascents of the mountain four times in only two weeks, bivouacking on three occasions. This is a monumental achievement. Barry Blanchard, who is now Canada's leading mountain guide (and no slouch himself), confided that even at his physical peak he would not have been able to match Kain's effort.

But the key to fully appreciating Conrad Kain is to acknowledge that—despite his great climbing achievements—he was human, with the loneliness and failings that we are all subject to. In these letters to his dearest of friends, Amelie Malek, Kain tells us of his travels and great adventures. More importantly, he reveals his child-like nature, his love of people and of life, his generosity of spirit, his almost inexhaustible love for the natural world, his anger at the injustice of life, and, above all, his terrible loneliness. In these letters we see Conrad Kain the great guide and mountaineer as Conrad Kain the human being.

ACKNOWLEDGEMENTS

Like most books, this one has a long history and has accumulated a XIII
long list of debts.

First, I wish to express my gratitude to Gerhardt Pistor—the son of Kain's long-time friend and client, Erich Pistor ("Dr. P," as he's called in *Where the Clouds Can Go*)—for recognizing the worth of the Kain–Malek correspondence and bequeathing it to the Whyte Museum of the Canadian Rockies. That acquisition got the ball rolling.

I wish to heartily thank my collaborators on this project, Chic Scott and Don Bourdon. I could not have wished to work with two better colleagues. Both have supplied this volume with wonderful essays of their own.

I owe a great debt of gratitude to Maria and John Koch, whose careful translation and transcription was simply splendid. As well, I am grateful to the Eleanor Luxton Historical Foundation, and particularly Peter Poole, for financing the translation project.

Accessing research materials in archives scattered around the world—from Banff, to New Jersey, to Vienna, to Dunedin—required considerable assistance from archivists and librarians, all of whose efforts I greatly appreciated. From the Whyte Museum, I particularly wish to thank Elizabeth Kundert-Cameron, Lena Goon, and Jennifer Rutkair.

For detailed comments, close readings, and other kinds of critical help and advice in the creation of this edition, I wish to thank Steph Abegg, John Allen, Zoe Avner, Ernst Bergmann, Ted Bishop, Renate Buchner, Suzan Chamney, Isabelle Daigneault, Ron Dart, Karen Fox, Bob Harris, Brad Harrison, Ted Hart, Sean Isaac,

Conrad Janzen, Arnor Larson, Ian MacLaren, Hermann Mauthner, Peter Midgley, Pat Morrow, Barb Neraasen, Joseph Patrouch, Liza Piper, Manfred Rotter, Karin Schmid, Stephen Slemon, Anna Thompson, and Brendan Wild.

This book has been published with the help of a grant from the Federation for the Humanities and Social Sciences, through the Awards to Scholarly Publications Program, using funds provided by the Social Sciences and Humanities Research Council of Canada.

MAPS

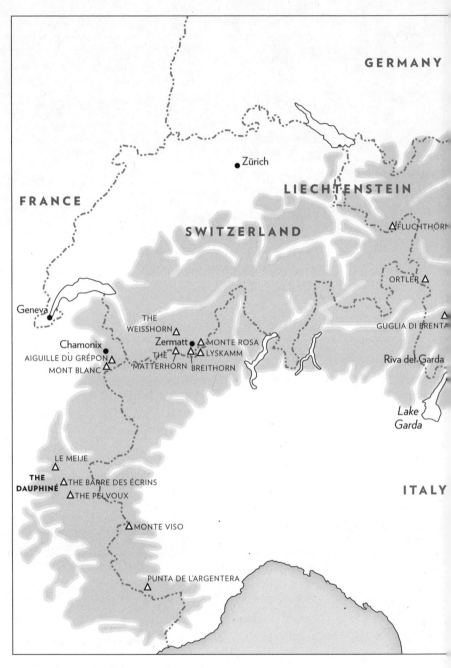

∧ *European Alps, pre–First World War (1914)*

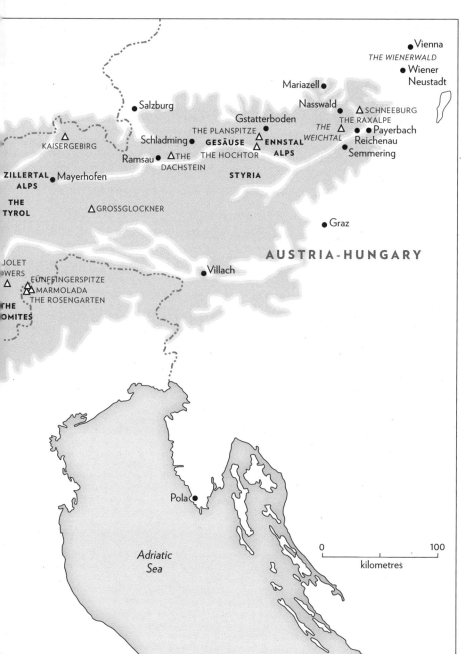

Vienna
THE WIENERWALD
Wiener
Neustadt

Mariazell

Salzburg

Nasswald

Gstatterboden

SCHNEEBURG
THE RAXALPE

THE PLANSPITZE

△ Payerbach

Schladming

GESÄUSE

ENNSTAL

THE
WEICHTAL

Reichenau

KAISERGEBIRG

Ramsau

THE HOCHTOR

ALPS

Semmering

THE
DACHSTEIN

ZILLERTAL
ALPS

Mayerhofen

STYRIA

THE
TYROL

GROSSGLOCKNER

Graz

JOLET
WERS

FÜNFFINGERSPITZE

AUSTRIA-HUNGARY

MARMOLADA
THE ROSENGARTEN

Villach

THE
OMITES

XVII

Pola

Adriatic
Sea

0   100

kilometres

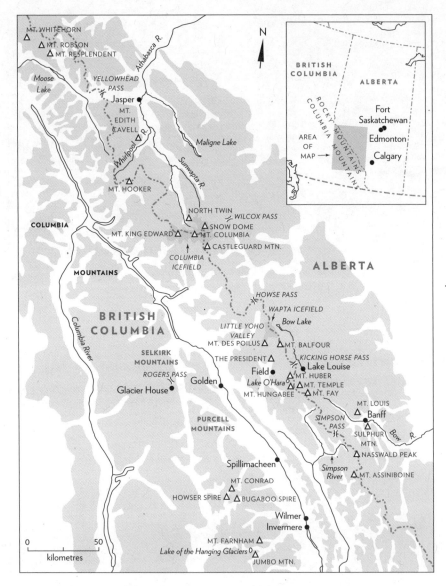

∧ *Rocky and Columbia Mountains of Canada*

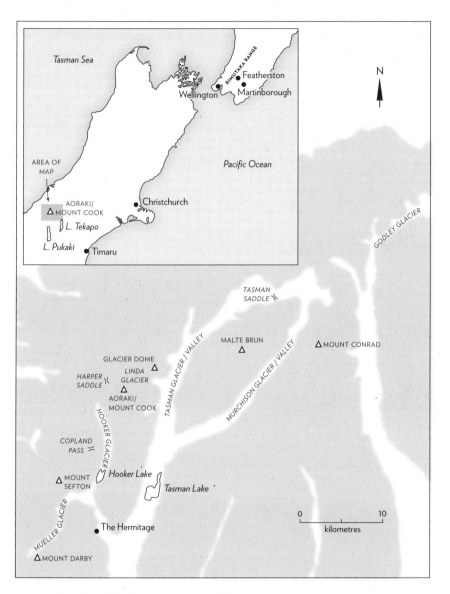

∧ Central Part of the Southern Alps of New Zealand

INTRODUCTION

Letters from the Archive

According to travel writer Ted Bishop, "what governs all archival events is serendipity." Bishop should know. The English professor/ motorcycle vagabond has spent enough time in archives the world over to accept that while we often speak of sound research methods and good detective work, "the real discoveries seem to come from nowhere, to be handed to you, after days or weeks in which (it appears in retrospect) the insight has been perversely denied, as if there were not just curators but some other power controlling the archive."[1] Bishop was referring, of course, to Sheshat (Sesheta, Sefkhet-aabut, and half a dozen other spellings), the ancient Egyptian goddess of writing, libraries, mathematics, and architecture, as well as archives.

In the spring of 2005, Chic Scott and I had both the Goddess and Don Bourdon on our side. Don was the head archivist at the Whyte Museum of the Canadian Rockies in Banff. He's the type of person who, if he calls to say he's acquired "something you'll want to see," the chances are that what he has is good. Really good. We got the call. And we descended upon the archive like junkies to the source—Chic in his old rusty truck, me in my equally decrepit hatchback. Iron oxide couldn't sway our course. Don had a set of letters written by Conrad Kain (1883–1934).

Of course, mountaineers familiar with the Canadian Rockies and Purcells need no introduction to Kain. The Austrian mountain guide was perhaps the singular, most superlative figure of climbing's earliest age in Canada. He was Esther Fraser's "prince of Canadian alpine guides"; Hans Gmoser's "master of the art of mountaineering"; even Canada's distinguished poet and novelist Earle Birney (1904–1995) honoured the "mountain man" in poem.[2] Standing five feet five inches, he had a stocky build with broad shoulders; his moustache and pipe were regular features. In camp and on the trail, he could be charming, harmlessly flirtatious, and an entertaining storyteller. An expert axe man and cook with a great capacity for carrying weight, he was patient with novices and discreet in his treatment of over-zealous climbers disinclined to appreciate natural splendours. His number of first ascents in the Rockies and Purcells exceeded 60. His new routes and other climbs are countless. Many know the roll call by heart: Robson, Louis, Bugaboo Spire....That this guide first arrived in Banff, Alberta, a little over 100 years ago at the age of 25, with nothing to his name save the promise of employment with the Alpine Club of Canada (ACC), makes his accomplishments all the more remarkable.

Chic Scott had noted the significance of these particular letters a decade earlier. In an article titled "Mountain Mysteries," printed in the 2001 *Canadian Alpine Journal* (*CAJ*), the writer and guidebook author, still basking in the warm glow of his *Pushing the Limits: The Story of Canadian Mountaineering* (2000), had set down the ultimate Canadian tick list—the *grand cours*, so to speak—for any alpine historian in this neck of the woods. It was the kind of "to do" list that, were it written in the early 1990s, might have been reverently stuck to the inside of my high school locker. The article is instead tacked on the wall in my office at the University of Alberta. It awaits unsuspecting students in need of a challenge.

High on Chic's list was what he called "perhaps the greatest single treasure in Canadian mountaineering": Kain's missing letters, journals, and diary.[3] We knew J. Monroe Thorington (1894–1989) had them in 1935, when, after the Kain's death, the Philadelphian edited and published Kain's autobiography, *Where the Clouds Can Go*. But the trace ended with him. Thorington died in 1989, at the age of 94, and his notes were sent to Princeton University, his alma mater. What next became of the Kain material remained unclear. No record of it existed at Princeton; the Thorington collection, however rich, was incomplete. Now in duplicate at the Whyte Museum, the collection consisted primarily of literary works, other correspondence and diaries, photographs, maps and scrapbooks, as well as the manuscripts for three books: *A Climber's Guide to the Rocky Mountains of Canada* (1921), the region's first mountaineering guidebook; *The Glittering Mountains of Canada* (1925), in which Thorington laid to rest what little remained of the century-old Brown-Hooker problem; and *Mont Blanc Sideshow* (1934), a biography of Albert Smith (1816–1860), a renowned mountaineer, showman, and founding member of The Alpine Club.

The archives and library of the Whyte Museum is a special place. Custodian of the ACC's rich archival fonds, it was established in 1966 to serve the mountain region bounded by the forty-ninth parallel to the south, the Peace River to the north, the Front Ranges in the east, and the Columbias in the west. The Eleanor Luxton Reference Room itself is nothing grand: long and narrow, it hardly covers 1,000 square feet. Catalogues of Byron Harmon photographs near the front entrance are enough to keep the wandering museum visitors occupied; but it's in the back of the room—windowless but for the giant 1:200,000-scale maps of Banff and Jasper national parks on the walls—where the real work is done. Here, white-gloved researchers quietly chatter to one another about their respective projects. Others sit alone, often bent over old parchment or lantern slides, lost in silent contemplation broken only by busy archivists returning from storage with loaded trolleys of requested material.

We sat and yakked about skiing. The archive was nearly empty. "Here they are," Don said, strolling into the room. "Nearly 300 pages." He set the thick folder on the table before us. I nervously wiped my hands, which turned out to be cold and dry with anticipation, and flipped open the cover:

Nasswald, 8. November 1906.

Sehr geehrtes Fräulein,

Erst nach längerer Zeit kemme ich dazu, Ihnen mitzuteilen, dass ich Ihre Sendung erhalten habe, wefür ich Ihnen meinen besten Dank ausspreche....

"Er, can either of you read German?" I whispered, staring at the yellowed typewritten pages.

The Goddess had left the building.

The correspondence before us consisted of 144 letters written between 1906 and 1933, the span of Kain's adult life, more or less. They were ordered chronologically and addressed to a single correspondent, Amelie Malek (1871–1941). From what little attention Malek received in *Where the Clouds Can Go* (1935), we knew she was an early client and "a friend from Conrad's youthful days in the Alps." Thorington had credited her as having "the wit to preserve the scattered notes and letters which he [Kain] continued to send her."[4] These were those letters.

Kain first guided Malek and her younger sister, Flora (1873–1931), up the Hochtor (2,369 m [7,772 ft.]), the highest mountain in the Ennstal Alps, near Gstatterboden, in the autumn of 1906. Their meeting was noted in Kain's autobiography:

> In the evening the headwaiter in the Hotel Gesäuse told me that there was a party of two ladies requiring guidance in the morning. I introduced myself. I was to be ready at about four o'clock.
>
> On leaving the table where both young ladies were seated with their momma, it occurred to me that I could not have made a good impression upon them with my patched stockings, blue shirt and broad-brimmed hat. We left the hotel about four o'clock in the morning and climbed up the waterfall route, to Hess Hütte and the Hochthor. I discovered at once that the girls had seldom been on a mountain excursion, and they were very happy at the Emesruhe, exclaiming about the view.
>
> One of the women was an excellent botanist. She collected flowers which I had never seen or noticed. We went down to Johnsbach, and back in a carriage to Gstatterboden. Both girls were highly contented with the excursion, and I was as well. For it was the first time in three weeks that I had been on a mountain with good people.[5]

1.

Nasswald,8.November 1906

Sehr geehrtes Fräulein,

Erst nach längerer Zeit komme ich dazu ,Ihnen mitzuteilen,dass ich Ihre Sendung erhalten habe,wofür ich Ihnen meinen besten Dank ausspreche.Es hat mir eine grosse Freude gemacht von Ihnen etwas zu hören.Mitteilen kann ich,dass das Wetter immer schlecht war,was Sie ja selbst wissen.Erst jetzt einige Tage ist es sehr schön.Derzeit machte ich nur 2 Partien,jedesmal den Wiener Neustädter-Steig. Mit einem Fräulein sollte ich im September ins Ennstal fahren um Touren zu machen, aber das schlechte Wetter machte einen Strich durch die Rechnung.Aber jetzt ist die Witterung sehr schön.Es ist wirklich eine Freude,jetzt in die herrliche Got= tesnatur zu schauen: alle Farben sind in den Laubwäldern zu sehen! Ohne schmei= cheln möchte ich Ihnen vergönnen,einige Tage in die schöne Natur zu schauen,in den Bergen,da ich bemerkte,dass Sie eine wirkliche Freundin der Berge und der Na= tur sind.- In Wien war ich auch seit der Zeit,bei Herrn Gerngross wegen der Rei= sebeschreibung von Korsika.Es hat mich aber etwas beleidigt,dass der Herr einiges Interessantes gestrichen hat,und das war von dem alten Herrn Pfarrer,von dem ich Ihnen erzählt habe,(wie ich mich erinnern kann): wo die Schweine in die Wohnung des Pfarrers eindrangen.(Weil sie hoffentlich auch neugierig waren auf die Ausländer, die ihrem Herrn einen Besuch machten !!).Als ich den Herrn G.fragte,warum er das gestrichen hat,gab er mir nur Antwort,indem er ein Jude ist,kann er dies nicht alles niederdchreiben.-- Falls Sie vielleicht einmal nach Reichenau kommen und eine leichte Raxpartie machen wollen,so bitte ich mir es mitzuteilen,denn es würd mir eine grosse Freude machen,wieder einmal eine gemütliche Tour zu machen. Sie wissen ja,wie meine"gewöhnlichen Partien sind,und dass sie oft das "Gemütliche" überschreiten!Sollte ich einmal nach Wien kommen,werde ich einen Besuch machen, wenn ich die Ehre habe. Meiner Mutter habe ich den Brief vorgelesen,den ich erhal= ten habe.Die Mutter hatte die gleiche Freude wie ich,da Sie mir alles Gute wün= schen.Von Lechner habe ich auch einen Brief erhalten,wo er mir mitteilt,dass sie alle glücklich in ihrer Zillertaler Heimat angekommen sind.Auch von mehreren Tou= risten habe ich Briefe erhalten,dass sie von ihren Hochtouren zurück sind. Und jeder,schrieben sie mir,ist mit Unlust in die Grosstadt Wien eingezogen.Aber es muss sein!Mit dem besten Dank und herzlichen Grüssen an Sie und Ihre Angehörigen

∧ Amelie Malek transcribed Kain's original letters at Thorington's request in 1935. Her typewritten transcription of the letters is all that remains. See Don Bourdon's epilogue in this volume for further commentary on Malek's transcription. Photo by Zac Robinson.

[WMCR, M160/7759]

∧ *Flora (left) and Amelie Malek, unknown date.* [Courtesy of Manfred Rotter]

Kain never forgot "the ladies from Gstatterboden." And, a year later, again in the Ennstal Alps, he was overjoyed when, from across the dining room of the Hotel Gesäuse, Amelie Malek recognized him and called out, "Why, there's Mr. Kain." A week later, they together climbed the Planspitze via the Petern route.[6]

A dear, lifelong friendship through correspondence ensued. The very differences in social class that brought them together—Kain a guide, Malek a tourist—likely precluded much of a relationship beyond friendship in the morally rigid climate of pre-war Europe. He nevertheless mailed her flower petals from the different ranges he visited throughout his travels. He signed off in English as "your friend in the western woods," "the wanderer," "your Conrad." Her replies remain lost. As readers, we had a one-sided conversation that stretched over 27 years.

What would the letters uncover? Surely Thorington would have carefully finessed any revelations into Kain's autobiography? We chuckled at the futility of our situation while slowly flipping through pages and pages of correspondence in a language we couldn't read. And then, little by little, passages in English appeared.

∧ *Conrad Kain and Amelie Malek on the summit of the Hochtor, the highest mountain in the Ennstal Alps, near Gstatterboden, 1906. [Princeton University Library, J. Monroe Thorington Collection, WC005]*

"Ahh, look," Chic said. "She's teaching him how to write."

Writing in broken English from his birthplace of Nasswald in 1909, just months before making his initial voyage to Canada aboard the *Empress of Britain*, Kain expressed his "great anguish for the slip of the pen in English" and begged Malek to point out and "korrekt" the pratfalls in his prose. Kain's English was limited to what he had picked up as a young man leading venturesome tourists on outings in the mountains southwest of Vienna. His father's death in a mining accident in 1892 left his mother, Franziska Kain (1866–1944), alone with four young children. Conrad, the eldest, could scarcely write his name when he left school at the age of 14. He took employment as a goatherd on the nearby slopes of the Raxalpe. Later, with only sporadic guiding work, he laboured as a quarryman, a livelihood he supplemented by poaching game. He purchased a writing pad with his first paycheque.[7]

What began as a desire to better his writing became a lifelong tutorial through correspondence. Malek carefully commented upon, corrected, and edited Kain's words—those English passages scattered throughout his letters to her, but also his diary, still lost, and the articles he later wrote for magazines and alpine journals, many of which Thorington used as chapters in *Where the Clouds Can Go* (1935). "It is very hard for me that I have nobody who helps me like you with your letters," Kain wrote to Malek in 1909. Later, in 1933, now writing solely in English, he told her, "Remember that, whatever I do, it will be little in comparison to what you have done for me."

Letters and archives are a means to directly access history, as much as that's possible. They bring history closer because they're not an interpretation or an intellectualization of past events, but the *actual stuff* of past events. We sat in silence reading what fragments we could. Mount Robson. The Great War. The Depression. The writing was raw, at times clumsy, but always exhibiting a genius for description and an all-abiding passion for Nature. Other passages were unbearably personal, tragic, and not meant for us.

We quietly sat with the letters for no more than a few hours that afternoon, but in the interval we had been blasted back to the early decades of the twentieth century, back to the romantic days of the pack train, when Banff was just a fledgling town within Rocky Mountains Park. The archive's closing time jolted us to the present. With a century still roaring through my ears, we called it a day and walked out into the brilliant sunshine.

Δ This edition presents the Kain–Malek correspondence in its entirety. Kain's letters are ordered chronologically and annotated to provide context. The sections in English remain, nearly word-for-word, exactly as Kain wrote them, while those in German have

been carefully translated and transcribed by Maria and John Koch
of Edmonton. Belonging to a later generation of European immigrants to western Canada, Maria and John share much in common
with Kain. Both grew up in mining areas of Germany: Maria in the
Ore Mountains of Saxony, and John in the coal-mining district of
Lower Silesia, only a stone's throw, in fact, from the town where
another influential immigrant to the Rockies, Martin Nordegg (1868–
1970), was born. Having taught German at the University of Alberta
for nearly two decades, Maria, now retired, was well positioned for
the task of translation—she immediately recognized Kain's regional
dialect and strived to retain the flavour of both his language and
style. As the project progressed, a warm affinity for the Austrian grew.
"You have an incredibly remarkable fellow here," John excitedly wrote
in a 2009 email. "He did so much. He was just so full of life!" Kain
was as endearing in his correspondence as he was purportedly in life.
And, not surprisingly, the letters revealed a richly detailed, first-hand
account of that very remarkable life.

Hundreds of thousands of immigrants came to western Canada
from around the world in the late nineteenth and early twentieth
centuries. The unprecedented influx was sparked, in part, by a
changing global economy and deteriorating working conditions
throughout Europe and Asia. Changing realities within Canada, too,
played a role. The completion of the Canadian Pacific Railway, the
invention of a more resilient wheat variety on the prairies, an "open
door" immigration policy, and, of course, the hyperbolic outpouring
of press agentry selling the "Last Best West"—these all served to
entice those seeking new opportunities in Canada. Perhaps even
more effective in populating the West were immigrants themselves,
who, through their letters home, convinced family and friends to
join them.

Writing letters was incredibly important to the immigrant experience in Canada. It was often the only link that connected families
across the Atlantic. For Kain, they were the physical connection that
allowed him to share his adult life and experiences with those at
home, the vessel by which to send flowers to Malek or money to his

mother. Today, these important documents provide us with a unique and personal view of what it meant to immigrate to Canada in the early part of the twentieth century.

But it's too easy to read this correspondence as simply "immigrant letters." The designation is too rigid, too narrow. Kain didn't leave Austria with the intention to permanently settle anywhere. He extolled his Canadian citizenship—granted to him in 1912—mostly for the increased mobility it afforded him abroad. Siberia. The South Pacific. New Zealand. Even near the end of his life, he bore no great desire to remain in the Columbia Valley, where he and his dear wife, Hetta Ferrara (1884–1933), bought land and a small farm in 1920.[8] As far back as Kain could remember, his "chief ambition was to travel." As a boy, despite the constraints of unremitting poverty, he never missed an opportunity to speak with tourists who passed through the alpine valleys near his home. "I would ask a great many questions," Kain wrote. "Where he came from, where he intended going, what the place was like where he stopped last, and so forth. I never forgot to tell them that I meant to be a tramp myself when I became a man." Mountain guiding became Kain's ticket to mobility, to the "open road," the so-called "carefree life," a romantic wanderlust that was always tempered by a deep melancholy and longing for *home*— Nasswald, the Rax, his Zikafahnler Alm.

Not inconsequentially, the tourists Kain so often sought to emulate also (though in different sorts of ways) shared the urge to narrate, to depict, to memorize, and communicate. The phenomena of tourist narratives over the past two centuries include a wide range of creative expression that in most other situations would be quite unthinkable. Here's an arena where the nonauthors and nonartists don't hesitate to try their hand at producing a travel diary, a watercolour, perhaps, or a photo narrative. Thus, the line between tourist amateurs and professionals of the trade—travel writers, poets, landscape painters, and photographers—often blurs. "Travels, to be good for anything, must be literary" was the opening editorial statement of the new *American Magazine of Travel* in 1859.[9] And publishing houses of the period plied a voracious reading public with *Diaries*, *Gleanings*,

Glimpses, *Impressions*, *Narratives*, *Notes*, *Rambles*, *Sketches*, *Travels*, and *Wanderings*. Travel books and guides formed a vast literature, a genre that deeply impressed Kain.

Victorian mountaineers—a specialized type of tourists—were further impelled to write by the institutional structure of their sport. Interest in geology, glaciology, botany, and cartography motivated much of the early exploration of the European Alps. Enshrining these scientific traditions, The Alpine Club in London—the forerunner to hundreds more like it—thus constituted itself in 1857 in the image of a learned society. Its well-heeled members read peer-reviewed papers about their deeds at club meetings, and these were subsequently printed in its journal, not inconsequentially subtitled "a record of mountain exploration and scientific observation." Even the ACC constituted itself, nearly 50 years later, with a claim of science in the first instance.[10] And the inaugural volume of the Canadian club's journal heralded the call for both book donations and a library.[11] Publications mattered. They established a mountaineer's claim to a particular ascent; for just as priority was a matter of prime concern and debate in science, so it was in mountaineering.

The printed word served another necessary function. In the sciences, a shared ethos was elaborated and maintained through journals. The same could be said about early mountaineering, which, unlike most sports, had neither a centralized body to formulate the "rules of the game" nor a system of refereeing to enforce them. Mountaineering was characterized by a series of complex, tacit rules (climbers now call them "ethics") that were recognized, sustained, and debated in an emerging literary genre of journals, guidebooks, and monographs. Of course, not all Victorian mountaineers were scientists, nor were they all writers. But the fact that alpine club culture emerged at precisely the same time that mountaineering-as-sport evolved from an older tradition of mountain-exploration-as-science is, well, noteworthy. The subsequent spread of club culture around the globe and the development of mountaineering practices thus gave rise to an immense body of literature. Mountain climbing today remains perhaps "the most literary of all sports."[12] It's the one sport that's most likely to have its own section in bookstores. Mountaineers talk about their favourite climbing books with almost as much enthusiasm as they talk about their favourite climbing routes, and mountain book festivals have become an annual highlight on many climbers' social calendar. And why not? The sport has been predicated upon the printed word since the mid-1800s.

As with most travel writers, there was a unified class dimension underlying the urge to narrate mountaineering exploits. The leisure classes—especially the trend-setting groups of academics, writers, and artists—were the trade's top achievers with few exceptions. Consider, for example, the first individuals to produce monographs concerning the Canadian Rockies. A.P. Coleman (1852–1939) and J. Norman Collie (1859–1942) were both academic scientists; the former was a geologist from the University of Toronto with an aptitude for photography and landscape painting, the latter a renowned British chemist. Another Englishman, Sir James Outram (1864–1925)—a Cambridge-educated clergyman—inherited familial distinction from his grandfather, an English general who fought in the Indian Rebellion of 1857 and was considered a British hero. Likewise, Americans Mary T.S. Schäffer (1861–1939) and Walter D. Wilcox (1869–1949) were also born into wealth and privilege.[13] Beyond their writings, Schäffer and Wilcox were both celebrated for their photography. Schäffer, in fact, hand painted many of her now-famous lantern slides.[14] My point, here, is that it was almost exclusively the representations of the urban middle (and upper) classes that became *the* experience of the Rockies to the exclusion of others. Their sketches, travelogues, and guidebooks captured and filled out much of the landscape, whereas those groups that didn't feel the need to record or elaborate their experiences (or lacked the possibility) were muted in the process.

Where the Clouds Can Go (1935) was thus a unique and important publication. It widened the view of Canada's western mountains, which, until the 1930s, remained narrowly constrained—figuratively, anyway—as a landscape of leisure and fantasy, not of productive labour. Beyond the confines of North America, the experiences of Swiss guides Mattias Zurbriggen (1856–1917) and Christian Klucker (1853–1928) were well known, but their autobiographies were similarly atypical of the genre.[15] Only Kain's remains in print. Its fourth edition was recently issued in 2009. Not bad for the self-disparaged "unlettered fellow," who so dreamed of being a writer.[16]

The Kain–Malek correspondence takes us beyond *Where the Clouds Can Go* (1935). Gone is Thorington's kind and careful editorial hand. The few passages he reprinted for Kain's autobiography, here, are indeed much rougher. But we can forgive the Philadelphian for discarding that which he perhaps felt was too personal, maybe too political or provoking, even defamatory. Well-intentioned, his goal was commemorative, celebratory—and he published hardly a year after his friend's death. Today, the passage of time grants us certain liberties—an "objective" distance, so to speak—that would not have been so easily afforded some 80 years ago. Of course, whatever conclusions we draw from these letters today are equally and unavoidably subject to *our* own place and times, our own history and memory. It's uncomfortable to read Kain's anti-Semitic remarks, or his early impression of Aboriginal peoples as "savage." We meet a Kain who sometimes, in contrast to his rosy depiction in *Where the Clouds Can Go, was* deeply bitter, who *was* afraid.[17] We're left to wonder about Kain's wife, Hetta, whom he married in 1917. What was her impression of Kain's close relationship with a wealthy, single woman from his home country?

Whatever conclusions we draw from these letters must also take into account their intended audience: Amelie Malek. These are letters written to someone whom Kain was deeply enamoured with, someone with all the privileges and biases of an affluent society into which he could never ascend. A love for travel and mountains (as well as books on the subject) was the bond they shared. It enabled and sustained their remarkable friendship. But it's only here, as a romantic surrogate to wilderness, that Kain was ostensibly welcomed. In this context, Malek's own haunting words from

1908—"We are far apart but our thoughts often cross in the beautiful alpine world"—perhaps carry a much deeper meaning beyond just geographic distance.[18]

Few traces remain of this extraordinary woman's life. Her wealth was inherited from her father, Franz Carl Malek (1842–1909), who, ironically, was a Viennese paper manufacturer specializing in letter envelopes. She died at the age of 69, in 1941, and was buried in Reichenau, a popular alpine resort town in Lower Austria not far from Nasswald.[19] She never married, nor did she have children. The Maleks' "summer villa" in Reichenau, where Amelie lived out her last years, stands to this day. It's a veritable castle in contrast to anything she would have found in the Columbia Valley during the Great Depression had she ever accepted Kain's repeated invitations to visit.

Δ In its entirety, the Kain–Malek correspondence places on view not only the romantic "carefree life" that so many popular representations of Kain reproduce and cherish, but also the complex life of a person who has suffered, loved, and worked, and who consequently deserves to be remembered as accurately as possible. His letters were a medium that made valid and valuable his life and his multifaceted role as a mountain guide, a labourer, a friend, a tourist and traveller, an immigrant—a writer. They are a small but important piece in a more open and inclusive understanding of the past. Conrad Kain deserves nothing less.

Four months after his last letter to Malek in August 1933, Kain became ill. It had been a particularly hard year. Hetta had passed away in the winter. Life on the farm was lonely. And so it must have been with muted joy that he was able to lead some long-time clients and friends across the Wapta Icefield, just north of Lake Louise, that summer. His fiftieth birthday was spent climbing Mount Louis (for a third time) near Banff. He reconnected with old friends at the ACC's Paradise Valley Camp. A final trip to his cherished Purcells was made in the fall. Fittingly, his last climb was a long first ascent of the

>Λ *Mount Conrad, Purcell Mountains of British Columbia. Photo by Steph Abegg, May 2012.*
> *Constructed during the summer of 1908, Amelie Malek's summer villa in Reichenau stands to this day. Photo by Zac Robinson, December 2009.*

highest summit in the Bobby Burns group. It now bears the name
Mount Conrad (3,279 m [10,758 ft.]).[20]

Kain died of encephalitis lethargica—now a rare degenerative
disease—in the Cranbrook Hospital on 2 February 1934. Despite his
final wishes to be buried beside his dear Hetta, who was interred in
the Roman Catholic section of the Cranbrook Cemetery, Conrad's
final resting place was over 100 metres away, separated by a fence, in
the "commoners" section. There, a lovely block of granite is marked
with the epitaph "A Guide of Great Spirit."

Introduction

1. Ted Bishop, *Riding with Rilke: Reflections on Motorcycles and Books* (Toronto: Penguin, 2005), 111.

2. Esther Fraser, *The Canadian Rockies: Early Travels and Explorations* (Edmonton: Hurtig, 1969),
   201; Hans Gmoser, "Foreword to the 1979 Edition," in *Where the Clouds Can Go*, ed. J. Monroe
   Thorington, 4th ed. (1935; Vancouver: Rocky Mountain Books, 2009), xx; Earle Birney, "Conrad
   Kain," *The Canadian Alpine Journal* (hereafter CAJ) 34 (1951): 100.

3. Chic Scott, "Mountain Mysteries," CAJ 84 (2001): 101.

4. Kain, *Where the Clouds*, xxiv.

5. Kain, *Where the Clouds*, 126.

6. Kain, *Where the Clouds*, 152–55.

7. Kain, *Where the Clouds*, xxi.

8. Kain was not well known throughout the Columbia Valley. Local newspapers, for example, regularly mistook his nationality for Swiss or Hungarian; a posting from 1922 incorrectly referred to him
   as a CPR Guide and an invitee on the second British Mount Everest Expedition. I am grateful to the
   chair of the Conrad Kain Centennial Society, Pat Morrow, for this information.

9. Quoted in Stanford E. Demars, *The Tourist in Yosemite, 1855–1985* (Salt Lake City: University of
   Utah Press, 1991), 14.

10. Writing in the 1907 CAJ, ACC co-founder Elizabeth Parker (1856–1944) set down "the objects of
    the Club" as "(1) the promotion of the scientific study and the exploration of Canadian alpine and
    glacier regions; (2) the cultivation of Art in relation to mountain scenery; (3) the education of
    Canadians to an appreciation of their mountain heritage; (4) the encouragement of the mountain
    craft and the opening of new regions as a national playground; (5) the preservation of the natural
    beauties of the mountain places and of the fauna and flora in their habitat; (6) and the interchange
    of ideas with other Alpine organizations." Elizabeth Parker, "The Alpine Club of Canada," CAJ 1,
    no. 1 (1907): 3.

11. "Alpine Club Notes," CAJ 1, no. 1 (1907): 162–63.

12. Bruce Barcott, "Cliffhangers," *Harper's Magazine*, August 1996.

13. A.P. Coleman, *The Canadian Rockies, New and Old Trails* (Toronto: Henry Frowde, 1911); Hugh
    Stutfield and J. Norman Collie, *Climbs and Explorations in the Canadian Rockies* (London:

Longmans, Greene, 1903); James Outram, *In the Heart of the Canadian Rockies* (New York: Macmillan, 1905); Mary T.S. Schäffer, *Old Indian Trails of the Canadian Rockies* (New York: G.P. Putnam's Sons, 1911); Walter D. Wilcox, *Camping in the Canadian Rockies* (1896), and later reprised as *The Rockies of Canada* (New York: G.P. Putnam's Sons, 1900).

14. Michale Lang's *An Adventurous Woman Abroad: The Lantern Slides of Mary T.S. Schäffer* (Vancouver: Rocky Mountain Books, 2011) features more than 200 of Mary Schäffer's colourful, hand-painted lantern slides, now housed at the Whyte Museum in Banff. These unique works of art detail some of the Indigenous peoples and landscapes of the Rockies, along with images taken on travels in Japan and Formosa.

15. Mattias Zurbriggen, *From the Alps to the Andes: Being the Autobiography of a Mountain Guide* (London: T. Fisher Unwin, 1899); Christian Klucker, *Adventures of an Alpine Guide* (London: John Murray, 1932). See Kain, *Where the Clouds*, xxii–iii.

16. Kain, *Where the Clouds*, xxi.

17. Of *Where the Clouds Can Go*, Hans Gmoser wrote in 1979 that "I read the words of a man who had been through the hard school of life. Yet he was never bitter; he was never afraid, even when, with torn shoes, infected feet, hungry and cold, he was tramping the roads of his native Austria, perhaps even unnoticed by other mortals." Kain, *Where the Clouds*, xix.

18. See Letter 15 in this volume.

19. Phil Dowling incorrectly noted that Malek "died of starvation in 1945." See Phil Dowling, *The Mountaineers: Famous Climbers in Canada* (Edmonton: Hurtig, 1979), 81.

20. Five mountains bear the impress of Kain's presence. A finger-like peak in the Mt. Robson area, which Kain himself selected, bears his surname. Nasswald Peak (2,995 m [9,827 ft.]), in the southern Rockies, near the Assiniboine group, was first ascended by Kain and named for his Austrian birthplace. Birthday Peak (3,233 m [10,607 ft.]), in the Purcells, was first climbed by Kain on his forty-second birthday, 10 August 1925. And a second Mount Conrad (2,598 m [8,521 ft.]) honours his memory in the Southern Alps of New Zealand.

PART ONE

A Young Guide in Europe, 1906–1909

- guiding in the Dachstein Mountains (1906)
- ski tours on the Rax (1907)
- guiding in the Ennstal Alps (1907)
- the Vajolet Towers (1907)
- guides course in Villach (1908)
- a trip to Vienna to study English (1908)
- guiding in the Ennstal Alps (1908)
- accident on the Barre des Écrins (1908)
- a birthday on the Vajolet Towers, the south face of Marmolada, Monte Rosa and the Matterhorn, and Mont Blanc (1908)
- rock slide on the Rax (1908)
- ski jumping injury (1909)
- accepts an offer of employment in Canada (1909)
- sails from Liverpool to Quebec City aboard the RMS *Empress of Britain* (1909)

1

Nasswald, November 8, 1906

My Dearest Miss:

Only now do I find the time to tell you that I received your remittance
for which I thank you very much. I was so pleased to hear from you!
I can report that the weather was bad the entire time, a fact that you
know yourself. Only now do we have some nice days. This time, I only
undertook two excursions, both to the Wiener Neustädter Steig.[1] In
September, I was supposed to go to the Ennstal with a young lady
for an excursion, but the bad weather destroyed our plans. However,
now it is beautiful. It is really a joy to look around in God's beautiful
nature: one can see all colours in the deciduous forest. Without exag-
gerating, I wish you could see the beautiful nature in the mountains,
because I know that you are a true friend of mountains and nature.
I was also in Vienna and saw Mr. Gerngross because of the travelogue
on Corsica.[2] I was upset, though, that the gentleman left out some
interesting tales about the old priest, whom I told you about—particularly about the time when a pig invaded the priest's apartment.
(Because it too was curious about the foreigners who paid a visit to
its master!!) When I asked Mr. G why he crossed this out, he replied
that as a Jew he couldn't write all this down. If you ever come to
Reichenau and want to take an easy climb of the Rax, please let me
know; for a change, I would be happy to take an easy tour.[3] You know
how my usual trips are, and that they often go far beyond a comfortable tour! Should I ever get to Vienna, I will visit you, if I may. I read
the letter I received from my mother. She was as pleased as I was
since you wish me all the best. I also received a letter from Lechner,
in which he tells me that they all arrived safely in their Zillertal
home.[4] I also received letters from several tourists telling me that

they returned from their alpine tour. And each of them, as they wrote me, did not cherish returning to the big city of Vienna. But it has to be!

With thanks to you and your family, I close my letter hoping that I will find the time again to write you about the mountains.

Your grateful Konrad Kain

1. The *Wiener Neustädter Steig* is a climbing route in the mountains that form in the southern corner of Lower Austria, also known as the Süd-Alpin (Southern Alps), where the hills rise from the plains to meet the European Alps.

2. During the spring of 1906, Kain guided Albert Gerngross of Vienna in the mountains of Corsica, a French island in the western Mediterranean, 160 kilometres southeast of the French Riviera and 80 kilometres west of the coast of Tuscany, Italy. The chief results of their excursion were the first recorded ascents of Capo Tafonato (south summit), Punta Castelluccia (northeast face), and the Cinque Frati (east face). For Gerngross's account of the expedition, see "Auf Korsika's höchsten Gipfeln," *Österreichische Touristen-Zeitung* 39, nos. 20, 21; for Kain's account, see "My Journey to Corsica," in *Where the Clouds*, 105–14.

3. Approximately 20 kilometres down the valley and southeast of Kain's birthplace of Nasswald, and 90 kilometres southwest of Vienna, Reichenau was a popular alpine resort town for wealthy Viennese tourists. Rising between Reichenau and Nasswald, the Raxalpe (or the "Rax") is Lower Austria's second highest point at 2,007 metres (6,585 ft.).

4. The custodian of Hess Hut in the Ennstal Mountains of northern Styria, Hans Lechner lived with his family in Zillertal Alps of northeastern Tyrol. Kain first met Lechner in 1904, while guiding in the Enns Valley. Amelie Malek most likely met Lechner at the Hess Hut in September 1906 during her and her sister Flora's first tour with Kain. See Kain, *Where the Clouds*, 34, 47, 126.

2

Nasswald, December 7, 1906

To the Dear Misses Malek:

With my best greetings, I am sending you some snow roses. I made some progress with the Italian language, but I am a little lazy—just like with writing. Lately, I was twice in the Dachstein Mountains with a lady. This time, we were lucky with the weather. We watched a sunset that one cannot describe. There is very much in Vienna, but Vienna certainly does not have such beautiful nature!! Therefore, I wish that you very soon can leave the big city.

With many greetings and Bergheil,[1]
Your most grateful
Konrad Kain

---

1. *Bergheil* is a traditional Alpine greeting Kain often used when he reached the summit of a mountain. With no direct English equivalent, it loosely translates to "salute the mountains," "hail to the mountains," or "long live the mountains."

3

Nasswald, December 29, 1906

To the Dear Misses Malek:

For the New Year, I wish Miss Amelie and Miss Flora, and their
father and mother, all the best. For mountain climbing, I wish you
very long holidays, good weather, nice company, much money, and
no bad luck.

> *Best greetings and thanks,*
> *Konrad Kain*

4

Nasswald, April 6, 1907

My Dear Miss:

Yes, yes, Kain is really lazy with writing! There is no other excuse. The
winter and the nights are long enough, and I now have the writing
paper! But if I have to write the truth, I can only mention being
bored. Mostly, I worked in road building, which was not easy work.
Every day, I needed two-and-a-half hours to walk to my place of work.
Often, it is a beautiful day, and I long for the Alps. But not one free
day passes without doing something. I often thought of writing the
Misses, but, on weekdays, I often was just too tired in the evening.
Now, I am free for several weeks. I go skiing, and have taken some

very nice tours. I am sorry that I cannot take photographs—they would be beautiful pictures. When I ski through the snow-covered forest and no trace of human beings can be seen, Konradl feels like God Himself!![1] Only I cannot help anybody like God can. If I could, you would be the first one to get her wishes fulfilled. Your pictures pleased me so much. My heartfelt thanks. Unfortunately, I was not in the Zillertal with Lechner. I could not take the course for guides, because it was overbooked, and the visit to Zillertal did not happen.[2] What is going on with the contract for Corsica, I do not know. Once last winter, I saw Mr. Gerngross—he told me that Mr. Hess had not returned the papers to him. I am sure Mr. Hess is very busy. For the summer, I already have accepted some bookings for other countries. But I would also be pleased if the ladies would come to visit me. Then, we surely will find a nice and easy route up to the Rax. At Easter, I was on the Rax and I looked over to the Semmering. I was full of joy about the beautiful weather. I called out a "Ski Heil," which was meant for the MISSES WHO HAVE FLED THE STONEWALLS OF THE CITY!

With alpine greetings to you, your sister, and parents, I am closing my letter,

A rivederci!
Your grateful Konrad

1. *Konradl* is a term of endearment for Konrad.
2. Kain earned his *FührrerBuch*, the book/passport that served as official recognition of professional guide status, on 10 October 1906. Weeks later, he received the guide's insignia of the German-Austrian Alpine Club and the badge of the Touring Club. See Kain, *Where the Clouds*, 126.

5

Nasswald, June 20, 1907

To the Dear Ladies:

I answer your letters with a joy, but I regret that I am not free on
Sunday, but will be sure to be on Monday. Therefore, I want to make
the following program for you: If you go to Nasswald on Sunday and
see the innkeeper, Mr. Binder, and still want to go ski touring, then
he will go with you. I will then join you Sunday evening. Of the tours
you mentioned, I would prefer the Wildfährte in the Kahlmäuern
because it really is one of the nicest climbs on the Rax. To descend,
he will choose another route on the south side. You won't regret
going to Binder because it pays to spend an evening there. It reminds
you very much of the Gesäuse. It will be my last tour in my homeland
mountains for quite some time. On June 27th, I will go to the Gesäuse
and then to the Tyrol, etc. On my trips, I will often think of you. To
prove my point, I will send you some postcards. If you ladies come by
car, you could still take a tour to the Reistal, but otherwise the time
will be short. But I have another idea: I will try to be already free by
noon on Sunday, then we could hike together to Nasswald or could
do a Höllental tour in the afternoon, perhaps up to the Preintaler and
down the Wachthüttelkamm. That will be the best! We could meet in
the Weichtalklamm. In the morning, you could take a little walk into
the Weichtalklamm. If you ladies like this plan, we will do it so that
you don't even lose a day. I would be in Weichtal between twelve and
one o'clock.

Best greetings and Berg Heil!
Konrad Kain

6

Jamthalhütte, July 15, 1907

Dear Lady:

Since I am spending a boring day in an alpine hut, I use the opportunity to tell you about my summer trip. Up to now, I have been lucky with the weather and with the touring. I started in the Ennstal, went to Reichenstein and Totenköpfel, Planspitze-Nordwand (Inntaler, Kamin).[1] From there, I visited the beautiful Hess Hütte. The picture in the nice frame that you donated to the Ennstaler people creates a really beautiful impression in the cottage. Lechner is pleased about it, too. There was a tiny flaw that I did not notice. There is oilcloth for only two tables. I was not smart enough to measure the length and width of the tables. Such covers would please Lechner and the Ennstaler. — The beautiful Ennstaler mountains and hut I greeted for you, but with such devotion I cannot put in words. With a goodbye, I left the Ennstal and visited with great joy the Dachstein via the south side and also the Kleines Dirndl. With longing, I looked at my dear Bachelalm, but I could not get there. In the Kaisergebirg, I did the Totensessel, Totenkirchel, and the Predigtstuhl (via Betzen-Kamin) twice. Then, we travelled to the Dolomites, where I received your card with great pleasure. Thank you so much. I climbed the three Vajolet Towers, but under very bad conditions. Then we went to Campitelle, to the Sella-Joch, where I thought of you along the way because of the beautiful alpine meadows with the small delicate flowers. They made me think of you. In my mind, I saw you in these meadows. They are to your taste and to mine, as well. In the case of beauty and nature, I believe we have the very same perceptions. I would be curious to know how much we would admire together if we could travel together for a few weeks in the beautiful alpine world. We

∧ *Built in 1893, the Hess Hut sits beneath the Hochtor in the Ennstal Alps of Upper Styria. Postcard, c. 1910.*

would never get tired. I hope you also see such beauty on your travels in the summer, and I will be very happy for you. Right now, I am sitting in dense fog in the Jamtalhütte in front of the Fluchthörner. After climbing them, I will travel to Chamonix and will stay there for some time. If you want to please me very much, then write to tell me how your summer travels turn out. I wish you beautiful weather and much fun. With many greetings and joyous Berg Heil, also to your sister and your Mama.

> *The old mountaïn nut Kain*
> *Address: Hotel des Alpes, Chamonix*

1. The ascent of the Planspitze by the north wall is among the more daring mountaineering undertakings prior to the turn of the twentieth century. The first ascent of the wall was made in 1885 by Austrian Daniel Innthaler (1848–1925), who, also from Nasswald, is credited with mentoring Kain in the guiding profession. Kain, in fact, was often mistaken as Innthaler's son. See Kain, *Where the Clouds*, 153.

7

Nasswald, October 6, 1907

To the Dear Misses Malek:

Since I imagine that your last mountain flowers are wilted, I am sending you a small leftover of the wonderful Rax flora. I also have to ask forgiveness that I did not write for a long time. I was in the Dachsteingebirge again with a lady, this morning I returned home, and in an hour I have to leave my mother again. Times are so beautiful that I was at home one night only. I am my own master now. I hope we will see each other on the 9th, when I will tell you of my wellbeing. I am invited to Vienna on the 8th for a celebration at an alpine society.[1] I look already forward to the travel before I even started. With many thanks for the beautiful news and remittance.

With alpine greetings,
your grateful Kain

1. The Austrian Alpine Club formed in 1862. From its inception, the club was very different in concept from the British original—The Alpine Club, formed in 1857—being an organization open to all (men and women), organized into local sections, and owning mountain refuges or huts in which its members could stay for a nominal fee. Whereas The Alpine Club (England) had 475 members by 1887, the Austrian and German club (they combined in 1874) had 18,020. See Walt Unsworth, *Hold the Heights: The Foundations of Mountaineering* (Seattle: The Mountaineers, 1994), 69. Prior to 1911, the Malek family lived at 2 *Elisabethstrasse* in the first district (or *Innere Stadt*) of Vienna among the grandiose buildings of the Ringstrasse. In the last half of the nineteenth century, the city's nobility and plutocracy rushed to build showy mansions in the area. Today, the district is a United Nations Educational, Scientific and Cultural Organization (UNESCO) World Heritage site.

8

Nasswald, October 18, 1907

Dear Miss:

I was so sorry that I could not go to Vienna on October 8th—and
that you, Miss, thought that I might have been there, but found the
distance too far. Since the day we parted in Weyer, I returned to the
Ennstal. The first days were very boring, nobody to chat with, so I
went walking a lot, to the waterfall, to the little Moonshine Bench; I
thought also of the Malek family, how they'll be busy getting everything in order in their house again. But you will be relieved to be
done. From the mountain air to the city air and then the disorder! —
Twice, I was in the Dachsteingebirge with the sisters Benedikt. Did
the south wall with each of them. And where do you believe, dear
Miss, I was on October 9th (since I could not come to Vienna)? You
know this mountain very well. "Could it have been the Planspitze?"
— Yes, it is! — We had a beautiful day crossing the Nordwand. But
the view was not as beautiful as the last time I was up here. I should
have been in Vienna at that time, yet I was so far away. At eleven
o'clock, we reached the top, the time I would have been with you in
Vienna. This time we descended via the Petrapfad. (Stop, stop!) The
next day we were at the Reichenstein und Totenköpfel. Should we
meet again by chance in the Ennstal, dear Miss, we will for sure pay
a visit together to the Reichenstein, won't we? Your Mama will allow
it for sure. Today I cannot write more; it will be too much. I can add
that Michl B. in Lahnsattel is now engaged. But I am fine—have
still lots to do. Last Sunday, I was at the Neustädter Steig, Tuesday
at Hochschwab, and Thursday at Inntaler-Band. With best greetings
and many thanks, a rivederci!

Konrad Kain

9

Nasswald, November 19, 1907

Dear Miss:

Perhaps you thought that Konrad forgot about you? This is not true. I thought of all of you every day, especially when the weather was so beautiful and one could see from the Rax to the Dachstein Mountains. Once I saw the Ennstaler Mountains at sunset. At that moment, I saw in my mind a mountain-loving Vienna lady standing next to me. Who could that have been? How are you keeping, dear Miss? Did you already adjust to city life again? It is also possible that I will have to adjust because I plan to study English, and then I would have no choice but to go to the city.[1] I have you as an example, because you too would rather stay in the beautiful Alps, and yet it is not possible. How long will it be until we see each other again in the mountains? Sixty-nine days disappeared already! Time goes fast, doesn't it? How is your dear family? Is everybody well? I was a little sick, but I am fine again and that is the reason why my long prom-ised note arrives only now. I must apologize for not letting you hear from me for so long. You know, the reason was as follows: My notes are from 1904, written with many mistakes, and I don't want to bother you too much. So, I will send three pages—the others I want to correct myself a bit so you don't have so much work. They won't be perfect anyway. You can do with the notes as you wish, because you understand them better than I do. The matter is not urgent.[2] Here in Nasswald, we have snow already, but not enough to ski. When will you try to ski again? Saturday, I was at the Nasskamm, the place where I once felt like God himself. I finish my letter with the best of greetings to you and your family. With alpine greetings,

your grateful guide Kain

1. Kain's desire to learn and improve his English is a recurring theme throughout much of the Kain–Malek correspondence. Not long after the writing of this letter, Kain, with the assistance of former clients, moved to Vienna and spent the early months of 1908 studying English under the tutelage of Sara Pistor (d. 1930). Kain had been hired as a guide by her husband, Dr. Erich Pistor (1873–1954), in 1904. Kain was again hired in 1905 as a guide on the Pistors' honeymoon trip to the Dolomites, Milan, Courmayeur, Chamonix (Mont Blanc, Aiguille de Grépon), Zermatt (Matterhorn, Monte Rosa), and Interlaken. A long friendship ensued.

2. Malek, like Sara Pistor, agreed to help Kain with his English. What begins here as a desire to better his writing becomes a lifelong tutelage. Years later, Malek sent much of Kain's notes and letters to J. Monroe Thorington, who, after Kain's death in 1934, made use of them for Kain's autobiography, *Where the Clouds Can Go* (1935).

10

Nasswald, December 27, 1907

Dear Miss Amelie:

Very tired, I returned from the Rax today. The skiing was exhausting with this poor snow, and maybe, too, it was also my "Berg Heil," which, with all my strength, I made from the Scheibwaldhöhe to the Semmering! There was a good view at that moment. It was the 25th around 2 P.M. But the dear Christmas gift, which was waiting for me, cheered me up again. So, I am saying my big THANK YOU to the dearest lady, also in my mother's and my siblings' name, who are all very pleased. How are the holidays at the Semmering?[1] As far as I could see, the snow is missing. You might not even do any sledding. I spent the holidays in the Habsburg-House; 185 people were there overnight. You can imagine what that means. My "bed" was in the front house on the bare floor. No chance at sleep. There was dancing until 2:30 A.M., and it wasn't until 4 o'clock that people began leaving. On the 26th, we were more than twenty people on skis. It was fun. There were more stars than in the sky that night. One family of six, and all with skis, were with us, too. The mother—at fifty-six years—was the best. On Sunday, the 29th, I will go to the Rax again. If the weather is nice, you could easily see me if you have your good binoculars with you. About 1 P.M., I will be on the Scheibwaldhöhe, near the tower. My watch is fifteen minutes faster than the railway clock. Wouldn't it be nice to be able to see each other from the far distance! I give signals with my coat like the one time on the Planspitze, where, unfortunately, you did not see us. Did you and Miss Flora receive my card from the Rax? On the 3rd or 4th of January, I will come to Vienna; therefore, I must go to the Rax often to enjoy the last days of the beautiful alpine world. If the weather is nice on Sunday, don't forget the Scheibwald.

With greetings and Berg Heil to you, Miss Flora, and your dear parents. My mother also sends greetings and thanks you,

Konrad Kain

1. Lauded for its clean air and grandiose peaks, Semmering, like the nearby town of Reichenau, was a popular destination in Lower Austria among Vienna's bourgeoisie. Its chief highlight was the winding railway over Semmering Pass, which, completed in 1854, was Europe's first Alpine railway. The line gained UNESCO World Heritage status in 1998.

11

Villach, March 14, 1908

Dear Lady:

You might think Kain is too lazy to write! It's true, but you must excuse me for what I tell you. It is not as easy as I had anticipated. First, the trip from Vienna to Villach. It was an unforgettable day for me. Everything was covered in snow, and it was so much more beautiful! In Weyer, I thought of the farewell from you and your family in September. From Hieflau on, I stood by the window half frozen. The Ennstaler Mountains had quite a different character. The Planspitze, in its nice "winter clothes," laughed down to Gstatterboden that we both know. The Hochter, the Festkegel, and the Ödstein looked proudly down to the Haindlkar, which reminded me of many beautiful hours. Nothing beats our beautiful mountains, doesn't it, dear Miss? Late in the evening, I arrived at Villach. Among my colleagues in the course, there is no one to talk with about the beauty of nature.[1] Most are quite ignorant, so I have to teach them in the free hours. Now, I will surprise you with the following: A few days ago, I was in the Kaiserpanorama and saw with joy and surprise the following: Weissenfelser See; the Peritschnigg Waterfall; the town of Veldes, with the picturesquely located Rock Castle; houses in Veldes; view from Hotel Mallner across the lake; the picturesque villa and scene at the lake; the Hotel Petrass with the lake; an island with church; Rotwein-Fall and bridge; and so many more beautiful things whose names I knew. I liked it all and can understand why you long for this <u>beautiful</u> Veldes as I do. If I had a chance, I would go there for a season and would also visit you. By March 11th, we were on the Predil-Pass (via Raibl) for map reading. The lake was snowed in unfortunately, so one could not see it. I called out greetings from you to the Mangart and the Wischberg. How are you in Vienna? Are you all well? Next Tuesday, I want to take an English lesson from you or Miss Flora, if it is possible. We will then discuss an excursion, which perhaps we can do next Sunday, if you both get permission, because YOU have to guide me, so that I can see whether you can get the guide certificate! I forgot to mention that I also greeted the Ennstal Mountains in your name. With best greetings and Berg Heil to all of you. Till seeing you Tuesday at 4 o'clock.

Konrad Kain

1. By invitation, Kain participated in a two-week guides course in early March at Villach in the south of Austria. The 13 students were housed at the Hotel Lamm, where the candidates sang mountain songs each evening to the delight of the proprietor and patrons. Daily instruction was provided in map reading, natural history, first aid, and mountaineering technique. A final examination was held on 15 March. See Kain, *Where the Clouds*, 171.

12

Nasswald, May 27, 1908

Dearest Miss:

How did you get home? Were you cold on the trip? And what did your
Mama say about the weather? It was not so bad after all. I only was
very worried about you because of the cold during the trip. I wrapped
my warm coat around myself and, yet, I had a strange feeling. You
had to leave so quickly with the car and were all alone. Was it boring?
You will have thought about the whole excursion: arrival in Weichtal,
heavenly peace in the Klamm, which was disturbed only by my poor
English, also the quietly rushing Schwarza and some zither music.
Then, the next morning, the merciless "Get Up," the weather that
did not promise much, the hike to the Grosse Höllental for the first
time in trousers that fit you so well.[1] The Akademiker-Einstieg, all the
familiar walls, the scree, a short but beautiful rest, from where we
saw the chamois. The Fensterl, the beautiful descent, the hike to the
Otte-Haus, the horrible thunder and lightning, the way back to the
Preintalersteig, the rain, the standing under trees, across from the
Klebenwand, which was covered by fog, then the roped section, the
bad scree and rain again, the small chimneys, the descent by rope, in
a few minutes on the path again, which we had come upon at six in
the morning. And now through the beautiful forest, surrounded by
rocks, before you reach the road. Then to the feeding station for the
elks, changing clothes, coffee in the Weichtal, then the postponed
job of writing: the postcards. It was possible to mail them, farewell
in a hurry, and the tour ended. Actually a short time, but when you
think how much of beautiful nature you pass, which you only see in
the mountains...! This I think after each tour, and I am happy. I wish
you the same attitude towards the beautiful nature. But you have that

already. Goodbye. If you get sick of city life, think of the beautiful mountains you will see again!

With greetings, also to your Mama, and thanks,

K. KAIN

1. Popular ideas of fashion, gender, and health for middle- to upper-class women in the late nineteenth century severely restricted the range of women's physical leisure activities. Many female mountaineers, for example, either climbed in dresses or wore riding breeches under their skirts, removing the latter only when they were at a safe distance from the trailhead or hostelry. However, as historian Colleen Skidmore recently noted in reference to women travellers in the Rockies, "stepping out of the domestic sphere into the new and comparatively unregulated social activity of travel not only tested women's independence and resilience, it offered them opportunity to mobilize latent abilities—whether physical, intellectual, or creative—and whetted the appetite for greater personal freedom." Colleen Skidmore, ed., *This Wild Spirit: Women in the Rocky Mountains of Canada* (Edmonton: University of Alberta Press, 2006), xxiv. In wider sporting culture, beyond mountaineering, trousers were generally not accepted as everyday wear for women until the 1930s.

13

Gstatterboden, June 9, 1908

Dear Miss:

I was sorry that I could not write, but now comes a long letter. First,
I thank you for your letter and card. Here is my report. After the
excursion with you, I went with a lady for three days: did Malersteig,
Wildes Gamseck, Danielsteig, Grosses Übeltal. Then, I went with a
gentleman over the Innthaler-Band, down the Katzenkopf-Steig. I
then spent a day for my pleasure at the Gschaidl at the Neuwald. I
like it there. It is simple and peaceful and quiet, all which I love so
much. Then, I took a gentleman to the Neustädter Pass, where we
had a mishap and good luck. While we were climbing, the gentleman
wanted to take a picture, and the camera dropped about thirty
metres. Luckily, it didn't break (it had cost 500 Kronen!). After that,
we had a good lunch in the Otto-Haus. Then I hiked alone to the
Habsburg-Haus. It was hard to leave my home mountains, as it was
so beautiful. I cannot remember to have seen the Rax with so many
flowers. No need to mention that I thought of you and your sister. In
the evening, there was a storm, and I had to stay in the Habsburg-
Haus overnight. It was a cozy evening. At five in the morning, I
left the Rax and went to the valley thinking that being a guide is a
terrible business, but ——— SO BEAUTIFUL! At home, as I said
Goodbye, it was not as sad as often before; my mother did not cry,
and so I felt better. When I stood on the Nasskamm, I felt like new-
born, since I looked into the beautiful green Steirerland! I thought,
again, about my life and compared the present with winter and told
myself: it will be alright. During the short time at home, I earned
enough and almost paid all my small debts. I am happy. I had to go
via Vordernberg-Eisenerz. In Vordernberg, I had to wait three hours.

I was tired and lay down in the forest, and slept and missed my train. So, I had to stay overnight—could only leave the next morning. It rained as if the sky had opened, and on the mountains one could see the snow. No way could I do any tours! In the Hotel Gesäuse, I was welcomed warmly by Mr. Arlhofer and by the locals; so, in spite of the bad weather, I am in a good mood. Yesterday, Monday, I took a walk to the Johnsbachtal and met Dr. Beck (will tell about it later). I had quite a surprise at the Bachbrücken Inn, where I met the old Johnsbach priest, and, when he saw me, he shouted: "Yes, my dear mountain guide is here!" And he embraced me. There were many tourists. It really touched me, I must admit. Then, I went home via the Schwammerlwald (as your mother called it). At the Moonlight Bench, I stopped and everything came back to me: sunset, moonlight, resting, exchanging thoughts with people who also love nature.

Today, I will visit my friend, Lechner, and chat about "hibernating," which I did not do. The hotel owner, Arlhofer, asked about the Malek family, whether they will come this summer. In good weather, I will do the Hochtor-Nordwand. Monday, June 15th, I will meet a gentleman in the Austria Hut, and we will stay the whole week in the Dachstein area. Then, I return to Gstatterboden and will go hiking with Mrs. Dub and Mrs. Pister for six or seven days. I would love to invite you, but it will not work. But, it will be possible in September. If you think of the beautiful Ennstaler Mountains, keep thinking, "Kain will do that in the mountains for me, too," which I will certainly do.

How is your Mama's health? I wish a speedy recovery and not too much excitement about the parade. I have to say many thanks to your Papa for the shoes. They fit quite well.

Best greetings, thanks and Bergheil!
K. Kain, Hotel Gesäuse, Gstatterboden

14

Gstatterboden, June 20, 1908

Dear Miss:

Since I am in Gstatterboden again, I'll tell you about my tour:
Monday, noon, I went to Schlabming, where I met my gentleman.
We went via the beautiful mountain village Ramsau, about which I
told you before. I cannot describe the beautiful alpine flora. We had
to hurry to the Austria Hut, but I still stopped several times. It was
so beautiful! Again, I thought of the poor city people, as I always
do being in such beauty. And I have to repeat that I am a rich and
happy man. In the hut, I met Landgerichtsrat Müller, who had examined me at the guides course in Villach.[1] We had a nice conversation,
which had been impossible in Villach. At three in the morning, we
left the hut, where I wrote a card to Miss Flora. The moon was out
and soon the cuckoo and the other birds were there. We climbed the
two Dirndln, the Dachstein, where we rested for more than an hour,
and then down climbed to the Adamek Hut. There I met friends, as
well. The sunset in the evening was brilliant—my heart was almost
breaking. I think, you've never seen <u>anything like it</u>, dear Miss. I've
seen a lot of sunsets, but nothing like that. Next morning at three,
we left the cottage for the Thorstein, where we spent two hours.
Unforgettable! I looked over to the Stoderzinken and thought of you
and Miss Flora. Then, we climbed the often forgotten Mitterspitze.
Another two hours of rest. I slept for half an hour, because the sun
meant too well! We stayed again in the Adamek Hut. Next day, we
climbed the beautiful Eiskarl-Spitze in wonderful weather. (It was
a bit difficult for the gentleman). Then, we hiked to the beautifully
located Hofpürgl Hut. I was heartily welcomed there, which pleased
the gentleman very much. He said: "Where can I go with you where

nobody knows you??" The hut is run by the Zillertaler people. In the midst of our conversation, the sunset occurred. Naturally, everything had to be interrupted. I lay down in the green grass. The reflection of the sun lasted over an hour. When I went to the kitchen, the Zillertaler people asked me: "How can a sunset interest you?! Sundown —— You see it every day!!" — You know, one cannot explain that to everybody, otherwise they would not ask such a dumb question, don't you think? I only said: "People, you don't understand!" At three in the morning, we approached the Bischofsmütze, and, at six, we stood on top of the Kleine. Beautiful view! Then, we climbed the Grosse. Back to the hut. The gentleman did not want to leave, and neither did I. In Mandling, we did not get a car and had to walk to Schladming. That was hard! After being high up for so long and now, one has to walk a dirty road! Fortunately, we reached the fast train at four o'clock. The tour was really beautiful, and we were both happy. I said goodbye to the gentleman, whom I should expect in France on August 16th, but there is something I had not thought of....When I got off in Gstatterboden, everybody came with the question "What happened, there is a telegram that asks if Kain is dead. You can imagine that I got scared! They gave me the telegram: "Please advise if Kain is dead. Franziska Kain." Hotelier Arlhofer sent this telegram: "Kain left Monday, not known where to." I went to the post office and wired home. My poor mother will have been so scared! — Therefore I wish, dear Miss, if you have time, write a few lines so that she is comforted. She believes you more than me, if you write that I am very cautious on my tours. If it were true, then it would be a terrible accident, if Mother would lose me, her darling, in this way. It must have been some misunderstanding. If I hear more, I will write to you immediately. —— Now, I have to thank you for your English letter. I understood it quite well and ask you, if you would honour me with another letter, to write it in English. Regarding your summer quarters, I congratulate you that you come to Reichenau.[2] I am only sorry that you are in my home mountains and I am away! I would have invited both of you for a nice Rax tour. Concerning the Stadtwaldgrat, I must tell you with pleasure that I will be able to do this tour with you and Miss Flora. It is better to have two people for this tour, like our tour on the Rax with Miss Flora. If there are more, you have to pay attention to more people and that disturbs the pleasure. I don't write this because of the money, but because I want to please each tourist, especially you, whom I have to thank. I will also bring notes along. What about the villa? Is it being built already? I dreamt that I visited you in your new house. Don't you think with this long report that I deserve an Emperor Virginier? In five minutes, I will lie under a tree and smoke it with pleasure. I still have a package of cigars from your dear Papa. With best greetings to you, Miss Flora and parents,

Konrad Kain

1. Kain's examiner, Landgerichtsrat Müller, of Munich, attended the guides course representing the central committee of the German-Austrian Alpine Club.
2. The Malek family had a holiday villa constructed in Reichenau during the summer of 1908. It was located at Schulgasse 27 and stands to this day.

15

Gstatterboden, July 3, 1908

Dear Miss:

How is it in hot Vienna, you friend of the mountains? Every afternoon, I think of you and can imagine how you have to struggle. I wanted to write sooner, but I've had no time, as you can tell from my report about the tours. Saturday morning, I took the Waterfall path with a gentleman. In the afternoon, my brother came with the gentlemen and took the Waterfall path again. My brother loved it, which pleased me, since I saw that he is a friend of nature, too, and will be much more so if more opportunities arise to see the mountains. Sunday was Hochtor-Ödsteingrat, Gstatterboden. Monday, again, the Waterfall path, Hess Hut, Johnsbach, Gstatterboden. Tuesday, I did hard work: We had to secure the Teufelszacken at the Hochtor-Ödsteingrat. I carried an iron cable of eighteen kg across the rocks, which were difficult. Wednesday, I was so tired, as never before, and I went to Gstatterboden. At 4 P.M., Miss Benedikt arrived, and we went to the hut. Yesterday, we did the Grat. That was very hard, hot, and the lady was not in a good mood. The descent to Johnsbach is really tough. In the evening, I went home with my friend, Zettelmeier, from Johnsbach, past the Moonlight Bench just when the sunset reflected in the rocks of the Haindlkar. As always, I had to think what a lucky man I am to see such beauty in nature, yet when the poor city folks come to my mind, I must say it is impossible to describe this feeling. Today, I rest and washed my clothes. If you were in Gstatterboden, I would have, as in the past, asked you politely to help me. Now, we talk about the future. I am happy you will soon be relieved of city life and come out into free nature.[1] But, I would wish for you a different stay in summer than the Thalhof in Reichenau.[2] It is very nice there, but, for a friend of nature like you, too city-like. But one has to be glad to have that. I am even more pleased, dear Lady, that we arrive at the same day: July 11th at Reichenau. I would be happy to meet you. I arrive with the 3:30 train from Mürzzuschlag and then go to the Weichtal, Sunday, up to the Rax. Monday, I would be free for you and your sister. But Monday it would not work, as your Papa is there. If all fails, I will find an excuse to be free on Wednesday. What do you say to this? I look very much forward to seeing you once more before my summer trip. It is really like you once wrote me in Zermatt: "We are far apart but our thoughts often cross in the beautiful alpine world," which I too believe. So you write to me about the excursions and try to make it possible. With best greetings and "Bergheil," Goodbye at the STADELWAND-GRAT!!!

Konrad Kain

1. "Nature," for Kain, was imbued with the powerful, romantic attraction of primitivism—the belief that the best antidote to the perceived ills of an overly refined and civilized modern world was a return to a simpler, more primitive nature. Dating back at least to eighteenth-century philosophers, primitivism gained renewed impetus in the late nineteenth and early twentieth century as a response to the mass industrialization and urbanization sweeping the Western world. In North America, this was most strikingly embodied in the myth of the frontier. See William Cronon, ed., *Uncommon Ground: Toward Reinventing Nature* (New York: W.W. Norton, 1995), 76.

2. The Thalhof was a hotel that dated back to the seventeenth century. During the 1800s, it was regularly frequented by Viennese artists and nobility, including even the Austrian Emperor, Franz Joseph I, in 1851.

16

Gstatterboden, July 9, 1908

Dearest Lady:

For your name day, I am sending you some flowers, which I picked near the Hess Hut.[1] It is not a big present, but, since you are a great friend of flowers, I know that you will be pleased to see these flowers on your table. In the meantime, until your name day comes again, I wish you all the best. And for those years, when you will already live in your house in Reichenau, I wish that on your name day your parents permit you to take a beautiful mountain tour—THREE CHEERS TO MISS AMELIE!

Konrad Kain

---

1. Often valued more than a person's birthday, a "name day" was the tradition observed in many European countries of annually celebrating the feast day of the Christian saint whose name one bears. Like her mother, Amelie Malek was named for Saint Amelia (AD 741–72), whose feast day fell on July 10.

17

Weichtal, July 12, 1908

To the dear Misses Malek:

I wanted to call you from the Otto-Haus, but you were not at home; so I asked you to phone me later, but I never heard from you. So, here is the following: Tomorrow, Monday, I am in the Weichtal and will expect one of the two of you. I am sorry I could not speak to you. With pleasure, I can tell you that I only leave Saturday and am thus free all week. I hope you two ladies can also spare some time? How the tour will go? I don't yet know. I don't want to offend either of you. Miss Amelie wants to go alone. I cannot contradict, but I will not help her, because you ladies might believe that I arrange it this way because of the money. You ladies will have more fun, if each one of you comes alone, and then your dear Mama is not alone all day.

With fond greetings,
Kain

18

Nasswald, September 15, 1908

Dearest Miss:

During the summer, I thought of you very often and tried twice to write to you, but could not because I wanted to tell you the truth. But so many thoughts came to me that my heart was breaking. I never have had such a bad summer regarding the weather and otherwise. The day I said goodbye to you and your family (July 15th) was beautiful—then I got to Villach in the rain. No mountains were visible, but I greeted them through the fog. Then we drove on to Bruneck, but, since it still rained, we continued on to Terrin. From there, to the See-Alpen. They are not so difficult and don't have such beautiful shapes as the Dolomites, but they have something that you, dear friend of the mountains, love: the grand, beautiful lakes and the solemn, quiet stillness. I climbed the highest peak in the group named Punta de l'Argentera. Two gentlemen were with me. Nobody got mountainsick. The next tour was the Monte Viso via the West Ridge under very poor conditions, then via the Col de la Traversette to Adries (France). There, we did the Barre des Écrins, the highest mountain in the Dauphiné.[1] It went well until we reached the Col des Écrins on the descent. There was a steep chute that took time. We had a local guide, who led us on, and I went last. Suddenly, boulders came tumbling down! Two men were safely behind the rocks, but one gentleman and I had to look death in the eye. One could not jump aside. It is impossible to say what one thinks at such a moment. I only knew that one rock hit my shoulder. When they got me behind the rock and I became conscious again, I was lying in blood. After a while, we continued, very slowly across a steep snowy slope.[2] When we were in the valley, I looked up and really thought of you when, earlier in Gstatterboden, I lay stretched out in a meadow near the hotel. I slept. But you saw me from your window and later told me the thought you had at this sight: "It looks like somebody had fallen down a mountain." In La Bérarde, I rested for two days, and then we went to the Meije in poor snow conditions. I had to take two people without a guide on my rope, in all making us five people—and I was the only guide! As a result, we were on the rope for sixteen hours and had to sleep in the open. This would not have been necessary if the gentlemen would not have been so stubborn when they were tired. After two days, we did the Aiguille d'Arve méridionale, a very difficult tour. After that, we went to the Mont Blanc group. The bad weather began there, and we had to turn back. We then went to the Dolomites, where, on my 25th birthday, I did all six Vajolet Towers. Next came a very difficult tour: the south wall of Marmolada. This has been my most difficult tour. Then came another critical moment: the guide, Piaz, and his gentleman started sliding and fell—and we were on one rope![3] Fortunately, I had a good hold with very good security. On August 14th, I met my second gentleman in Zermatt. We did the Monte Rosa with seven peaks. As a result, we both suffered eye problems and had to stay in a dark room for several days. After three days of waiting we climbed the Matterhorn. We needed eight hours going up and seven coming down. There was fresh snow. I saw two tourists fall, sliding actually. Nothing happened, but I feel I have to tell you sometimes. I did the Breithorn, too. Then, we drove to Chamonix. Three nights and two days were spent snowed under in the Cabane Tête Rousse, but finally we could reach "the King of the Alps." So, the Mont Blanc was the last tour. Believe me, dear Miss, that never before I liked going home so much as this time around. I travelled from Chamonix to Gstatterboden! The fast train went too slow for me. What yearning! Add to this that I had planned to meet somebody in Gstatterboden whom I could entrust with my problem. But nobody was there. Well, so what! The family Malek is coming! But I waited in vain for each train until I received your postcard. On September 9th, I went to the Haindlkar at five in the morning. It was a beautiful day, but the sun did not rise as beautifully as in former

Gesäuse:
Wasserfallweg, Ennstaler

times. I wanted to do the north wall of Festkogel, thought about it, and went via the Peternpfad. It was a happy day for me, because I am in the Ennstal and could escape the cruel death that followed me. So sad was I, thinking "a year ago, who was with you?"[4] What happy eyes your trusting tourist showed when she saw all this beauty! And how happy were you that she liked your guiding! And today you sit alone and lonesome on the Scharte! A few songs came to mind. I then had a long time at the lake, after which I visited my friend Lechner in the hut, where everybody was sad because of an accident in the Zillertal. Did you read about it? I went home in the evening via the Waterfall path like a year ago, but it was not as beautiful. It began to snow and the forecast was bad. For you and Miss Flora, I bought a little memento that will arrive in a few days. It is not much. Further, I can tell you that I am not as satisfied with my earnings as I had been earlier. The bad weather is to blame. If it were so awful every year, I would look for another occupation, because, otherwise, I could not save for my old age. But one must not give up—it can improve again, don't you think? I close with my best greetings to all,

Konrad

1. The loftiest summit of the Dauphiné, Barre des Écrins (4,102 m [13,454 ft.]) was first ascended on June 25, 1864, by Edward Whymper (1840–1911), A.W. Moore (1841–1887), and Horace Walker (1838–1908), with guides Michael Croz (1830–1865), Christian Almer (1826–1898) the senior, and Christian Almer the junior. Located in the French Alps, it is the most southerly alpine peak in Europe that exceeds 4,000 metres. Kain had ascended the peak once before in 1907.

2. The incident is an early indication of Kain's strength and professionalism as a mountain guide. The 24-year-old Kain, bloodied and bruised with a serious head injury, guided the whole party down safely without the assistance from the local guide, who had expressly joined the party to assist with the descent. Of the ordeal, Kain wrote as follows: "Our local guide lost his head, his nerves failed and he could not act as last man during the descent of the remaining 400 metres of steep snow. So I had to do it! We remained roped until the moraine was reached." See Kain, *Where the Clouds*, 183–85.

< A popular hiking tour from Gstatterboden to the Hess Hut, the Waterfall Route was taken by Kain and the Malek sisters in 1906. Postcard, c. 1910.

Located in northeastern Italy, the *Marmolata* (or Marmolada in English) is the highest peak in the

 Dolomites at 3,343 metres (10,965 ft.). Kain and his client had originally intended to climb the east

 wall of the Rosengarten, but were invited by Giovanni Battista Piaz (1879–1948), better known as

 Tita Piaz, a renowned Italian mountain guide, to join him and his client on the mountain's steep

 southern wall. According to Kain, their ascent was the nineteenth. "It was the most arduous tour I

 had made," he wrote; "it is one of the hardest in the Alps." Piaz would later recommend Kain as a

 guide to clients wishing to visit Austria. See Kain, *Where the Clouds*, 189, 197.

4. It was one year earlier that Kain first guided Amelie and Flora Malek in the Enns Valley.

19

Nasswald, November 10, 1908

Dearest Miss:

I wanted to write earlier, but I've had lots to do since the weather has been so beautiful. Winter has arrived now, which is the worst for me: too much snow for climbing and too little to ski. So, I stay in my warm room, writing in my diary of which you, my patient lady, are getting a few pages. What do you think about winter? Will you be able to spend a few days in beautiful winter nature? I don't know what to do. I have to continue my English, which is dear to me, but I don't know—should I go to England, or should I look for work somewhere where I also could take a few days for guiding? Such two good lady teachers as I had last winter I might find again, but I cannot live in Vienna with my earnings. As I told you in my last letter, I will be able to put away a few savings from the bad summer—I did have a few good excursions. If I had nobody to look after, I would be able to live in Vienna for three to four months at my own expense in order to learn English.[1] But now, I shall go to England two or three months earlier, before I travel to America. I think that is the best. Perhaps later this winter I can save a few Kronen. Last Sunday, I was supposed to do the Stadelwandgrat, and looked forward to the beautiful tour (on which I had already experienced many happy hours).[2] However, what appeared was not joy but minutes of fear (that turned into a whole hour)! Slowly, we hiked to the Gassl, when, about twenty metres into the gorge, a big slide of boulders mixed with timber suddenly came down. I shouted to the two gentlemen: "Take cover! Take cover!" One had a fairly good spot, and I gave the other mine. So, I was without protection. I moved as far as I could, but it quickly got worse and I had to jump across the rocks —— and luckily found a good protected spot. While standing there, trembling and looking with fear for my gentlemen, I saw that one of them was tumbling down the rockslide path. Fortunately, the slide diminished, and I got my two gentlemen to a safe area. One of them was only slightly injured, while Mr. Weinberger (Weihburggasse) was much more hurt. I was fine. I must have a good guardian angel? When we looked after Mr. W., he seemed much better. He also could walk to the Weichtal without much help. I had been at the Gassl at least twenty times and had <u>never</u> noticed a rockslide (and perhaps never again!). How is the house building progressing in Reichenau? Will it soon be done? I have had no opportunity to see it. Saturday, I attended a nice presentation about the Dachstein Mountains in the Reichenau area. Perhaps we shall meet when you come out here because of the construction and take a little trip to the Weichtal. I wish you good luck for the construction, that everything goes quickly, and then you can spend nice and pleasant days there.

With alpine greetings,

K. KAIN

---

1. Kain's father, Eugen Kain (b. 1857), perished in a mining accident in 1892, leaving his mother, Franziska Kain (née Reisenauer, 1866–1944), alone with four young children. Conrad, the eldest at nine, was forced to leave school five years later in order to support his family. At 14, he became a goat herder on the Rax and, a year later, began work as a labourer in a nearby stone quarry. He sporadically worked as a quarryman from 1903 to 1907.
2. Easily accessed from both Nasswald and Reichenau, the *Stadelwandgrat* was a popular rock climbing route up the Schneeberg (2,076 m [6,811 ft.]), which, just 70 metres higher than the neighbouring Raxalpe, is the highest peak in Lower Austria.

20

Nasswald, December 29, 1908

Dear Miss Amelie:

[In English from hereon] It is a very long time since I wrote a letter to you, because I always must be by work on the holidays, but I have no work and have time to writing and learn English. I will go in spring to America. I have got a letter, and I have a place as Swizzer guide in Montreal, Canada.[1] *[In German from hereon]* For today, I will write no longer in English to you, because there will be too many mistakes. I would beg you to point them out to me. Above all, I want to thank you for your Christmas gift that pleased my whole family, especially my mother. She wanted to write, but has difficulty with letter writing, so I say thanks, again, for her. Excuse me that I only wrote a card in answer to your letter, but I really had no time, no free days—I even had to work on holidays. And now work has been stopped. This made me very angry, because I was supposed to go to the Tyrol over the Christmas holidays, but thought I should instead stay at work all winter. And now, I have no work! I will have to find something. Maybe I go back to my old trade: breaking stones in the quarry! —— You will be curious about my trip to America. Just think, I suddenly received a letter from Dr. Pistor, who was happy to send me a message. I had been angry at myself for not hearing from him for so long and thought I might have offended him. But that seems to be out of the question. I also received the passport. Now it depends on the war.[2] What a pity it would be if things didn't work out. Now, we have to talk about last year. That went by so fast, don't you think? There were some sad and nice ones among the 365 days. I wish the nice days to come back in the New Year. For you, it has not been so good, as you had to do without things more than in other

years, such as the mountains and the lakes. But as far as I know, you had some beautiful days, too. When I watched you at the Grat, at the Akademiker, and the Stadelrand, your eyes were shining with joy about the nice weather and your free hours in nature. Will we do a tour in the coming year? I would be pleased if your parents permitted it early in spring. —— In winter, I will be in Vienna for the meeting of the Vienna Section.[3] Perhaps, then, you could show me another nice tour through the Wienerwald.[4] I would be very grateful. For New Years, I wish you the best, health, happiness for your whole life, good weather for summer holidays, wonderful mountain tours, nice company, and no accidents. The same to your sister and parents.

With an alpine greeting,
your grateful K. Kain

1. The Canadian Pacific Railway (CPR), which had its headquarters in Montreal, began employing Swiss mountain guides in 1899 to safely lead hikers, sightseers, and climbers from its grand rail-hotels in the Rockies and Columbias. The CPR's decision to hire professional guides and bring them to Canada partly stemmed from the death of American climber Philip S. Abbot (1867–1896), who fell during an attempt of Mt. Lefroy (3,423 m [11,231 ft.]), near Lake Louise, in 1896. Abbot's death caused considerable debate in Canada concerning the dangers of mountaineering. See Charles Sproull Thompson, "Mt. Lefroy, August 3, 1896," *Appalachia* 2, no. 1 (1897). Like the hotels, the acquisition of Swiss guides was also part of an aggressive tourism campaign to construct the mountain west as a safe, comfortable, and thus a desirable holiday destination for those whom the CPR's general manager referred to as "the class that travels." Railway advertisements strategically highlighted the European ethnicity of its guides in order to promote the Rockies and Columbias as the "the Canadian Alps" and "Fifty Switzerlands in One."

2. Kain was referring to the annexation of Bosnia and Herzegovina by Austria-Hungary in October 1908. The crisis was not resolved until the following spring with the amendment of the Treaty of Berlin, which accepted the new status quo. Nevertheless, relations were permanently damaged between Austria-Hungary and Russia and Serbia. Reactions to the annexation are considered to be a contributing cause of the First World War.

3. The Vienna Section of the German-Austrian Alpine Club.

4. The *Wienerwald* (or "Vienna Woods") encompasses the gentle, heavily wooded hills to the west and southwest of Vienna. The area covers over 1,000 square kilometres and includes the northern-most parts of the Alpine chain.

21

Nasswald, January 15, 1909

Dear Miss Amelie:

[In English from hereon] Thanks for your long letter. I have a great anguish for the slip of the pen in the English letter, but you are a good teacher and have patience with your poor pupil. There are many days we were not in the beautiful nature. It is just past one half year. Could you still remember the nice days? Perhaps it is possible we could have so a day next spring. To morning, I shall go to Nasswald from Hirschwang. I asked about the work in the old stone breaking. Perhaps we come together one time in Reichenau. I make you a visit in your home. I hope that I do not all week go to Nasswald. I must write again of German, I think there are many slip of the pen and that you could soon to make angry with my bad writing. A English letter is much difficult as a German one. My best thanks for your Korrektur, and please you have the kindness and write me the slip of pen again. *[In German from hereon]* It is not going so bad with the English writing, but if you help me, it will improve! Don't you think? All beginning is hard. How is Vienna? Are you all well? I can understand that you have lots of work, but then you can rest when all is done. We have awful weather today, a snowstorm, one cannot see as far as a hundred metres. But perhaps it is good for the water shortage we wish to end, but people in the city are worse off! As to the notes, I must tell you, that I am working on them. Right now, I do nothing with them but let only my best friends read them. Otherwise, there is nothing new. Saturday, January 9th, the Reichenau Section offered a lecture: "The forest with its beauty."[1] Unfortunately, I had no time to attend.

Best greetings,

your grateful pupil K.K.

1. The Reichenau Section of the German-Austrian Alpine Club.

22

Nasswald, January 21, 1909

[In English from hereon]

Dear Miss Amelie:

My best thanks for your letter and for the Korrektur. I am very sorry that I made so much mistakes in my English letter! Now I have not learned English three days, I was on Sunday on a nice ski tour (*Sonnleistein*). One thousand six hundred and thirty eight yards over the sea, And Steinappel retour over the Ameiswiese to Nasswald. I think on you. It was a beautiful day, the best snow and good weather for a ski party. Monday and Tuesday I made exercise with ski on a meadow. A week ago, I was in the old stone breaking quarry to ask for work. It was for nothing, they have people enough. The master told me, they want nobody till the month of March. In the month of March I do no more want a work in the stone breaking. If it is a beautiful spring, go much people to climb on the Loswand and in the Reisstal. My brother is still in Hirschwang busy. With the best thanks and greetings,

Yours truly,

Konrad Kain

Best compliments on your parents and sister.

23

CONRAD KAIN

[In German from hereon]

Nasswald, February 3, 1909

Dear Miss Amelie:

You will forgive me that I write in German again. You can imagine how glad I would be if I already knew more English. It is very hard for me that I have nobody who helps me like you with your letters. There is an innkeeper in Nasswald, who speaks English, but one has to eat and drink and pay a lot and I don't have that. I also had to help my friend with a large sum of money, since all her three children came down with scarlet fever. One child died, another child might not survive. Her husband earns only 2 Kronen 20 Heller. She lives in Traisen. That also cancelled the trip to Vienna. Even if I live free of charge at the Kränzchen, one still needs some money. I am always healthy as are the others, and everything will be alright because spring is coming. I often write down my notes and get my exercise with ski jumping almost every day. However, my Norweger are broken, so I have to jump with the Lilienfelder, and they are not good skis for jumping.[1] Tomorrow, Sunday, I will again do a Hochwald tour. Sometime, I want to lead you in such a forest, because I cannot believe that you ever saw something like it. Other tours are very dangerous now because of avalanches. In Altenberg, two huge ones came down. They are nice to look at, however they create so much damage. In Lahnsattel, a stable with four cows was buried. My two school friends who speak English are now waiters in Cairo. I hope my English will get me that far, too, that I can manage in a foreign country. With best greeting and Ski Heil,

your grateful pupil
Kain

1. According to ski historian E. John B. Allen, "the word *Norweger* was often used in a generic fashion for any Norwegian ski. *Lilienfeld*, on the other hand, refers to a particular ski made by Mathias Zdarsky, called Lilienfeld, Austria, because that was where he made his home and to which many people came to learn from 'the master.' In an advertisement for his ski, Zdarsky was quite clear that it was different and better than Norwegian skis in nine different ways. The most important, here, for jumping at least, was that (a) the ski was shorter, hence Kain did not like it much, and (b) that it had a heavy, complicated metal binding" (Email communication, 2010). Also see E. John B. Allen, *The Culture and Sport of Skiing: From Antiquity to World War II* (Amherst: University of Massachusetts Press, 2007), 126–29.

24

[In English from hereon]

Nasswald, February 13, 1909

Dear Miss Amelie:

My best thanks for your letter and the corrections. I am sure that I made too many mistakes in my letter again. I have often a word in the head quite right, I should like to bring it on the paper, and there is one mistake after another! Some days ago, I got a long letter from Mrs. Pister. She is pleased to see that I have not forgotten all what she taught me a year ago. What is with your cough? Is it already better? And the catarrh of your sister? What made your mother always? Is she sound? It is a pity that you have not seen the pictures from Mr. Haid about the Julischen Alpen a year ago. I read the last Mitteilungen. It must be a dangerous tour. The three days were not so nice as you think. On the 1st Feb. we went on the Gaisloch. This tour is one of the worst in winter wegen der Eiswall. Have you heard of that? And what so much new snow. We went from Weichtal till Ottohaus in nine hours. 2 Feb. we made exercises on the plateau, but it was not well for ski, too much snow. At Mittag, we went over Thörl to Edlach and with the railway to Mürzzuschlag. Stay overnight in Hotel Post. 8 o'clock in the morning, we start up to Pretulalpe. The way was very bad. One o'clock we arrived in Rosegger Haus. It was very stormy and cold. The Abfahrt was very beautiful. We want one half hour to Mürzzuschlag. Returned to Payerbach, stay overnight bei Königseder. The next day, I went on foot to Nasswald (9 hours). The snow was on the street nearly one yard high. Thursday we got a rain and water, we have the same need as in Vienna. We must fetch the water 10 minutes from our house. On the 7th Sept. I was on the Zikafahnler Alm und Kesselgraben. Do you know I like very much the Alm. But I did not have a nice Abfahrt. Gratuliere your Papa that he escaped the misfortune with the lamp! And you can see, how easy it could be possible to meet a misfortune in the city just as in the mountains! I have seen your house, it is quite nice. I have papers for letters still enough. Today I think I have answered all your questions. Excuse my bad writing and the many mistakes. Please have the kindness and write out the mistakes for me. With best thanks and greetings,

K. Kain

25

[In German from hereon]

Nasswald, March 12, 1909

Dearest Miss:

Beginning my letter, I have to beg your pardon for my long silence
and that I do not write in English. Thank you so much for your last
letter and the corrections of my foolish mistakes. On February 17th,
I had an unhappy day, because, while ski jumping, I sprained my
muscles in my right foot and had to stay in bed with terrible pain.
I could not get a doctor, as there was a terrible storm and snowfall.
But a friend gave me a Schwarzwallnergeist, the name derives from
the well-known Healer of Leg Fractures, who also made a healthy
man out of the mountain guide Reisenauer.[1] It helped me a lot, so
that on March 3rd I already could do the Stuhleck, although with a
lot of pain. It would have been a nice tour, but, with a sick foot, it
is not so nice. Then we climbed the Rax and had beautiful snow. In
the evening, I almost cried with pain while skiing, but I could not
show it, because it concerned my earnings. Luckily, I got better overnight, so that I could dare the Kesselgraben, since the gentleman
was not a very good skier. But, in the evening, I had enough and
thanked God that the three days were over. I almost think the
tours were good for my foot, because it felt fine the next day. Last
Sunday, I took a tour: I skied to the Ameisenwiese—Weisse Wand—
Waldeben—Gschaidl—Preinetal and Nasswald. I often told you about
the Hochwald in winter, so that perhaps you already had enough
of it. But I cannot help saying it again: I was the happiest man on
earth! Rax, Schneealm, Schneeberg ahead of me were so beautiful,
as if I were in the really high mountains! And then the BEAUTIFUL

FOREST at the Gschaidl! Not a trace of people, no birdcalls, solemn, quiet winter silence. The houses at the Gschaidl are almost hidden in the snow. Since Christmas, nobody was there. I was sorry that I had disturbed the people in their Sunday mass. —— This week, I cut wood so that I am free when something comes up. And I made a new ski binding which will replace the Norwegian one, although jumping might be impossible since your feet need to be in top shape. In eight days, the Dachstein tour will finally take place. We want to go to the Gosau–Adamek Hut via the Steinerscharte to the Simony Hut and to Hallstatt, all depending on the snow. We will send you a card from Hallstatt. Winter scene! You will be surprised provided I get the one I had seen. How are you all? You will still have much to do with your house. Are your teeth okay again? And your dear Papa's eyes? In a few days, I will send you snow roses. Now there is still too much snow, but soon spring will come. I already heard a bird. And I know you love flowers. Do you remember my first letter to you? It was two and a half years ago, but I still remember almost everything I wrote. Good memory, don't you think? A year ago, I was in Villach for the course. There we did (that is today—) the tour Reibler–Predil, where there is a lot of snow today, what you probably read every day. If I am lucky on the Dachstein and can do everything, I will take a little detour to Gstatterboden, perhaps to the Hohe Scheiben. That should be a splendid tour! The snow-covered rocks and the beautiful forest! Do you think we will once more meet in the Ennstal? It would be interesting if I came flying in from America. I don't know yet what will happen with going to America, but I hope for the best. Many people want to talk me out of it, but they are mostly those who consider me a good and cheap guide. But I think as follows: My mother doesn't mind, as long as I don't forget her (which I won't). During the summer, I am away all the time anyway, and in fall I can go home again, if I wish. In America, I will earn more money. And I can see a piece of another beautiful country. The main reason is that I can also greatly improve my English. And if I am born TO MISFORTUNE, misfortune will be in America just as here. I enclose the copy of a letter that also went to America. When I read it, my heart was beating so fast. Firstly, I am pleased that Dr. Pister recommended me so much[2]; secondly, while reading through the list of my tours, I remembered many joyful and serious and also sad hours, which I experienced in all these mountains. How hundreds of people entrusted me their lives, and, among them, there were so many good ones, and also ungrateful ones, who estimated their lives in millions and mine in only a few pennies. But I will nevertheless remain true to my profession. With best greetings and a hearty Berg Heil, your grateful pupil,

K. Kain.

1. "Schwarzwallnergeist" likely refers to a type of schnapps liqueur.

2. Earlier in the year, Pistor corresponded with both the CPR and the Alpine Club of Canada (ACC) on Kain's behalf to inquire about employment for him as a guide. "Conrad is not only a good, competent man," Pistor wrote, "but a first-class guide and exceptional because he is just as good on rocks as he is on glaciers. He is clever and sympathetic too, he is a 'gamin' with people who like dangers, and careful like a father of 50 with people who are in want of care." Erich Pistor to Arthur O. Wheeler, ACC President, 9 April 1909, WMCR M200/ACoM/52.

26

Nasswald, April 7, 1909

Dearest Miss:

Many thanks for your last letter and postcard. I wanted to send a letter with the flowers, but did not get around to it. I am pleased that the flowers arrived in such fresh condition. I picked them in the morning, when they were still closed. I am angry that my Dachstein tour did not happen. Two weeks ago, I was also made a fool. It was Sunday, March 23rd. I was not at home, but on the Ameisbühel. The weather had changed, and I was back home at two o'clock already. A telegram had arrived saying: "Expect me Sunday Otto-Haus. L.W." The telegram was sent at seven o'clock, and, in Nasswald, the post office closes at six o'clock. Since I could not leave anymore on Sunday, and I thought that it is good enough to be there tomorrow morning at eight, I went Monday at three in the morning to Kaiserbrunn and up via the Brandschneid. There was no path, a real torture. On the Ebenwald, I met a gentleman I knew, who told me they had expected me yesterday noon. Since I did not come, they went on their own. Such things one has to take with patience. Where I will be at Easter, I don't know; maybe I will visit you in Reichenau. Miss Flora sent a letter about the war. I must say, I did not think much about it, because so much thinking is good for nothing. I would have cared if it had hit me. But you cannot do anything, you have to go. My only consolation would have been that the officers are friendly and have to be so at wartimes. Did you read the joke where one soldier says to the other: "Now it will be serious!" — "Why?" — "Two more wagons with ammunition arrived!" — "I am telling you, there won't be war!" — "How do you know?" — "That's easy, when there was danger, our sergeant addressed us as 'my dear children.' And now he says again 'you dumb oxen!'" —

I am longing for a letter from America. This winter was the last
winter I plan to spend in Nasswald. No more! I would not get enough
money together for my old days. If travelling were not SO BEAUTIFUL,
I would look for another occupation where one is more secure in
one's old age. But everything has a downside—I must apologize that
I don't write English. Do not think that I get worse. My notes are
ready. You will still have enough work, although I copied them. And
now, you have no time. I wish you a very pleasant Easter, nice
weather, and much fun. My mother wishes you the same. I think she
would be glad if I were in America. She only is afraid of the water,
·otherwise she knows no fear. With my best greetings, also to your
parents and your sister,

your grateful
K. Kain

27

Nasswald, April 14, 1909

Dear Miss Amelie:

Thank you very much for the parcel, which pleased me and Mother very much. How was Easter? The weather was quite good. My Easter was also better than expected. Every day I waited with longing for the mail, always in vain. Sunday afternoon, I went for a walk with my brother, and we met the tourists from Brünn, who took me along to the Weichtal. There I asked whether the family Malek was there. No. Monday morning, we went up the Stadelwanggrat. It was very nice, but strong winds. At noon, we were in the Weichtal again. I waited till five o'clock. Each car that came I thought would bring YOU! But unfortunately not. YOU were all probably too busy. I gathered some flowers for you and Miss Flora, and, since you did not come, I sent them in a big cardboard box by car to you. Don't know whether you got them. If not, I would be sorry, because I know you would have taken them to Vienna. I saw one chamois in the Stadelwandgraben. When I came home, a letter from Dr. Pistor was there. With my heart beating, I opened it. The president writes that unfortunately no position for a guide is open, but he had no doubt that I would be a special guide for the Alpine Club of Canada when I came, only I had to pay for the trip myself.[1] Dr. P. writes that the trip would be around 150 Kronen, which should not be too much (if Dr. P. did not make a mistake!). But what does the cheap trip help me? I cannot do it at this point. No doubt, there are many who owe me money, but I don't get any. The president of the Club writes that he would have work for me for the winter. And Dr. P. believes that I could certainly get a position as a hunter. I would like to send you the letters, but don't know whether I might need them. You would see that things don't look bad. You can imagine how I feel. Not too good. I don't know where to find the money, it is very hard. If I ask those who know and trust me, that I would repay the money—these would be people I always guide. But I don't dare to say anything to them. I shall not be mistaken in my thoughts, how I would fare with them (but do not want to praise myself). I fear the answer will be "one should give you <u>money</u>, so that you can see a new country? And in the end, we have no decent guide in our area except for Innthaler!" Many believe that you can get rich in the Rax area as a guide, but that is not so. Times have changed very much in this area. Now, I will write once more to Dr. P. for advice. He would like to forward me the money, but I fear that he cannot afford that. AND THESE KINDS OF FRIENDS I HAVE MANY, who would like to help, if they could. My grandfather would have the money, he could lend it to me, but he is not mentally quite fit anymore otherwise I would ask him. And I don't want to do it because of the family, because I am convinced that they might think, then, that they won't inherit as much!! — With friends, I will not touch matters of money, because I've already learned that lesson. I would like the trip to America to materialize. Who knows how earnings at home will be next year? And those people who helped me with English so much, and supported me: I want to show that it is not all in vain. If I still stay at home, it is obvious that I won't easily meet an Englishman, who would take me along into the world.[2] I am <u>known</u> as a mountain guide in Vienna and in other cities, but who does take such big trips here?? Yes, if I could manage to sell some of my talent as a mountain guide then MANY A RICH JEW WOULD APPLY!![3] — And I soon would have the money to travel! — However, I will leave it to fate. My mother was in Mitterberg at Easter, as her sister had died. She came home only today. She was so pleased with the linen and asked me to thank you for it very politely. And thanks to your dear Papa for the cigars, which I enjoy very much. <u>One</u> each day! We have bad weather now. So I finish my letter with my best greetings and thanks.

Yours,
K. Kain.

1. Kain refers to Arthur O. Wheeler (1860–1945), a bearded, energetic man with a forceful personality, who, along with Elizabeth Parker (1856–1944) of Winnipeg, was the principal founder of the ACC. A Dominion Land Surveyor by profession, Wheeler served as president of the club from its 1906 inception to 1910 and was its director until 1930. The year he and Parker founded the ACC, Wheeler also prepared the first issue of the *Canadian Alpine Journal* (published annually since 1907) and was its editor until 1927. See "Arthur Oliver Wheeler," *CAJ* 29 (1944–1945): 140–46.

2. Members of The Alpine Club (England) were often considered the best clients because they were generally regarded (not altogether accurately) as the wealthiest and finest climbers in Europe—a generalized cachet associated with, and no doubt promoted by, the pretentious ranks of The Alpine Club. By the turn of the century, the so-called "golden age" of mountaineering in the European Alps had long sputtered to an end. In fact, as early as 1865, the contest for first ascents, having spread throughout the European ranges, had more or less exhausted the Alps in the minds of many climbers. Wealthy mountaineers thus began to seek first ascents beyond the confines of Europe—carrying with them British standards and prejudices—into the mountain ranges of New Zealand, Africa, Asia, and the Americas. They also brought with them their European guides. See Unsworth, *Hold the Heights*, 72–74; Ronald W. Clark, *Men, Myths and Mountains* (London: Weidenfeld and Nicolson, 1976), 48; Fergus Fleming, *Killing Dragons: The Conquest of the Alps* (New York: Grove Press, 2002), 290–93; and Reuben Ellis, *Vertical Margins: Mountaineering and the Landscapes of Neoimperialism* (Madison: University of Wisconsin Press, 2001), 26–27.

3. Fuelled by the rise of the conservative Christian Social movement under Austrian politician Karl Lueger (1844–1910), anti-Semitism was widespread in late–nineteenth-century Vienna and had gained power throughout much of Austria by the turn of the century. Its causes are complex, but among them was an association between Jews and liberalism. Far from being the persecuted and relatively poor minority of the 1850s, Jewish people were, by the 1880s and 1890s, increasingly prominent in such fields as literature, the press, music, and other liberal professions, adding to the established Jewish prominence in banking, commerce, and industry of Vienna. Many Jews lost money in the 1873 Stock Market crash, but some managed to salvage their holdings. The envious were attentive only to Jewish success. According to historian Steven Beller, "Much of anti-Semitism's power arose from the envy of the largely Catholic populace, who would not accept that Jews, condemned in Christian theology to abasement, could legitimately deserve their new prosperity." Steven Beller, *A Concise History of Austria* (Cambridge: Cambridge University Press, 2006), 155.

28

Nasswald, April 19, 1909

Dearest Miss:

Forgive me that I have to ask for another favour from you. In the newspaper, I read about an expedition to the North Pole, and I want to ask you if you could translate the enclosed letter for me.[1] I don't think that I can go along, but at least one can write and ask, don't you think? I only go for good pay. Today, I received your card. As yet, I am reassured about the America trip. I did try something regarding money, but unfortunately for nothing. I heard that my grandfather was free to meet. With my heart beating, I begged him for help. He said: "Yes, you want to go to America? You already were far away. And from there you will never come back!" —— He did not say yes or no, just wondered about it, and I had to leave. Can you imagine how my heart sank? I could have cried. Now I wrote to Mr. Weinberger. Perhaps I will get a good answer from him. Tomorrow, Sunday, I will go to the Rax. If the weather is nice, I'll watch the sunset, so I can think of something else.

With best greetings and Berg Heil!
Your grateful K. Kain

---

1. The exploration of the North and South Poles—or, more specifically, the race to be there *first*—reached new heights by the end of the first decade of the twentieth century. The Cook–Peary controversy of 1909 over the "discovery" of the North Pole, as well as Roald Amundsen's historic journey to the South Pole in late 1911 and Robert Falcon Scott's tragic death on the return from the South Pole in early 1912, garnered extensive publicity.

29

Dear Miss Amelie:

My best thanks for your card from Pola.[1] I can only imagine how happy you feel at the seashore, and I think you really deserve it because at home you always have to work so hard. I wish for good weather. It will already be warm in Pola, because we have fine days now. A few days ago, I received a letter from Miss Flora that astonished me very much, because I did not know how to react. I don't know whether you know about it; if not, don't mention it to her. She writes, I should not be afraid, that she would not tell anybody. Inside the letter was 30 Kronen "to get to America easier." — I was not pleased since I thought she probably took my last letter for one that was begging for money. Perhaps you think the same about my second last letter? And I have to beg that you don't think of me as such a naughty fellow. You know, if one is bothered by something, one feels better to confide to someone. And that is the case with me. That does not seem anything new to you, I think, because I told you so much already of my good and bad times. — Miss Flora writes that we should perhaps go climbing in May. I already know a route that is not too difficult and yet very beautiful and new to you. I would be happy to do this tour, because it soon will be a year that I had the pleasure to guide the ladies. — Will my trip materialize? I don't believe it will in the near future. I wrote and got no answer till now. I thought everything over. What do you think of my new plan? There it goes: If I do not get the money, I will stay here another summer, save as much as possible, and ask for more money for guiding. In the fall, I will then have so much money that I won't need anybody and can go to America without problems, don't you think? Was my letter forwarded to you? And will it also reach you in Pola? If so, please look out over the sea sometimes, because I too love it.

With my best greetings,
K. Kain.

Two days ago, we had a big forest fire in Nasswald. I helped for twenty-four hours.

1. Situated on the southern tip of the Istria Peninsula (of what is now Croatia), Pula was an Austro-Hungarian port town that, until 1918, was known under the Italian name Pola. Its large, natural harbour became Austria's main naval base and a major shipyard during the nineteenth century, and, later, during the First World War, the port was the main base for Austro-Hungarian dreadnoughts and other naval forces of the empire. See H.P. Willmott, *First World War* (New York: Dorling Kindersley, 2003), 186–87.

30

On board *Empress of Britain*,[1] June 5/6/7, 1909

Dear Miss Amelie:

For the past few hours, I have seen nothing of the European soil anymore. — First, I have to tell you about my departure from Vienna: When I left you May 29th, I sat down on a bench. You have no idea how I had to force myself on Saturday to show that I am a man. Inside, I was weak like a female. At the station, I met Mr. Beer, who departed for Africa, and Dr. Kratochwill, who accompanied me to Leipzig. He did not talk nicely about my trip. He said that "the money for the trip I could have given you, too, but I will not send a guide away, whom one needs <u>here</u>! But to get you back, I will give that to you!" (Not bad!) In London, I looked around a lot. The city is beautiful, but I would not want to live there. In Liverpool, I could not see much, and time was too short. I did not imagine the boat to be so big.[2] I had to take third class. That is not pleasant, but it is the cheapest. As an Austrian, I got no ticket and had to pretend to be a Swede. There are no Germans on board, at least in third class—only English people, Swedes, Norwegians.[3] If possible, I won't go third class again. One has no idea about this racket if one does not see it oneself. Children cry, most people are seasick. Just think of a pigsty! The children and girls of Mr. Pearl are very sick. I have not been seasick yet. Mostly, I stay on the deck with my sleeping bag. I saw a sunset, very beautiful, but that is all you see: <u>Only</u> sky and clouds and water. And in the mountains you see <u>so</u> <u>much</u> <u>more</u>! — The air I like a lot. I am always hungry. The food is not first class. Oh, where are you Wiener Schnitzel and you my good beer? My only good things are the dark bread and the cigarettes from Vienna, which I smoke with great pleasure. Thanks a million for them! But with time, things will

∧ *The* RMS Empress of Britain. *Postcard, c. 1910.*

improve. I met a very decent Norwegian, and we talk about mountains and skiing. Today, June 7th, it is foggy. I am sitting in the smoking room, writing letters. I feel fine. Write soon to me to this address: A.O. Wheeler, Calgary, Alberta, Canada. Dr. Pister sends me a card with a Vienna horse-drawn carriage on it: "Let's drive Your Highness a little ways to Canada!!" I received the card yesterday. I had not known that letters are forwarded! Farewell, greetings to your dear parents and sister.

With best regards,
Your Konrad Kain

1.   The RMS *Empress of Britain* was a transatlantic ocean liner built in 1905–1906, in Scotland, for
     the CPR, which, in 1903, had expanded its Great Lakes steamer service to transatlantic service.
     This ship—the first of three Canadian Pacific vessels to be named *Empress of Britain*—regularly
     traversed the transatlantic route between Canada and Europe until 1922 (the war years excluded).
     This Empress was distinguished by the Royal Mail Ship prefix because the British government and
     CPR had, decades earlier, reached agreement on a contract for subsidized mail service between
     Britain and Hong Kong via Canada.

2. The 14,500-metric-ton vessel had a length of 140 metres, and its beam (or width) was 20 metres. The ship had two funnels, two masts, twin propellers, and an average speed of 18 knots. On its maiden voyage, the ocean liner provided accommodation for 175 first-class passengers, 473 second-class passengers, and 809 third-class passengers. See George Mush, *Canadian Pacific: The Story of the Famous Shipping Line* (London: David and Charles, 1981), 162.

3. According to Canadian historians R.C. Brown and Ramsay Cook, "Most European nations were hostile to Canadian immigration agents, and attempted at least to limit their capacity to induce their citizens to emigrate, and in some cases prohibited their activities outright. The government of France actively campaigned against immigration to Canada, while Germany, among other countries, prohibited immigration agents and set heavy licence fees for steamship lines carrying emigrants." Robert Craig Brown and Ramsay Cook, *Canada, 1896–1921: A Nation Transformed* (Toronto: McClelland and Stewart, 1974), 62.

PART TWO

Your Friend in the Western Woods, 1909–1912

- arrival in Banff (1909)
- A.O. Wheeler and the ACC Club House (1909)
- the ACC's Lake O'Hara Camp (1909)
- Glacier House (1909)
- surveys in the British Columbia interior (1909)
- Fort Saskatchewan (1909)
- railway construction for the Grand Trunk Pacific (1910)
- booming Banff (1910)
- the ACC's Consolation Valley Camp (1910)
- a Bow–Yoho traverse and a birthday on Mount Habel [Mount Des Poilus] (1910)
- survey of the Purcell Range (1910)
- a labourer in Banff (1910)
- Banff's first ski club (1911)
- winter sports festival (1911)
- into the Little Yoho (1911)
- bear hunting near Spillimacheen (1911)
- survey of Jasper Park, Yellowhead Pass, and Mount Robson (1911)
- winter trapping with Curly Phillips (1911–1912)
- an offer of employment on a trip to Siberia's Altai Mountains (1912)
- Canadian citizenship (1912)
- departure for Europe and Asia (1912)

31

Dear Miss Amelie:

[In English from hereon] Your letter was the first which I got in this country. My best thanks for it. I'm not doing too many mistakes in English, it is better I write in German. *[In German from hereon]* You write that you got no mail from me. It is possible you did not get anything until June 9th. But you should have received my letter (written in pencil, because I had no ink. I hope that did not offend you?). I'll tell you more about my trip. On the 8th and 9th, we had a storm and one could not lie on deck. I did not get seasick. The 10th was beautiful. On the 8th, I met a Norwegian, who had lived in Vienna for a long time, and, after a long talk, he asked me whether I could dance the waltz. As I am not a good dancer, I told him the truth. He did not let me go, and I had to dance! He danced very well and so I learned how to dance!! On the 11th at 5 P.M., we landed in Quebec, not in Boston.[1] I said goodbye to Dr. Berl, who was very kind to me. If it had not been for him, I would have been hungry. I will explain this to you. Upon leaving Vienna, I had more than 500 Kronen. I bought a travel bag for 10 Kronen, the trip to Hannover 33 Kronen, the trunk 26 Kronen, the trip from Hannover to London 42 Marks, food (I don't know how much), for the dentist 45 Kronen, which was very cheap. In London, I paid 33 Shillings for three days, for the trip 11 Pounds 11 Shillings. Since I went sightseeing, I needed a few Shillings. — Dr. Berl had given me 120 Kronen at our farewell, so I would manage. The trip from Quebec to Winnipeg is wonderful.[2] For almost two days, you drive through forest and pass a thousand lakes! You see no houses for hours. Not like at home, every two kilometres a little house, a signal box station. In Calgary, I got off after

NE CLUB HOUSE

∧ The ACC Club House on Sulphur Mountain in Banff, Alberta, c. 1920s. Photo by Malcolm Geddes. [WMCR, M39/N756/PS-17]

a five-day trip, and since President Wheeler was not at home, I had to wait. — I was received very friendlily and was in a hotel for three days. There were some tourists who asked politely how I was. I am addressed as a Swiss guide. On the 20th, I got to Banff, where I met President Wheeler. He is a very friendly man and made a very good impression. And so does everyone else. The mountains are very beautiful, and so also are the forests and many lakes, which you love so much. I often think of you while I look out of my tent in the evening. Since the ocean trip, I love the stillness of the water very much. I cannot name a town to compare with Banff. Some things remind me of Cortina d'Ampezzo. Banff is in a park that is cut by the Bow River.[3] I work at the Club House and my job is to clean the forest.[4] I live by myself. For meals, I go to a little hotel twenty minutes from here. There are hot springs. Many guests are here with rheumatism and

gout.[5] I am treated like the guests, who are mostly rich people, but that does not matter here. As a labourer, you are the same and have the same rights. I like that. Of course, you come to the table cleaned up. A rich Swiss is here, too, who every day teaches me the most difficult English words and introduces me to the people—as "guide." He likes me a lot and says I am a smart guy. "You will amount to something!" It is strange that everybody who speaks German says "Du."[6] One family lives in the tent beside me. He is a carpenter at the Club House. These people are very friendly. They invite me over every evening and are offended if I don't come. They are really concerned about me. I must say that we Austrians are not as friendly towards foreigners, especially among the working class. Alcoholic beverages I have not yet had here—the bars are closed from Saturday night to Monday morning. It should be like that in Austria, many a labourer would be better off. Yes, you are right, I will return a different man! I am grateful to myself that I have come here. But to be called "Mister" at work is most strange to me. I am also "Mr. Kain!" I am sure I will soon be known here as a guide, because Herr President W. said that my list of tours is longer than that of the Swiss guides. He can hardly believe that such a young man has already seen so much. I don't think I am mistaken that he likes me. At work, I hardly feel to be so far away from home and from my friends. Only in the evening, when I crawl into my sleeping bag, I have such secret thoughts, but not homesickness. That would be bad for me. I will tell you about it later, because, as you know, I tell you a lot that I don't tell anybody else.
—— Your precious name day is coming up. This time it is impossible for me to send you alpine roses, but, believe me, I would love to do it if I were not so far away. In the meantime, I wish you all the best until your next name day, which you stay well and healthy, and never lose your good humour. You will be already in Reichenau when my letter arrives. I will close for now, but you will soon hear from me again.

With heartfelt greetings and thanks to all, and many greetings to Miss Flora and your parents,

your Konrad Kain
Address: K.K. guide, Banff (Alta) Canada.

1. Kain landed at Quebec City, the oldest port in Canada, where crowds of families and friends of those aboard greeted the *Empress* at the docks. Wheeler, believing Kain spoke little English and no French, sent a letter to dock officials requesting the guide receive assistance. Kain, *Where the Clouds*, 210.

2. Of his impression of the CPR and his journey across Canada on the railway, Kain later commented that "the employees of the Canadian Pacific are very kindly, and it does not at all agree with what I heard of foreigners being handled like cattle. But it is true all right that, in Austria, outsiders are treated like animals." Kain, *Where the Clouds*, 210.

3. In 1885, Prime Minister John A. Macdonald set aside a small reserve of 26 square kilometres as a public park known as the Banff Hot Springs Reserve. Under the Rocky Mountains Park Act, enacted on 23 June 1887, the park was expanded to 673 square kilometres and named Rocky Mountains Park and, in 1930, was renamed Banff National Park. It was Canada's first national park and the second established in North America.

4. In 1909, the Dominion government gave the ACC a building site for a clubhouse midway between Banff and the hot springs on the nearby Sulphur Mountain. The Club House was finished in 1910, with a lounge, dining hall, and a second-floor library; tent cabins were erected to house climbers. According to long-time Banff resident Eleanor Luxton (1908–1995), "It was a delightful place, and much used by all climbers." Eleanor G. Luxton, *Banff: Canada's First National Park* (Banff, AB: Summerthought, 1975), 95. Also see L.C. ("Jimmie") Wilson, "The Club House, 1909–1959," *CAJ* 42 (1959): 112–15. In 1973, the ACC built a new clubhouse in nearby Canmore, although the old building stood on Sulphur Mountain until 1974, when it was demolished by Parks Canada.

5. The Victorian fascination with warm mineral waters and health drove the early development of Banff. Stumbled upon by three prospectors in 1883, the Cave and Basin hot springs were similar in content to the renowned waters of Bath, England. As at Bath, at Banff it was commonly held that either drinking or bathing in the waters improved one's constitution. Town boosters hoped Banff would be as popular as Bath. R.G. Brett (1851–1929), the CPR company doctor and sanatorium/hotel owner (later the lieutenant-governor of Alberta), decreed in 1909 that "the popularity these Springs have attained among invalids for the cure of rheumatic and neuralgic afflictions, skin diseases and disorders of the blood, leaves no doubt as to the fact that a most profitable return will be made on this outlay." Quoted in Leslie Bella, *Parks for Profit* (Montreal: Harvest House, 1987), 16. By 1916, the largest outdoor swimming pool in Canada was in full use at the Banff hot springs, though few tourists likely knew that its construction was completed by labourers interned at the Cave and Basin during the First World War.

6. *Du*, meaning "you" in German, is used for those with whom one is on first-name terms, such as family, close friends, and children. *Du* is also used in informal situations, in particular among young people. *Sie* is more formal and is used with people whom one would address by their surname.

32

Banff, July 10, 1909

Dear Miss Amelie:

Today is your name day. I will tell you what I did since I last wrote to you. First, once more, congratulations on your name day, a cheer that you won't receive for another fourteen days. But you can see that, even from far away, I did not forget my calendar and the people who did such good things for me. I will <u>never</u> forget. —— Mr. Wheeler and his family are here now. I do not eat at the hotel any longer. We are all around one table, and I am very well received. It is as if I belong to the family. Mr. Wheeler is a high employee with the government, and his son is an engineer, but at work there is no difference. Everyone uses the desk as I do. They are proud of their work and of what they do. Once we unloaded crates from a railway car, and I said to Mr. Wheeler, "Let us do it. We'll manage," and he answered, "Conrad, I am not a European! Here, the best man takes the axe and fells the tree that is in his way!"[1] His wife is a very good woman[2] for the house and the people, and something else is very nice here, too: a good interpreter! The maid speaks very good German. She is Russian, very nice, and very clever. She loves nature and the mountains. She is happy to speak German, although she speaks English quite well because she was born here. I have to avoid her sometimes, as she is falling in love a little. Mrs. Wheeler noticed it, too. It is too dangerous here. Mr. Wheeler made that clear to me. I won't be in the Club House much longer. In two days, we will be in the camp.[3] I look forward to that very much. Last Sunday, we climbed a mountain, not high, about 7,000 feet. I thought of you when I saw the big mountains and the small lakes. I picked the first flowers, took them home, and put them in my big dictionary. Today, I put them in this letter and send them to you, you great friend of flowers. I discovered that about you on our first mountain tour, a good lady, just like I wrote you in my first letter 1906. Time goes by —— Today, I was at a hot springs, two hours from my tent. I have to be honest with you, since I know that you understand and will not tell anybody. <u>For the first time</u>, I got homesick, quite suddenly. Not really homesick—I don't know how to describe it, but I'll try. To reach this spring, I had to go through high forest, then I reached a clearing: A small deep blue lake to the left, and to the right high mountains, snow-covered, but what really got me were the many flowers, lilies by the hundreds. I lay down by the lake in the flowers. I was all alone and thought of good friends with whom I often spoke about the beauty of nature. And now, there is <u>no one</u> to share the joy with! Yes, thunder without rain!! One says the silence of nature is best when one is alone. But not always. If somebody had been here, it would not have been so hard. I picked some flowers, and I am sending you one as a keepsake. At the spring I took a footbath. On the way back, I avoided the nice spots. Although my English has improved, I cannot yet express myself well enough to talk with somebody about the beauty around us. Yes, you have to go through a lot if you want to move from a simple a labourer in a rock quarry to something higher in an honest way. What pleases me is that President W. is very satisfied with my work and me. In the evenings, he always says, "Konrad, sit with me. Enough for today!" Then, we smoke a few pipes. A lady, who often comes here, told me that I have made a good impression upon him. She translated my guidebook. That I watched like a hawk, as you can imagine! — The Americans are easy to handle. You have to agree with them, and you never want to say that "at home this or that is better," because Americans always seem to claim that their country is the best at everything. There is enough food, but not prepared like at home. But you must not say that if you want to keep them in a good mood. In Canada, what I like best is the equality. Nobody asks for your religion or profession, only a lady asked me about it. But she first said "Please don't be cross about my question." She thought I was a failed student, and not a breaker of stones, because my manners around people impressed her. She said, "You cannot have learned that in the quarry!" I told her about my trip, and said that, as a guide, I am most interested in manners because you deal with so many different people. I told her, too, that I had planned to work since summer is too short to live from guiding alone. She thinks that, here, I would manage, especially working in winter. Whenever she comes in the evening, I accompany her home, and she has told me quite a bit already. She said that if I ever get into difficulty, I could trust her and to let her know. She is a single woman and spends the summer here in a fine hotel, the "Springs Hotel,"[4] which I showed you in the little book. What is bad here are the mosquitoes. There are millions. Almost unbearable! My shoulders are swollen so badly that I can hardly work. These little animals drive many people away. A few days ago, the cook left because of them. Now, I have some netting, and it is a bit better. The next letter I will write from the camp. Since your first letter, I have had no more mail.

With the best greetings,
yours truly,
Conrad Kain
Alpine Club, Banff

1. This is the first indication that Kain changes the spelling of his first name from "Konrad" to "Conrad."

2. Clara Wheeler (1864–1923) was the daughter of the famous Canadian botanist John Macoun (1831–1920), who had made numerous trips to the northwest to survey the railway and evaluate the land for westward expansion in the mid-to-late nineteenth century. Arthur married Clara in Ottawa, Ontario, in 1888. Elizabeth Parker remembered Clara as a "capable collaborator" with a "talent for affairs and a faculty for detail that amounted to genius." Elizabeth Parker, "Clara Wheeler: An Appreciation," CAJ 13 (1923): 181. While much of her life was plagued by bouts of illness, Clara attended many of the ACC's early camps.

3. First held during the summer of 1906, the ACC's annual summer mountaineering camp was already an honoured tradition in 1909. But the 1909 camp, held at Lake O'Hara in Yoho National Park, was a particularly special camp for Wheeler and his club. In that year, the British Association for the Advancement of Science held its annual meeting in Winnipeg, Manitoba, and because a great number of its members were also members of The Alpine Club (England), an invitation was

convened through Wheeler extending such courtesies as might be possible for the ACC to provide the visiting mountaineers. Twenty people accepted the invitation and arrived at the Club House on 27 July, stayed for a few days, and then moved on to the Lake O'Hara Camp. The party consisted of many famous British climbers, such as L.S. Amery (1873–1955), Prof. H.B. Dixon (1952–1930), Geoffrey Hastings, who had been a companion of Albert Frederick Mummery (1855–1895) on Nanga Parbat, A.L. Mumm (1859–1926), with his Swiss guide Moritz Inderbinen (1856–1926), and Edward Whymper of Matterhorn fame.

4. Known to many visitors simply as "the Springs," the Banff Springs Hotel was built between 1887 and 1888 by the CPR at the instigation of its president, William Cornelius Van Horne (1843–1915), who envisioned a chain of luxurious hotels that "capitalized the scenery" of the Canadian west. The famous *Baedeker Guide to Canada* (1894) listed the Banff Springs Hotel as one of the top five hotels in the Dominion. (The four others cited were the Château Frontenac in Quebec City, the Windsor Station in Montreal, and the Russell House and Grand Union in Ottawa.) The Banff Springs Hotel was filled to capacity with 450 guests during the summer of 1909. Bart Robinson, *Banff Springs: The Story of a Hotel* (Banff, AB: Summerthought, 1988), 5, 37, 42.

33

Glacier House, Hotel System. September 8, 1909, Glacier, B.C.

Dear Miss:

Forgive my long silence. It was really not possible to write, because I have been in the deep forest for much of the time and with much to do. So, I want to tell you about it. July 23rd, I went to the camp at Lake O'Hara: Two hours by train from Banff, then a whole day on horseback to the lake. Once there, we set up camp. There was so much work for two weeks that it almost made me angry. On August 1st, the real camp life began. There were many tourists, and I had to guide every day, which I did not like: Nothing for a long time, and then too much of it. Mostly, I went up Mt. Hoover (11,100 feet),[1] a beautiful mountain and not too difficult. Well, I did not imagine life here like that! We set up forty tents. That is work. We had twenty to twenty-five horses, three Chinese cooks, waitresses, and many workers, hunters, and often more than 100 tourists. I was guide, waiter, cobbler, tailor, and barber! Up to August 25th, then we went to another valley. Six days through forest, over glaciers and rocks without path or trail.[2] Bedroom and food on the back! Sleeping under trees or amongst rocks. That was great, but not the carrying of the heavy loads! ——
I must tell you about the beauty of the campground at Lake O'Hara. A small meadow to the left and right dense forest. Snow-covered mountains above the forest, some beautiful formations, like the Swiss or Tyrol mountains. Further down, a large deep blue lake (Lake O'Hara), surrounded by forest. To the right in the forest, two very long lakes, one dark blue, one light green. Higher up, a small lake, which is frozen most of the year, Lake Oësa, the "Ice Lake." An hour

> Conrad Kain (far left) with an ACC group at the Lake O'Hara summer camp, 1909. Photo by Byron Harmon. [WMCR, V263/NA-49/E-33]

further lays a glacier and in the middle a beautiful lake, you need two hours to walk around it. You can imagine the sight of it. I like the green lake best. I often went there in the evening, laid down in the soft moss, and listened to the stillness of the lake. Often, I thought of things from home, funny things and sad things, and then I dreamt about the future. In my mind, I often saw a good friend next to me; often I thought of you and said to myself, "What would you say, listening to the stillness of forest and lake? And I would have someone to talk about the beauty of nature! That would be so beautiful." —— Then, I would go into my tent, close up, put the gun at its place, and dreamily fall asleep. Once in a while, a porcupine comes inside. That provokes a hunt! August 5th was my lucky day, because I showed how much depends on a guide. We were about fifty-five people, who all went up a mountain, Mt. Huber (11,000 feet). I was the last one with my party and went on an easier but longer path. When we got there, a snowstorm started and everybody went back. One Englishman, who also led a group, said to me "Konrad, we will go on, there is still time to turn back. We wait out the weather." It got better, but the Englishman had to go back, as a lady got sick because of the cold. People are all poorly equipped. I had several pairs of gloves in my knapsack, and that was the best, otherwise, I too would have had to return. I had three ladies and a gentleman, and got them up there very well in spite of the fresh snow. Coming down was dangerous, but went well, and the people did not know the danger that they were in. I feared Mr. Wheeler would be angry, because I did not return with the Swiss guides, but it turned out differently. When we returned, Mr. Wheeler met us. His first question was whether we had been on top or not. And the ladies hollered: "Conrad is a good fellow!" — Mr. Wheeler shook my hand with the words "You did well, Conrad!" Then, they all came, more than one-hundred people. Suddenly, they grabbed me and carried me to the campfire shouting "Hip Hip, Hurrah!!" Then, Mr. Wheeler said to everybody, "Yes, it is like Mr. Pister wrote to me, that Konrad does not rest until he has done his job, if it is possible." The Swiss did not like that.[3] They were a little miffed, but they cannot do anything because the Club stands behind me, and they know this very well. From that day on, the ladies always wanted to go with me. It is not good to talk about oneself, but I must tell you that the people here like me very much. As proof, I can report that in a short time I made over forty dollars in tips, and got suits and shoes, mostly in very good condition. And another thing: Everything is fine, but the season is too short for me. Someone suggested I should stay, that they will help and provide a business for me (tourist equipment) because you cannot buy anything here. I said, "That pleases me a lot, but I don't like to operate with someone else's money." I will think about it carefully. It does not sound bad. But one thing I don't understand, you probably can guess! It is marriage! If I have a business, I cannot stay at home. And so I would have to have a wife. I am afraid of that, although I don't fear to get a wife. But who would be the right one in such a hurry? She should be loving and clever, a lover of nature and who knows what else! It would be great if one could do magic! So, I think about it a lot, what I will do, because I will not end my free life in a thoughtless way. One lives only once and life is short (and it also can get too long!). My best thanks for your dear flowers, because they are not as beautiful here. Your letters pleased me very much. I got them all together. I would have loved to enjoy the Rax day with you and Miss Flora. I am happy you had a nice day and thought of me. Your lost jacket, I would have surely found, even if it is in Zerben. I can well imagine what is going on in your house. I am glad everybody is happy. One's own home is worth a lot. I will gladly contribute to your garden, but I am too far away and cannot easily send something. I am really sorry about it. But I have a good idea: In the fall, I will send you seeds for flowers and trees. Perhaps you, a careful gardener of flowers, can do something with them. One very straight Canadian spruce tree would fit well in your garden. That would be the best memento, unforgettable also for me when I come visiting. What do you think about that? I was surprised that your dear Papa sold his business.[4] But I can see it: Man lives only once. And so he should enjoy himself. He probably won't travel to Canada for pleasure, because it is so far. It would be nice, but not everything can be as one wants it. I am convinced you would like it

∧ *Franz Carl Malek.* [Courtesy of Manfred Rotter]

here. I am curious when I will see you again? Not for two years for sure, because I changed my plans. But today, two years ago (September 8th, 1907), I saw you in Johnsbach. Further, I want to tell you, that I am on a trip in the west towards the Pacific Ocean until the end of November. Then I will be paid. I don't know yet how much I earn. It will be about 2,000 Kronen (this is net pay). That is enough, because I know that you cannot reach that in my home country, in Austria. I have to tell you, too, what the entertainment situation around here is like: There is nothing except for the dollar and the alpine world. It's the pits! It makes me sick that there is nothing here like our Sunday. People are very full of bigotry. One talks about the Holy Bible, but it is not right. I realized this early on, that the bigots are not the best human beings. If they stop talking about the Bible, they start with the dollar. I know the Bible, too. And it talks about the opposite. On Sunday, I usually get a little homesick. But I easily get over it: I also am conscious of the dollar!!—and calculate it in Kronen. One dollar is worth more than four Kronen. Up to now, I got fifty-eight dollars in tips: That is about 250 Kronen. That does not happen in Nasswald!! That is the American way! There is nothing to spend money on here, so you have to save. I already lived merrily, and I also went hungry. So I tell myself, "Now you have to watch your money!" That is how one has to look at it as a cheerful Austrian, as a "Nasswaldler." If that weren't so, I would soon return home. Now I benefit from knowing how it is: you either have money or you do not. I bought a Kodak, but only take the most beautiful pictures, if I feel like it. When I am bored, I collect beetles. Often, I feel like an old bachelor, and yet I am a young one! I can treat the Americans in a fine way!! The Swiss guides are far behind us in this regard! — Often, when I explain something or tell something, I think of Dr. P. when he said, "You are oiled with all ointments, now you can go out into the world!" —— I like the older gentlemen and younger ladies best. There is no need to write this to you, because you don't want to become a guide!! I think I wrote about everything. I am writing in the Glacier House, which is known all across America.[5] I am sitting in a beautiful room on a soft chair in a black suit, with a stiff collar that I dislike. "Like a little snob," your Mama would say. The mountains are pretty nice, more so the wonderful glaciers, lakes, and huge trees. I sent a card with a lake on it. Forgive me that I don't write in English. It takes too much time. But I can already speak it well. I speak it better than the Swiss, who have been here a long time. That is what people say, that I have a better pronunciation. I will soon let you hear from me again, with best greeting and a German Bergheil!

Your Konrad
Address: Alpine Club, Banff.
They forward my mail, since I travel with Mr. Wheeler.

1. Kain mistakenly attributes the name "Hoover" to Mt. Huber (3,368 m [11,049 ft.]), which, as the official "graduating climb" of the camp, was popular with those seeking "active membership" in the ACC. See Arthur O. Wheeler, "Report of the 1909 Camp," CAJ 2, no. 2 (1910): 147–63. Set forth in the club's 1906 constitution, active membership required, in the first instance, "an ascent of not less than ten thousand feet above sea-level in some recognized mountain region," and "a summer camp...shall be organized in each year" for just that purpose. See "Constitution," CAJ 1, no. 1 (1907): 179, 181.

2. The six-day expedition, which followed the Lake O'Hara Camp, was organized to enable Wheeler's British guests to see more of the glaciated terrain of the region. In all, 33 people (ten of whom were guests, with the remainder comprising club officials, volunteers, and guides) travelled from Sherbrooke Lake, north over Niles Pass, and then across the Daly Glacier to the western slopes of Mt. Balfour and its outlying spur, Trolltinder Mountain. Descending to the toe of the Yoho Glacier, the party investigated the Little Yoho Valley and later exited via Yoho Pass and Emerald Lake. See Wheeler, "Report of the 1909 Camp": 159–60.

3. Kain was in the professional company of Wheeler's "old standbys," Swiss cousins Edward Feuz Jr. (1884–1981) and Gottfried Feuz, who were annually loaned each summer to the ACC camp as mountain guides through the courtesy of the CPR. In addition, for the 1909 camp, the ACC hired from the CPR Ernest Feuz (1889–1966), Edward's brother from Interlaken, who was guiding for his first season in the Rockies. A.L. Mumm, a member of the visiting British delegation, also made available his personal Swiss guide, Moritz Inderbinen, on a number of occasions.

4. According to records at the *Wiener Stadt- und Landesarchiv*, Franz Carl Malek was the owner of a prominent paper manufacturing company located near his home in the first district (or *Innere Stadt*) of Vienna. The company, registered *Firma Malek F.C.*, specialized in letter envelopes.

5. Two years after the completion of its transcontinental main line in 1885, the CPR built Glacier House near the summit of Rogers Pass, BC, in the Selkirk Mountains—where the Great Glacier (now the Illecillewaet Glacier) spilled down to the valley bottom—to serve as a restaurant and hotel for its passengers. Dining cars were too heavy for the engines to pull on the steep grades. So popular did Glacier House become that, by 1906, the original structure—a dining room and six small bedrooms—was expanded into a large, lavish hotel with 90 rooms, lawns, fountains, and billiard rooms. Throughout the 1890s and afterwards, skilled mountaineers from around the world gathered at Glacier House, to the extent that alpine historians today recognize the area as the "birthplace of Canadian mountaineering." See Chic Scott, *Pushing the Limits: The Story of Canadian Mountaineering* (Calgary: Rocky Mountain Books, 2000), 105. Trains, however, were re-routed in 1916 with the completion of the Connaught Tunnel. Protected from avalanches in what was for decades the longest railway tunnel in North America, trains no longer came near Glacier House. Though it continued to be popular destination with climbers, its best days were over. The hotel was closed in 1925, and, in 1929, the buildings were dismantled. What could be salvaged was removed and sold; the rest was set ablaze. M. Daem and E.E. Dickey, *A Short History of Rogers Pass and Glacier Park* [cover title: *The History of Rogers Pass*] (Revelstoke, BC: Vernon News, 1968), 33–34.

34

November 30 to December 1/2, 1909

Dear Miss:

You cannot possibly imagine the way in which one must travel
around this country, especially considering that it has been surveyed.
As I wrote to you on October 30th (a card), I had absolutely no more
time to write. Ten days ago, I received two letters and a card from
you. Letters touch me very much. Especially yours, since you did so
much for me and since your unforgettable father was so dear to me.[1]
As you know, I got several hundred cigars from him. I can imagine
very well how you must felt when you heard from the doctor that
nothing could help anymore. — And I also know how it is when one
sees their father die. I was with my father to the end and cried many
tears. But there is no way against the laws of nature. I don't want to
open your wounds again. It is easily said, "Console yourself." But it is
not easy to find consolation at first. You will feel like I do when I am
homesick. I often think I have to get it out of my head and not think
of home, but the old thoughts return whenever one sees something
familiar and that is how you will feel. I don't know whether you know
homesickness? I tell you it is horrid! No food tastes good, no smoking
helps, and not even work. My homesickness I could call mountain
sickness, since I think of the mountains more than of home. Recently,
I was in a boring area, and it was terribly cold.[2] No bird could be
heard. Camping is pleasant in summer, but not this time of year. In
spite of my good sleeping bag, I was cold every night. When one gets
one's head out from under the blanket in the morning, everything
was white. Hoarfrost was thick on the blanket, and long threads were
hanging down from the tent. I was, of course, the first to be up. I
heated the stove, and then made a fire outside for cooking. All the

food was frozen, and it was hard work to get water. Today, I also want to tell you about the Indians. At home, one has no idea about their lives. The Indians' huts are built for the cold. The roof is covered with soil and around the house is horse manure. Only the better ones have a floor, but it is not a Vienna dance floor! I get along well with "the brown ones." It is more interesting to see them than to read about them in books. If you enter a hut, the first thing that the man gives you is the pipe, directly from his mouth. Not to offend anybody, you take it and smoke it, even if it <u>disgusts</u> you.[3] It is a sign of friendship. The tobacco consists of dried leaves and tastes very good. The woman seems no more than a slave. One does not greet her when entering the hut. It takes very long to become friends with an Indian woman. They love the white people if there is a chance of marriage. Next to our camp was a settler who had married an Indian woman. I observed myself that she loves him very much. An Indian woman who marries a white is called a "crutch." The opposite is the case with the male Indian. He does not like white women, so none of them need to fear him. With the blacks in South America, it is a different story. They are crazy about white women. You may have heard about that. That the Indian is the best hunter is an old story. I tried hunting with Indians. I shot three deer (elk), and two were very beautiful. This was a joy. But then I often think of the dangerous hours in my home country. Often, I thought of you. I don't know whether you remember our talk when we climbed the Akademiker. It was on the path to the Speckbacher Hut. We talked about hunting. One half of it has become true, but where is the other half? *[In English from hereon]* Yes, you have found the right words: "These happy times will never come back." — Oh, but I hope, sometime in the future I will see you again. It will be very nice to spend some hours with you. And then so many happy hours will come back for me! I would like Haindlkar and the Peternpfad and so many other interesting trails. I remember everything what we have seen together. I often think of it. I feel happy, and sometimes unhappy. I think it is better I write in German again, because there are too many mistakes. But I will write every time a little English. I take lessons in English writing.

[In German from hereon] I'll further tell you that the Indians are not as poor as many believe. They all own a lot of land. Around here, there are some who are really rich. They could have more, but they don't like to work, just like all the Blacks, because they believe that people do not have to work for more than what they need for themselves. Indians are not very good workers. In winter, most of them live on fish and potatoes. That is their main food. But there are many Indians who have a big farm and wear the nicest clothes on Sunday. The women love jewellery. It is interesting how they carry their little kids. They have a little board, nicely done with carvings, which they put the little one on and then tie it on their back. The child lies better there than in their arms. Only, when they cry, the white people get a bad impression. It is amazing to see the little kids alone on the water in the Indian canoe. In the beginning, that was hard work for me— carving a tree into a canoe. You may have seen one of those prepared trees? Now, I am in Calgary for a few days. This afternoon I got paid. I will write you about it. I sent 50 Dollars to my mother, which is 240 Kronen. I was pleased that you visited my mother. I can imagine how she felt. What impression did you get of that little tiny room? One can hardly believe that six or seven or eight people find space there!! Many, many miserable hours I spent there. But mother does not want to move. I will see to it that good and pleasant hours are spent in this little room, since I make good money now and can help her. Yes, dear Miss, you will not know and not believe what a family costs and the worries one has. It is difficult to provide. And yet, family life is beautiful, more so than wandering about on your own without a real home. I know you are a sympathetic, good lady. I can say you are too good. At our farewell, you sent me off with some good advice: "Don't borrow money and give none away!" And now you want to do so your-self for my mother! That is so lovely of you. And I'll tell you, you don't have to do it, because I now support my mother very well. But I'll tell you something else. I am sending my mother now more than 200 Gulden, so altogether it is about 700 Kronen, and when you are in Reichenau in wintertime and have the opportunity, visit my mother in Nasswald and share the joy and serenity of my people. There will

be a different mood in the little room than the last time. I know my mother cried about every letter she received from me and that she thinks of me a lot. So I want to do the best I can for her and she should cry for joy in the dear old home country. —— Now I can tell you how things are with the money. An hour ago, we shook hands, Mr. Wheeler and I. He talked to me in good words. He was a bit tense when he thanked me for my services. He gave a speech. There were some committee members present

(I write it in German): "So, dear Konrad, here is your bill and the money, and I thank you for what you did for me, and I thank you in the name of the Alpine Club of Canada for your diligent work at the clubhouse and for your careful guiding. Especially for August 5th, when you climbed Mt. Huber with three ladies and one gentlemen. On that day, you proved that the Alpine Club has one of the best European guides, since out of fifty five only five reached the top, and they were under your guidance. Among the fifty, there were also the Swiss guides. We wish that you can stay with us for a long time. We will do the best we can so that you become a rich man!!" Then everybody shook hands with me and offered words of thanks. I thanked Mr. Wheeler and Secretary Mitchell[4] for the great effort they made on my sake, and said that I was very satisfied with everything and that I will always try to do the best for the club. Wasn't it nice of the President to acknowledge that much depends on the guide and that it is a profession, where you have to protect the lives of other people more than your own? I copy the bill. I got paid from June 20th to September 2nd, for all days, also Sundays:

71 days ($2.00/day)[5]	$142.00
Guide bonus	$38.00
Travel funds	$50.00
	$230.00
Advance	$80.00
	$150.00

Tips	$60.00
Tips	$20.00
Work for survey	$186.00
TOTAL	$416.00

Altogether, I made about 1,000 Gulden in half a year, and they say next year will be better. The money is the net amount since I always had free meals. What do you think? Can you earn or save this at home? No? —— Oh, yes!! But not as a mountain guide. This thought is medi- cine for my homesickness. At the moment, I have $320.00. I sent $170.00 to Austria ($100 for my mother and $70.00 to my good friend Gerngross, who actually is the focal point in the whole story). So I keep $150.00. With this, I will buy a nice suit to make me look more like a gentleman. Then, there is my trip to Edmonton. On the whole, that will leave me $80.00, which I will deposit in the bank. Next summer, my brothers are supposed to come.[6] Next winter, I am supposed to keep the clubhouse in Banff in connection with winter sports. I cannot agree with the club on all matters. They think I should get married. I said I don't know any women. I thought that would get them off my back. But no! They know two women!! (I know them, too, but I don't want to marry them!!). I said I couldn't keep a woman, since I have to worry too much about my family. I think that, if you don't have the right love, it is better not to marry. I like many girls very much, but none that I care to marry: I mean that I don't have the right love for them, not even for one of them. Please forgive me for writing all this so openly, but I know you are interested in this matter. That is all I know for now. I will write more often now. I will also write to your sister and your dear mother for the New Year. I wish you a pleasant and merry Christmas! Excuse my ink spots. I have to buy a new fountain pen. There is too much ink flowing if I press it down a little too hard. And don't tell about my homesickness in Reichenau, because they don't understand this and nobody needs to know. I wish you much pleasure so that you don't always have to think of your unforgettable father.

With a German alpine greeting,
your Konrad

1. Franz Carl Malek died on 9 September 1909. He was buried at the cemetery in Reichenau, Austria.

2. From mid-September through to late November, Kain worked for A.O. Wheeler on land surveys in the BC interior. While the Cariboo gold rush of the 1860s and the construction of the CPR line in the 1880s had encouraged Euro-Canadian settlement in the region (the City of Kamloops, BC, for example, was incorporated in 1893 with a population of 500), much of the interior was inhabited by the Secwepemc or Shuswap Nation, which formed part of the Interior Salish language group, and homesteaders brought to the region with the fur trade decades earlier.

3. Kain is writing to an audience that is assumed to already know what "Indian" lives are and mean. For example, novels by Karl Friedrich May (1842–1912), "possibly the most-read German author of all time," single-handedly invented the "Wild West" for countless generations of Europeans and entranced Germans with the idea of "going Indian." See "Ich bin ein Cowboy," *The Economist* 26 (May 24, 2001): 84. German literature of the time was especially redolent with the binary of the Noble Savage (the romanticized "natural man," unencumbered by the stifling cloth of civiliza-tion or divine revelation) on one hand versus the zero-degree-of-civility stereotype on the other. Notice, for instance, how this binary appears in Kain's own self-positioning: Watch me do some-thing genuinely human, generous, and inclusive, despite the fact that my sensibilities are like yours (upper class), and I'm actually disgusted. Kain, here, is writing in accordance to the times.

4. Glasgow-born Stanley H. Mitchell (1863–1940) came to Canada as a young man and took up residence at Winnipeg, where he was associated for some years in the lumber business with his brother, who was also a member of the ACC. A keen lover of the mountain wilderness, Mitchell took part in the founding of the ACC at Winnipeg on 27 and 28 March 1906, and was one of its original members. In 1907, he was appointed secretary-treasurer, an office Mitchell held until 1930. His peers at the club remembered him as "a living embodiment of our motto: *Sic itur ad astra* [thus you shall go to the stars]." Completed shortly before Mitchell's death, and named in his honour, the alpine hut in the Little Yoho Valley stands as his memorial. See "Stanley Hamilton Mitchell, 1863–1940," *CAJ* 27, no. 1, 1939 (1940): 101–06.

5. Kain's 1909 wage was half that which the CPR paid its European guides. During the first years of the CPR guiding program, the Swiss guides were paid two dollars a day for their service at Rogers Pass. It was an attractive sum of money in those years—good enough, at least, to entice Christian Häsler (1857–1924) and Edouard Feuz (1859–1944), the first railway-hired Swiss guides in western Canada, to return summer after summer for over a decade. By 1909, the CPR paid its guides four dollars a day. Those rates rose to five dollars per day for much of the 1920s and 1930s. See R.W. Sandford, *High Ideals: Canadian Pacific's Swiss Guides, 1899–1999* (Canmore, AB: Alpine Club of Canada, 1999), 26.

6. The Baptismal, Marriage, and Death Registries held at the Evangelische Church in Nasswald indi-cate that five children were born to Eugen and Franziska Kain: the eldest was Konrad; a second son, Franz, was born in 1886 but died at five months of age; Theresia was born in 1887, Auguste in 1890, and Eugen in 1892. After the death of Eugen Kain Sr., Franziska had two more children: David (b. 1895) and Rosina (b. 1898). The editor is grateful to Karin Schmid for this information.

35

Fort Saskatchewan, December 20, 1909

Dear Miss Amelie:

Now, in the short time since I wrote the last letter, I have done a lot. Since I know that my experience so far away interests you, I use the first free minutes to tell you about it. I wrote to you that I did not find Dr. Berl here, and that I will work here.[1] I took a job with a hunting outfit and went far north. I left this place on the 12th and went with this group for two months (but I am back already). From here, we went for one day on horseback. In the evening we put up a tent in deep snow. The night we spent there was terribly cold. On the 13th at 4 P.M., we reached our destination. Everything there was prepared, but not the way I had anticipated. I had thought they had a little hut there, but it really was a cave in the ground. We pitched a tent as a kitchen. We slept in the cave. I could not sleep. On the 14th, we went out to set traps. It was very cold. Right on the first day, one of us shot a grizzly bear. In the evening, we were very merry and ate Schnitzel. Again, I could not sleep. On the 15th, I stayed in camp alone to cut wood and cook. That day, nothing was shot. Another bad night. On the 16th, we went hunting. I shot a blue fox, another man a marten. "Good luck," everybody said. On the 17th, I had to stay at a particular place for six hours, nothing came and they would not believe it. I almost froze to death. The cold is strange here: everything is still, no air moves. And the ice grows on your body like hoarfrost. That night was the worst. Not one of us five men could sleep (one of them spoke German well). In the morning on the 18th, another group joined us. One of them, an Indian, went home, and I joined him. He had frozen his hands. A very dangerous thing. I also froze a sensitive part of my body. Two hours ago, I saw the doctor. I thanked God that it is not dangerous and will not have any bad after-effects. On the 18th, at 9:30 in the morning, the two of us left the camp and hoped to reach the last homestead by the evening. But it was impossible. We had to spend the night outside by a huge fire that I made. We jumped around like idiots the entire night. Oh, how it was a long a night. In the morning, we continued at a brisk pace. At 1 P.M., we reached a farm. The farmer had to get his horses and took us to Fort Saskatchewan. He did not want to take us, but I told him the condition that we were in. At 5 P.M., we got to the hotel, where I had been earlier. The people there are very kind to me. I had the doctor called from the hotel, but he was not at home. He was at a meeting in Edmonton. I spent the night in a very agitated state. This morning, I saw the doctor. He told me not to worry, that such frostbite often occurs in the strong cold.[2] He spoke German. I will stay a few weeks and spend the holidays here, since I got skis here. It is quite cheap here. Some letters were here for me, too. One from my good friend Gerngross and a card from Dr. Pister. Mr. G. wrote a very dear letter: "Dear K. You cannot believe how I love to get your letters and how it pleases me that I did some good for you, and that you are well etc." Yes, he did a lot of good for me and I will be grateful for the rest of my life, just as with the others. I also got pictures from the mountains that I climbed in summer. I will send you some, so that you get an idea of how the mountains look here. You and Miss Flora should keep them as a memento. On the back are the names and numbers. I will explain that to you:

No. 201 is the lake where I often was lying in the moss and thought of my dear home country and the good friends there. I know you will understand me.

No. 210 is the lake about which I wrote you that the glacier reaches into the lake (little me is the second.)

No. 217 is the tea tent and eating area (the start of it). One can hardly see me.

No. 204 is Mt. Huber, which I climbed six times.

No. 213 is its backside. A steep wall of ice which does not look so dangerous in the picture.

No. 200 is of Lake O'Hara, the large lake next to the camp.

No. 322 is a picture of the six-day trip. You can see how we carried things.

No. 252 shows a beautiful lake near Banff.

No. 205 is a picture with the view from the camp.

No. 304 shows one of the most beautiful waterfalls in the Rockies.

No. 211 is a lake two hours from the camp, frozen almost all year (7000 feet above ocean level).

No. 218 the dining room,

No. 325 scene on the six-day trip. I am the 3rd man from left.

No. 400 a waterfall on the six-day trip.

No. 311 a memorable climb which reminded me of the Stadelwandgrat.

No. 401 is at a crevasse. I was the leader. The last tourist is the son of the president of the English Alpine Club, who will recommend me highly. So, that is it.

If possible, please show the pictures in the Section. But be careful that they don't think that Konrad, who has a bad reputation with the ladies, has sent pictures from Canada to the two Misses Malek!! Please forgive me this remark, you know what I mean. But you can show the pictures to Mr. and Mrs. von Haid. I don't think they consider me a bad person. So take the pictures and decorate your mansion or do whatever you like with them. I give them to you from my heart and will send you more later because I now have my own Kodak. Next will be the diary notes. I pity you! I have to improve them, since I am a little ashamed of them! My exact address is: Alpine Club, Calgary, Alta, Canada. They forward my mail. Who knows where I will be roaming around until next spring. And what will I experience, I wonder! I have a good and yet also not so good life. But I have money! So this winter won't be anything like the last ones and I can give my mother more for her support. I will soon write to you again. This winter, I won't be hunting anymore. There is enough work and I shall find something. How are you? Have you calmed down more about your misfortune? I always think of you, and I don't know and don't want to influence you, but don't you think that it would be better not to visit the grave of your unforgettable father so often? I imagine it always opens the old wounds. I know this from myself and my mother. Too bad I am not at home. I would visit you often. I would teach you to see so you could forget this terrible accident a little. Don't you think? — Now it's time for bed. I have to catch up with sleep. But I will mail this letter today. So I greet you and Miss Flora and your mother many times. With alpine greetings,

your K.K.

1. Located on the banks of the North Saskatchewan River, 25 kilometres northeast of Edmonton, Fort Saskatchewan was "a rather large town," according to Kain, "with two hotels and several businesses. Eastward, in the Beaver Hills, there are only German farmers and, to the north, only French ones. In the hotels, German, French, and English are spoken." Edmonton, the young province's quickly growing capital, was similarly diverse in its cultural makeup. In fact, Kain noted of Edmonton that it was "customary to hear six or seven languages on the streets and in the hotels." Kain, *Where the Clouds*, 245. Between 1896 and 1911 more than a million people poured into the western interior of Canada. The promotion of immigration and western settlement during this period was believed to be, according to historian Gerald Friesen, "a crucial 'national enterprise' akin to the construction of the transcontinental railway or the passage of the BNA Act itself." Gerald Friesen, *The Canadian Prairies: A History* (Toronto: University of Toronto Press, 1998), 246.

2. The doctor sent Kain's companion to a hospital in Edmonton, where the man lost a hand and some fingers due to the severe frostbite. Kain, *Where the Clouds*, 246.

36

Fort Saskatchewan, January 15, 1910

[In English from hereon]

My dear Amelie:

Right on New Years Day I got your card. My best thanks for it. I am very sorry that you did not get my letter which I wrote the 30th of October from Kamloops. I wrote the address to Reichenau. Did you get the one I have sent from Calgary and the other one I have sent from this place? Did you get the pictures which I sent you three weeks ago? Later I was very angry about myself that I have not sent it per Express. I wrote behind on the parcel: If the adressant is not in Vienna it may be sent to Reichenau N-Ö. — I hope the best. Did you like these mountains with snow and ice? And the many beautiful lakes? — So nice it was in this country in summer and so sad is the time for me here now!! —— No good friends and no mountains, no weeds—all is gone—on X-mas day I was homesick, you can believe me, because I have not seen anything I liked in the old country. How was Xmas to you? It was the first Xmas without your father. Next year I think I will be at Banff. Perhaps it is better there. But if it is like this one, I cannot stay here. It is too sad for a young man. I think it is better I write in German again. Goodbye. Write soon. If I get some news from my dear good friend I feel better ——— Will you be kind enough to send some alpine papers? Please do. *[In German from hereon]* This was my first Christmas that I spent far away and amongst strangers. On my former trips, I was <u>never</u> far away from home at Christmas. Here, Holy Night is not considered so holy. It is taken as almost any other day. On Christmas Eve, the foreman at the construction site where I work asked whether I would "work tomorrow."[1] I did not know how to answer. Some people really did work. The people here are pious and bigoted. It's a mistake in my opinion. On a Sunday, the bar is closed, and on Christmas Eve and New Year it is <u>open</u>! And they <u>all</u> get sloshed. — In that condition, the people here are much worse than at home in Austria. Christmas Day I spent in the presence of ladies, and therefore I drank nothing. Sunday: I ski jumped for the ladies,[2] and I observed already that the British and American ladies are not as cool as they are described in books. I am well known here and often get invited for supper in several houses, even by a Russian family once. There, I tutor two girls in German. Four miles from here there is a German village: mostly Austrians from poor and infertile lands of Galicia.[3] But the people don't resemble their country's population any more. Many are well schooled and very popular, and they live <u>happily</u>! They came from a poor area to a fertile country especially for cereal crops. They received the land for nothing, started poor and small, and now most of them are rich farmers and know how to work their fields.[4] But you cannot talk with them about the beauty of nature or of mountain touring. But they want me to talk about Austria, since most of them have been over here for a long time. They all encourage me to start a farm. It wouldn't be bad, but you cannot serve two masters, and I won't give up my occupation. You know that, dear Miss, and you will understand why. It is interesting to observe their marriages. They don't often marry English people and always look for their compatriots. They also have a gentleman who brings people together: The inspector for German settlements. He knows everything, and he matches the right people. Of course, these are not love matches, but this custom is established and the people live happily together. I cannot quite understand. A few days ago, I got many cards from many parts of Austria, also a letter again from Mr. Gerngross.

Hearty greetings with alpine hello,
yours truly, K.K.

1.   Earning 35 cents an hour, Kain worked in Fort Saskatchewan as a carpenter, which, he felt, provided him with the opportunity to improve his English. Kain, *Where the Clouds*, 246.

2.   Skiing was widely introduced by European immigrants to the mining towns of western Canada in the late decades of the nineteenth century. Ski jumping, in particular, captured the imagination of locals and quickly became a popular spectator sport. This would not be the first time that Kain would impress locals with his skiing skills. See Chic Scott, *Powder Pioneers* (Calgary: Rocky Mountain Books, 2005), 19–35; and Jorgen Dahlie, "Skiing for Identity and Tradition: Scandinavian Venture and Adventures in the Pacific Northwest, 1900–1960," in *Winter Sports in the West*, ed. E.A. Corbet and A.W. Rasporich (Calgary: The Historical Society of Alberta, 1990), 99–111.

3.   Highly aggressive in the years leading up to the First World War, Canada's immigration policy was not without prejudice. As Americans promoted their country as a haven for the downtrodden, the Canadian government welcomed only those who could contribute to the nation's wealth. Responsible for western immigration, Clifford Sifton (1861–1929), the minister of the interior under Sir Wilfrid Laurier, did not want "the wretched refuse of your teeming shores"; rather, he wanted sturdy farmers, agricultural settlers of "good British stock." But few English yeomen wished to gamble their future on the cold prairie steppe. Unable to attract the English, Sifton settled for foreigners, but *northern* foreigners, since it was his belief that southern Europeans would not make good farmers. Germans and Scandinavians were deemed acceptable, and so were the sheepskin-clad serfs from northeastern Europe—Ukrainians, Poles, and other Austro-Hungarian Slavs. All of these were lumped together under a single ethnic name, Galician, because so many—150,000, in fact— came from the old Austrian province of Galicia, where life had become unbearable and land impossible to obtain. See Ninette Kelley and M.J. Trebilcock, *The Making of a Mosaic: A History of Canadian Immigration Policy* (Toronto: University of Toronto Press, 2000), 111–63.

4.   Between 1896 and 1911, wheat production on the prairies rose from 29 to 209 million bushels a year. The price of grain and fodder, too, rose steadily and considerably. During these years, the terms of trade moved in favour of prairie farmers, who were also learning to grow new quick-maturing kinds of wheat and to cultivate arid lands with new dry-farming techniques. Settlement, therefore, spread quickly over the western interior along with a network of railways. Small mercantile towns rose up along the tracks. The wheat boom transformed the region and its people. In the process, millions of acres passed from large owner to small occupant. Robert Bothwell, Ian Drummond, and John English, *Canada, 1900–1945* (Toronto: University of Toronto Press, 1998), 55–84.

37

At an Austrian farm, March 10, 1910

My dear Miss Amelie:

[In English from hereon] I have to write a very long letter, and so I think
it is better, I write in German. I like to write in English, if I have more
time. *[In German from hereon]* I am not surprised that you are still in
Reichenau. In your place, I would do the same and turn my back on
the city for a long while. I can believe that the lecture by the North
Pole traveller Payer about "Cook and Peary" was very interesting for
you and also for the others. Here in Canada, one also knows the name ·
Payer, in general one respects the Austrian scientists very much here.
I cannot send you the book now, since I am far away from a larger
city.[1] — From Calgary to Fort Saskatchewan, the train takes about
fifteen hours and now I am twelve miles east of the Fort in the
country. I am with an Austrian farmer and am gaining a general
knowledge about agriculture in Canada. I work at everything. You
might not believe that I feed pigs, milk cows, and take manure to the
fields. During my last years at home, I would have never thought
while wandering through the forest that I could stand to be inside for
a whole day. Yes, much has changed in my life. But it is no shame to
do all this work! Now, I have to tell you the reason why I am on a farm.
I plan to acquire land together with my brothers, Eugen and David,
who will follow me here in June. I received a letter from President
Wheeler, who advised me that I should let my brothers join me here.
The Alpine Club accepted many new members, Mr. Wheeler wrote,
and the possibilities are very good for us. I would stay in Banff and
the brothers would go to the farm. Of course, it will be hard work in
the beginning. First, we have to build a little house. You get 100 acres
from the government for free, and, after three years, you own it and

can do with it what you want. Each year, you have to live on it for six months, and that we can accept.[2] In summer, my brothers shall do mountain guiding, and that would be a way to earn something, if everything goes well. The people in the Club are helping me along if I need something. Mr. Wheeler writes that the whole club is pleased about my good plan and my promise to stay several years. The Club realizes that not every Swiss guide is suitable for this country and these mountains—many Swiss guides have come here to work, but only one guide has come back for ten consecutive years.[3] I already told you that one has to put up with a lot while camping here in summer. But as a guide from the Rax, I have to take it since this is the easiest way to get ahead. But I still remain a good old German and will not stay away from my beloved home for my entire life. I hope that I will be able visit Austria in the winter of 1912 or 1913. It costs less than one thinks, for each winter there are pleasure cruises to Europe with tickets that are good for six months. Oh, it will be nice to see my homeland again. I am very healthy—like the elk in the forest! Only the homesickness—there is no help for that! Sometimes it goes away, often it quickly returns. I am annoyed about sometimes being ridiculed about it. And how do I look otherwise? In the fall, I got rid of my little moustache. I looked like eighteen or nineteen years old again. Some people said I should always shave. But I will let the moustache grow again. I have no thermometer, but there is one at each house, so one always sees how cold it is. One feels it, too. It is <u>always</u> cold here! Winter lasts six months. Normal shoes are not good. You need to have fleeced shoes and rubbers, and, if it is forty below, one stays in the house. You hardly need maps here, which you won't understand, but it is true! When you go to the mountains here, one sets up a camp, and then climbs the mountains close by. The routes upward are not entered in the map, because the mountains are not climbed often enough to make this necessary. There is a map that Mr. Wheeler made—that's his profession. But there are also many unnamed mountains, where one cannot be sure about the route. The snow rose from the base of the Rax pleased me very much. There are none here. I put it carefully with the others. You are right,

dear Miss. Pressed flowers are a nice keepsake, especially if they
come from your home country.

Many thanks for the last letters etc., etc.,
K.K.

CONRAD KAIN

1. Julius von Payer (1841–1915) was an Austro-Hungarian arctic explorer, mountaineer, cartographer, and landscape painter. He authored the *Second German North Polar Voyage* (1874) and *New Lands within the Arctic Circle: Narrative of the Discoveries of the Austrian Ship "Tegetthoff" in the Years 1872–1874* (1877). Although Payer gained some celebrity as a mountaineer in the Central Alps of Italy, he was best known for the "discovery" of the extensive Franz Josef Archipelago. In recognition of the achievement, Payer received the Gold Medal from the Royal Geographic Society in 1875. "Julius von Payer," *The Geographical Journal* 46, no. 4 (1915): 322.

2. Beginning in 1871, prairie settlers, by choosing a quarter-section of land and filing a claim with the government's land office, entered a contract to break at least 30 acres of land, construct a house worth $300, and to reside on the land for half of each year for three years. If these conditions were fulfilled, 160 acres of prairie land—valued at perhaps $10 or $15 an acre on the open market—would be theirs at the end of the three-year period. See Friesen, *The Canadian Prairies*, 306; Bothwell et al., *Canada*, 64–65.

3. After the CPR initiated its guiding program in 1899, Christian Häsler and Edouard Feuz, in fact, both returned each summer season until 1911. Although Edouard Feuz ultimately retired in Switzerland, Häsler returned to Canada in 1918 to live with his son, Christian Häsler Jr., in Golden, BC.

38

Calgary, May 4, 1910

My dear Miss Amelie:

I did not write for a long time—almost two months. You probably think I was too lazy, but that isn't the case. I will tell you of my experiences during that time. I left the farm on March 20th after the farmer had an accident that affected me, too. His two best horses perished, and so he could not pay my wages. So, I travelled to Edmonton, the capital of Alberta. It was impossible to find work there, so I had no choice but to go far north to a railway construction site 200 miles northwest of Edmonton.[1] We could travel 100 miles by train, but then had to walk for four days. Never in my life will I forget this. Mostly, we went through bush, and twice we had to ford a river full of water— melted snow! Finally, we reached the camp. That was a joy, but it was short-lived. During the first night, I noticed lice all over the place. And that was that! Yes, everybody had lice, even the gentlemen. If you are removed from the civilized world, it is normal to have to do without many things. People only have one suit. On Sundays, most of them clean their clothes as best as they can. There are no women around. I was hardly there a week, when a bad accident occurred, which almost caught me, too. Because of a mountain slide, three labourers were killed: a Swede and two Galicians, who also spoke German. All nationalities can be found in railway construction. Now imagine such a funeral: 200 miles away from church and cemetery!! — It is almost impossible to transport the bodies so far, and it is not the custom. It took four days until the police came. They were buried on the sixth day. It was eerie—without a priest! Over 300 labourers were present. A beautiful resting place was found in a meadow for them. There were no coffins. They were wrapped in bags, and all three were buried in one grave. Eulogies were given in four languages: German, Swedish, English, and Polish. Can you imagine, dear Miss? I had to be the representative for German! I could not get out of it. I had two days to prepare the eulogy. This was not difficult, as there was enough material for the speech. The two Galicians were married, and their families were still in the old country. But the whole affair affected me very much. I don't want to give another eulogy. After the funeral, many Germans thanked me. One even asked me whether I could not hold the sermon next Sunday? — One could not determine what religion the two Galicians belonged. The Swede was Lutheran. On April 29th, I left this work and went back to Edmonton, where I finally got mail again from the dear old home country. Yesterday, May 3rd, I went from Edmonton to Calgary, where I am now presently in the office of the Alpine Club President and am writing to my friends. You are the first, dear Miss, and I know I still owe you answers from the last letter. But, unfortunately, I have your letter in my suitcase, which is on its way to Banff. But I will write about that later. I know where I stopped: At self-education. You can imagine how surprised I was about your two dear cards from Dalmatia! I am happy for you to have taken a beautiful cruise and wish you many more great days, because I am convinced that the beauty of nature and the distraction do a lot to brighten one's life and one forgets, even if not totally but at least for some time, the sad parts. It also pleased me that you thought of me at the beautiful shore of the sea. Yes, dear Miss, you can believe me that, quite often, my heart is beating loudly and my thoughts are with the fatherland. And when I get such beautiful cards from home, it always begins again and many airships bump into each other in my mind! Then each airship is damaged so badly that it cannot be used any more. Of course, it is no problem to build another one right away! — While working on the railway, I met a German-Hungarian, who told me the story of his life. The first part was not very nice, but the last part, his experiences in America, was very interesting. He also told me that homesickness makes you very old, and I really believe it. He said that I can be sure that whoever loves their home country gets homesick, and whoever doesn't love their home country is a bad person who has nothing to offer. I agreed. I made many interesting observations. Here, one meets many interesting people that have no need to be so far away. There are also people of nobility here, people who have committed bad things at home and are taking refuge in America. ———

Spring here is not at all as lovely as at home! It is already May 5th and not much green grass can be seen, let alone flowers. The song of the birds is not as lovely as at home. How pretty it will be around your mansion in Reichenau! Please write more about your lovely spring trip. I have already told you about my spring trip!! We only spent one spring day together, you and me, outdoors in nature. Around the Vienna Woods! — I hope that my summer trip will be beautiful. The Club has a big program.[2] Many Germans and Americans are coming to the camp, as well as some famous tourists from England. In a few days, I will be all alone in the clubhouse in Banff. I long for good news from my brothers regarding their trip to Canada. I don't know anything definite yet. I wrote to them that they should say Goodbye to you when they depart. Take a look at these young travellers carefully!! I am sure that they will learn a lot so far away. They'll return as changed boys.

——— I had to interrupt writing for a few days because I had to go away. I was at a ranch because of horses. It is already May 10th, and it stormed and snowed like in winter! I would not want to live here in Calgary. Everything is boring. There are no beautiful parks like at home. Of course, these cities are still very young. — Tomorrow I will travel to Banff. I think it will be nice there. Now, I will send you something to read about the Rocky Mountains. What do you think, dear Miss? Would you perhaps come over here to visit? You can imagine that it would be an indescribable joy for me to show you all the beautiful lakes in the forests and to talk with you in our true mother tongue! But this will probably not come to be! So I wish you a cozy life in

Reichenau and many beautiful hours in God's wonderful nature, where we met and tied the ribbon of friendship. And may it last a long time and not tear and end even across the big ocean! I greet you from my heart with a German Berg Heil to you, and your dear mother and sister.

Yours truly,
K.K.
Address: Banff, Alta.

1. Kain was labouring in the construction camps of the Grand Trunk Pacific Railway (GTPR), which had its westbound clearing and grading operations near Wolf Creek (near present-day Edson, Alberta) in April 1910. The GTPR, a wholly owned subsidiary of the Grand Trunk Railway, was formed in 1903 with the mandate to build a railway connecting Winnipeg, Manitoba, to the Pacific coast at Prince Rupert, BC. By spring of 1910, much of its track had been laid across the prairies; all that remained of the job was to close the mountain gap from Wolf Creek west to the Rockies and over Yellowhead Pass to Tête Jaune Cache, where eastbound crews from Prince Rupert were headed. Thousands of teams—a veritable army of workers, many of whom were immigrants—were engaged in the expansion. "Work on the N.T.R., Progress Made on the Big Road is Encouraging," *Globe and Mail*, Tuesday, March 8, 1910, 2.

2. The ACC held its annual summer mountaineering camp in the Consolation Valley, near Moraine Lake and Laggan (now Lake Louise Village), which was the "jumping-off station" for the camp. For an account of the camp, see A.C. Galt, "Consolation Valley (Rocky Mts.), Annual Camp, 1910," *CAJ* 3 (1911): 137–46.

39

Banff Alta, May 17–21, 1910

Dear Miss,

Since May 12th, I have been back in Banff and very happy. I am the master of the house, nobody else is here. I am quite alone in the big club house until June 15th. It pleased me very much when Mr. Wheeler handed me all the keys. Everything is open for me, even the piano is unlocked!! But, unfortunately, I cannot play. — In the mountains, there is certainly a different life than in the flat country and the big city. Firstly, you are freer in everything and, second, the people are friendlier in the mountains, here just like at home. I have enough work, but nobody pushes me. Of course, I work hard anyway, because I am happy that the Club trusts me so much. Friends in Banff welcomed me very warmly, and everybody wanted to know how I spent the winter. Even an Indian came. He said that he often thought of me in wintertime. Then we had supper together. Really a dear man! He is also kind of a guide, speaks English well.[1] I sent you a picture of him. The first Sunday I stayed at home: The weather was bad and there is a still a lot of snow on the mountains. I washed clothes, but enjoyed it, which is often the case with women! — How do you imagine this, Miss Amelie, the mountain guide washing clothes! It works well. In the afternoon, I went to the pool. I met many friends there. I then went for a walk in the forest. Great! Fresh air after a hot bath, the birds singing, blue violets, fresh greenery, and in the background the high mountains, which still wear their winter clothes. The violets were the first spring flowers here. I thought of you and picked a few. I will include them in the letter. Banff is really a beautiful place. It's very pretty now with the fresh green and the snow-covered mountains in the background, but most important—the little flies are not here yet!! I would be happy if they never came again. Yesterday, Monday 16th, I ironed my clothes. I worked well, but folding things was hard. I folded some pieces so often that I had to iron them again! But I was not angry. When I was finished, I sang the old hiking song: "If mother would know how things are in the foreign land!" ——— I think, my brothers will not be pleased when they see that you have to do <u>everything</u> yourself in this country. Today, the 17th, I washed windows and tidied up the house. At noon, I tried to bake a pie, which turned out well, only too brown. Next time, I'll know better!! In the evening I went to the post office in the village. Nothing there for me. — Now it is 10 P.M. and I will finish. Continue tomorrow.

——————————————— *[In English from hereon]* May 18 Today I was working hard and at once Mr. Wheeler is standing behind me! I did not know that he is coming up today. So we had dinner and supper together. He was very happy. He said: "I am just as glad, Konrad, as you, if I can stay at Banff again." He gave me order to put up more sleeping tents. And that is not so easy. But I hope I will fix them alright. And then he told me that so many Germans and English will be coming this summer. And there are coming two German girls and a lady, who will look after everything, who is German too. And so it will not be too bad for my brothers. —— I think I am going away from here on the 1st of July. I am going in the Yoho Valley. I was there last fall. It is a fine place. Ms. Wheeler cannot go to Banff this summer, she is very sick. I am very sorry for her, because she is a good and friendly lady. Well, what do you think about my English writing? I think in one or two years it will be alright. *[In German from hereon]* But German is always easier! Did you get my long letter and the book? How do you like it? It is the best that I could find in Calgary. There is another nice book: *Camping in the Mountains*.[2] But I could not get it. I am reading a very interesting book: *A Guide to Zermatt and the Matterhorn* by Ed Whymper. If I owned it, I would send it to you. But I can give you the address: John Murray, Albemarle Street, London.[3] It also describes the first accident on the

Matterhorn. You could easily travel to Zermatt. It does not cost much and it is one of the most beautiful places in the Alps. And, if I were there, I'd say, "Now, dear Miss, if you want to come and have courage, then we go up to the Matterhorn. It is not hard, but long!" When I read descriptions of mountains that I have visited, I remember the beautiful impressions. I have had such good times as a guide and as a traveller. The other days of my life were not the best. But I anticipate better times when my brothers come, and when they find their right place in the world. I can then finally keep my money for myself. If it would only be true that the Hotel Association introduces winter sports here next winter, then I would be in good shape. Then I could earn as much money in winter as in summer. They are building two more hotels in Banff, and a highway from Calgary to Banff. In ten to fifteen years, Banff will be a world-renowned mountain village, perhaps like St. Moritz or Grindelwald.[4] —— I told Mr. Wheeler that, in two years, I want to go home in winter. He said, "Konrad I am sure, you won't have the time. In two years, we will have much to do for you, and you soon will become a rich man." And he continued, "I am sorry we could not do more for you and that we have a short season. It will be better from year to year. We have six hundred members now and more tourists are coming out from the old country every year." ——— Who can say that he is right? It would be a pity to lose that money. I told you before of my plans for the future. Until I am forty-five or fifty, I want to work, but then I want a quiet life. Up to now, I have nothing for my retirement, when I want to live on the Zikafahnler Alm.[5] I have twenty-three years to see what can be done. Who knows whether the future will bring more bad things than good ones? —

————————————— May 20. Yesterday, I was down in the village and received several letters. Yours was there, too, the one you wrote in Reichenau on April 15th. Many thanks for it. You know I am a friend of travelling and want to see a lot of the world. I am so pleased for a good friend, or lady friend and good acquaintance, when they get to know new places. It pleased me a lot that you liked your trip to Dalmatia so much and that you feel better. I had heard a lot about Ragusa and can believe that, according to your description, it must be very beautiful.[6] I can see it like a picture now. I don't think I'll get there myself. I won't become that rich to take such trips at my own expense. I wish that your impressions stay with you, your dear mother, and Miss Flora for very long. However, there will always be something leading you back to sadness. Just like now when the fresh young green of spring reminded you of the great loss your father's death meant to you. I sometimes feel like that when I am alone and see the new awakening of nature. — This time, you didn't have many questions. About the Russian girl, you are right: I don't like her. One loses trust for real love with some people. One judges wrongly after such experiences. I have other things on my mind: How can I best use my money? When winter sports start here, I think I might open a business for supplies: "Outfitting." I am also planning a nice trip (perhaps in a few years) to New Zealand and Australia. If I were married, it would be good to stay in one place—you wrote something in your last letter that I had not asked for: your age. Forgive me a little remark about this. I did not trust my eyes and put the letter away. "Is it possible, is it possible?" I asked myself. Yes, everything is possible. I can congratulate you, Miss Amelie, that you still look so young! I sometimes thought, "How old can the lady be?" I never guessed more than thirty-three or thirty-four years.[7] —— I again have a moustache and am convinced I would recognize you right away and you would recognize me. I would want to be recognized AS AN OLD FRIEND OF THE MOUNTAINS AND AS YOUR GRATEFUL STUDENT! With best greetings to you and yours,

yours truly, K.K.

1. The Siouan-speaking Stoney (Nakoda)—who arrived in the region after 1790, and perhaps not until the mid-1800s—knew the Bow Valley and the eastern slopes of the Rockies well by 1870. In his annual report of 1879, for example, Indian Commissioner Edgar Dewdney wrote that the Stoney "are good hunters and trappers, and spend a good deal of their time in the Rocky Mountains, between the [US–Canada] Boundary line and Jasper House." Edgar Dewdney, "Report of the

Indian Commissioner," Annual Report of the Department of Indian Affairs (ARDIA), 1880, 80. During the late nineteenth century, surveyors and explorers commonly turned to Stoney guides, and, as a result, many landforms in Banff National Park are still known by their Stoney names. Despite the prominence of Stoney place names, however, after two decades of park building in the late 1800s, Aboriginal peoples were actively excluded from Rocky Mountains Park (Banff) in the interests of game (not wildlife) conservation, sport hunting, tourism, and Aboriginal assimilation more generally. See Theodore (Ted) Binnema and Melanie Niemi, "'Let the Line Be Drawn Now': Wilderness, Conservation, and the Exclusion of Aboriginal People from Banff National Park in Canada," *Environmental History* 11, no. 4 (2006): 724–50. To this day, the Stoney Nation's crucial role in the early tourism industry of the Rockies remains notably absent from popular histories of the region.

2. Kain could be referring here to Walter Dwight Wilcox's popular *Camping in the Canadian Rockies: An account of camp life in the wilder parts of the Canadian Rocky Mountains, together with a description of the region about Banff, Lake Louise and Glacier, and a sketch of the early explorations (1896).* The book's appeal—which Neil Wedin recently argued "played a key role in spurring on the world's fascination with the Canadian Rocky Mountains"—warranted a revised and enlarged edition, re-titled *The Rockies of Canada*, in 1896. See Neil Wedin, foreword to *The Rockies of Canada*, by Walter Wilcox (New York: W.G. Putnam's Sons, 1900; Surrey, BC: Rocky Mountain Books, 2008), vii. It was, for all intents, the first real guidebook for climbers and explorers of the Canadian Rockies, and its creative non-fiction narrative style no doubt enthralled a largely urban reading public with a thirst for the excitement of mountain and polar travel.

3. John Murray, the famous publishing house on Albemarle Street, specialized in books of travel, exploration, and adventure, such as Edward Whymper's *A Guide to Zermatt and the Matterhorn* (London: John Murray, 1897).

4. By the turn of the century, Banff was still a very small, one-industry frontier town situated in the fledgling Dominion park. Not yet a year-round destination, the park virtually shut down during the cold months that followed September: many local businesses closed, and commerce was brought, almost, to a halt. But, by 1910, the financial benefits of winter sports generated increasing interest from the CPR, which, after expanding and modernizing its Banff Springs Hotel, turned its extensive advertising efforts toward promoting Banff as a year-round destination. Over the next decade, prominent local businessmen took notice, as well. Their efforts, along with the CPR's, would soon create a wintertime image of Banff that has long since been the standard stock-in-trade of Banff's modern tourism industry.

5. Near Nasswald, the Zikafahnler Alm was alpine pastureland on the slopes of Raxalpe.

6. Ragusa (Dubrovnik) is a city on the Adriatic Sea coast of what's now Croatia. With its luxury hotels and medieval walled city, Ragusa became a popular tourist destination in the nineteenth century. With the fall of Austria-Hungary in 1918, Ragusa was incorporated into the new Kingdom of Serbs, Croats and Slovenes (later the Kingdom of Yugoslavia) and renamed Dubrovnik.

7. Amelie Malek was born on November 17, 1871. She was 38 years of age when Kain paid her this compliment and 12 years his senior.

40

Banff, June 22–25, 1910

Dear Miss:

Today, June 22nd, I received your card. Thank you so much. And since you are writing so often, I have to answer your last letter. I want to be a good pupil and answer all your questions. The place where I worked and where the sad accident occurred has no name. It is still wilderness. But on the map you will find the Yellowhead Pass and perhaps Wolf Creek (70 miles from Yellowhead Pass). You know almost my entire life. Except for the trips in the mountains with good people, good friends, among them I put you first, dear Miss, most of my life has been sad and serious. — Yes, it was very exciting for me after the accident to give the eulogy. Now, I am again in the right-fully called <u>beautiful</u> Banff.[1] But for a few days, I was sad. Again, I got bad news from home: it is <u>impossible</u> to bring my brothers to America! — I got so embarrassed in the Club, because we expected them here any day! — And now this! All my good and feasible plans fell into the water, and I have to remain alone so far away. At the end of the letter, my mother hints that she would like me to come home. That I cannot quite understand —— although I struggle with home-sickness, a hard struggle. But I don't want people here to know this. I can only say that "home is home, never a place like home——." Yes, you poor lady, I know your soul, and I wish that you could forget your sad thoughts. It will be easier from day to day. Good things are happening for you and they will drive your sad thoughts away, so you can enjoy life. —— Since most of my dreams always crumble, I will give up my planned outfitting business for an indefinite time!!

> *Conrad Kain, 1910. Photo by Byron Harmon. [WMCR, V58/NA66-408]*

— Your "surprise in the camp" came to my mind a few nights ago—a dream which pleased me. It was the first time that I saw you in my dream so clearly and so real. The day of May 29th, I also thought of you. Much came to my mind. I cannot believe it has been a year that I said farewell to my Vienna friends. Did you receive my card from May 29th? It was Sunday, and I had to work. I did not notice anything about the Pentecost Holy Days here. I don't think they are celebrated here. News in Banff: the one interesting event is that two big bears came into our house in broad daylight! Shooting is not allowed because this area belongs to the protected nature park. I have to calmly let my hunting fever pass. But on the 20th (two days ago), one of the bears was actually shot from our reading room. What impression does that give you? To shoot bears from the clubhouse!! Yes, there are many bears here, but they are not to fear people. I had visitors every day because of them. People came just like in winter to the Höllental for the elk observation. You are right: the days when we went to the Akademiker und Stadelwandgrat belong to the spring season—also the spring of my life that I will never forget. I don't know yet when we will listen together to the songs of the birds in the Weichtal. But if things work out in the future, it will one day happen. We will take a nice tour together again. — I read about the hunting exhibition. It must be very beautiful. I am always pleased to hear from good friends and it is good that one can put one's thoughts to paper. However, I decided to stop writing so many letters, since so few people are writing back. Of course, you are not included!! I am happy to have one person—you, dear lady—who understands my letters! — Recently, I received a letter from an acquaintance who offended me a bit as it concerned homesickness. You know, I write everything as it is, and so the yearning for the old dear mountains of home was stressed too much. I admit it. So mostly, I will send cards now, and then people will know that I haven't forgotten them. But for you, I permit myself to complain a bit, don't you think? — I saw the Halley's Comet very clearly in the winter, but not any longer now, since our house stands amidst mountains so that you don't see much of the sky.[2] I think I have now answered all your questions. Now, I have to tell you some things about me. I had my photo taken and will send you a picture so you can see how I look as a guide in Canada![3] I think I look the same as before: the old hat, the old suit. —(No, that one you don't know). Otherwise, I will be the same as always. Since my brothers cannot come, I have a tent house to myself. I call it my home. You would be amazed how nicely I fixed up the simple tent. Full of pictures from home. A rope, two ice picks, and my gun hang on the wall. The tent is on a hill, but, unfortunately, trees block any view. I made a hammock, but cannot use it much; there is no time, and, in the evening, the little flies are very bad. I cleared the forest around the clubhouse nicely, and everybody who sees it is pleased because they don't know beautiful parks like we have. But I have the right to give everybody a piece of my mind: when they throw away things and aren't aware of the fussy caretaker who is around. — It is too bad that we have hardly any people here. The season is too short. Soon, though, I will depart for work and you won't hear from me for a while. But when it is possible, I will write. Your name day is on July 10th, and I think this letter will arrive at Reichenau in time. You will see that, even from far away, I don't forget much. And so I wish you all the best from my heart. May you be very well until that day arrives again. I am sending you my picture and two photos (waterfalls), the yearbook of the Alpine Club of Canada, a book with scenes from Banff, and a few little books for keepsakes. Please accept them and don't think they cost too much for me. Please write to me when Miss Flora's name day comes up. A hearty German Berg Heil to you on this beautiful day! Farewell, my dear good friend Amelie!

Yours truly,
K.K.

1. This moniker was no doubt made popular by local boosters. In 1912, for example, Norman Luxton (1876–1962), the owner of Banff's *Crag and Canyon* newspaper, published Banff's first comprehensive visitor's guide, a promotional booklet titled *50 Switzerlands in One: Banff the Beautiful.* Earlier, James Outram, in his *In the Heart of the Canadian Rockies* (1905), uses the phrase "Banff the Beautiful" as the title of his second chapter. See Outram, *In the Heart of the Canadian Rockies,* ix.

2. The year 1910 saw considerable public interest in the predicted return of Halley's Comet, which reached perihelion on 20 April. Kain, perhaps, confuses the Great Daylight Comet of 1910 for Halley's apparition. The Great Daylight Comet surpassed Halley in brilliance and was actually visible in broad daylight for a short time about four months before Halley made its appearance. The appearance of the Daylight Comet, therefore, came as something of a surprise and made an extremely strong impression on an expectant public.

3. Kain's endearing guide photo was taken by Byron Harmon (1875–1942), the official photographer of the ACC since 1906, who first arrived in Banff and the Canadian Rockies from Tacoma, Washington, in 1903. Through his photographs, Harmon is widely credited for "capturing the golden age of mountain exploration" in the Rockies. His collection of images, which exceeds 6,000, is maintained by the Whyte Museum of the Canadian Rockies in Banff.

41

Golden, B.C. The Columbia Commercial and Tourist Hotel,
August 30, 1910

My dear Amelie:

You will hardly believe me when I tell you that, for two months, I
have been in no bed or in a proper room, where one could comfort-
ably sit at a table to write a few lines to one's good, dear friends. A
chair has become a foreign object. Now, I am back in a nice hotel,
but unfortunately only for a short while, therefore you have to excuse
the shortness of this letter. You know that I love to write long letters
to you and tell you all the details if possible. Now, I have to tell you
quickly about my long silence. At the end of June, I left the club
house in Banff and went to the Yoho Valley, where we set up camp.
From there, it was back to Laggan, where I received your little parcel,
which was a great joy for me. Then, I wrote you the card with the
pipe, and I hope you understand the meaning. It was a miracle that
I found such a fitting card! From Laggan, I went to the Consolation
Valley. There, we had a large camp, which required a lot of work.
On July 10th, I did a first ascent with young Wheeler.[1] How often I
thought of you! I thought how beautiful it would be, and what joy for
you, to do a great first ascent on your dear name day! When we got
back to the camp, I wrote a card in great haste. On July 11th, I did a
first ascent of an unnamed mountain of over 10,000 feet. Afterwards,
it was named Mount Konrad.[2] On July 21st, life in the camp began.
But to my surprise, it was quite dreary: only ninety people, which
was quite different from last year's two hundred. On the whole, it
was a disappointment for me. On August 1st, we went on an eight-
day trip into the Bow Valley. From there, it was off to the Little Yoho
Valley, where I stayed until August 23rd.[3] I then went to Banff for two

days, and am now on a one-month trip that has to do with hunting into a totally unmapped area south of Golden.[4] I received your cards and letters, and will answer them properly on my return. With best greetings,

Yours,

K.K.

1. In the company of A.O. Wheeler's 20-year-old son, Edward Oliver Wheeler (1890–1962), Kain arrived at the Consolation Valley Camp on 9 July. Already a capable climber, the young Wheeler would later participate in the first topographic survey of Mt. Everest in 1921. He wrote accounts of his first ascents made from the 1911 ACC camp, specifically of Mt. Babel and Chimney Peak, but they were ascents made in late July. What he climbed with Kain on 10 July was not recorded. See E.O. Wheeler, "Mount Babel and Chimney Peak," *CAJ* 3 (1911): 73–79.

2. Again, the peak that Kain refers to here is not clear. From the Consolation Valley Camp, various peaks stand in excess of 3,048 metres (10,000 ft.)—but, of these, few were unclimbed in 1910 and none were unnamed. A "Mount Conrad" does exist in honour of the guide, but nowhere near Consolation Valley. In the 1930s, a celebrated English alpinist and professor of literature, Ivor Armstrong Richards (1893–1979), applied the name to a 3,251-metre (10,666-ft.) peak in the Purcell Mountains, which, south of the CPR line, rise between the Rockies and the Selkirks in south-eastern British Columbia. See Glen W. Boles, Roger W. Laurilla, and William L. Putnam, *Canadian Mountain Place Names: The Rockies and Columbia Mountains* (Calgary: Rocky Mountain Books, 2006), 70.

3. See B.S. Darling, "Up and Down the Yoho," *CAJ* 3 (1911): 157–71.

4. In late August, Kain left Banff in the employ of A.O. Wheeler, Byron Harmon, and Dr. Tom Longstaff (1875–1964), an English doctor, explorer, and mountaineer, famed for being the first person to climb to elevations exceeding 7,000 metres in the Indian Himalaya in 1907. Longstaff also employed two packers, W.B. "Bert" Barrow and Charles Lawrence. Their objective was to survey the Purcells from the Columbia Valley to the Duncan Valley, and north, so that the survey could connect with old stations on the Prairie Hills, and then return to the Columbia by another pass. While the terrain turned out to be too difficult to tackle given the time available to the party, it was nevertheless one of the earliest recorded explorations of the Purcells, bringing mountaineers into close contact with the Bugaboos for the first time, an area soon to be famous for its granite spires. Originally printed in the *Geographical Journal*, Longstaff's account was reprinted in the 1911 *CAJ*. See T.G. Longstaff, "Across the Purcell Range of British Columbia," *CAJ* 3 (1911): 26–39.

42

Bugaboo Valley, September 9, 1910

My dear, good Miss Amelie:

Far from all human habitat, far from railroads and postal services, in one word, I am in the wilderness! But I am not a savage yet! It is September 9th. A beautiful day of memory for me took place almost 7,000 miles away from the beautiful mountains, when we were together three years ago! I am sure you too remember. You were only a few miles away from the mountains, which were so mysterious in the fogs of fall. I remember everything so well, even though I am far away from there—in the Bugaboo Valley! But my heart and thoughts are where I was three years ago! Everything returns before my eyes—I smoke my pipe and it is like on the card that I wrote to you. More I need not write, because you know yourself how beautiful the day was, the time on top of the mountains, the view, and how you felt the first time in your life being on the rope. I can only assure you that I will think of this beautiful day all my life and thank fate that I experienced such a day as it was. With German Berg Heil,

your K.K.

43

Banff, October 22–25, 1910

My dear Miss Amelie:

[In English from hereon] I can understand that you already looking for a long letter and I will write one today. I will tell you about my last trip. There have been so many new experiences and some days with very hard work, and the nights sleeping outside, that means without blankets. The weather was not the best. Most of the time, there was rain and fog. I think it is better I tell you all that in German, for writing in English is not so very easy, you know. But you can believe me that I can <u>speak</u> pretty well. —

[In German from hereon] Was my last letter not long enough? It seemed very long to me, and I think I wrote about everything. On the whole, the camp was not bad, but it was hard, hard labour. We were not enough people, so the hard work was left to the two of us: Mr. Wheeler's son and myself. We set up fifty tents again, and there was not much wood. The campsite was near a really beautiful lake (Consolation Lake). But it was not as beautiful as Lake O'Hara, and the mountains were not so easy to reach. We had bad luck on the very first day of climbing. I had two ladies and one gentleman for Mt. Bident. The man and one of the ladies had never climbed before, so we moved very slowly. Eighteen hours had passed until we reached the camp again. The same day, one of the Swiss guides and a group went up the same mountain————. The next day, we were out again for sixteen hours and did not even reach the top of Mt. Fay. On that day, I had a few complete "greenhorns" with me, among them a lady who was in the mountains for the first time and almost too heavy for this tour. She was a teacher at a university in Chicago. That

day, we were altogether twenty persons. After this tour, we set up a "high camp." From there, I took a very easy tour up Mt. Fay. We then set up camp on the other side, in the Larch Valley, from where we climbed Mt. Temple (11,624 feet), the highest mountain of this group. The camp was at a beautiful site near two lakes, Mt. Bident (10,000 feet), Mt. Fay (10,600 feet), and many alpine flowers. I met a friend of flowers there, just like you. When I noticed that she loved flowers, I picked some for her and she was so pleased. I told her little stories and noticed that she really is a friend of nature and flowers, and is a very good person. And so I finally had the same experience as I had in the old home country. Can you remember what I wrote to you in my very first letter: all people who love nature and flowers are good to others. I can say that about you. About the American friend of flowers, I know nothing, not even her address. I climbed Mt. Temple once, and was once up Mt. Eiffel (over 10,000 feet). On that one, I had a "poor" party, one very heavy lady, a gentleman who was almost blind, and two young lads. One thought that I would not get this group to the top, but I did my best. Afterwards, I got a big ovation. After that day, I had a day of rest. In the evening, I had to give a lecture at the campfire. I did not want to, but the people said that my English was good enough! So, I told them about a night at the Ödstein (Ennstal). Afterwards, I went with two gentlemen up on Mt. Fay. A splendid day. The same day, Dr. Longstaff broke a finger on a first ascent with Mr. [E.O.] Wheeler, who named the unnamed mountain "Chimney Peak." When we felt sorry for Dr. Longstaff, he said, "Oh, there has to be an accident sometime!" Dr. Longstaff is a model for everybody who goes with a mountain guide. On July 31st, we left the main camp and went on a six-day trip. The first day to Laggan, where we camped by the river, then along the Bow River—this year we had ten horses—to Bow Lake, then six miles across a snowy pass to the Yoho Valley. The day before, I was on a small easy mountain. The Bow Valley is very pretty and was new to me, but there are many mosquitoes and hornets. Horrible! We were expected up in the Yoho Valley. I stayed in the camp with several people. There, I found your letter and card. We climbed several mountains. I did a first ascent.

On my 27th birthday, I climbed Mt. Habel (10,000 feet). It was a beautiful morning and a good view. Habel is a German name, named after the first man who climbed it.[1] At noon, the weather changed, and we got caught in an electrical storm so strong that I thought that it might be my last birthday. My hair stood straight up. We were on the top of rocks. When we got to the snow, it was much better. My ice axe was ripped like grass in the wind. You would never have experienced this! — In the camp, there were two British ladies with whom I climbed six mountains. These ladies had climbed many mountains in the Tyrol, Salzburg, and Steiermark, but could not speak German. I enjoyed talking about the mountains in my home country. The ladies will go to the Tyrol again next year. One day, we took the Emerald Pass (9,800 feet) to the Emerald Lake Chalet and back via Summit Lake to the camp. A pretty long trip. On August 23rd, we closed the camp. That day, I went with a couple through fresh snow up Mt. President (10,200 feet) to Emerald Lake and to Field. The woman was on a mountain for the first time and did well, better than the gentleman. I don't know whether I ever wrote you that ladies do better here than the men?[2] In Field, we missed the train and had to stay overnight. I was very offended that evening by the Club people, but I don't want to write about it. Then, we went to Banff, where we stayed a few days. I had to cut wood. On August 27th, we went to Golden. I wrote to you from there. Then further into a new, uncharted area. It was very interesting, but hard work, especially for me, because I always had to lead with the axe. I also was the cook, which meant I had to work while the others rested. I had not envisioned this, but now I know the meaning of "the first party through." The first days were not so bad since we followed a trap line. But when it ended, and we had to find our own way, many hard hours followed. On September 4th, I went out for meat. I succeeded in shooting a mountain goat. I also took the skin and the four feet, and so I had a heavy load. In addition, I had to climb down a whole rock wall (very cautiously)! When I got to the ground, there was quite a stretch of open alpine meadow, and there I saw a brown bear, which I followed but could not get. Twice I shot, but it was too far away. I ran until my heart and my lungs gave out, and I had to lie down for a while. Then, I went back to carry the meat. It got dark. I did not think that this evening I would have to sleep under a tree. But it had to be, since moving in this forest with numerous windfalls and bushes went too slowly. Laden with load, I fell and rolled down quite a stretch, and a long time passed before I found my gun. I had no lantern (my own fault). I was so tired that I could not go any farther. My load was thirty to thirty-five kilograms. Then it started to rain. I sat down under a tree and tried to make a fire—no luck! Matches half wet, wood, too. With a deep breath, I tried the last match, and it failed. What a worried feeling. I lay down, and covered myself with the goatskin, which protected me from the rain. But I got so cold that I had to get up. Long were the hours! No stars visible, eerily dark. — At five in the morning, I left. Within five minutes, I was soaked through. At 6 A.M., I reached the camp. Everything was quiet, everybody slept. I made breakfast and changed my wet clothes. I was astonished to hear that Dr. Longstaff had shot three grizzly bears. Later, we congratulated each other. It snowed—stormed—impossible to climb a mountain with instruments, because there was no visibility. So I went with Dr. Longstaff and a packer for the bearskins. It was cold work; one cannot wear gloves!! I went to the camp with one skin and cooked a good soup: goat meat, rice, and potatoes with a little flour stirred in. Dr. L. was exhausted when he came back, the packer too, and he said the soup saved his life! Mr. Wheeler was in a bad mood because of the weather, and we had to cheer him up. We did an "Indian dance." Dr. Longstaff and the two packers wrapped themselves into a bear-skin and I myself into a goatskin. Mr. Harmon was the musician. Instruments: one pan! And so we danced around the campfire for a long time with terrible screams! Next day, the weather was no better, so we stayed in the tent. I baked a lot of bread and the others worked on the skins. Next day, the weather was a little better, but too windy for surveying. I went up a mountain with Mr. Wheeler to get to know the area. I had my gun along, but did not see anything. On top, we had a pretty good view of so many unclimbed mountains. I was sorry to only look at them and pass by the most beautiful and highest ones. We had climbed a few small ones. The following day, we took a rest at a small mountain. Very fine weather. We spent more than five hours on top. I had nothing to do. When Mr. Wheeler was ready, I got the task of building a stone man, five feet high. The view was marvellous: a beautiful glacier and very fine spires, which would not be easy to ascend.[3] I thought of the date, which was September 8th. I remembered the time a few years ago—and on September 9th. Today, Mr. Wheeler and I ascended another peak. Right after getting up in the morning, I began to think about the Ennstalerberge three years ago. I went climbing with a young lady who was entrusted to me when she needed the rope. And how well she managed! For four hours, we stayed on the peak, from 11 A.M. to 3 P.M. ——— I knew our thoughts would meet somewhere. In the evening, I wrote a few lines and this was not so easy, so I kept it short, because had I written more I would have mentioned your situation and your mourning. But I did not want to spoil these beautiful memories. But today, I can tell you about it and that I was thinking, how my dear good Amelie is? She can no longer be as happy as before, especially on September 9, 1907. I would be glad if once in my life that I could spend another day in the mountains with you. And I hope for that. With you in my mind, I thought about your situation and thought of the days which brought you unexpected events. I keep your dear father in my thoughts. And with these sad thoughts, the day of memories ended. ———

Today, our horses had very hard work to do. They had to cross a pass (I will send a picture, so you will get an idea). Mr. Harmon and Dr. Longstaff, as well as the two packers, also had hard labour to do. At one spot, they had to rope the horses just like tourists. It is impossible to believe what the horses mastered, unless you see it with your own eyes! —— On the pass, Dr. L. stayed with one tent and made camp. That was exactly at the timberline. We had to climb another mountain from there. It was a cold evening. The next morning we

> ∧ *Granite spires of the Bugaboos, 1910. Photo by Byron Harmon. [WMCR, NA71-0859]*
> *Conrad Kain, Tom Longstaff, "Bert" Barrow, and Charles Lawrence. The Longstaff-Wheeler Purcell Expedition, 1910. Photo by Byron Harmon. [WMCR, V263/0840]*

had a foot of snow. So we could not get out on the mountains. The horses continued with all the supplies and we had enough food for only one more day. So I went to another valley, on the other side of the pass, to get supplies since we had to reach that mountain for the survey. Soon, I reached the camp, since I could go downhill. I saw fresh big bear tracks. Mr. Harmon and the two packers had breakfast only at 9 A.M. I went back to the camp at the pass and shot two grouse with the pistol. So we ate *malecken* (an Indian name) in the evening. Do you know this food that comes close to your dear name?! — We sat by the campfire until eleven at night. Dr. Longstaff told us about his trip to the Caucasus. The next morning, the weather was bad again, and we did not want to spend another day on that windy pass. So, we went to the main camp, our tent on our backs. We left the instruments behind on the pass. It was better in the main camp. The next morning was beautiful, so we returned to the pass and from there up the mountain. We returned to the other side. It was hard going. We hit such a steep stretch that we rolled downhill. Never before did I see bushes on such a steep stretch. Next day, we climbed another mountain. It was a very long day. The others improved the trail. The day before, Dr. L. and Harmon went hunting. For nothing. On the mountain, today, we got a totally different view. You can see hundreds of mountains that have never been climbed. Quite tired, we returned to the camp. We had been gone for thirteen hours. The next day, the camp was moved as far as the trail had been cleared. Since we had no meat left, I went hunting for a goat, which I liked, so I shrugged off any weariness. I climbed around for a long time until I could see something. I then saw two goats, but they were too far away and I could not get closer. I headed for them, climbed quite a bit. I thought I would return with empty hands. The sun was setting, and I had nothing and didn't want to return to the camp empty handed. So I crossed another clearing. There, I saw an old buck, but he was far below me and difficult to hit. I tried, and the second time, the poor animal fell over high rock walls. I was sorry to have to be cruel, because of the meat—these wild goats are so nice. Perhaps you saw one on your hunting exhibition? This time, I did not take the whole goat, and the path back to the camp was not so bad. I arrived before nightfall. In the morning, we had a good breakfast: bacon and liver. Then, we went up a mountain with the instruments. Dr. Longstaff came along for a grizzly, Harmon had washday, and the packers looked for a decent path, though they came back with long faces. We reached the peak after six-and-a-half strenuous hours. On top, two young goats came very close. Dr. L. saw a grizzly, but did not get it. I think he was very excited because he was alone. I heard the shots. On the descent, I took some more meat (from yesterday's goat) since we passed the spot where it lay. We did get near a small bear, but Mr. Wheeler had only one pistol, so we could not kill it. After this day, hard work and new experiences began. No trace of a trail to the area that we had to get to for the survey. The valley was very narrow and the shrubbery so dense, you hardly could see as far as five metres. We had to wade through a very wild creek. We cut down a tree to get across easier, but tough luck! The tree hit a rock, broke, and floated away. One bad thing after another. For instance, we walked the trail a half- or a quarter-mile, encounter an obstacle, and then return. The similar example is the stretch Payerbach-Nasswald, no pass or trail! — On one day, we crossed a creek six times, had rain, wet sleeping bags, and cold temperatures. The next morning, again wet clothes and again into the waist-high water. This for five days. Suddenly, we hit a good trail. Hello! Everything over! Hurrah, Hurrah! But how long? The good mood lasted one hour. I went ahead and met a man. I happily called out to him. He was astonished and said, *[In English from hereon]* "Where do you come from?" — "We come from the Bugaboo Valley!" He said, "How many are you in your party?" — "Six men and ten horses." — "Oh, you cannot go farther with the horses. It is impossible!" — "What is the name of that creek?" — "That is the Howser Creek." — "So, and we were thinking we are on Reno Creek!" We laid down, and the man told me about the country. He was a trapper. At last, the horses came after, and everyone was disappointed to hear that we are on the wrong trail. And Mr. Wheeler would not believe it. But it was true. The trail had been made by a few prospectors. So we reviewed the whole situation and found out that there is only one way to come out and that is to go back. *[In German from hereon]* To go back took much time. Dr. Longstaff and Mr. Harmon could not accompany us any longer. They had to search for the nearest path to civilization. The trapper took them to the Howser Lake, and, as I heard later, they had to spend a long night in wet clothes under a tree. So we were left with four men. It was very exciting because of the Pass. We asked ourselves, "Could we take the horses across the pass with the fresh snow on the ground?" It did not look so good: rain in the valley and snow on the mountains. Worst of all, the creek was high because of the rain. Already bad luck on the first day of our return: one horse fell in the creek with its pack, and my warm coat was in it. I thought the horse would be dead. It was underwater for a long time: there were trees across the water and the poor animal had been pulled under. After two hours of hard labour, we brought it ashore. We had to cross the creek three times that day. We rode across twice, but the third time the horses could not come back: it was too risky. So, at a narrow spot, we cut down a tree. But unfortunately, the tree broke in the middle and floated away. The second tree did the same; it was not long enough. It was getting dark as I walked along the stream to find a good place to cross, and, finally, it looked good. I went back and called Mr. Wheeler, who was already dead tired. When I showed him the place, he said it was too dangerous, and that it really was not ideal! But more searching proved useless, so I jumped across ——— the water was higher than I thought. It splashed high above me. So I had to fell a tree to make it easier for the old man. And now we were wet from top to bottom, and we still had to walk quite a distance until we reached the camp. The campsite was not very good. The poor horses had to be tied, since it was too dangerous to let them roam overnight. Without being fed, they had to stand up all night. We had no time to set up camp. Very tired, I still had to make supper. It was very quiet that evening. Everybody was glad not to have to talk. All four of us were lying behind a tree, covered with a tent. There was a heavy thunderstorm. The lightning was eerie in the darkness. The next morning, we were all quite stiff. So we only took a short trip, and we stopped at the first good site where there was grass for the horses. The next day, we had another long hike, again, of course, very wet. But we came close to the pass. It did not look good: fresh snow! Mr. Wheeler and I went ahead with the instruments, since he needed measurements from the pass. How will the horses come up? That was the question. Luckily, the sun came out and made things easier. At the pass, I left Mr. Wheeler and went off with the gun. I had Dr. Longstaff's Mannlicher from Steyr "Made in Austria"![4] I thought I would soon get something as I had found fresh tracks. It turned out differently. I had a difficult trail, and I had to keep my eyes on the ground. Also, my boots hurt terribly! I saw a goat but I did not want to climb too high in the fresh snow. Slowly, and with hope, I crossed the alpine meadow and each little hill. I saw seven different bear tracks. One was so big that I almost got scared. I followed a grizzly track for quite a distance, but it led into the thicket. So, I continued on the alpine hill and hoped for a deer, which, by evening, luckily got near camp. It was almost too dark to shoot, but the Austrian rifle from Dr. Longstaff went precisely where I had aimed it—the head—so that the elk died instantly. That evening, things were different at the camp-fire. A few minutes after I arrived, the good looking meat sizzled in the pan and we had a good supper. "A drink!" The packers were very glad that the horses easily crossed the pass and that we would soon be again on a "human" path. The next day, we were to climb a moun-tain, but it was too foggy. So, we went further and found the trapper's trail. That was pleasant. Then we climbed a peak for surveying. Mr. Wheeler worked for four hours. Oh, they were four long, cold hours! As pleasant a rest is in good weather, it is awful in bad weather. The next day we went five more miles, then we had a day of rest (the weather was bad). I went out with my gun and aimed at a big eagle but missed. With the bullet in flight! — I was not a good hunter! Next day, we climbed a very steep and brittle mountain, and, when we reached the top, the fog set in so there was nothing to see. We waited three-and-a-half hours, but in vain. The next morning, we were to see people again. We did after fifteen miles. It was very pleasant to see a set table again and even a good bed with linen sheets. It looked so nice, but I could not sleep. It was too soft and comfortable! The others said so, too. The place was called Spillimacheen Stopping Place, forty-one miles from the Golden railroad station. Since Mr. Wheeler wanted to combine his work with a survey line, we went out early in the morning. A man told us that if we climbed the hill on the other side of the river, we could see some spots where we had travelled. That was convenient for Mr. Wheeler. It looked as if everything would end well. So I want to report on the "good ending." We took our lunch, crossed the river in a boat towards a cleared line, and everything looked easy. Reaching the other side of the river, there was a bog. We went around it and so we lost our line. Having it back, we reached a channel, which was too deep to wade through. After a long search, we found a suitable spot to cross. But where is the line now? A second channel caused us great difficulties, and there was such high grass that one could see nothing. It is dangerous to go through such high thicket. Finally, we reached the slopes of the small mountain, and we would have reached the top soon if we did not have to go along the line. "Today we can do nothing anymore," the old man said! "I am sorry, but I cannot help it, we have to sleep outside this time." — We looked for a good site. Thank Goodness, we had an axe with us. So we built an Indian hut out of little trees and made a big fire. How was supper? Brief and simple. No cooking, no dishes to wash: two little slices of bread for each, and enough tobacco. The night was clear. Now again, the old familiar story: On one side you get fried, on the other you freeze. So, we turned about a hundred times. When it got grey, a warm wind came up and then rain. That's the end! We can do nothing but go back and look for the sleeping place again. Breakfast was poor: two pieces of Peter Chocolate.[5] Smoking was no fun either. In half an hour, we were drenched. But the dense forest gave us a breakfast; we still had a little luck, since we found a trail, which in two hours led us to a hot breakfast, which was a cup of good coffee. Now one thing was left: an opportunity to get to the train in Golden! The horses were gone already. But often unexpected things happen! So a little steamship came on the Columbia River that brought us to Golden on the same evening.[6] I had a hot bath and then slept fourteen hours very well. The next evening, I reached Banff, while Mr. Wheeler went west. But this season has not ended for me. I experienced a great disappointment which, unfortunately, I have to keep to myself, but I'm glad to tell you. I have to be more cautious with others. With many things, luck has been with me, but only smiles, and it is hard when luck turns around and again shows its old, boring and often bad face! *[In English from hereon]* If I did not know that you have always understood my writing and speaking, I would not tell you about my broken luck. But I feel much better, if I can tell it to one of my good friends. So listen: *[In German from hereon]* Didn't I write to you in spring, that this summer will go well with earnings? Luck smiled on me. I will save 2,000 Kronen! Yes, such a rosy picture was painted for me that I already felt 1,000 Kronen in my pocket, and the other 1,000 Kronen would follow easily. But it did not work out that way. I did not write to any friend in Europe about it, and they won't hear it. I cannot do it, because I would have to turn things around, and that I cannot do. I always wrote good things about Canadians, and they were good and still are. Only Mr. Wheeler was not quite honest. Of course, he looked for an excuse, but that doesn't help me. I'll tell you the matter was. I worked hard last spring so that the club house in Banff would be in shape and everything would be ready when the people came, at which time I left. One recognized, too, that I did more than my duty. At the end of June, an English tourist arrived, who needed a guide for fourteen days at Mt. Assiniboine. The Englishman talked to me before asking Mr. Wheeler, but Mr. Wheeler said, "I cannot let you have Konrad. I urgently need him here." That was what the gentleman told me when he returned. He was miffed about Mr. Wheeler, as he had believed to get the club guide. Because he didn't, he lost two days, as he had to wait for the CPR guides. That was the first case. — A few days later, Dr. Longstaff came with his sister to climb Mt. Assiniboine for twelve days, and again I could not go. I had hoped to go, because I met the packer, who takes the people and horses, and he is a good friend of mine. He painted me a picture of the most beautiful mountain, and said "you come along!" So I thought he had heard it that way. In the evening, Mr. W. let me know that I should wait for the Swiss guide, who would arrive by train in the evening. I went to the station and got him. Mr. Wheeler wanted him to sleep together with me in my tent. Mr. W. led him towards the club house and pointed the way. I had no room for him, and thus got very angry! Next morning, I had to clean the veranda and watched as the party left the club house with another guide. I threw down everything and went to my tent. I could not have endured to talk to anyone: I could not have talked, my heart was so heavy. So I went on strike and wanted to see old Wheeler, but could not catch him alone. He avoided me. His son comforted me and told me nice things, so I worked again. Had I had enough money, I would have left. But where to go without money? Then we did the trip to the Yoho Valley, and from thereon I wrote you everything. They also sent another guide to the Yoho, and I could work up to July 10th and 11th. I told you about those dates. Now, I am finishing my tours. There are few. And only now I learned that a gentleman wanted to take me to South America. For September, they'll pay me one dollar extra for cooking, and that I owe to Dr. Longstaff. He also gave me ten dollars and two pairs of shoes, and said, "I am sorry that you could not come with me in June." He gave the other guide a twenty-dollar tip for twenty days. But nobody said anything; it was as if nothing had happened. In another week, I will clarify things and will see how things go. I will tell Mr. Wheeler what I think, and demand a written contract for next year. It is also possible that I won't stay if they refuse to pay what I have asked. But I won't go home because of that. I plan to go home with nothing less than 1,000 Kronen. I speak English fairly well now, and I have friends and acquaintances on each continent. I'll find something if I need it. As soon as the Grand Trunk Pacific is ready, I will go there as guide.[7] So that is what hurt me. What do you think? These are "hard lines," right? But I am the guilty one. I am too good and give in too easily when it comes to business matters. Mr. Wheeler's excuse was that he could not find workers for the house. That is how it was. When I returned from the trip, I had my picture taken in work clothes. I also had a moustache. I will mail this picture, and the letter, and will enclose another picture from *Spring and Fall*. I think that will be the right title; I am curious what you think of it. Right now, I am clean shaven again, which my mother does not like. I will send you a picture later: how I look as "an Englishman." In spring, I will let my beard grow again. Now, you want me to answer all your questions. I'll postpone it this time, since this letter is already pretty long! — For one month, I will now do nothing but write and will really continue my diary notes and send them. You are right when you say that I am "too lazy to write." I took notes of everything and wrote a large part already. Forgive me this laziness. Today, I translated a German letter into English from the central library of the German and the Austrian Alpine Club. Those clubs want to become friends and exchange books. For now with best greetings to you and yours,

With alpine greetings and Berg Heil,

K.K.

1. Jean Habel (1839–1902) was a German mathematician and geographer. Famous mostly for his explorations in the Andes, he also made two lengthy visits to the Canadian Rockies where he mapped parts of the range. The peak was named in Habel's honour in 1900 but was subsequently changed by order-in-council during the First World War, when German place names in the Rockies became undesirable. The current name, Mt. Des Poilus, honours the contribution of French troops in the Great War. Incidentally, in 1985, the Committee on Geographic Names undertook a belated rehabilitation of the name "Habel," applying it to the nearby, previously undesignated north peak of Mt. Rhondda. Boles, Laurilla, and Putnam, *Canadian Mountain Place Names*, 79–80, 115. Mt. Des Poilus was the mountain featured in Lawren Harris's famous 1930 painting *Isolated Peak, Rocky Mountains* (Oil on canvas, 106.7 x 127.0 cm, Hart House Permanent Collection, University of Toronto).

2. In contrast with The Alpine Club in England, the ACC was enlightened insofar as it permitted women to be members. In fact, nearly one-third of ACC members in 1907 were women; by 1927, women constituted half. Gina La Force, writing in the 1979 CAJ, attributed this diversity not to the liberal nature of the ACC but to the innovations demanded by Canada's size and sparse population. Gina L. La Force, "The Alpine Club of Canada, 1906 to 1929: Modernization, Canadian Nationalism, and Anglo-Saxon Mountaineering," CAJ 62 (1979): 40. The Alpine Club (England) did not permit women members until 1974.

3. This is Kain's first view of the granite spires of the Bugaboos. Later, in 1916, Kain made first ascents of two of these "nunataks" (Bugaboo and Howser Spire) and claimed they were "as interesting and difficult as any I have encountered in the Alps." Kain, *Where the Clouds*, 429.

4. The bolt-action Steyr-Mannlicher rifle (1895 model) was the standard issue rifle of the Austro-Hungarian army.

5. Perhaps not fully appreciated by Kain for breakfast, Peter Chocolate was an international sensation in Europe during the last decades of the nineteenth century. A Swiss candlemaker by trade, Daniel Peter (1836–1919), with the help of his neighbour, Henri Nestlé (1814–1890), was the first to blend milk with chocolate. The company opened its first manufacturing facility in North America in 1908. Later, in 1951, the company was renamed as the Nestlé Chocolate Company.

6. From 1886 to 1920, steamboats ran on the upper reaches of the Columbia River in the Rocky Mountain Trench from Golden, BC, south all the way to Jennings, Montana. Steamboat captains Armstrong and Blakley regularly serviced the Golden–Lake Windermere section. According to William Dennison Lyman, "over the hundred miles between these two points, the Columbia is a slack-water stream, having a descent of but fifty feet [15 metres] in the distance from the extreme head waters to Golden." See William Dennison Lyman, *The Columbia River: Its History, Its Myths, Its Scenery, Its Commerce* (New York: G.P. Putnam, 1909), 278.

7. Wishing to emulate the southern CPR—which had built fine hotels along their line, imported European mountain guides, and promoted tourism and trail-riding—the advancing westbound GTPR, along with its rival company, the Canadian Northern, promised new opportunities for the Athabasca Valley and the environs of Jasper Forest Park, created by order-in-council in September 1907. See Peter J. Murphy, "Following the Base of the Foothills: Tracing the Boundaries of Jasper Park and its Adjacent Rocky Mountains Forest Reserve," in *Culturing Wilderness in Jasper National Park: Studies in Two Centuries of Human History in the Upper Athabasca River Watershed*, ed. I.S. MacLaren (Edmonton: University of Alberta Press, 2007), 87; and C.J. Taylor, "The Changing Habitat of Jasper Tourism," in MacLaren, *Culturing Wilderness*, 200.

44

Banff, November 19, 1910

[In English from hereon] My dear good friend:

[In German from hereon] That is all I am writing in English today. I think you will have received my last letter that I sent by registered mail. Perhaps an answer is already on its way, and somewhere our letters will cross paths. After the letter, I sent a card, which you probably also received already. Unfortunately, I already know that you will be disappointed again because of the picture I wrote about. This time, it was not the photographer's fault, no. I don't know myself how it happened. Suddenly, the parcel appeared among my books. I really thought that I had sent it to your Vienna address, VIII Josefstädterstrasse 64.[1] — I am now down in the village and have an apartment for myself: a kitchen, a room, cook myself, only go to the hotel at noon, as there is no time to cook. I live with a fellow, whom I met in the mountains. In the summer, he is a "packer," which is what one calls the guides here. He has a brother; they are both unmarried, my own age.[2] Between the two of them, there is a big difference. One saves money like mad, the other uses his money for travel in winter time. He already was on most continents. This winter, he will be in Honolulu for several months. I would love to join him!! But I have to be content with the trips I take as a guide. And the main thing is the money, about which I will now tell you more. It turned out a bit better than I had thought and calculated. But I am still disappointed, because it could have easily been more.

Account: October 31, 1910

May: 27 days at $2.00 = 54.00

Jun: 30 days at $2.00 = 60.00

Jul: 31 days at $2.00	=	62.00
Aug: 31 days at $2.00	=	62.00
Sep: 30 days at $3.00	=	90.00
Special climbs:		30.00
Expenses in Calgary:		9.00
Expenses in Field:		1.20
October: 31 days at $2.00	=	62.00

430.20

Cash E.O. Wheeler	15.00
Cash book	100.00
Blankets	7.00

122.00

Remainder	$308.20
Exchange	.50

$308.70

I made about sixty dollars in addition. On the whole, it is not as bad if one has this money in the old country. But one also has to calculate the work I did for it: often fifteen to sixteen hours a day! I purchased several things: food for two months ($25), rent $10, and wood for a few dollars. Thus, much of money is used up. At this time, I have $200.00 in the bank, $60 I have with me, and will send money to my mother, but I'll wait for her message to see how much she needs. I sent her $50 in the summer.

On November 2nd, I started to work as a carpenter and, except for a few days, worked all the time. This week, I was at home for three days because I did not feel well. But since people came every day, I should go to work if at all possible. I tried again today. I think it will be okay for a while. But I have to take the cure this winter. I won't write home about this. If they knew this country and the strenuous conditions here in summer, they would ask what is wrong with me. I am proud of my health and can stand quite a bit of stress, which I have proven. But I have no resistance to this Canadian wilderness sickness, although I fought it for a season. This illness is das *Reißen*, meaning the rheumatic ripping and pinching in the bones. Staying in wet clothes and lying on frozen ground in the fall in the mountains are the cause. But this illness is said not to be dangerous. If you go to the hot springs and bathe there, then one gets rid of it.[3] And that must be true, otherwise all the old trappers and packers would be crippled! As long as the weather is good, I shall work so that I have enough for the winter and don't need money from the bank. In winter, I probably won't be able to save. Here in the West, everything is very expensive and therefore the wages are a little better than in the East. So, now I have to tell you my definite plans. I will only stay one more season with the Alpine Club, then I get a position as a guide for the new railroad (Grand Trunk), which goes through the Rocky Mountains and will be completed in spring 1912. I hope I get to the Yellowhead Pass.[4] But before I get there, there is something I will "guide." Next fall, I will see my good old Vienna friends! As a surprise, I will knock at their door, "who is there?" — "Oh, an old fellow!" will be the answer, and they will know who it is because I will answer in the old <u>Nasswald dialect</u>!! I will stay only a few weeks in my dear home country, since I am going to France for the winter to learn the language and have a change. If you were in Reichenau during my visit, I would be very glad to take French lessons from you. I think you won't be as angry anymore as before. But I don't think I will be so good that I won't deserve the ruler as a punishment once in a while!!! — I hope to leave Canada with 2,200 Kronen, and I need not spend it all in Europe.

With best greeting to you and yours,
your K.K.

1. Records at the *Wiener Stadt- und Landesarchiv* indicate that in 1910, a year after her father's death, Amelie Malek purchased an apartment at VIII Josefstädterstrasse 64 near Vienna's wealthy *Innere Stadt* (or First District). She lived here alone until 1931.

2. Kain is likely referring to brothers Bruce and Closson Otto, who arrived in Banff from Ontario around 1904 to work with their older sibling, Jack Otto, who had been outfitting in the region for a decade. The Otto Brothers organization was officially formed in 1907 and, in 1909—because of their excellent service to the ACC's 1908 Rogers Pass Camp—they were appointed the valuable position of "Official Outfitters to the Alpine Club of Canada." Kain worked with the Otto brothers at the ACC's camp at Lake O'Hara in 1909 and in the Consolation Valley in 1910. Not long after, the Ottos relocated their business to Fitzhugh (Jasper), where railway activity promised new opportunities for outfitting. E.J. Hart, *Diamond Hitch: The Pioneer Guides and Outfitters of Banff and Jasper* (1979; EJH Literary Enterprises, 2001), 83–84, 138–42.

3. If one believed the Banff Springs Hotel's publicity drive, Kain's warm estimation of the waters was not far from the mark. By 1910 Banff was known internationally for its hot springs, which were thought to be "especially efficacious for the cure of rheumatic, gouty, and allied conditions," as well as for conditions of "the liver, diabetes, Bright's disease, dyspepsia." Quoted from Robinson, *Banff Springs*, 30.

4. One of the half-dozen main corridors through the Rockies, the northernmost Yellowhead Pass connects what is now Jasper National Park in the east and Mount Robson Provincial Park in the west. Due to its modest elevation (1,110 m [3,642 ft.]) and gradual approaches, the pass was recommended by Sir Sandford Fleming (1827–1915)—the Scottish-born Canadian engineer widely known for proposing standard, worldwide time zones—as the best route across the mountains. The CPR rejected the proposal, largely for political reasons, in favour of a more direct and southerly route over the much steeper Kicking Horse Pass.

45

Banff, January 15, 1911

My dear Miss Amelie:

You will have received my New Year's card on which I promised you a longer letter. Yesterday, January 14th, I got to Banff and have to return to the camp at 2 P.M. I have little time and will sometime tell you about camping in a tent in winter. You will hardly believe that one can survive in a tent in winter, since it is much colder here than in Austria. Last week, I withstood terrible cold. There was a storm, and it was so cold that the birds fell down from the trees. If I do this survey, then I will have enough experience about the life "out of doors!" —— I get $45 a month plus food. Half of the earnings one needs for clothes. I will answer your last letter from camp. I have more time there, since we often can only work for a few hours. Of course, often it is impossible to write from camp because of the cold. Now I get many letters from Europe, New Year's wishes, etc., etc. Last week, we had -40 degrees every day. —— Best greetings and Berg Heil,

yours K.K.

Your Friend in the Western Woods, 1909–1912

46

Banff, March 8, 1911

Dear Miss:

I am now back in Banff after the survey and will tell you about my newest experiences. I had planned to write you once from camp, but it was too cold and often I was too tired. December 20th, I started with this group; December 22nd, after five miles, we made the first camp. We worked hard during the day. We had to cut trails through the bush, which makes the snow fall off the trees. That would be okay, but for the cold snow that falls in your face and often on your neck. We were wet almost every day. Over Christmas, we were in Banff. In the second week of January, a horrible storm developed during terribly cold temperatures. For three days no train could pass. The coldest day was -52. In the tent at night, it has been a little warmer, but not much because we had a very poor stove. It did not want to burn, but one evening it burned too well. A fire started in the tent and burned it down. Luckily, we saved almost everything, but my blankets got burned very badly. I suffered the most damage of all. I was not in the camp that evening. I was in Banff with the dogs to get provisions and only returned after midnight half frozen to the camp. Of course, we were on skis all the time. The snow was four to five feet deep. One always sleeps fully dressed. One gets conditioned, that is true! -20 does not seem so cold, but when it drops below -30, that is too much, and in such weather our thoughts turn homewards or to another warm area. One guy had frozen his hands and ears, and some men simply left. I would have continued to work in spite of the cold, but work was stopped. The engineer, who leads the work, wanted to take me to the Hudson's Bay for two years; but I told him I did not want to go that far away from the mountains. He recommended me highly to the government in Banff. I often worked with the surveying instruments and never made big mistakes. It is not that difficult, but in Austria one would not let a labourer do it. Now I work in the ice for $2.50 a day. I did not speak German for a long time, but I don't worry about forgetting my mother tongue! — Strangely enough, I don't have the Nasswald dialect together when I speak German. A week ago, I founded a ski club in Banff![1] People seem very enthusiastic about this sport. Sundays we practise skiing and ski jumping, and many people gather on the football field to watch. My longest jump is fifty feet, twelve feet more than the last record. Are you going skating? I remember well when I was in Vienna and often watched the skating club in the large arena. I always identified you in the large crowd. "There is the miss," I told myself when I had spotted you. Oh, how poor I felt there and then! — Couldn't skate and couldn't go in, but it will be different when I return to Vienna. I can skate and have the admission money, and so I also may have the honour to skate a few laps with you. Now you will think that Konrad still suffers from homesickness. It is more or less true; however, there is a big difference between this winter and the last. I can easily overcome what I could not do last winter, but —— I still long for home, for my mother, the good friends, and the typical German ways of doing things in the mountains. But I still don't want to stay at home forever, because it is certain that Canada is much better for a working man: one has more freedom and better opportunities to earn money. It will soon be two years that I left Vienna. How fast time went, and how much has happened in these two years! Next fall, I am supposed to go on a survey party again until January. There won't be time for learning French!! But I still ask you to give me a few lessons when I return home, perhaps in spring 1912. Maybe we can do a nice climbing trip towards the end of April! Hearty greetings to you.

Yours very truly. K.K.

1. Although the first skis arrived in Banff around the turn of the century, Kain's ski club was no doubt the first in Banff. See William B. Yeo, "Making Banff a Year-Round Park," in *Winter Sports in the West*, ed. E.A. Corbet and A.W. Rasporich (Calgary: The Historical Society of Alberta/University of Calgary Press, 1990), 87; Chic Scott, *Powder Pioneers*, 36.

47

[In English from hereon]

128

My dear Miss Amelie:

I just took a letter for you down to the P.O. and received one from you, written on the 18th of Feb. My best thanks for that long nice letter. It makes me very happy to hear that you will be so kind again to me and that you will give some lessons in French when I come home. Now, it is no more so cold here, and we have all kinds of fun with winter sports. It is a very long time I did not write in English to you. Now we had better talk the mother-tongue. *[In German from hereon]* I was very sorry that you lost another in your group of friends. I feel with you every time you write something like that, since I know how good and compassionate you are. But death is the law of nature, which all of us have to accept. I am happy to hear that you feel well and that you are healthy. I am now healthy again, too, but I still take a bath every other day in the sulphur springs. The pool lies 1,000 feet above Banff, so I take my skis along. I have a pretty good run downhill afterwards.

March 25. A long break in writing. First, our winter sport festival interfered, and I have had a terrible toothache for two weeks. I am now okay again. The winter sport festival turned out very well. We had over four hundred visitors. It lasted almost all night. We had more than one hundred lanterns. A tent was set up, where refreshments were sold. We made $55. It was a good start. People are serious about winter sports here. Yesterday, a lady from the CPR came to me to find out what could be done on our terrain with skis and toboggans. For more than two hours, I told her about that great sport. I

had to give her pictures, one of me, too, which she needs for advertis-
ings in books. Tonight, I will meet the lady again. I have to introduce
two trapper friends of mine, who also will give her information.
Now, I will answer your letter and once again be a good pupil! ——
On May 1st, I will join the Alpine Club again. The end of June, a big
trip will be made to the North in order to make a map.[1] My rheumatism has vanished. While taking the cure, I learned how to swim,
and it was wonderful to jump into the hot water from the cold snow.
Spring is coming and nature is putting on her beautiful green dress.
Everything is new and refreshed. And so it is with people, isn't it?
The long winter makes our memory sleepy, and spring wakes us up
again. Everything returns to our memory that once used to be there.
I remember that three years ago today, with two dear Viennese ladies
(you and your sister), I took a beautiful tour into the Wienerwald.
Perhaps you think of it too at this moment? Of course, the time is not
the same: here it is 4:40 P.M. March 25. In Vienna it will be about 1:30
in the morning on March 26. — In three weeks, it will be Easter. You
will then be in Reichenau and perhaps pick spring flowers and listen
to the birdsongs of spring. I wish you a very pleasant time. I mail
this letter to Reichenau and finally, finally my notes, too. But not yet
all of them! But it won't take much longer. I still keep my word, dear
teacher! You also will soon receive another letter. You will remember:
last spring, too, I was writing often. That is due to the already
mentioned lovely spring! —

With heartiest greetings.
Yours forever,
K.K.

Addendum: I am sure you have heard about the great mystery of
hypnosis. I have never believed in it, but I saw a miracle! In fact, I
was hypnotized myself. Afterwards, I knew nothing about it. I gave
a long lecture about tourism and about the beauty of nature. The
audience later told me that I spoke so clearly and distinctly that one
would never believe that I was under hypnosis. A lady, who was also

hypnotized, told us about her first love affair, AND not in an indiscreet way. We were roaring with laughter!! She said, "When he held my hand and I gave him my first kiss, I felt twenty years younger!" — (And, at that time, she was only eighteen years of age!) Then, two strong men went under hypnosis at the same time. They had a workout boxing. Also very amusing! And there were more similar acts. Goodbye, K.K.

1. Kain's ambitions to visit Yellowhead Pass were soon to be realized. With rival railway companies planning lines across Yellowhead Pass, the ACC needed no reminder of what railways through mountains meant. One of the primary objectives of the club—"the encouragement of the mountain craft and the opening of new regions as a national playground"—had been achieved in the south, particularly around Banff and Lake Louise, where the thoroughfare was bustling and prosperous. Parker, "The Alpine Club of Canada," 3. Things were quieter to the north. Only a handful of climbers had explored the mountains north of Yellowhead Pass. If reports and rumours of "magnificent peaks, great icefields, wonderful glaciers, and gloriously coloured lakes" bolstered club enthusiasm, the idea of a special mountaineering camp at the foot of Mt. Robson—the highest peak in the Rockies—prompted the ACC to investigate on its own behalf. If completing a survey and map of the region could help settle the lingering problem of the boundary between British Columbia and Alberta, then so much the better. Arthur O. Wheeler, "The Alpine Club of Canada's Expedition to Jasper Park, Yellowhead Pass and Mount Robson Region, 1911," CAJ 4 (1912): 3.

48

Banff, Alta. April 23, 1911

My dear Miss Amelie:

[In English from hereon] What kind of Easter did you have in
Reichenau? I hope you had a good time out there. Did you get my
letter in R. or Vienna? I had a very fine trip at Easter and I must tell
you about it, but I think it is better, I do it in German. *[In German
from hereon]* Easter Sunday, I left Banff with an acquaintance, a green-
horn for the coming exertions. At noon, we reached Field by train and
went to Emerald Lake, where a hotel is open in summer.[1] The snow
was very good and I did not put on the skis. In three-and-a-half hours
we covered eight miles. I had marked our campsite on the map. The
lake, of course, was frozen. On such trips you have no blankets. One
mostly sits up at night or you make two fires and lie down between
them. It was a splendid night. At two o'clock, the moon came up.
Everything was calm and still. My friend, who was tired, slept very
well for a few hours. I woke often and put more wood on the fire. I
smoked my pipe and some beautiful memories went through my head.
I thought of you, that you might have been looking at the mountains at just that moment or listening to birds. And should you have
thought of me? You could not have known that I was sitting on snow
by a good fire and enjoying the sleeping nature in its stillness. At five
A.M., I began to cook breakfast. It was very simple: coffee and bread,
a few pieces of bacon, which I fried over the open fire. I don't know
whether you already have had the experience of cooking meat on a
stick over the fire. How it tastes so very good. At six A.M., we left our
camp and proceeded towards Summit Lake to get to the Yoho Valley.
At 10 A.M., the sun was shining so warmly that we laid down on a
rock and fell asleep without wanting to. We reached Summit Lake at

one P.M. The snow was ten to twelve feet deep. We stopped for lunch. We could see wonderful winter scenery, unknown and new compared to what I had seen before in summertime. Now, we wanted to go to the upper trail to reach the "Little Yoho Valley," but, in the afternoon, the snow became so soft that we had to work hard with the skis.[2] We changed our plans and went down to the Yoho Valley and, at the Takakkaw Falls (of which I sent you a picture), we spent our second night (Easter Sunday). We had lots of wood and made a good bed with branches on the snow. We also built the fire on the snow. In the morning, it had burned to the ground. It showed how deep the snow was: the hole was eight feet deep! That is over two metres. That night was not so pleasant. A terrible snowstorm was blowing so that we could not sleep. At four A.M., we started our way back to Field. There was six inches of fresh snow, which did not affect our progress. When day broke, we saw enchanted pictures of winter before us. Truly indescribably beautiful! On the way to Field, we met Dr. Longstaff, who had learned that I would come out that way. We stopped for a rest, I made tea, and then we continued. At one P.M., we reached Field. My friend was dead tired, fell into bed, and slept right away. I went for a walk with Dr. Longstaff, my friend went home, and I went to Hector with Dr. L. From there, we went to Sherbrooke Lake, where the club camp will take place this year. In the evening, I returned to Banff. Today, Sunday April 23rd, my friend and I went canoeing on the Bow River, six miles from Banff. On the way back, we met friends and had afternoon tea in the bush with them. It was a beautiful rowing party. You see, Miss, what kind of sports I do here?! Tomorrow, I go to work for a week, and next Sunday I'll go bear hunting! When you receive this letter, I may have killed one already!! —— I go to British Columbia alone, because I have not found a suitable companion. It will be very hard work, because I have to carry all my luggage on my back for twenty miles, and not everybody can bear this. So I rather go alone, although it is not very advisable. But I hope for the best. Also on this occasion, I will do some first ascents. I want to write to you about my experiences, as soon as I return. If all goes well, I hope to be in Banff by the end of May. I am convinced I won't come back empty-handed. This journey, better called trip, cost me some dollars, but I think I will have wonderful adventures. With hearty greetings to you and your family,

yours always truly, K.K.

1. The CPR constructed a small hotel on the shores of Emerald Lake in 1902. A marked departure from the railway's established hotel design tradition, the hotel at Emerald Lake was the first in a series of lodges built in a rustic Swiss design, which was an alternative to the more grandiose properties in Banff and Rogers Pass. See R.W. Sandford, *Emerald Lake Lodge: A History and a Celebration* (Calgary: Canadian Rocky Mountain Resorts, 2002), 24–25.

2. This was perhaps the first group of skiers to visit the Little Yoho Valley, just north of Field, BC. It was extraordinarily early for a backcountry trip in the winter, let alone a ski trip. In fact, there is little evidence of backcountry skiing anywhere in the Rockies prior to 1928. Despite the growing interest in ski jumping in 1911, the preferred form of winter ambulation among local recreationalists, packers and outfitters, and early mountaineers was snowshoeing, not skiing. Thus, it may be the case that Kain's use of "skis," here, actually refers to snowshoes. Either way, just travelling in the winter backcountry in the 1910s was generally considered far too dangerous to undertake as a pastime. See Zac Robinson, "Off the Beaten Path? Ski Mountaineering and the Weight of Tradition in the Canadian Rockies, 1909–1940," *The International Journal of the History of Sport* 24, no. 10 (2007): 1322–29. In time, of course, this limitation changed. Beginning in the 1930s and 1940s, ACC ski camps would make the Little Yoho Valley a popular backcountry ski destination. See Scott, *Powder Pioneers*, 82–90.

49

Banff, Alta, April 30, 1911

My dear Miss Amelie:

Today, April 30th, I received your dear, long letter. My best thanks for it. I am in a great hurry today and yet I must answer your letter, otherwise you won't hear from me again for a long time! I am just packing because, tomorrow morning at 9:20 A.M. (by train), I leave Banff and go bear hunting. I told you in my last letter. For two days, I will have hard work with the carrying. There is still too much snow for horses and no fodder. It also would cost too much. But I will persist. I have to carry about 35 kilo. I expect exciting hours. A grizzly hunt is always exciting, because it's not easy to kill. I have no fear, because I am a pretty good marksman and have a good gun that I know well. That I will always sleep in the open on this hunt, I probably don't have to mention specifically. Each evening, I will write down my experiences, "Alone in the Wilderness,"[1] and, when I come back, I'll send a letter from the first post office. You will probably get the letter by the end of May. I received the report from the Austrian Alpine Club. From my old friends, I hear less and less. Last spring, I wrote to you that, of all my many friends, you write most often, and I pray you will continue to do so! Every time I hear from you, I am overjoyed. I just read the lines you wrote about your friend from St. Pölten and the dear children. I love you also like a sister, I should say. — Now I want to write about the Schneealm tour, which you want to take, and I am sure you will be very satisfied with it. I think you should do it at the beginning of July. They drive the cattle up there in late June. You'd stay in Nasswald overnight, go up to the Nasskamm and to the Karlalm, and on via the Ameisbühel to the Schneealm. You will easily find overnight accommodation up there. The woman who milks the cows and makes cheese has two or three good beds. Next day, you'd climb down to Kapellen and be home in the evening. The climb downward cannot be missed. I once marked all the trails across the Schneealm. But you can also do this easily in one day. If the weather is nice, I would recommend that you spend the night up there since the view is so beautiful: Rax, Hochschwab, and the Ennstaler Mountains! Very worthwhile to see the sunrise and sunset from the Windberg. Add to it the sound of the cowbells. How I would love to accompany you on this tour! You will find the alpine flowers just the way I described it in my diary, perhaps even much more beautiful. If the summer is late, then the alpine flowers remain very pretty until July 15th. I wish for you that you can do this tour in very good weather, and I am sure you will send me a few flowers from the beloved Schneealm. I will frame all the dried flowers that you sent to Canada for me. I have enclosed a flower, too. I picked it the day before yesterday: the first spring flower of 1911. I am very sorry I have to close now, but I run short of time! With dearest greetings to you and your mother and sister.

Yours truly, K.K.

1.   Stories of boyhood adventure set in the wild were in vogue in the first decade of the century. No doubt, if his Jack London–esque title is any indication, Kain was not unaware of the popular literary trend. These were, as historian I.S. MacLaren wrote, "heady times for young men. The Klondike Gold Rush had ended the previous century with a spirit of dizzying exhilaration, but there were less crazed and precarious ways of immersing oneself in the Back of Beyond. Charles G.D. Roberts, Ernest Seton, and Rudyard Kipling had begun a vogue for animal stories in the early 1890s; Jack London would publish his story, 'Call of the Wild' in *The Saturday Evening Post* in June and July 1903; and four years later Robert Service would publish his two entrancing volumes of poetry, *Songs of a Sourdough* and *The Spell of the Yukon*." I.S. MacLaren, with Eric Higgs and Gabrielle Zezulka-Mailloux, *Mapper of Mountains: M.P. Bridgland in the Canadian Rockies, 1902–1930* (Edmonton: University of Alberta Press, 2005), 52.

50

On my way to bear hunting nine miles from Spillimachine:
in the forest, under a tree, and at a good warm campfire.
May 3 (evening), 1911.

Dear Miss Amelie:

This morning at eight o'clock, I crossed the Columbia River and the
Spillimachine River by ferry. Soon after, I was in the beautiful green
forest, which I looked forward to seeing all winter. It is impossible
to describe the splendour of the newly-awakened spring. Flowers are
rare, except for the little March violets. The delicate grass can only be
a few days old. The air is pure! The mountains are still covered with
winter snow, which I did not expect, particularly on their southern
exposure. It is easily possible, that I cannot carry out my program
because of all that snow. I am tired and off to bed under a big tree,
four metres away from the fire. ———

May 4th, 1911: The night I spent well, for a short while the moon was
very bright, then lighter in the morning. For breakfast, I cooked
Nasswalder-Schmarrn, called Sterz,[1] and coffee. At six A.M., I left the
campground and followed the trail along the creek. It got harder all
the time: windfall and snow, and then rain. At ten, I saw a slide come
down on the other side of the valley. The wind almost threw me to
the ground. I was quite a bit higher than the valley bottom, where
the slide stopped. It reminded me of the slide in the Großen Gries at
the Rax. From noon to one, I stopped for lunch: buttered sandwich,
COCOA, bacon, onion. Then, after half-an-hour, I got back into the
green forest, where I clearly saw old bear tracks (black bear). I then
returned to the burnt down forest. The rain got stronger, and the
snow increased. At six P.M., I stopped. —

I camped under two dried-out trees near a stream. I tried to build a
tent with some linen cloth I had taken along for this purpose, but it
did not work; so I made an Indian hut from branches that I had taken
along for this purpose, but that did not work either; and, so, I built
an Indian hut from branches that I had to carry for several hundred
yards. In the "green" forest, there was too much snow for camping.
In the evening, I made makeshift snow shoes. At ten P.M., I bedded
down quite tired. After midnight, a storm developed with snow and
rain. My roof was not waterproof and I found myself in water——

May 5th: At 3:30 A.M., I cooked my breakfast, Sterz and COCOA. I was
wet and I was pretty cold. I took the tea kettle, the axe, and something to eat, and left the camp at 4:30, followed the creek for several
hundred metres, when I then had to fell a tree for a bridge across the
creek. I then followed a wild creek and reached a plateau, where I had
been with Mr. Wheeler last fall for a survey. I followed the plateau in
a south-easterly direction and came up on a pass, from where I could
see the mountain that I wanted to climb. I rested for twenty minutes,
made tea, and left behind everything except an ice pick and my snow
shoes, which held up very well. The mountain is very boring, a great
drudgery! I kept believing that I was close to the top, but always
something else was in between! Finally, at 2:30 P.M., I reached the
summit. It was covered with snow and had huge cornices, which is
why Mr. Wheeler named this mountain Mt. Cornice. I could not build
a stone man, since there were no stones around! The view was poor:
everything was in fog, and it started to snow. About 1,000 feet below
the top, I built a stone man and left a cocoa tin there with my name
in it. It is certain that I was the first one on this mountain. It must
be 10,000 feet high. On my way down, I enjoyed some nice downhill skiing. The snow in the forest was six-to-ten feet deep. At 9 P.M.,
I reached the camp. On my way, I saw six goats. I shot one of them
so that I would have fresh meat. I saw no bear tracks. I think it is too
early and too cold. ——

MAY 6th: Today, the weather is very bad: rain and a cold wind. I slept until 10 A.M. Am a little stiff from yesterday's tour. At noon, I ate liver dumplings, boiled and fried goat meat, rice and tea. Now, at 6 P.M., the sky is getting a little brighter. I am lying in front of my Indian hut and write about my day's work, which actually is not too much more than eating!! I fixed up my tent a little, and hurt my knee, but must also hang the fishing line in the water. The surroundings are very beautiful: up front, a burnt forest; behind it, green forest; and, further back, the snow-covered mountains and two big glaciers. The valley is narrow; the rocks are reddish, similar to the Dolomites. The creek is swollen high and very noisy. I like to hear the rushing water very much———

May 7th (Sunday): Last night I slept very well in my improved bed. At 5:30 I woke up. It was a beautiful morning. Before lighting the fire for breakfast, I went up a hill with my gun and surveyed the surroundings. But there was nothing to see except two marmots.

Continuing May 7th: Today, I consider myself a person well served by nature: a blessed man. I keep the Sunday according to the Commandments and have nothing to do. So, I want to write a little more to you, dear Amelie, because I know it will please you to know that a human being in the wilderness is thinking of you. I am really in the wilderness, and on top of it: I am all alone. In one direction, the distance to the nearest human being is 16 miles. How long the distance is to the next human being in the other direction, I don't know. All alone in the wilderness! What do you think? Is that beautiful? I don't want to hear the answer to this question from everybody! Many would say, this is stupid, etc., but I find it very beautiful. I know you understand my letters; you know my views about nature. At the beginning of my letter, I called myself "a human being well equipped by nature." That will be something new to hear from me, won't it? I think I have a right to say so, because if one is not well equipped by nature then one could <u>not</u> endure all the exhaustion, etc. Nobody can buy strength and health for himself, even if they are very rich. The pleasure to spend some time in the wilderness is not something everyone can achieve. Many are not healthy enough to endure sleeping under the open sky, others are not strong enough to carry all the things that you need for two weeks, many would not understand what to take along, how to not make the load too heavy and yet have enough to eat. There are many who cannot cook! How many have the health and strength, but fear the loneliness! They would stay alone in the forest, where there are all the wild animals, for one minute.

—————— In the language of Nasswald one would say "for that, one needs to have guts," and that I have always had!! I have never had the guts for only one thing, and that's to go begging (see my Diary about my Life in Vienna!) Now I will cook dinner ————— I am lucky: I caught a fish!! —————

Dinner is over. I had dumplings, rice, fish, roast goat, coffee and now my pipe!! A better life, one can hardly imagine! But the good does not last! One more week, and I have to work again. But I am very contended with my "holiday!"

Continued later: Dear Miss Amelie: I think you will now have gotten a picture of my beautiful "holiday." It is connected with strenuous effort, that is true. But being your own master for two weeks, you can only do it with great effort. And only this way is possible to be a totally free person. Wouldn't you love this freedom, too? Aside from the fact that it would be too hard for you, one could not enjoy all this freedom at home. First of all, you would have to ask many people, whether it was permitted to light a fire here or there. Not to speak about fishing and hunting. Besides, most people would laugh and say, "Oh, he isn't quite right in his head!" But I am convinced that life in a camp would please you very much, that is for a certain time. It is also nice and pleasant to get into a clean bed.

May 10th, Wednesday: Monday and Tuesday I had no time to write, but I will catch up. Monday, the weather was worse again. Fresh snow on the ground, and I wondered what to do. I would have loved to kill a grizzly bear, but it is too early in the season: that means it is a late spring here. A mile further from my camp, the snow is still two to three-feet deep. So, I decided to go further, where there was less snow, and I left the camp at 10 A.M. When I left the burnt out part, I met a black bear in the dense bush. I jumped, shot at him, and injured him. He made a horrible noise and disappeared in the bush quickly. I followed him and his tracks, but found no bear. It is very dangerous to follow a wounded bear into dense bush. I did it very cautiously. When I left the bush again, I was almost without pants. There was also not much left of my shirt: everything was tattered and torn. It really bothered me to have to get back to Banff in torn pants. I hoped somebody would lend me a pair of pants, at least until I could buy a pair!! — After this adventure, I went three miles further and got to near my first camp. Oh, how quickly nature changes in spring! From May 3rd to May 8th, the grass had grown visibly, and some of the moss flowers were also becoming visible. One can hardly believe that things grow so fast! In the evening, I was very tired, but all the beauty made me alert again. The birds once more sang so loud and so lovely. I slept in an old bear trap that night. (Of course it was not set for that night!!!). The most beautiful moonlit night! Tuesday, I got up early to mend my clothes as well as I could. Then, I returned to the spot where I had wounded the bear. After a longer search, I found traces of blood in the snow. I think I shot off one of his paws. I then made two new bear traps. Being alone, that was hard work, but I managed it. In the evening, I returned to camp, wet through and through. A warm rain. I made a hut from the old bear trap and slept very well.

Today, Wednesday, May 10th: In the morning, it poured. On the mountain lies new snow. At 8 A.M., the clouds broke, it cleared up, and it was a gloriously, beautiful day. In the morning, I went out stalking, first around the camp, and in the afternoon along the stream, and got to an old bridge and an old mine. The creek runs along a deep valley, very beautiful scenery. On the other side of the creek is a good trail that I followed for two miles. Then, I returned to the bridge, lay down in the warm sunshine, and let many nice thoughts and plans go through my head. I would like to tell you more about these beautiful surroundings, but where are the right words for this? — Beautiful and lovely above all! I could hardly leave that area! Did I ever see such fresh green grass? I really cannot remember. The canyon with the foaming water, the snow on the mountains, the sounds of the birds singing! Too bad that the cuckoo does not live in this country! On my way back, I saw a beaver dam. I think I already wrote you about these little animals. I claim they are the cleverest of all animals! Not even humans could build a better dam than the beavers. Then I shot a grouse. I pity these birds; I don't like to shoot them, but what shall I do? If you are in the wilderness, you have to live off what it offers, because it is impossible to carry along every-thing you need: beans, rice, grout with fried onions, a cup of cocoa. Now, it is a quarter past eight. The sun already disappeared behind the mountains. I think we have a full moon, but there are such heavy clouds in the sky that the moon will hardly come through. It will be best that I go to bed ——— big drops are falling already — Good night! —

Thursday, May 11th: Today was a so-called lost day. The sun did not shine, but it did not rain either. At six in the morning, I left the camp and took a long walk in very dense forest. Very hard work. I was very close to a mountain lion. What a pity I could not kill that bad animal because of the very dense brush. I only saw it for a second, tried to run after it, but it was impossible. From 1 to 2 P.M., I rested and then took an easier way back. I was at the bridge again and slept there a short while. On the way to the camp, I shot two grouse. One I fried for supper, the other is for tomorrow's lunch. Now, I bake bread. It seems to turn out well. The one yesterday was not good: too little heat or something else went wrong. What a joy for me, if you would surprise me, my dear friend! What do you think about it? The first minute you might not even recognize me, but later you would!! Particularly when I opened my mouth!! In minutes, I would have supper ready for you! And what a good grass hut I would build

for you! Then we would sit by the camp fire and listen to the birds.
——"Oh what silly thoughts!" you might say when you read these
lines. But you know what thoughts can cross your mind when one
is so totally alone! — The evening is very lovely now at 7 P.M. (In
Vienna, it is May 12th at 3 in the morning). Tomorrow, I'll take a
longer tour. I also have to check the bear traps.

Friday, May 12th: Today, I have had a very bad day. Rain from morning
to night without an end in sight. In the morning, I went hunting, but
in this weather it is almost impossible to see something. The fresh
snow lies far down in the valley. Tomorrow, I will go out into the
Columbia Valley. If I am lucky, I won't have to wait too long for the
boat. I have to go about ten hours by boat and then eight hours by
train. It is a pity that the weather has not been good for hunting, but
I will have other opportunities. Instead, I had more time to watch the
beautiful nature in spring. Actually, the trip isn't over yet, but I hope
that nothing more will happen and that I can call this tour a "beautiful" one. If I had time and money, I would do a similar tour in fall.
But in 1912, I am supposed to go home, and for that reason I have to
save my dollars———

Saturday, May 13th: In the evening in the boat. Today, I marched in
pouring rain along the valley. Wet to the skin! — Luckily, I reached
the boat that goes to Golden. We will only arrive there at 10 A.M.
tomorrow. In the evening, I will be in Banff and from there I will
write more to you.

With a German Bergheil!
your K.K.

1. *Sterz* is the Nasswald dialectic equivalent of *Schmarrn*, from *Kaiserschmarrn* ("Emperor's mish-
mash"), which was a light caramelized pancake popular in Austria.

51

The Clubhouse, Banff, Alta. May 14, 1911

Dear Miss:

I was annoyed to find my letter from April 30th, which I wrote in
great haste, in my apartment in Banff! Please forgive me for the delay.
I am now in the Clubhouse again, alone for the time being. How fast
the dear time passes! I remember so well when I wrote a few letters
from here to you last year and told you about my housekeeping. It is
still the same: cooking, washing, baking, writing, etc. But the mood
is like in nature, not the same as last spring. It is dark and cold, the
birds are hardly singing, no leaves can be seen, spring flowers only
where moss is growing, where the warm water runs through. In the
morning, there is always hoar frost and one has to wear gloves. It is
a very late spring. I have no great urge to work like last year. I worked
more than ever then! And, in the end, Wheeler was not very consid-
erate to me. When the tourists arrived, he called the other guides.
This summer, I already wrote you about it. So, I will not toil as much,
and I will only work as much as it is right: twelve to fourteen hours.[1]
I won't do any more. —— In the evenings, I now always go to the
village: to the post office and often boating with friends. All the hotels
are open already. The CPR hotel was enlarged by 120 rooms during
the winter.[2] There are already visitors here: a sign that spring is
coming, even though one does not see much about it here yet. The
seasons seem to move directly from winter into summer. You know,
I am a little spoiled after my trip into southern British Columbia.
Everything there was beautifully green, the flowers in bloom, the
birds sang so lovely, the women were busy in their gardens, and,
here, the frost has not disappeared from the ground yet! Today, I

wanted to make some flower beds around the house, but had to give up since the ground was still frozen.

May 21st, 1911—in the evening. What joy did your dear long letter and the special publication of the Reichenau Section bring to me! Many thanks for both. How do you think I felt when I had read the heading "Our Beautiful Rax"! Yes, there won't be many who know the Rax better than I do! The whole publication interested me very much. And it also touched me a bit, you understand how I mean that; it was not homesickness, but similar to it. I liked the third verse best, and I think it is the most beautiful! How many memories it brought back to me, especially from my times as a breaker of stones, when I often sought peace and quiet alone on the Rax and found it there. The description of the Rax by Mr. Benesch is very beautiful, and I was happy to read that he did not forget the Zikafahnler-Alm that I loved so much: "There lies the charming plateau of the Zikafahnler-Alm, a true pearl among the beauty of the mountains." Yes, that it is for sure! How often I think of the beautiful hours I spent there! They were even whole days. So do you, by any chance, know that little place? If not, I have to show it to you when I come home. How beautiful it would be to make camp there for some days! In early summer or fall! I would have liked to take part in the celebration and would have liked to see and hear the operetta *A Mountain Guide's Homecoming*. I hope my next homecoming will be beautiful, however I have to stop or you will really think that, again, I have melancholy thoughts of home! — I want to obey you. It is natural that I have very different ideas when the sun of spring shines warmly for a few minutes. I don't think about getting rich anymore, because that means wrecking your brain for nothing. But I am not cross because of that, oh no! In your letter, you mention my friend Lechner. He did not save his money by mountain guiding, but solely with running a tourist hut. I don't think Lechner could pay cash for the hotel, but surely he will manage. Who is now running the Hess Hut? The beautiful Gesäuse will always be an incomparable valley for me. It is possible that we will see the Ennstal together again, perhaps next year? On June 13th or 14th, the club members will arrive, and then I won't be alone any more. For two days, we had fresh snow again and it is pretty cold —— With my best greetings to you and your family,

yours very truly,
K.K.

1. While Kain attributes a 12- to 14-hour workday acceptable, labour movements across Canada were in fact, as early as the 1870s, striving to reduce the 12-hour workday that was standard across the country. Neither legally recognized nor nationally organized, the first unions in Canada made great strides throughout the 1880s and 1890s: the country's first labour laws and regulations were introduced, "Labour Day" was recognized as a national holiday in 1894, and blue-collar workers in Toronto even won a Saturday half-day off near the turn of the century. In certain industries, workers were even given Saturdays off. The fact that Kain is working more than 12 hours a day in 1910 and 1911 is, no doubt, due to the unique nature of his vocation.

2. If the season of 1910 was sublimely busy at the Banff Springs Hotel, the season of 1911 approached the ridiculous. Over 22,000 people stayed at the hotel that summer; this at a time when the combined population of Banff, Bankhead, Canmore, and Exshaw was only 5,250. Robinson, *Banff Springs*, 43.

52

On the way from Edmonton to Yellowhead Pass, July 1, 1911.

My dear Miss Amelie:

I am so sorry I had no opportunity to write to you. I had a load of work. A sudden departure caught me by surprise, and I had to do everything for the outfitters. On June 29th, we left Banff and took the train to Edmonton, where we met the other gentlemen. We stayed a day. Yesterday, we took the train to Edson on the railway that I worked a year ago. Sadly, I looked out at Wolf Creek and to the site where we buried the four accident victims —— We are now in a railroad coach and have to wait for a connection. We should be able to see the mountains from here, but the weather is so poor that one can hardly see as far as a mile. I hope we have a very pleasant trip. At least, I will learn something again, since it is a "scientific" trip.[1] We will gather rocks, plants, beetles, birds, bears, and other wild animals. I received your long dear letter a week ago. I agree to the publication of my diary; I leave all of that to you, and I will discuss further details when I come home. By that time, I should have all my diary entries finished. If I have an opportunity, I will write from the camp again.

With my best greetings, yours forever, K.K.

1. Made possible through the co-operation of the GTPR, which contributed handsomely toward the expenses, Wheeler's 1911 mapping expedition to Jasper Park, Yellowhead Pass, and the Robson region originally comprised Kain, Byron Harmon, and a cook; the transport and outfitting was in the hands of Donald "Curly" Phillips (1884–1938). Phillips was a young Jasper outfitter who had claimed to have climbed Mount Robson with Revd. George Kinney (1872–1961) two years earlier. Kinney, too, joined Wheeler's survey party; Wheeler decided to bring him along in an assistant

role. Subsequent co-operation and financial assistance by the British Columbia, Alberta, and Dominion Governments substantially enlarged the scope of the expedition to include an investigation of the fauna, flora, and geology of the region. According to Wheeler, "An attempt was made to interest Canadian scientists in the expedition, but without success, so the matter was submitted to Dr. Charles Walcott [1850–1927], Secretary of the Smithsonian Institute of Washington, who collaborate [sic] most heartily and sent a party of four to join and work with the Alpine Club." Wheeler, "The Alpine Club of Canada's Expedition to Jasper Park," 3–4. The supplementary party comprised Ned Hollister (1876–1924), assistant curator of mammals of the United States National Museum; J.H. Riley, also of the US National Museum; and the hunters of the group, Charles Walcott Jr. (1889–1913) and Harry Blagden, whose duty was to secure big-game specimens.

147

53

Ten miles past Yellowhead Pass in the jungle. July 10, 1911. 8 P.M.

Dear Miss Amelie:

I remember with joy your dear name day, which is today. I am sure that many of your friends and acquaintances will remember you today. I will be the furthest away from all of them. I am now about 350 miles north of Banff. Right now, I am sitting under a big tree, surrounded by moss flowers. I will send you some of them. They will, of course, lose their beauty by the time they reach you in Reichenau, because they will travel for months. We are now already quite far away from villages or towns, and I don't know when I will have an opportunity to send the letter on its way. But, nevertheless, you will receive it one day! You will see that somebody is thinking of you deep in the Wild West! I wish you many happy returns of your dear name day. May you experience many good things and may fate always bring you only the best. With warmest greetings I remain your *K.K.*

54

Moose Lake, July 23, 1911

Dear Miss Amelie:

I can now already tell you more about this "Wild West." It is called
the "Wild West" for good reasons. It is really still very wild here:
no houses, no roads, no pass, and only old Indian hunting trails.
Often you sink up to your knees into the wet mossy ground! We
have already climbed some mountains. They were not so difficult,
but to get to them is!! The climbing did not start very well. On our
first climb, we almost got buried by an avalanche. Mr. Harmon had
the audacity (!!) to photograph the avalanche at its most dangerous
moment!! —— We were four men. Two of the group were so tired
the next day that they could not come along. We were on the go for
seventeen hours. — Mr. Wheeler and I climbed another mountain
the next day, and Mr. Wheeler almost lost his life. It is an easy mountain, so we were not roped together. Some metres from the top, Mr.
Wheeler took a wrong step and, with a scream, he was rolling down
over snow and ice-covered rocks. I was only a few steps ahead of him.
I succeeded in reaching him by throwing myself on him with some
abandon. Because of that, he almost pulled me along. We stopped
with one metre to spare before falling into the depths of a crevasse.
I could hold myself on a small piece of rock and him, too. Since that
hour, we always take the rope—*the life line*—which, of course, creates
more work for me. We took the descent on another side of the mountain, and had to wade through a foaming rushing glacier stream. We
could not reach our camp before night and had to sleep in the forest.
The next morning (that is July 23rd), we arrived at the camp at 7 A.M.
In the afternoon, I shot a goat and Mr. Harmon took a picture of me
as "a hunter." I will send you the photo. It is past 9 P.M. here, and the

sun is still shining on the mountains. But I have to sleep, I am tired. Good Night. —

P.S. I don't know how I can describe the sight and the extent of this group of mountains. As far as the eye can reach, nothing but peaks, snowfields, glaciers, and valleys! All this is beautiful. If only the little flies were not here. They pester you so much that it is hard to admire the beautiful nature of the valley! How fortunate that they don't go higher than the edge of the forest. ——

With the heartiest greetings, yours truly, K.K.

55

On the watershed dividing Alberta and B.C.

And on a little mountain, 8,500 feet. July 30, 1911

My dear Amelie:

Since on almost every mountain that we climbed we have spent four to five hours surveying, with which I have nothing to do, I will use this time today to send you a few lines. For this purpose, I brought some paper and a pencil along. By now, we have almost been one month in these mountains, have seen many beautiful things, and have dealt with many hardships. During that time, I wrote two letters to you that, of course, are still in the camp and in the wilderness, far away from any post office. You will receive them all at the same time, perhaps in a month or so. At the moment, I am sitting on a steep rock with nothing but mountains around me. On the right, the rock goes down several hundred metres to a glacier. In the south-west lies Mt. Robson, "the King of the Rockies," clearly and well visible. Not far away is Mt. Kain and the Finger of Kain, which I am proud of and enjoy more each day. The Finger is an elegant rock, like a needle, which reminds me strongly of the Aiguille du Géant in the Montblanc group. Around the Finger are snow-covered mountains. Once the map and pictures are completed, I will show you all of it. From my friend Harmon, who is with us again and takes lots of photographs, I will get the pictures. In this entire range, only a few mountains have yet been climbed. The first climber of the highest mountain here, Mr. Kinny, a minister, is also with our group.[1] Up to now, we did eight ascents. The mountain from which I send you these lines is the eighth. Our camp lies on an alpine meadow at the treeline. The grass is fresh and green, and many flowers grow here.

∧ *James Shand-Harvey, George Kinney, Conrad Kain, Donald "Curly" Phillips, Charles Walcott Jr., Harry H. Blagden, Ned Hollister, J.H. Riley, and A.O. Wheeler around the campfire,* ACC–*Smithsonian Robson Expedition, 1911. Photo by Byron Harmon.* [WMCR, NA 71-1148]

Yesterday was Sunday, the first we were all together. We held services in the camp. We are twelve. Often, we camp at the treeline. It is interesting to see how things are collected for the museum. You use certain collection methods. For instance, traps are put up high in the trees. One of the professors said to me that "you can travel a hundred years in the mountains and still there are little unknown animals." Well, now, I have to quit, as Mr. Wheeler is ready. My job is to build a stone man when we move homewards to the camp. —————

On a mountain not far from yesterday's mountain. — August 3, noon. After I finished the stone man, we skirted over rocks and snow to the glacier on the right. At 6 P.M., we reached the camp, where everyone was in a good mood. Four caribou were shot. Harmon had taken many beautiful pictures. We went to bed at ten. A better night than the one before, since it was very cold. If the nights are warm, you don't sleep well, because the little flies are so bad that you can hardly protect yourself from these plagues. In that way, it is much worse here than around Banff. — This morning, at 6:30, we left the camp and hiked the first part of yesterday's trail across an alpine meadow. After an hour, we reached the glacier. From there, we had a beautiful view, the best one yet of Mt. Robson. For two hours, we followed the glacier, then we had to hike on the brittle top of a rock, which Mr. Wheeler and Mr. Kinny found very difficult. Both walked very poorly. ——— Now, I am sitting on top of a mountain a bit removed from the others and write these lines. The weather is not the best for photographs. Fog moves from one mountain top to the next. It is pretty to watch, and it is warm. I am in shirt sleeves. Miss Amelie! There is no day that I don't think of you when I am in the mountains! I hope that you are in good health and that you are doing well. How are the excursions to the mountains going? Were you already on the Schneealm, or on the Reifalpe? What will you think of my "autumn picture" after your return from the mountains? We are still on tour for two months, and during this time my beard will grow a lot. We will still have lots of hard work to do. —

Heartiest greetings. Yours truly forever, K.K.

1. Recognition of Kinney and Phillips's 1909 claim to have ascended Mt. Robson was withdrawn in 1913. While legitimate concerns arose over inconsistencies found in Kinney's 1910 account ("To the Top of Mount Robson, Told by Kinney and Phillips," CAJ 2, no. 2 (1910): 21–44), Wheeler doubted the claim from the beginning. Writing in the 1912 CAJ, Wheeler made his opinion known: "the route looked impossible, and certainly one of tremendous peril. The great wonder is that they returned alive....Kinney took a desperate last chance and succeeded. He has been criticized rather severely by practical mountaineers for taking on so extremely dangerous a climb a companion [Phillips] who had no previous experience." Wheeler, "Jasper Park, Yellowhead Pass and Mt. Robson Expedition," 53–54. Whatever the speculation, it is clear that Kinney trespassed on code, which made it all the more difficult for Wheeler and the mountaineering establishment to accept the claim. That, and, as Chic Scott wryly remarked, "We must remember that the [Survey] expedition of 1911 was laying

the groundwork for Wheeler's pièce de résistance—the ACC Camp of 1913. But that confounded parson had got in the way and had stolen the first ascent before the cameras and the ACC were ready." Scott, *Pushing the Limits*, 76.

56

Yellowhead Pass, B.C. August 30, 1911, in the evening.

My dear Miss Amelie:

Today, I received your long dear letter of June 14. Many thanks. The letter travelled for seventy-five days! It went through many hands before reaching mine. It is such a joy, when you live in the wilderness for some time and hear nothing about the world and then receive letters from friends! On August 26th, we emerged from the wilderness to Moose Lake. We climbed a mountain and then hiked back to the Yellowhead Pass. There, the letters awaited us. I got nine of them!! I didn't even finish reading your dear letter before beginning to write you just a few lines in a great hurry. Tomorrow, and the day after, we have hard work to do and then we say Goodbye once more to the civilized world! — I am healthy and doing fine. We took a trip around Mt. Robson, the "King of the Rockies."[1] Unfortunately, I could not climb the wonderful mountain. No time! But I climbed the second and third highest mountains.[2] By now, we have climbed twenty mountains with the instruments. All were first ascents. We were lucky with weather, but have been working hard since August 3rd, when we left Moose Pass. Did you receive my letters of July 10th and 30th? I sent them out with the packers who had to go back with the horses. We had to carry everything across a pass where the horses could not go. We had enough to eat and always had fresh meat: goats, caribou, bears, etc. I shot a big grizzly. Now I must close. I hope that your mother is well again and that you could carry out your travel plans.

With best greetings and German Bergheil! Your K.K.

1. In early September, when the expedition again reached the summit of Yellowhead Pass, via the Fraser River valley, a cairn was built and inscribed. It was the first monument marking the Alberta–British Columbia border. After two long months the expedition had completed the first recorded circuit around Mt. Robson, having travelled nearly 140 kilometres—by way of the Moose River and Pass, Calumet Creek, Smoky River, Robson Pass, Berg Lake, Grand Fork, and the main Fraser River—and climbed 20-plus peaks. In the months that followed, the survey produced the first published map of the region. The official height of Mt. Robson was reduced from 13,700 ft. [4,176 m] to 13,068 ft. [3,983 m] (an estimation within a mere 100 feet of its 12,972 ft. [3,954 m] height). Reports were printed in alpine and geographical journals in North America and Europe. While the work of the Smithsonian Institute made headlines in Washington, Wheeler spent the early part of 1912 lecturing to Canadians on the beauties of the Yellowhead region. His enthusiasm did not go unnoticed. In 1913, the same year the ACC held a special mountaineering camp near the shores of Berg Lake, Mount Robson Provincial Park was established by a special act of the British Columbia legislature. It was the second in the province's parks system and a jewel in what UNESCO designated, nearly a century later in 1990, the Rocky Mountains World Heritage site.

2. Kain is referring to Mt. Resplendent (3,425 m [11,237 ft.]) and Whitehorn Mountain (3,395 m [11,138 ft.]); it was the latter that Kain, much to Wheeler's chagrin, climbed alone, at night and without permission of the autocratic Wheeler, famously once referred to as "He Who Must be Obeyed." See Wheeler, "Jasper Park, Yellowhead Pass and Mt. Robson Expedition," 47; and Kain, *Where the Clouds*, 332–34; Esther Fraser, *Wheeler* (Banff, AB: Summerthought, 1978), 96–97.

57

Athabasca River, September 9, 1911

Dear Amelie:

Today is a day I like to remember. As you see, I don't forget it and have to write a few lines. You must excuse the poor paper. It is the best that I could find in the whole camp—only a few scraps. Today was a very hot day. We travelled fifteen miles. I remember all the details of our excursion to the Planspitze in the beautiful Enns Valley! *Oh Du alte Burschenherrlichkeit, wohin bist Du verschwunden?* Do you know this university song? I am sure that you, too, will today remember the tour, and our thoughts will meet somewhere out on the water.

Many hearty greetings. Yours very truly, K.K.

58

Swift's Homestead, Athabasca River, October 16, 1911.

Dear Amelie:

[In English from hereon] You will already think I have forgotten you,
but it is not so. I am still in the mountains and in the wood, where
you can't send a letter every day and where you can't even write.
Well, now listen: On the 30th of September I came to Banff, got my
post there, your letters too. My best thanks for them. I had to fix
some business there, had to be very busy the 30 hours I spent in
Banff. Then I started out again, first to Laggan, then to Yellowhead
Pass again on the same route. Now we are here at Swift's, where we
rest a bit.[1] I have to write some letters. I begin with a letter for you.
[In German from hereon] My last report was from the Yellowhead
Pass, wasn't it? So, I will report further to you. From the pass, we
went in a southerly direction. First east to Maligne Lake, which is a
very interesting mountain lake. There, the survey party ended, and
Mr. Wheeler went back to Edmonton. The rest of us went through
the mountains directly to Banff. 180 miles! It took us twelve days.
Unfortunately, we had bad weather part of the time. We had to cross
a high, difficult pass for horses, Wilcox Pass (9,000 feet), between
the Saskatchewan and Athabasca Rivers. For five nights, we camped
in snow and were very tired and overworked, especially me. This
summer, we have hiked altogether almost 1,000 miles. In the end,
we reached Banff in good health, and I intended to get a really good
rest, but it was not to be. The outfitter, who brought us to Banff,
came from the North and had to return. He was alone and could
not find anybody to accompany him, and so I went back with him.[2]
We went to Laggan, where we had our horses, but we did not find
them for two days. From Laggan to Swift's, we needed thirteen days,

and walked every day without a day of rest. —— I can say I know the Rocky Mountains now very well. And now, a summary about the summer of 1911: On the whole, we had a good summer, did several beautiful first ascents: saw a lot, but it was hard, <u>hard</u> work. —— I was not satisfied with my wages; however, I don't want to write much to you about my disappointment. It is mostly my own fault. I am too trusting, especially when somebody speaks nicely to me! But this has to change. I am through with the Alpine Club, as long as Mr. Wheeler is the director.[3] We parted on good terms, and the Alpine Club will not say one bad word about me, because I did my duty faithfully, and I am sure that I will be remembered often. Not everyone will serve in this way. I will now go seventy miles in northwesterly direction with my friend. We go trapping (marten and wildcat). By the end of December or beginning of January, we want to return, when the snow gets too deep. We hope for good pay. Then, I'll go back to Banff and write my diary. Finally, you will have the whole story in your hand. I don't know yet what I will do then. Perhaps I will work as guide for the CPR. If not, I will guide some groups myself in the mountains. Coming home will not materialize, since I went for this party. This summer, I sent my mother 100 Dollars, which equals almost 500 Kronen, and I know that she is very satisfied with that. From home, I heard that my grandfather passed away. I would have loved to see him once more, but for him this is better, because he was old and weak and could not enjoy life any more. ——— With very great interest, I read your travelogue. I am so glad that you had such a good time in Ischl. If only I could have been on the Simonihütte with you!! We sure would have reached the top of the Dachstein! You see, in cases like that, when you were in the hut and had no guide because they were all engaged, with <u>me as a guide</u>, you would have had a gentleman who surely would have taken you along. As a guide, I would have put in a good word with the group, since it makes no difference getting up to the Dachstein from <u>this</u> side, whether one has three or four people on the rope. I hope it's not boasting to say that, in such cases, I <u>always</u> handle things <u>well</u>. If it could be done, I always let people come along, especially ladies. From the top, you might then have seen the Bachel-Alm that I love so much!! Perhaps the opportunity will arise that I can guide you up the Dachstein! Your two Kodak pictures pleased me very much, of course. In the pictures, I see no changes in your appearance. I think you are still the way you were when I left you. I will always treasure you. When I get to Banff, I will send you many pictures of my summer trip. —— Last week, we "roped" a bear! Hope the picture turned out well. You will then understand what good nerves I have!! We found a black bear in his winter quarters and could not get it out any other way than pulling it alive with a rope out of his cave. Of course, we then had to kill him! That was my most interesting hunting experience! The nights are already pretty cold here. We mostly sleep in the open. I now feel as healthy as the stag in the forest. — Since June 30th, I was in a bed for only one night! My time runs out! I have to stop writing. Don't be surprised if you should perhaps hear nothing from me until the middle of January, but then a long, long letter will arrive!! My mail lies in Banff until I return. I hope to find some lines from you there. Heartiest greeting to you as well as to your family.

Your friend in the Western woods,
Conrad Kain[4]

1. Lewis John Swift (1854–1940), originally from Ohio, was the lone homesteader in the Athabasca Valley left after the lands comprising Jasper Forest Park were expropriated by the Dominion Government. Six Métis (mixed-blood) families, whose roots in the region stretched back to fur-trade times, were not so lucky. They were deemed "squatters" under the law and forced to leave with little compensation in 1910. Ironically, as I.S. MacLaren points out, "other and much more intrusive development was permitted. For instance, the park was home to hundreds if not thousands of railway workers in 1911, when lines were building." MacLaren, *Mapper of Mountains*, 102–03. Swift's became the only freehold land in the park, and he became the park's first appointed game guardian. His homestead—near the banks of the Athabasca River and under the rock wall of the great Palisade—was a focal point for the region. In 1908, another traveller, Mary Schäffer (1861–1939), likened the place to an oasis in the wilderness: "That pioneer's little house was very interesting. Thirteen years previously Swift and his wife had penetrated here to make a home. By degrees, he had brought in his stock from Edmonton over three hundred miles of as bad a trail as can well be imagined—cows, horses and chickens. His wheat field was yellowing, the oats were

still green and waving in the soft warm wind. By a mountain stream he had built a mill for grinding his flour, and a large potato patch was close by. His buildings were of logs, sound and solid, made entirely by himself, his residence composed of one large room. Here we were welcomed by our hostess who showed us how comfortable a family of six could be in so small a space." Mary T.S. Schäffer, *Old Indian Trails of the Canadian Rockies* (Vancouver: Rocky Mountain Books, 2007), 158.

2. The outfitter is Donald "Curly" Phillips.

3. By many accounts, Arthur O. Wheeler was a difficult employer. According to historian Leslie Bella, Wheeler's "aristocratic manner" was "imperious"; with a "short temper," he "blustered through life, impatient with those who could not match his pace." Bella, *Parks for Profit*, 43. Pat Brewster (1896–1982), a Banff outfitter, also remembered Wheeler as "a meticulous autocrat" and noted the great difficulty of "trying to find men who would be willing to go out with him on various trips." F.O. (Pat) Brewster, *Weathered Wood: Anecdotes and History of the Banff-Sunshine Area* (Banff, AB: Crag and Canyon, 1977), 45. Wheeler caused guides much grievance, as well. Swiss guide Edward Feuz Jr. recalled that, "towards his subordinates, indeed towards anyone he considered an inferior," Wheeler was "savage," and "those in his employ or at his orders often found him abusive, arrogant, conceited and autocratic. In short, when not on good behavior, he epitomized the anarchist turned tyrant." Andrew J. Kauffman and William L. Putnam, *The Guiding Spirit* (Revelstoke, BC: Footprint, 1986), 110.

4. From hereon, with few exceptions, Kain spells his first name with a C.

CONRAD KAIN

59

Banff, March 4, 1912

[In English from hereon]

Dear Friend Amelie,

I am sure you will be looking for a letter from Canada every day. Well, what do you think has been the matter that I did not write for such a long time? Now I can tell it you. It is all over, and I am well again. I have just come from the <u>hospital</u>! I had been there for two weeks. The first time after coming back from my trip I have been sick. I had overworked myself a little. I did not feel it so much out in the open air, but when I came in the house, I got worse every day, and so I had to go to the hospital. I am alright now. I did not write about it to my mother, and I will not tell her anything at all. You will surely be interested in my hunting trip, and I will tell you all about it. I had a very good time indeed, and I will write you a very long letter tomorrow and the day after tomorrow. I am working now in the wood on account of my health, and so I have only time for writing at night, and I have to write so much and <u>so many</u> letters! The other day, I had a letter from a gentleman of Washington, a naturalist and he asked me, if I would come along with him to Siberia and the Mongolian border next summer, and he says we shall see Vienna too.[1] And so I hope the day of a "Wiedersehen" will come. I send you a copy of the letter I am speaking of. *[In German from hereon]* Hah! A reunion, provided things go well, and perhaps a bit of climbing with my dear old friend from Vienna! (That's you!). Please excuse that this letter is so brief.

Yours very truly,
Conrad

1. The favourable impression Kain made upon Ned Hollister—during the 1911 Robson survey—prompted an offer of employment with a Smithsonian exploratory trip to the Altai Mountains of Siberia in 1912. See N. Hollister, "Camp in the Alti," CAJ 5 (1913): 73–81.

60

Banff, March 16, 1912

[In English from hereon]

My dear friend Amelie:

Fancy this morning I posted a letter for you and just now I got your dear letter from February 18th. So you must not have got the little photo I sent to you, when I came back to Banff and before I went to the hospital? I had no letters from home for a long time, but I believe they wrote me. I missed more mail. It must have been lost up North somewhere around Yellowhead Pass. Now I must start to tell you about my trip and I had better write in German, don't you think so? —— *[In German from hereon]* It is impossible to tell everything that I have experienced in the last four months as a trapper in the wilderness.[1] But first of all, I must say: the life of a trapper is one of the most beautiful lives and one of the most difficult. One suffers hunger and thirst, then lives like a lord with the best meat in the cottage. Happy and sad hours, and often very dangerous minutes, are all a part of the job. But *one is the free man of the woods* and also *the king in the forest* and *master over everything!!* ——— At the end of October, we (my friend and I) reached our winter quarters. In two days, we built our cabin near the Big Smoky River. My friend then left with the horses. I accompanied him across the Moose Pass to the Moose River. There, we made a lean-to in a sheltered spot under big trees, where I spent almost a month. — On November 3rd, I said farewell to my friend for a month and began hunting and trapping, all alone in the wilderness. Already on the second day, I had bad luck and yet also good luck. I was hunting goats and followed an old billy goat up a steep snowy slope. After a three-quarter hour climb, I had reached a sharp edge, and suddenly the slope broke away, and I knew instantly that I was in danger of avalanching. Luckily, I was only buried in the snow to my hips and stayed <u>on top</u> of the debri. In two to three minutes, I was in the valley, back where I had been three-quarter hours before!! The snow had gone through my clothes to my skin. I hurried back to the woods, made a big fire, and dried my clothes. Dead tired, I arrived at my shack at midnight. The next day, I started trapping. I set thirty-five traps along the Moose River, a ten-mile line, and then went back across the Moose Pass to the Smoky River. I had a tent there, but one without a stove. I made a fire in front of it. On this side of the pass, I had another trap line with about thirty irons, and so I regularly hiked back and forth across the pass to check the irons. And I was lucky: already the first time I took out three martens. *[In English from hereon]* Then I got a big caribou: so I had lots of fresh meat. On the second round I got known to the trapper's devil: the wolverine which, as every trapper knows, steals every-thing she gets a hold on, and sometimes is making great damages to the hard working trapper. The trouble is that the wolverine is very hard to catch. These beasts are very keen and wise. I caught two the first week, but they went away <u>with the trap</u> on foot! Then I caught them a spring pole. The time they upset the trap the spring pole goes up in the air and so they are helpless and have to die there. But the trapper likes very much to get a wolverine <u>alive</u>. (The skin is not worth much, only 5–6 dollars.) *[In German from hereon]* I wanted to write in German and slipped into English probably because I have not spoken my own language for so long and therefore I am begin-ning to <u>think</u> in English, too. You would hardly believe if I told you that from October 1st to the end of January, I spent about forty nights in the open, and even in terribly cold weather. The coldest day was 62 below zero. In the forest, it might not have been that cold, but, for sure, it was -50; yet, I froze nothing except a little bit of my face, and that does not count in this area! I was conditioned like any animal of prey in the forest. And when I arrived in Edmonton and stayed in a first class hotel, I caught a cold and it got worse every day. I stayed over a week in Edmonton and have a few acquaintances there. There are 3,000 Germans in Edmonton, also a few from Vienna, but I had no opportunity to meet anyone. From there, I went to Calgary for a day, and then I went back to my now beloved mountain village, Banff. I was so pleased that, here in Banff, I was welcomed so warmly. Old and young came to the hotel to greet me. My cold had become so bad that I had to go to the hospital. And that was good. The doctor told me that I was overstressed and had gone through too many strenuous situations. No wonder! I travelled for seven months through the wilderness! One has to go through stress and it cannot be avoided. Now I feel quite healthy again. Only my voice is still rough, but it also gets better with every day. I am in my old place. Below me live two Englishmen, who have a piano and play all the time. It makes me tired to listen to this constant noise, although I like music and songs. I am not really homesick, but often I find the world so boring. I am tired of this eternal bachelor life. During the day, I work in the forest, and when I return home into the cold apartment, tired and hungry, cooking bothers me the most. So, I often go for dinner to the hotel. In the hotel, there are no white cooks. All are Chinese, and the food is not good at all. All this cooking has no taste: a far cry from Viennese cooking. Yes, my dear friend, it has been a long time since I had the last Wiener Schnitzel with you on May 29th, 1909, hasn't it? ————— *Long Interruption*————— I just heard from my friend, Professor Hollister, that I will be able to accompany him, and so I have an opportunity to see my beautiful old home country and visit my good friends. Hollister writes to me to say that we will leave New York in the middle of May, travel from London to St. Petersburg, then further through Siberia to the Altai Mountains on the Mongolian border. Early in October, Professor Hollister has to be back in New York. I figured that by the end of September, I can be in my home country's mountains. Well, my dear friend, there is one more chance to climb the old nice Dachstein or some other mountain besides

the old "fashionable" Rax mountain. What do you think about it?
I won't stay at home very long. I must return to the Western forest,
where there is unlimited freedom and where I have the same rights
as anybody else. I think you will understand that one likes to go
back where one feels <u>well</u>. Perhaps I can take one of my brothers
along. As I read in the paper, there are very upsetting times in Europe
with strikes in the coal mines and constantly increasing prices. You
cannot blame the working class that people have become restless and
impatient.[2] What do you think? I don't concern myself with politics
here at all. In Canada, things are going well and all is calm. Canada
will probably one day belong to the best countries in the world.[3]
While at home, I hope that I can give some talks about my travels in
the Rockies. I don't know how I will do with speeches. Instead, I will
show lots of pictures. Some days ago, I met a Swiss man. First, we
spoke German, and then we turned to English and did not get out of
it anymore!! I was not pleasantly surprised to find out that I could not
speak German fluently, but I hope that it won't take much time to get
it back, once I hear the language again. In two weeks, it will be Easter
and you will probably be in your villa in Reichenau and stay there for
some days, weather permitting. I am already looking forward to see
your home in Reichenau, from where you always sent me messages
in such a friendly way. I have to close now, my dear good friend. I will
write again soon.

Yours very truly,
Con

1. The winter Kain spent trapping in the Yellowhead Pass region with Donald Phillips is also recounted
    in Kain's "A Trapper on the Athabasca," in *Where the Clouds*, 337–45.
2. By the late nineteenth century, coal mining in Europe had increasingly become a political and
    social issue. Coal miners' labour and trade unions became powerful organizations by the turn of the
    century and were often led by the leaders of the "Left" or socialist movements. In March of 1912, a
    National Coal Strike gripped England that saw 800,000 miners lay down their tools in demand of
    better wages. Similar strikes broke out in Berlin and Paris. It was front-page news in Canada.

3. Kain's optimism was widespread among immigrants to Canada in the first decades of the twen-tieth century. Immigration pamphlets titled *Canada: The Land of Opportunity*, for example, boasted in 1909 that "the Premier of Canada expressed the idea, which is that of all Canadians, that as the 19th century was the century of the United States, the 20th century is the century of Canada." Quoted in Brown and Cook, *Canada, 1886–1921*, 49. Underlying this new self-confidence were the comforting facts of economic success and the expectation that the future was limitless.

61

Banff, April 17, 1912

My dear Amelie:

[In English from hereon] I am sure you will think me unkind for not writing for such a long time, but I hope you will forgive me, when I tell you the reasons. Well, I am coming to Europe for sure. I have to be in London no later than May 25. *[In German from hereon]* Up to now, I have received four cards from your beautiful trip. My best thanks. With joy, I read your news that you travelled to Africa, and I am sure that you had a beautiful time there (if we leave out the seasickness!!). How I, too, would love to see Africa! Perhaps the opportunity will come sometime. By now you might be in your villa in Reichenau, enjoying the coming spring and reminiscing about your Mediterranean trip. You will not have stopped in Corsica—a pity! Had you been there, you would have remembered me. I remember that trip so well, as if it had been only a week ago. Your last card was from Malta. The street one sees on the card reminds me of many Italian mountain villages. When you receive these lines, I might be on my trip already. From the Mongolian border, we will go by steamer on the Obi River to the Altai Mountains. We will not climb mountains, but we will hike a lot. My work will be trapping and hunting, watching for little animals, collecting flowers, etc. I am already looking forward to it and will certainly have lots of new

experiences. The professor taking me on this trip holds me in high regard and trusts me very much. Last summer, I collected mice and beetles for him, and so we became friends out in the woods. And now, I have to tell you the most joyful news of the future trip: on the return trip, I can visit my hometown and stay for as long as I want, and I will get paid for my trip to America. *[In English from hereon]* What I do hope and expect is that I shall be in the old country on September 14–16, and I shall come home over München, Salzburg, Ennstal. And you know how much I do love the nice Bachl-Alm and the Ennstal, so I will stop there for some days. I would be the more glad, if it could be possible for you and your sister to come and meet me at Schladming and we would climb then together the old Dachstein from any side you like. I would like to be your guide on this mountain, and I know that you would like very much to climb with me, wouldn't you? — *[In German from hereon]* You see, it would be great if we could possibly do <u>that</u>! I think it won't be impossible for you and Miss Flora to get a little holiday? Should I discuss it with your mother? From the Ennstal, I would go home to see my mother and show her "a good son!" But then travelling begins again: back to Canada, and then perhaps farther on to New Zealand. About the latter, I cannot yet say anything definite. I am looking forward so much to seeing my mother, all of you, and my dear old mountains again! I also want to do some Rax tours with you and Miss Flora. I am longing for home very much. —— In early May, I will travel from here to Montreal, and, on May 9th, I take the ship to Liverpool. Please write to me to London. From there, we will travel to St. Petersburg on May 29th. On September 14th, the Professor has to be back in London. I can be at home from St. Petersburg at the same time, and I will take the shortest route. Around this time, all the huts are still open, and the alpine dairymaids are also still on the alm. I can already see Resi from the Bachl Alm, full of joy when I visit her![1] Resi likes me a lot. She writes me sometimes, and I have to laugh when reading her letters: she writes just as she speaks!! I am sure you would love the Bachl Alm just as I do. It is one of the most beautiful alms I ever saw. I hope we can stay there for a few days. I will write a nice letter to your mother about it, and I feel sure she will let you go for some days. Did you hear about the Big Disaster on the ocean? 1,500 people perished, among them some millionaires.[2] Most women and children were saved. The steamer cost fifteen million dollars. I want to close now with heartiest greeting to you and your family.

Yours truly,
Conrad

My address in London: K.K., Dr. William Phillips, American Embassy, London.

1. A dairymaid in the Bach Valley, Resi served tourist huts at the foot of the Dachstein. Kain befriended her in 1905, while in the valley with clients seeking to climb the mountain's southern wall. Their success marked, perhaps, the first time the wall was guided. See Kain, *Where the Clouds*, 91–93, 100, 124–25.

2. The RMS *Titanic* was the largest passenger steamer in the world when it set off on its maiden voyage from Southampton, England, to New York City on 10 April 1912. Four days into the crossing the ship struck an iceberg, south of the Grand Banks of Newfoundland, and sank in the early hours of 11 April. A total of 1,517 people perished in the cold waters of the North Atlantic. It remains one of the world's deadliest peacetime maritime disasters. Incidentally, one of the "millionaires" to whom Kain was no doubt referring was Charles Melville Hays (1856–1912), the president of the GTPR (and its main financial backer), who was returning to Canada from a visit to England; he was scheduled to attend the grand opening of the Château Laurier Hotel in Ottawa, Ontario.

62

Banff Alta, Canada, April 26, 1912

My dear good friend:

I am so sorry that I have to tell you that I face a big disappointment.
Full of joy, I wrote to you about my European trip, and today I received
a letter from the Canadian Consulate that states as follows: "In view
of your military duty, a passport will probably not be issued."[1] ——
What do you say to that? Without a passport it is impossible to travel
to Russia! I am very desperate and I have nobody here to complain to
about my troubles. Most would only laugh at me. Canadians are definitely the freest people and cannot grasp how one can be <u>hindered</u> in
any kind of travel! — I will try my utmost in order to get the permission to travel. Unfortunately, the time of the departure is already so
close. I am convinced that you will not be offended when I say that "if
my fatherland will make it impossible for me to take this trip, then I
will lose all my feelings for fatherland and patriotism and have no
urge for defending my country!" But in spite of it, <u>I remain German</u>
in word and meaning. And I am, and will remain, true to my home
country and my mountains from the viewpoint of nature. What shall
I do? I know you would love to give me advice, but, when these lines
reach you, I am already supposed to be on the ocean on my way to
England!! The expedition will not be postponed because of my passport!!! I will try to get protection and information from some higher
officials of the Canadian government, thanks to the fact that I know
some personally. Mostly, I feel sorry for my dear mother, who is
already full of joy and looks forward to our reunion. Please tell
nobody about this for the time being. I hope the best from a very
good recommendation from the Canadian government. Actually, I
should not even write to you about it, but it eases my heavy heart to

complain to <u>one</u> trusted person! I shall write by registered mail right away when I find out. I think my mother's heart would break if she knew about all that! I feel very agitated myself. It's unbelievable to think that a thirty-year-old man can be legally treated like a little child! To think that, at the same time, I could be expected to be a defender of my fatherland and, in case of war, would, willingly or not, give my life to the Emperor's country Austria. A sad situation. I am sure you agree with me that such laws control a person too much and that one is made to feel more or less like a slave. I will also try at the Russian consulate. Perhaps they would let me pass through without a passport? I hope you had much fun on your cruise and that the trip was good for you. With my heartiest greetings to you, your dear mother and Flora,

your true friend for ever,
Conrad

---

1.   Kain served eight weeks of mandatory training in the Austrian army in October and November of 1904. See Kain, *Where the Clouds*, 61–64.

63

Banff, Alta, May 1, 1912

My dear friend Amelie:

This morning, I received a letter from the Parliament in Ottawa, which stated that I have the right to apply for Canadian citizenship. I can then travel wherever I want to, and "Miss Canada" will, wherever I am, protect me! So, it is possible to take this trip, and I don't need a travel permit from the Austrian government to travel around Austria or any other country. And so I will board ship on May 17th in Quebec and go to Liverpool on the Empress of Ireland!! I already told you my address. When we leave London, I cannot give you any other address. At home, I will also show some photographs during my lecture. I think I will get the glass plates from Dr. Longstaff. For you, I will give a "special presentation!" The last part of your trip was from Venice. I am already eagerly looking forward to an extensive report about your beautiful trip.

With many dear greetings to you all,
yours very truly,
Conrad

PART THREE

The Wanderer, 1912–1916

- travels to the Altai Mountains of Siberia (1912)
- last visit to Europe (1912)
- aboard the SS *Orsova* bound for New Zealand (1912–13)
- labourer in a New Zealand bush camp (1913)
- an invitation to return to the Canadian Rockies (1913)
- aboard the steamer *Moana* bound for Vancouver (1913)
- work on the Alberta–British Columbia Boundary Survey between Vermilion and Kicking Horse Pass (1913)
- the ACC's Mount Robson Camp (1913)
- work on the Boundary Survey near Vermilion Pass and Mount Assiniboine (1913)
- adventures in the Southern Alps of New Zealand with Herbert Otto Frind (1913–1914)
- tragedy on Aoraki/Mount Cook (1914)
- return to Banff (1914)
- work on the Boundary Survey between Elk and Crowsnest passes (1914)
- return to New Zealand as an official guide in the Aoraki/Mount Cook area (1914–1915)
- imprisoned in New Zealand as an "enemy alien" (1916)
- return to Canada (1916)

64a[1]

Biskra, Siberia, June 17, 1912, at the Obi River

My dear good friend:

[In English from hereon] I just wrote a nice letter to your dear mother, and I do hope the best of our Wiedersehen and our Dachstein trip. How happy I shall be to see you on the station in Schladming! I do see you in spirit already! Well, now let me tell you a little more about my present time and where I am. Far away from you, my dear friend, but not quite so far as two months ago. — [In German from hereon] I hope that I answered all your letters well and you are satisfied with me. Now, I want to be quite good again, since I am already closer to my strict, but still dear, teacher! Before my departure from London, I received several letters, but nothing from you. We travelled with the Nord Express, first-class sleeping coach (fine!) to St. Petersburg, where we stayed for a few days. We had to run around a lot because of several permits. And, with so much to do, I could not keep my promise to write to you from St. Petersburg. We continued with the Express to St. Nikolai in Siberia for four days and nights. An indescribably vast country, grandiose forests. From St. Nikolai, we travelled by steamer on the Obi River to Biskra. Today, we were very busy with shopping. Tomorrow, we leave and travel 325 miles by wagon, then eight days by camel (or any other beasts of burden). A long stretch lies before us still before we start work. Then, we will have six weeks of hard labour. After that, we turn homewards: the two gentlemen to America and me via Moscow to Austria! ——— Up to now, everything has gone very well, but the difficulties begin. Both gentlemen are very good and friendly to me. In everything, I have been treated as an equal. So far, I have not been addressed or treated as a servant. I already know Mr. Hollister very well. And Mr. Lyman is almost the same: always friendly.[2] I try to be attentive and look out for things I can do for them. The people of the area here are very poor. And terribly dirty! I fear that, in a short while, we will all have lice! Amelie, I am happy that I see so much of the world! On the way to the Dachstein, I will be able to tell you many things. While climbing, however, there will be no talking!! At such times, one is serious! — It will be impossible to write when we are in the mountains, and so you will not hear from me for a long time. When I come back here again, I will write, and, from Schladming, I will send a telegram. Perhaps I'll go via Warsaw first to Vienna and afterwards to the Dachstein Mountains. I cannot yet say this for sure. — It is almost 3 A.M., I think, and I have to close now. Since this is my last letter for a while, I have to wish you the best of luck for your dear name day! I wish you the very best of everything from my heart and that God may keep you healthy, and you will live to see many name days and many beautiful days and hours in this world!

With my heartiest greetings and an "Auf Wiedersehen,"
I am yours very truly,
Conrado Caino.

1. Thorington (or Malek) mistakenly listed two letters—this one and the next—as "64."

2. The expedition to the Altai Mountains of Siberia and Mongolia was financed by American physicist Theodor Lyman (1874–1954), of Cambridge, Massachusetts. Lyman came from an old, wealthy Boston family and was educated at Harvard, where he obtained his PHD in 1900. After a short spell studying abroad at Göttingen, Germany, and Cambridge, England, he returned to Harvard where he served as the Hollis Professor of Physics (1921–1925) and director of the Jefferson Physical Laboratory (1910–1947). An avid sport hunter, Lyman was a member the Travelers' Club, an organization founded in 1902 "to promote intelligent travel and exploration, especially by Harvard men." Although conceived for the purpose of collecting fauna in the Altai Mountains, which, at that time, were unrepresented in American museums, the expedition soon split after reaching the Siberia–Mongolia border: Hollister and Kain stayed put to collect the smaller mammals and Lyman pushed on alone into Mongolia for large game hunting. He brought back specimens of sheep, ibex, and gazelle. P.W. Bridgman, *Theodor Lyman, 1874–1954: A Biographical Memoir* (Washington, DC: The National Academy of Science, 1957), 245–46.

64b

At the Siberia/Mongolia border, July 11, 1912

Dear Amelie:

It is a shame to use such paper to write and send it to a good friend!
If I didn't know you so well, I simply could not do it! But I know
you enjoy getting a few lines from so far away and knowing that I
remember you on your dear name day. *[In English from hereon]* Now,
my dear friend, so many miles I am off from you, I often don't know
what time and date we have, but I watched for the 10th of July!! And
now here we are: It is one day over already, but I could not write
yesterday, but in spirit I had been with you at your happy home
at Reichenau. I had been thinking of you all day long, and I gathered many flowers for you. I shall give them to you with great joy
and happiness the first hour we are together, or I shall send them.
Flowers from Mongolia! ——— *[In German from hereon]* They will not
be so beautiful and fresh anymore as they are now, standing before
me, but I know you will take them anyhow, won't you? Yesterday
was a beautiful day: beautiful in nature and beautiful for my soul
and mood. I thought of all the good suggestions you gave me. Yes,
there were many, many! And for this, the beautiful flowers you love
so much. If you could only see them yourself! I think the flowers
are the most beautiful things one can imagine. May you live in good
health and see many more "Tenths of July!" This day, for me, too, will
always be a joyful day, even though I am miles and miles away from
you. But, in spirit, I can always be with you and nobody can take that
feeling from me. — Now, I have to give you a better idea about my
whereabouts. We are just at the border of Siberia and Mongolia. I am
healthy, and so is my friend, Hollister. We work very hard, go hunting
daily, and I am very tired. The area is mountainous, not much forest,

and is very cold. We have rain almost every day, and often snow. I am always alone during the day and come back to the camp with my prey in the evening to discuss the events of the day with my friends. We have a Kalmyk native, who looks after the horses and supplies, and takes care of the firewood and cow dung. My work is very interesting. I like it better than mountain guiding. Hollister is one of the best people anywhere: a gentleman, top to bottom. He teaches me a lot and is always kind and friendly. Mr. Lyman and the interpreter travelled still further and will be back in a month. From Biskra to here, we needed eight days by wagon. A horrible vehicle! We stayed in one village for two days. Then, we needed a couple horses and another two days to get here from the last village. We'll travel further to Mongolia from here. We have captured and collected more items than we had anticipated, so there is a possibility that perhaps I can come home earlier in September. I would love to see a bit more of the autumn in my home mountains. Oh, if I could give wings to these lines! Who knows <u>when</u> you will get them? We are cut off from mail service here. Please forgive me for the dirty paper. I cannot find anything better. Now, Addio my dear friend!

With heartiest greeting to you, your dear mother and sister,
yours very truly,
C.K.

65

St. Petersburg, Grand Hotel d'Europe, August 26, 1912

My dear friend:

Only a few more days and I will have the pleasure to see you and my home mountains again. I just arrived in St. Petersburg. Tomorrow, August 27th, I will take the train to Vienna and stay in town for maybe one or two days. I will let you know of my arrival at the Payerbach station, and, if you are not too busy, please come to the train!! I would be so pleased to greet you and your sister when leaving the train! Nobody knows that I am coming!! Even my mother does not know. The poor lady will be overjoyed to see me again! Between this letter's arrival and mine, there will be no great difference in time. First, I wanted to surprise you, but then I thought it over. What will happen with our planned Dachstein excursion? Would you get holidays? I am so pleased that I can come two weeks earlier than I had originally thought. We worked very hard so that we could return as soon as possible. Therefore, you must not be surprised if I don't look "very fat!" But I am as healthy as always. Special greetings to your dear mother and Miss Flora. This time I can write: see you soon—see you soon—see you soon—!

I am yours truly,
Conrad Kain

66

Miss Amelie Malek Reichenau N.Ö.

Telegram from Vienna –76–4447–11 31 10 25M August 31, 1912

ARRIVE 3 O'CLOCK—TRAIN PAYERBACH STATION KAIN[1]   179

1. Kain visited Austria from 31 August to 12 November 1912. "I made a few difficult climbs," he wrote,
    "quenched my three-year-old thirst with beer and had a jolly time, living my youth over again."
    Quoted in Kain, *Where the Clouds*, 351. During his stay, he also visited with Albert Gerngross—the
    "Mr. G" of Vienna—and no doubt shared many stories about his time in Asia and North America.
    This was Kain's last visit to Austria. He never saw his mother, Amelie, or his home in the Alps again.

67

Bonn's Hotel, 1 Craven Street, Charing Cross, London [no date]

Dear Miss Amelie:

[In English from hereon] This is my third letter I start to write. I have to be a man now, but these days I sometimes felt like a little child, who has lost his mother and is alone in the world. — *[In German from hereon]* Well, I give you my travelogue. I went from Vienna via Innsbruck, Buchs, Zürich, Basel, to Paris. I have an acquaintance there who I unfortunately could not find. Paris is a beautiful city. Unfortunately, I had very poor weather. From Paris to London. Here, I live very well, staying with friends. On Sunday, Dr. Longstaff brought me your dear letter for which I am very grateful. These are the first lines from my old home country. — Dear Miss, I owe you many, many thanks for all the thoughtfulness you offered me during my holidays in the mountains of my home country. I don't find the right words. I wish you that dear God may bless you and keep you well. For myself, I wish that I may have the pleasure again to see you in your beautiful home in Reichenau. ————— And now ——— what next? ——— You will not trust your eyes!!! I go via the Orient Line to Australia and New Zealand!! A long trip! You know my wishes and plans. It is my greatest wish to see as much as possible of the world. <u>And I will do it.</u> I go to New Zealand to get to know the conditions there. What experiences and observations will I have in the far South? I am ready for everything—good and bad. I will get through it. I will keep a good diary and write lots. One day, I will return home as an *experienced traveller of the world.* — I have good references for New Zealand. Yesterday, I was invited to the Alpine Club for dinner and got acquainted with very fine people. They all admired my adventurous spirit! Just now, Dr. Longstaff phoned: "A letter!!" It surely

It is not much the world can give
With all its subtle art,
And gold and gems are not the things
To satisfy the heart,
But oh! if those who cluster round
The altar and the hearth
Have gentle words and loving smiles
How beautiful is earth!

In remembrance of
                    yours truly
                         Conrad Kain
October 31ˢᵗ 1912

Reichenau

∧ The inscription Kain left in Flora Malek's diary, October 31, 1912, from C.D. Stewart's "Gentle Words." [Courtesy of Manfred Rotter] will be from you!—?—Right!!! Oh, how grateful I am to you! It will be the last for a long time. Mail from New Zealand takes five to six weeks to get to Austria. It will probably be the longest voyage one takes. I am pleased that you were well entertained at the theatre and concert. And now, I have to beg your pardon, that I did not send a card for your birthday. Do you still accept my wishes? I wish you the best for everything, especially good health, and that you stay young and yet will become very old!! I am quite well except for a cough. Now about my address in New Zealand: "c/o Mr. Ross, Wellington N.Z."[1] Please write more often. I can imagine everything so well, when you tell it in a letter. It is as if I hear it from your mouth. Did you already visit Mr. von Payer? Please greet him from me, even though I am not known to him. When you go to Reichenau at Christmas, I will be just arriving in New Zealand. Of course, I will go third class again (costs 21 Pounds), and the ship is booked to the last seat. I only got my ticket by chance, because one traveller decided to wait for the next boat. But even though I travel third class, it does not matter: I already endured a lot and so I will be able to manage this! If I don't like New Zealand, I will return to Banff in June. I wrote to my good friend there asking him to watch over the things I left there. As people tell me here, New Zealand is supposed to be much better than Canada. I will see for myself. *(Interruption)* ——— Well, it is my last night in England, I can say in Europe. It is 10:30 P.M., and these lines are the last ones which I write ashore. You will, of course, get news from the ship. I think you can even write to me a few lines and I will get them on board. On November 30th, we will get to Naples. Tonight, I went to the theatre with Dr. Longstaff. They played *The Girl Who Sells Flowers*. I would have rather not seen that play, since it affected me as a lover of flowers. You must excuse my bad handwriting, dear Miss. I am lying in bed and my suitcase is my table!! On the dresser, I have some pictures of my good friends and some letters. There are also the flowers I forgot to give you in Vienna, so I take them along to New Zealand! I will keep one half of them for myself, and, the other half, I will certainly send to you. Now, I must sleep. Good Night. ————

November 22, 5 o'clock in the morning. Good morning! I hardly slept. Another four hours and I am on the *Orsova*.[2] I will do my best concerning the Canadian diary entries. I also wrote to all my friends because of pictures. I know my book cannot be in any better hands than yours. I am very grateful for your effort and work, you never-tiring teacher! — Farewell! God may protect you until I see you again. Forever Goodbye! — Farewell, all my dearest friends and dear home,

———

Yours very truly forever,

K.K.

1. An avid mountaineer and journalist in Wellington, Malcolm Ross (1862–1930) helped found the New Zealand Alpine Club (NZAC) in 1891 and later served as vice president and the editor of its journal. Ross's greatest mountaineering achievement was perhaps the first traverse (and fourth ascent) of Aoraki/Mt. Cook in 1906 with Englishman Samuel Turner (1869–1929) and guides Peter Graham (1878–1961) and Tom Fyfe (1870–1947). It was an ascent made in difficult conditions over a 36-hour "day." Ross published several books, most notably *Aorangi; Or, The heart of the Southern Alps, New Zealand* (1892), *A Climber in New Zealand* (1915) and, with his son, Noel, *Light and Shade in War* (1916).

2. Built in Scotland for the Orient Steam Navigation Company, the SS *Orsova* was an ocean liner that provided passenger service between London and Australia (via the Suez Canal) from 1909 until 1915, when it was commandeered as a British troopship. Although torpedoed and beached in 1917, the vessel was repaired and, in 1919, resumed passenger service along the UK–Australia route. The 12,026-metric-ton vessel had a length of 163 metres and its beam (or width) was 19 metres; it had a maximum speed of 18 knots. The ocean liner provided accommodation for 280 first-class passengers, 130 second-class passengers, and 900 third-class passengers.

68

On board the *Orsova*, November 22, 1912. 8 h 45.

Dear Miss Amelie:

At 1:10 P.M., we departed. Hundreds of people sent us off with their good wishes. The boat is big and very clean. I like it better than the "*Empresses.*" It is full of people everywhere, even old people emigrating, and all are English. I haven't heard one word in another language. The food is good —— it will be good if it stays like that. It was a foggy day, until the sun came through. Now it is perfect and very calm. The moon shines brilliantly. I sit on deck, feel very well, and look in the direction of home. How will it be there? My mother and many a friends will think of me. This morning in London, I mailed a letter to you: you should receive it on the 25th in the afternoon. *[In English from hereon]* Perhaps our thoughts are crossing on the wide ocean.

I do feel sleepy, so Good Night, Conrad (8 hr. 15 min.)

69

[In German from hereon] Orsova, November 23, 1912. 8 h 45 o'clock.

Dear Miss Amelie:

Now the second day has already passed. Today, it was not so nice, a bit stormy. Many people are already seasick and look near dead. I am healthy as a horse. I just comforted an old lady, who is 57 and still takes such a long trip. She wants to see her three children, who live in Australia. Today, I was busy with my diary entries. Just think, I already wrote two pages and am only as far as July 10, 1909, and my first case of homesickness. I have to praise myself, since nobody does, because nobody knows me and <u>what</u> I write!! I hope that I achieve something with writing on board and get ahead with my diary. The trip will take six weeks, so I will have Christmas at sea. Could be nice, don't you think? But the Christmas spirit cannot find anybody here! —— Well, it did not find me last year at Smoky River either! So, it probably crossed my name off its list. ————— As long as I don't take the names of my friends and acquaintances off *my* list, and they don't hear from me for too long! I wonder what you are doing now? Maybe you are reading some nice books or the newspaper? I would like to know more about poor Austria and the war.[1] I am sitting in the smoking room, and they are playing very nicely in the music room. The steamer is fine. Now Good Night, I am reading the book you gave me (Schiller).[2] Thank you ever so much! *K.K.*

1. The First Balkan War, which lasted from October 1912 to May 1913, pitted the Balkan League (Serbia, Greece, Montenegro, and Bulgaria) against the Ottoman Empire. It marked, as historian Richard Hall noted, "the beginning of an era in European history dominated by nationalism and conflict" and was the first concerted effort of the Balkan peoples to emulate the Italian and German examples and form large nationalist states. Richard C. Hall, *The Balkan Wars, 1912–1913:*

Prelude to the First World War (London: Routledge, 2000), ix. While the Great Powers of Europe intervened to help shape the resolution and settlement of the Balkan Wars, the skirmishes in south-eastern Europe were never fully resolved before the whole continent was engulfed in war by July 1914.

2.   Johann Christoph Friedrich von Schiller (1759–1805) was a German poet, philosopher, historian, and playwright.

70

On the *Orsova*, November 24, 1912, in the *Bay of Biscaya*

Dear Miss Amelie:

Today was a beautiful day, not cold. Dinner was very good, as was the tea. I hope it will stay like this: I could stand the six weeks easily. Today, I found out that we will be on board more than six weeks to get to Wellington. To Brisbane, it is 13,198 nautical miles. I don't know how many miles it is to Wellington, probably another few thousand. When you receive my letters, you will probably follow my travels on the map. Our next stop is Gibraltar. But I don't know whether we stop long enough to go ashore. In Naples, we will surely go ashore. There, I will mail the letter and diary entries. I think I did well by this long trip. I hope to catch up with my diary notes, which is your wish and to my benefit, don't you think, dear Miss? What will you have done today? Perhaps you were in a concert and were entertained. How are your nerves behaving? I often think about this, because I often noticed that your nerves are fragile. Why is it so? Do you follow my advice not to read all these unjustified, often dumb and exciting, newspaper articles? Maybe I am a bit pushy with my advice, but I know you as such a good lady that I believe you just cannot be cross with me! ———— Now it is a beautiful evening (moonlight). The beacons of the lighthouses can be seen on all sides. The passengers are all in a good mood, and one hears singing from all directions. I believe there is also a church service tonight. Now, I will go to the dining room and later write a few more lines and notices. I am now at Mt. Huber.[1] Good night, dear Amelie. *K.K.*

1. Kain's diary (1904–1909) would later constitute the first half of Thorington's edited *Where the Clouds Can Go* (1935). Chronicling much of Kain's early life, the diary, which remains lost, received its last entry in the spring of 1910, when Kain was 27, near the conclusion of his adventures on the Canadian prairies. Here, though, in the dining room aboard the *Orsova*, off the shores of Spain and Portugal, Kain is perhaps writing his most charming entry for 1909, "Hip-Hip-Hurrah!," which relates his first summer with the Alpine Club of Canada (ACC) and its mountaineering camp. See Kain, *Where the Clouds*, 220–22. The entry was subsequently reprinted in Bruce Fairley, ed., *Canadian Mountaineering Anthology: Stories from 100 Years at the Edge* (Vancouver: Lone Pine, 1994), 108–09.

71

Orsova, November 25, 1912

Passing the coast of Spain and Portugal

Dear Miss Amelie:

Another day has already passed, never to return: a beautiful day, and
so warm that one could sit on deck almost without a coat. All is well
and happy. In the evening, I saw something new. Perhaps it would
have been new for you, too! On one side, the sunset; on the other, the
full moon coming up. The ocean was so calm one can hardly notice
that the ship moved forward. You know my descriptions of sunrise
and sunset, don't you? When I watched the sunset I thought ——
Oh, if only I could write about such beauty the way I have it in my
memory and keep it there for the future! In the evening, it is always
quite merry here: today, there was a gathering to elect a committee
for sports. In the afternoon, I spoke for a long while with two
gentlemen, who already had been in Australia for forty years, and had
come to visit their home country for the third time. They, of course,
spoke very well about the country. I will see for myself! I do everything where there is money to make, because I have to think of my
old days. I already told you about it. I want yet to spend a few years in
my old home country near my Rax. Now, it is time once more to go to
bed! Good night!

Conrad

72

Orsova, November 26, 1912

Dear Miss Amelie:

Today is November 26th. I am sure you think of my name day![1] Today,
you will have received my letter from London. At 11 A.M., we reached
Gibraltar and stopped for 2½ hours. It is a wonderful place! I did not
go ashore because the boat was far from the coast, and going and
coming by boat takes a long time. In the evening, we saw a beautiful sunset again. I talked with a sailor who said that we will see even
more beautiful ones in the evenings to come. The name day was
quite nice. I made it nice for myself by building castles in the air![2] I
am looking forward to hearing from you in Naples. Good Night!

1. Catholics celebrate the name Conrad as a Saint Day on November 26 in honour of St. Conrad of
    Constance (975–900 BC).
2. The popular expression "to build castles in the air" usually means to daydream of unattainable
    goals.

73

Orsova, November 28, 1912

Gulf of Lyon

Dear Miss Amelie:

Yesterday was a rough day and most passengers were seasick. I had
some headaches, which got better in the evening. No sunset, at least
not a visible one. The moon rose late. I could not write, but I read
something by Schiller. Very beautiful and interesting. The old lady
about whom I wrote you is not doing well. I am worried that she will
hardly last through this long trip. Today, we reached Toulon, where
we stopped for four hours. Most passengers visited the city. I didn't
disembark, because I thought there was not enough time. Toulon
lies in a beautiful setting and is popular for a honeymoon trip. —
Now I am out of writing paper! How dumb of me not to be prepared
for that! In Naples, I will buy enough of it. Tonight, there will be a
concert on board. I bought a newspaper and read under "Vienna"
that yesterday there was panic at the stock exchange. Some shares
fell by 30 to 50 Kronen. This morning, I talked with a very clever
gentleman about the situation. It is amazing what fine people can be
found in third class! I hope and wish that this money crisis does not
concern you too much. How are you all? Are you all well? Now Good
Night! *K.K.*

Orsova, November 29, 1912

Oh! What a fine day! I see Corsica!! —— Beautiful memories go
through my mind: My trip with Mr. G., which I will never forget. I
also think that you and your dear family crossed this ocean in the

spring of this year, only your path would have been more southerly. The mountains of Corsica are all covered with snow: I think I see the Monte Cinto range!! I hope once in my life to see Corsica again! When I am so lucky, I will invite you and Miss Flora to join me. But first comes the Dachstein, doesn't it? Tomorrow at 6 A.M., we are in Naples and will stay there until 2 P.M. I have to mail this letter today by steamer mail before 9 P.M. Now it is past 8 h and so I must close, hoping that you are healthy and well. Many greetings to Miss Flora; I kiss your dear, good mother's hand. With a hiker's greetings and thanks, I am yours very truly,

Konrad Kain

74

Orsova, December 1, 1912

Dear Miss Amelie:

Yesterday, when I came back on board at Naples, I received your dear card and letter, which I opened with much joy! Unfortunately, you could not tell me much good news. I couldn't trust my eyes when I read the sad news about your best friend! Dear Miss, in my mind I feel with you and wish that things will turn out better than you believe. I put myself in your place: if *I* would lose my best friend in the world like that —— it would certainly give my heart a lot of pain, because I know what it means to have a good friend, an honest friend, a faithful friend! One does not find one like that every day. At least I don't, even though I meet many people and perhaps have more experience in this area than you, and so I can easily feel with you during your anxious, sad hours. I pity the poor husband of your friend. They both were so good and kind to me when I visited them. Dear Amelie, I have known you for six years and know that you are a charming, kind-hearted lady and that you only choose the same kind of people for your friends and best friends. I wish I could be near you. Perhaps I could do something to distract you. Please write me everything. It is much better to confide your worry to someone who feels with you. I am very sorry that Miss Flora is ill, and I hope she recovers soon. I was very pleased that she wrote to me and will answer today. Unfortunately, I did not receive the letter from your dear mother, perhaps I will in New Zealand. It can take weeks! I am convinced that she sent me good wishes. My letters to Vienna left yesterday, and the day after tomorrow, December 3rd, you will receive them. Maybe they'll give you a little joy. Naples is beautiful, as the enclosed picture will show you. We were ashore for five hours. I was the "leader" and had a group of two ladies and two gentlemen. I was so pleased that I could make myself understood so well. We visited the poor districts, the churches, museums, and the palace San Martino. The most interesting place was the old church, where the remains of the royal family are buried. The two ladies were frightened. In my party, there were only "greenhorns." They only know what is happening in England. They did not like the dirty streets, but Naples is not the dirtiest place I've ever saw. Tired out, we returned on board. I will mail this letter in Otranto. Too bad, we will go through the Straits of Messina at night. Right now, we see land, but not clearly (it's raining). At 11 A.M., there is a "service" that I will attend. You know my opinion about religious services. It is in nature where I unite my soul with God. From Suez, I will write again. My address is: c/o P.O. Wellington. That is enough. Please write a lot to me! Goodbye, dear poor friend Miss Amelie.

I am yours truly,
K.K.

75

Orsova, December 3, 1912

Dear Miss:

Yesterday, I got to my cabin at 4 o'clock and found two letters with your beautiful handwriting. I thought somebody might have broken into my suitcase, but saw that the letters were not opened. First, I opened the big one. Thank you, my dear good friend from my old home! Unfortunately, already the seventh line started with the sad news. I can imagine what poor Miss Flora has to go through with the Erysipelas![1] I wish her a quick recovery from the bottom of my heart so that she is well for Christmas. It would be such a pity if you could not go to Reichenau. —— Yes, the boat is okay, food is good, only the cabins are too overcrowded. I see so much that is beautiful! Now, we are along the coast of Greece. —— You write about the war-like mood. Yes, I too wish this threat of war will have a good ending, because, even without war, there is enough misery in Austria. Thank you for your prayer on my name day. *[In English from hereon]* I remember I told on our way back from Baumgartner-Haus (Schneeberg) through Krummbach-Graben about the best girl I met in my life. I am glad I told you all these kind words in the time I was at home. Go ahead with correcting me, dear Miss Amelie, I like it and I will be thankful for it. I wish I could look on the blue sea with you and your dear mother and sister! But I will look at it with you all in spirit as I do now. I would be pleased, if I could nurse you and yours when you are seasick! To-day we have a bath-day. Many are sea-sick, but I am alright. It is a sign that I am a healthy fellow! I have your letters before me to answer them. *[In German from hereon]* Which words to use now? I don't know because now I have read your second letter—the one from your dear mother. I was so pleased about it that I was quite moved and still am, because I know how to appreciate good friendship! You know that I was always so pleased about the hospitable welcome at your home. I will keep your dear mother's letter in a safe place, because it is a proof of her graciousness and friendliness. I wish for you that you will have your mother with you for a long time, and that I will still see her in the best of health upon my next return home. My heart is heavy. —— I have to take a break to recover ——

Orsova, December 4, 1912 — in the morning.

One has to part with what one loves most! These are the words I send to you on the sad loss of your dearest lady friend. My most sincere condolences. Nobody can say how life will end. It is the law of nature. Of course, we all want to live long and bemoan the passing of those friends who should have lived longer. If only I could spend a few days with you during this sad time to tell you things to distract you and also because I would like to be near to Flora! The poor lady. I feel so sorry for her! I will write a few lines to her today. Dear Miss, console yourself and don't dwell on it too much. Think of your nerves. And believe that it had to come, that it was perhaps God's will. Even a person committing suicide you cannot condemn. (I know you don't do that!) It wasn't your friend's fault. Perhaps her mind was overstressed and she lost control over her will. — Dear Miss, may God protect you from further sad events! This is my prayer to God for you. Tonight, we will arrive in Port Said. From there we can send mail. The next station for mail will be Suez. Then you won't hear from me for a long time. But I might write a few lines every day, *[In English from hereon]* so that you know what kind of trip I had. I am writing on my notebook. Hope you got my letter from Naples already. A very fine morning, rather warm. Soon we get to the Red Sea. ——
[In German from hereon] We will stop in Colombo (India) for approximately twelve hours. I will go on land there. *[In English from hereon]* On Xmas evening I shall think of you. I shall try to think myself into your nice, little, white room. We shall be in Freemantle on the 24th of

December. *[In German from hereon]* The time difference to London—six hours. Once more, my sympathies for your unforgettable loss. I feel with you, just as if the deceased had also been my best friend. It is good that you were prepared for this loss. With the best and fondest greetings to you, my poor friend, I am yours truly, *Conrad.*

————————————

Orsova, December 4, 1912

To Reichenau Villa Malek from Suez Red Sea

Though distance divides,
Still friendship abides.
With all good wishes for a bright and happy Xmas. —
All the best that one can wish, I wish for you, dear Miss, and your family for New Year. Health and happiness throughout the year!

Prosit 1913! Conrad Kain

1. Also known as "holy fire" or "St. Anthony's fire," erysipelas is a type of skin infection that appears as a red, swollen rash typically on the face, accompanied by fever. Today, the infection is easily treated with penicillin. Prior to the development of antibiotics, the condition was very dangerous and, in its most severe form, could result in lymphatic damage, septic shock, gangrene, and death.

76

Orsova, on the way to Suez

December 5, 1912

Dear Miss Amelie:

Tonight, we were in Port Said. I went ashore. Now, we are in the canal from Port Said to Suez. The weather is great, and the landscape very interesting. You know the Suez Canal, don't you?[1] I feel quite well except for the fact that I always remember your sad loss! In Colombo, I will mail the next letter and hope that you get these lines in Reichenau. In my thoughts, I accompany you up to the grave of your unforgettable father (via the Haberg, which is perhaps already snow-covered).

Yours very truly for ever!
K.K.

1. Connecting the Mediterranean and the Red Sea, the Suez Canal, an artificial sea-level waterway, opened in 1869. It stretched over 160 kilometres, from Port Said on the Mediterranean to Suez on the Red Sea, and allowed water transportation between Europe and Asia without having to navigate around Africa. Its opening provoked international celebration. Historian J. Forbes Munro calls it "one of the most important landmarks in nineteenth century maritime history." J. Forbes Munro, *Maritime Enterprise and Empire: Sir William Mackinnon and his Business Network, 1829–1893* (Suffolk: Boydell, 2003), 121. Egypt reaped little immediate benefit: the engineering feat not only cost thousands of lives but also left its government deep in debt, forcing a new dependence on foreign investment. Britain eventually bought Egypt's canal company shares in 1875 and established an informal protectorate that would last until the First World War. William J. Duiker and Jackson J. Spielvogel, *World History: From 1500* (Belmont, CA: Thomson Wadsworth, 2007), 576.

77

Orsova, December 8, 1912

Dear Miss Amelie:

Tonight, I saw the first sunset at the Egyptian Coast! It was like a picture never seen before. We were at the end of the canal Port Said–Suez. The ship moved slowly through the canal. It was lovely to see camels grazing on the strip of land. A nice foreground. It took long before the splendid colours of the sunset disappeared. Now we are stopping in Suez, but only for a short time. It is 8 P.M. I mailed a letter for you and your Mama and hope that you got it. All is well and happy on the steamer, except a few children. Now Good night!

————————————————

Orsova, December 10, 1912

Today, I re-read all your letters to me. The time drags after a few weeks, and it is terribly hot. The sea is calm and deep blue. I sit on the upper deck and write my notes, and in the evening I read Schiller. At night, we sleep on deck, because the cabins are too humid. We are too many passengers in third class. The food is still good. I did not make friends with anyone yet. One talks to many people. It is a pity that there are many ill-mannered among us, who only now begin to show their true colours.

Orsova, December 13, 1912

It was another beautiful day: calm, almost too calm, not the slightest breeze. A beautiful sunset! I wish you could see this spectacle! I don't know whether you have seen such beautiful sunsets at the ocean?

When I next come home and have to leave again, perhaps you would travel with me to the water!! It would be a pleasure if I could see you looking with cheerful happy eyes towards the blue ocean! This afternoon, we saw a beautiful island and a green bay! Oh! Lovely to look at. ———— Good night! ———— Just a few more lines.

78

Orsova, December 11, 1912

In the Arabian Sea

Dear Miss Amelie:

[In English from hereon] Well, where have we been two months ago at 10:30?? We were between Katzenkopf-Steig and Oberen Zimmer-Steig-Riss. It had been a nice day, and I shall remember the 11th of October for my whole life. This day is in a way familiar to the 9th September 1907, when you had been on the rope, and after more than three years there had been a nice day once more again. I thanked the Lord that I could have been so happy. The next time on the 11th Oct., we were roped together. Dear Miss Amelie, it had been a day of benefit for me and my future life. I can see it now already since I have left you and my home. Now I am so many miles from you! I am sitting in a corner on deck. It is rather warm, the sun is shining, the sea is quiet and beautifully blue. The people around are reading and writing, and I am thinking on the 11th Oct. over and over again. I remember quite well what we spoke of, I can hear your voice, I can see you! I am glad I told you so many things about the book. I am just thinking how long it will last, till we can see the old Rax again together? Yes, I wonder when? When? —— We can't say anything about it now, can we? I trust in the future, that it will be some day. Then I shall be able to tell

you more from the world. It is too bad, that the beautiful hours are so short, too short, and it is still more terrible for me to think, that you are so unhappy now in losing your best friend in such a dreadful way. Miss Amelie, I am feeling very strongly with you, because I know you would do the same, if I would lose a good friend of mine. Well, it is over now, and I wish you might get over it too. Of course it is not so easy to get over such bad things. The bell is ringing ————— Afternoon. Well, we had a fine lunch, but it is so hot in the dining room. Oh, how good it is to get up on deck again! I am smoking my pipe now. There is going on some sport in the afternoon, but I will stay where I am now. I don't like to speak with anyone, I am thinking backwards and forwards, you know. It is nice to think some things over and over. I always find something new. I am just thinking of the happy hours I spent with you and yours on my holidays. I remember what I spoke in these hours, I might say days. I feel glad I emptied my heart out to you, and I am glad to say, you have listened to me. When I saw you on the 31st of August again, I found you just the same as when I left you on the 29th of May 1909. You were not changed, and I hope to find you the same in the future, when we see each other again. I am looking out on the sea and can say to myself: Thanks God, that I got known to you, otherwise I would <u>not</u> be here perhaps on this Steamer, and I would have not seen so much of the big world. And so I will keep what I promised and will be a good fellow, so that you will not hear anything bad of me. I will look up at you all my life and will be thankful to you for all your kindness you have done for me and will still do for me. My best friend in the world, I will pray to God that I do not lose you, and that you stay my best friend forever! Good bye, dearest friend, dear, good Miss Amelie!

I am yours wandering friend C.K.

——————————————————

[In German from hereon] Addendum: Just a few more lines. At 11 A.M., the post office will be closed. Between 12 and 1 P.M., we are to land in Colombo. I look forward to be on firm ground again. Well, how are you? Did you have a great time at Reichenau? I am sending some notes, as well. I kiss your dear Mama's hand and best luck to you and Flora.

I am yours, C.K.

79

Orsova, January 1, 1913

Dear Miss:

Happy New Year! It is ten o'clock in the morning. The difference in time is now about ten hours between here and Reichenau. So, it will be midnight for you. Maybe you are still awake or at a New Year's Eve celebration with your family? I was satisfied with the past year. I took a beautiful trip, learned a lot, and saw many new things. Yes, I even saw my dear old home country again, my good mother, my siblings, and my best friend. I have to write something else or I will get homesick, and, as you said, I must not get homesick! —— On December 30th, we landed at Melbourne, one of the largest cities of Australia. A wonderful city! The streets are wide and very clean; the harbour is very beautifully designed. My travel companions left ship here. I accompanied them to their new house, which was very beautifully located; but I am sure they will be <u>very</u> homesick! I visited the museum and the Botanical Garden.[1] Oh, it was splendid. At sunset, I was among the most beautiful tropical flowers and plants one can imagine! I thought of you, great friend of flowers, picked a few petals to send them to you. It will be a long time before they are in your hands! I hope you are well, and also that Miss Flora and your dear mother are in good health. Once more, the very best for the New Year. Good bye!

Conrad

1. As in North America, in Australia the "colonists of the New World"—as they increasingly saw themselves in the mid-to-late nineteenth century—wished to emulate and best the models of old. Their cities became their showcases. As historian Stuart Macintyre put it, "Melbourne's Parliament House had to be the grandest in the Empire outside Westminster, the ballroom of its Government House had to be larger than that in Buckingham Palace. 'Marvelous Melbourne,' a title conferred by a visiting British journalist, embarked during the 1880s on a heady boom." Stuart Macintyre, *A Concise History of Australia* (Cambridge: Cambridge University Press, 1999), 111. In this vein, Melbourne's Botanic Gardens was established in 1846 near the Yarra River south of the city. Over the next 60 years the swampy site was transformed into a world famous landscape that equaled the gardens of London.

80

Sidney, Australia, January 2, 1913

Dear Miss Amelie:

At 2 P.M., we landed at the capital of Australia.[1] Sidney is really a very beautiful city. The harbour is incomparable. It's the most beautiful part of Sidney (i.e. the harbours), but the streets and alleys of the city are not as grand as in Melbourne. We plan to take another boat to New Zealand on Saturday afternoon. These lines I am writing here in Sidney, sitting on a bench in a beautiful park. I am tired already from all that walking around the streets. I still sleep on board the *Orsova* and take my meals there. The *Orsova* continues to Brisbane. But I don't know when. Today is a very hazy day; there will be rain. There are many gardens and parks here. Sidney has the most beautiful harbour I have seen so far. Much more beautiful than Naples! No comparison! I will now visit a picture gallery.

Goodbye!

————————————

Sidney, January 3, 1913

Yesterday, I was in the picture gallery, and, to my surprise, I saw
a picture of the Dolomites! This morning, I went for a walk with
an acquaintance from the ship. I am now lying on a little hill and
watching the ocean and the many ships. I don't think you might have
ever received a letter from so far away. I see in the newspaper that
there won't be war after all. I would have liked to know how you are?
I hope you are well. How are your nerves doing after the death of your
dear lady friend? You will write me about it, won't you, dear Miss?

203

————————

Sidney, January 4, 1913

Tonight at 8 P.M., the ship leaves for Wellington. I was already on the
ship with my baggage. A very beautiful ship. It has only 1st and 2nd
class. I had to pay 10 S extra and now my billfold is pretty empty. I
have to turn each penny around before I spend it, but I expect money
from Canada in Wellington. I hope it will be there when I arrive!! If
not, I will be in trouble. At 3 P.M., the *Orsova* will depart, it is time to
go and say Addio to the ship and the people. ——

1. Kain is mistaken in attributing capital status to Sydney, but it was, perhaps, an easy enough mistake
    for a newcomer to make in 1913. In 1901, when six Australian colonies federated to become the
    Commonwealth of Australia, it was agreed in Sydney that the site for the national capital *should
    not* be in New South Wales but somewhere to the north. It wasn't until 1909 that a vote of the
    Federal Parliament chose Canberra, a site on the high country between Sydney and Melbourne.
    Bureaucratic delays hampered the transfer of national government and administration to Canberra
    until 1927. But it was Melbourne, in fact, that remained the temporary capital for the first quarter
    of the twentieth century. Frank G. Clarke, *The History of Australia* (London: Greenwood, 2002), 6;
    Macintyre, *A Concise History of Australia*, 146.

81

Wellington, January 8, 1913

Dear Miss Amelie:

Now, I am at my destination in New Zealand. I write these lines in a miserable room. We arrived at 1 P.M. I went to the gentleman to deliver a letter. Unfortunately, he is away travelling. I went to the post office ——— no money ——— no letter! The next mail from Canada will come in two weeks. I own 3 S 4 d.[1] I am miserable and poor. I am not in good shape. I have to figure something out for tomorrow —— Good Night ——

—————————

Wellington, January 9, 1913

It is 2 P.M. I sit in the Botanical Garden.[2] My heart is broken. I only want to write to you to tell you how I am. I could not sleep all night. For bed and breakfast, I paid 1 S 9 d. I inquired about the Canadian consulate, but there is none since New Zealand is British. There also is no Austrian consulate. I inquired about work. There is plenty, but not in Wellington, and one has to pay 4 to 10 S for service at the Labour Office. I cannot talk about my troubles with anyone. I am a total stranger. I want to try and trade my watch and ring for money. Not sure I can get anything for them. I don't dare look for a bed ———— don't know what to do —————

Later: —— I met an acquaintance, from the boat, who is not doing well either, but he still has enough money! He took me to his hotel. I slept in his room on the floor, secretly, of course. We told each other

our problems. He is for the first time in a foreign country and feels it more than I do. Tomorrow, I will go to the German consulate. Will see whether I will get lucky there. —— That is my last resort. ———
Good Night.

————————

I am sitting on a bench with birds and flowers around me. I feel a bit better. This morning, I was at the German consulate. I am supposed to come back at 4 P.M. The consul could not receive me, and I told his secretary everything. He believes they will help me for sure! So I live with this hope and wait with great anticipation for the hour mentioned. Wellington I don't like especially. It is too hilly, but the Botanical Garden is very beautiful. These wonderful flowers!! Also the view of the harbour is very beautiful. As you see, the year 1913 has started poorly for me. What would my dear mother say, if she knew———

8 P.M. January 10, 1913

Dear Miss Amelie:

Hallo! My dear friend! I am alright now! I am out of the water, thank the Lord! At 4 P.M., I met the consul, explained the situation, made a good impression, and showed him my guidebook. Luckily, his own son is a tourist. He lent me 35 Shillings. I went to the Labour Office and accepted work as a "bushman." Tomorrow at 4 P.M., the train will leave for Featherstone,[3] and from there it is forty more miles by carriage. These 35 S will just get me there. I don't know how the work will be, but I surely will survive. Now I say Addio, and *[In English from hereon]* I will write soon more to you. I am healthy and all right, and I will take care of myself and will come back to my best friends again. Good bye. *K.K.*

1. Three *shillings* and four *pence*.

2. The Wellington Botanic Garden was established in 1868 and soon became a distribution centre for useful exotic tree species, such as Californian pine and cypress. See Paul Star, "Humans and the Environment in New Zealand, c. 1800 to 2000," in *The New Oxford History of New Zealand*, ed. Giselle Byrnes (Melbourne, Australia: Oxford University Press, 2009), 52–53. Coincidently, during its first 21 years, the garden was administered under the leadership of James Hector (1834–1907)—a name not unfamiliar to travellers in the Canadian Rockies. Hector was a Scottish geologist, naturalist, and surgeon appointed to the British North American Exploring Expedition (1857–1860), which, under the leadership of Capt. John Palliser (1817–1887), sought to explore possible railway routes for the Canadian Pacific Railway (CPR) and collect new species of plants. While a mountain of more than 3,300 metres (10,827 ft.) northeast of Lake Louise now bears Hector's surname, his presence in the Rockies is also ascribed to Kicking Horse Pass, the route chosen by the CPR to cross the Rockies in 1885. Shortly after surveying the pass, Hector was kicked in the chest by one of the party's horses, rendering him "senseless for some time." See Irene M. Spry, *The Palliser Expedition: The Dramatic Story of Western Canadian Exploration, 1857–1860* (1963; Calgary: Fifth House, 1995), 155. Hector, of course, survived both the kicking horse and Palliser's expedition, and he was, in 1865, appointed director of the New Zealand Geological Survey and Colonial Museum.

3. Lying in the eastern shadow of the Rimutaka Range, Featherston was a small town that serviced the rural communities in the southeastern corner of New Zealand's North Island.

82

Martinborough, January 24, 1913

My dear friend:

Now I am in the "bush" in the camp, and work as a bushman. It is
hard work, but I can stand it well. The people are good and kind. We
work nine hours per day, that makes 10 s (1 s 1½ d per hour). The
board is 2 s a day. We are forty miles from the P.O.[1] *[In German from
hereon]* My camp is deep in the forest. I am healthy and am able save
money. The money I expected from Canada also arrived. This letter I
send as registered mail and enclose a letter for my mother. Please be
so kind and send it to her. You can read it if you like. Please send the
two envelopes with my address to my mother, so that I receive her
letters for sure. There are also black people in the camp. In a few
days, I will write a lengthy letter. There is not much time today, since
someone is leaving camp very soon. You will wait eagerly for news,
won't you? What I experience! Not even money for a stamp!! ——
That never happened to me before!! — Now how are you and yours?
How did you spend the holidays in Reichenau? I thought of you so
often. Excuse the short letter. The next one will be very long. With
heartiest greeting to all of you, I remain your grateful, *Conrad Kain*

Address: c/o G.P.O. Wellington, New Zealand.

---

1. Post office.

83

Camp, February 2, 1913. <u>Washday</u>!!

Dear Miss Amelie:

Today was washday, but don't fear that I am in a bad mood! It's all done. I had only three shirts, two pairs of pants, two hankies, three pairs of socks, and a towel. Can you imagine that? Washday in the camp? It would be interesting if you could see this and could hear the conversations of the bachelors on washday. I refer to the quote from the Bible: "It is not good that the man is alone and so God created the woman." ————— But, unfortunately, no woman was created for life in the bush! It would be beautiful if one could rest on a Sunday instead of washing and mending! As I heard, the New Zealand women are not very good housewives! (Too noble!) As long as I am healthy, I will keep my clothes clean by myself. I have to end this subject or you will think I am homesick! Up to now, I did very well. Of course, my thoughts often fly across the wide ocean, but not for homesickness, Miss Amelie! On January 29, I received your lovely long letter, the first in New Zealand. It needed lots of time for the long trip, but it reached its destination. I really thank you many times. Soon, another one will arrive, don't you think, dear lady? As I see, the affair about the war has settled down well. Thank you for the newspaper clipping. I am really pleased to hear that your nerves are in good shape. I agree: tears cannot re-awaken the dead. — The old lady on the *Orsova* about whom I wrote survived the trip very well. A week ago, I got a letter from her. She writes in a marvellous style. She feels quite well in Australia. One of her sons also wrote me a few lines. He said that his mother often talks about me and has said I was <u>the best gentleman</u> on board. She asked me for a picture of myself and so, on some occasion or other, I will send her one. And now about the questions in your letter. Yes, Corsica, I could clearly see it on this trip. With "castles in the air," something might be possible! The Dachstein is a sure thing, also the Ortler is quite possible. But, in the end, <u>nothing</u> is impossible!!! Because I will remain a free man, perhaps I even <u>have</u> to remain one! All the sunsets I have in my head and also in my notebook. Very dear of you that you are thinking of my mother. I am convinced that it will be a great joy for her if you visited her. She is always happy to see some of my friends and acquaintances. Often, I am very sorry that I cannot be with her. Motherly love—you only really know it when you do not have it. We human beings all share something that we can hardly express in words, about happy minutes and about sad hours and days. I am now 14,000 nautical miles away from my home mountains, and I have to try hard to be sensible. I am alone, and I have nobody to share my feelings. I can only write to one single person who understands what I express on paper. Now, I have to tell you what the country looks like: nothing but hills! When we get to a hill, we see the ocean. There are many birds here that sing beautifully in the morning. I did not see many flowers here. The land we clear is for a sheep ranch.[1] I wrote two cards from the trip to the priest in Reichenau, but did not get an answer, so I will not write anymore. Did Mr. P. send you the pictures (Dachstein)? I hope he kept his word. You must surely enjoy them! Please correct my mistakes, dear teacher, I like that. With the heartiest greeting to you and yours, *your grateful Konrad.*

---

1. Sheep farming was established in the 1850s and, for several decades, wool accounted for over a third of New Zealand's exports. Following the first exported shipment of frozen meat in 1882, sheep meat became a significant source of revenue for New Zealand as it forged a role as Britain's farmyard. The process of deliberate environmental change for purposes of agriculture in New Zealand, however, was dramatic: it decreased the area of native forest from an estimated 8.3 million hectares in 1883 to 5.1 million hectares by 1923. Such transformations led the increasingly urban, and perhaps more leisured, population of New Zealand to adopt their Scenery Preservation Act of 1903, which, by 1915, resulted in the creation of 430 scenic reserves comprising over 111,000 hectares. Star, "Humans and the Environment," 61.

84

Camp, February 10, 1913, late in the evening.

Dear Miss Amelie:

I could not send my letter of Sunday (washday) off, since the postman, who comes only once a week, did not come. For some reason, we received the mail yesterday. I received a long dear letter from Miss Flora (23/12/1912). She really wrote a letter that one cannot wish any better of from your best friend. Right away, I wrote her a long letter as an answer. Your sister writes that you have a cold. Poor Miss, and even over the holidays! I hope all is well again. I hope to receive a letter from you tomorrow. Oh, how many beautiful things you will write, faithful Comrade. I hope you had a good time. Perhaps you even were up on the Rax? There, you must have thought of me? — The last week was very good: we could work the whole time. So, I saved 46 S. Now, I have to tell you of a very good idea of mine, and for this I have to ask for your kindness again. I know you won't say no. The fact is that I now need you as "a banker." Of course, as "a banker," you won't earn any money (!!!), but many, many thanks. I have to begin to save regularly, and, from now on, I will save 10 per cent of my earnings from each pay. It's for my old age. But I have to be certain and send the money away with firm will power. IT HAS TO BE. Will you be my banker? — I know you will praise me for this good idea! I will follow through. You will see. And you are my best friend, and so I know you will put the money in a good place. The next letter will be a registered one with my diary notes. And you will find a letter amongst them. Tomorrow is February 11th. Where were we four months ago? On the Rax! How quickly time passes! And how much did we have to experience during that time—such sadness! And I travelled many thousand miles and had lots of experiences. Now we hope for the best. With dearest greetings, I am yours truly, *Con.*

85

Camp, 15/02/1913

Dear Miss Amelie!

Last week, I got your dear card from the Otto-Haus (Jan. 1). My best
thanks for remembering me—"on top of our beautiful Rax." I have
been waiting for three weeks for a letter from you. Since I got the
card, I know that you are well and healthy, or you would not have
been on the Rax! I received a letter from my brother telling me that
you and Miss Flora visited my family (on December 28). That was very
kind of you, and I thank you very much, because I know that my good
mother feels better when you tell her that she does not have to worry
about me. I assume that you had a good time and nice weather in
Reichenau. I hope you could go for nice walks and all three of you
were happy in your beautiful home. Will you take a cruise again this
spring? If so, I wish you very happy hours and that you don't get
seasick!!! As I read in the newspaper, there is still no peace on the
Balkan.[1] One is shocked to read about the many murders. I hope that
Austria is out of danger. Now what shall I tell you about here? We all
moved our camp. Last Sunday, I was hunting and shot a young boar.
The weather is not too nice: rain and wind. In five to six weeks, just
when you will receive these lines, we will be finished with the work
here, and I already will be somewhere else. I will still be working with
the man I work for here, perhaps all through the winter. He is very
good to me. Should I hear, however, about something suitable from
America, I will travel there. I will sell my cottage in Canada.[2] I am
waiting from a letter from Mr. Hollister in Washington. There isn't
much going on with mountain guiding in New Zealand. I made thor-
ough inquiries about it. I would prefer again to travel with the
naturalists. I love to travel with them. ——— Now I will give you a
little joy and reveal to you my beautiful "plan," a plan for the future:

WHEN I RETURN. —— I can already see you smile —— when I return ——! Yes, when I return. I will come in spring, when the days are long and the flowers bloom and the birds are singing! I will plan it in a way that I will have work all summer long: from July 15th to the end of September. I will try to keep the time free to July 15th. And I invite you and your sister for a nice little trip. Your dear good mother will give you holidays. On this trip, your wishes about mountain climbing will be fulfilled. By the end of June, the shelter huts will be open, the cattle will be in the alpine pastures, and life on the mountain begins. Now let us travel! — By train through our unforgettable Ennstal to Schladming. From there, we climb the beautiful Dachstein. Downhill to the Bachl-Alm. There, we will find the camp in the evening and a fire. I will show you my good cooking. You and Miss Flora will sleep in the tent, and I will provide a good soft bed with lovely smelling spruce branches. On the Bachl-Alm, it is beautiful. We'll stay for a few days, listen to the rushing of the little creeks, the songs of the birds, the bells of the alpine cattle, and SEE the AWAKENING OF NATURE in each little blade of grass and each little flower. And then —— one has to part with what one loves best: —— and then, Addio Dachstein, back to Schladming, but not home! Oh no! The time is not over yet!! We drive to Meran, from there to the king of Austrian mountains—the Ortler! In Sulden, we first take a good look at the Ortler from below, then we go up to the Payer-Hütte, where we stay overnight. The next day, we'll climb to the top and look at the "King" from above: as far as one can see—we will look into three countries——.[3] One voice will reach your ear: "Miss, do you feel happy??!" —— "Yes, TRULY happy!" (So am I!). That was our goal and your wish. Now we return home? Oh, not yet! Here are the beautiful peaks of the Dolomites! We must not ignore or neglect them! And we still have time. We'll take a nice easy hike across the Joch, and, in order to not forget and neglect climbing, we climb up to one of the inviting peaks: the Winklerturm or the Fünffingerspitze, or the Rosengarten, the little king, we will pay him a visit, too. — The garden with the roses, yes, and around this time will be your name day, and it will be a big joy for me to congratulate you with the words of a friend. I will hand you a bouquet of mountain and meadow flowers, yes, freshly blooming flowers that you love so much. ————— Now our trip, our holiday, comes to an end. Happy hours pass quickly. I will accompany you and your sister back to your beautiful home, to your mother. "Here, dear lady, I am bringing back your dear daughters, healthy and well. I thank you from my heart for giving the ladies a holiday. It was beautiful, it was wonderful."

————— Well, what do you say to this plan? Isn't it a beautiful one? If we are healthy, it can easily be done. We need 18 to 20 days. —— Next Wednesday (mail day), I definitely expect news from you. I hope it will be a long letter. Take these diary notes. There are not many. There could be more, but writing in camp is not as easy as in a house. And, for a few weeks, I haven't felt my best. I am somewhat depressed. I will soon write again. Now Good Bye. I hope you are well. Best to your dear mother and sister.

With love, I am your wandering friend, C.K.

1. While an armistice in December 1912 briefly interrupted fighting, skirmishes resumed in the Balkan Peninsula around two besieged cities in Albania, one besieged city in Thrace, and in eastern Thrace until the spring of 1913. A preliminary peace treaty was signed in London in late May 1913, officially ending the First Balkan War. See Hall, *The Balkan Wars*, 80–97.

2. It remains unclear whether this is the apartment in Banff that Kain mentioned in Letter 44. He is not known to have owned property in Canada until 1920. See Letter 127.

3. Standing at 3,905 metres (12,812 ft.), the Ortler is the highest mountain in the eastern Alps outside the Bernina Range. It is the highest point of the Southern Limestone Alps, of the Italian region of Trentino-Alto Adige/Südtirol, of Tyrol overall, and, until the end of the First World War, of the Austro-Hungarian Empire. In German, the mountain is commonly referred to as König Ortler or "King Ortler."

86

Camp Kaiwaka, New Zealand [no date]

Dear Miss Amelie!

Take a thousand thank yous from me for writing to my dying brother, David, in Wiener Neustadt, and that you gave him my address, because, otherwise, I would not have heard anything from him. Miss A., that was a good noble deed that you extended to my brother and me, a deed that only a good kind heart can accomplish! May God bless you for it! You can probably imagine what I feel in my heart. I know that David, whom I love—and he does so likewise—is not healthy anymore. Diabetes! — I know well what that means.[1] I hope that nobody disclosed that to him. And my dear sister, Rosina! She, too, will not escape death, as I gather from the letters from home. And what else will be behind it all! I fear my good mother's heart is broken, and all this may kill her. It is very hard to have such thoughts in one's mind. I know our family situation so well, and I am so far away! I will send you the two sad letters I received from home, so that I don't have to read them anymore. Please keep them for me. I will send money to my mother for all that requires expenses. She does not mention it in her letter, but I know very well that she needs it. I know you will agree with me, dear Miss. The saddest news, which I already anticipate, is only now to come. I thought much about him, and had great hopes for him, since he, too, was to be a friend of nature and always very kind with Mother. And now this incurable disease let this radiant boy end like that! It would not have surprised me so much to hear something like that about Rosina, who always was sickly. I always doubted her recovery. If I were not so far away, I could hurry home instantly to console my poor mother, because she would feel a little relieved if I were by her side since she thinks a lot

of me. In her letter, she calls me "My good faithful son." As unsophis-
ticated as she may be, she knows what it means to be "true." When I
come home again, I have to tell you in person about how she managed
the problems of bringing us up after father's death. I was the oldest,
so only *I* know this among my siblings. She should have seen better
and happier days, and now this happened! I always want to do the
best for my mother, if only I don't lose her too soon! I myself am now
better than I used to be: I quit smoking and drinking tea. Besides,
now I have dangerous work (felling trees), so that, in contrast to
former times, I cannot let my thoughts wander away from my work.
Every evening, my thoughts are with my dear mother for a while and
with my best friends in the world. I am sure you will, for my sake,
console my mother with a few lines. I know she thinks a lot of good
about you and yours, after you always have been so kind to her.
Perhaps you yourself observed that kindness is received with more
gratitude by poor people. And so I thank you with all my heart for
your graciousness towards my mother. My program for the next
month is as follows: on May 9th, I go on board ship in Auckland, get
to Vancouver on May 27th, and then to Banff on June 3rd. Please
forgive me that I include no notes in this letter. I have to write several
letters. Hearty greetings from your grateful,

C.K.

1. Although recognized since antiquity, diabetes mellitus remained poorly understood at the turn of
   the twentieth century. It was a death sentence before the discovery of insulin in 1921–1922, when
   medical scientists at the University of Toronto, under the leadership of Canadian Frederick Banting
   (1891–1941), furthered research toward an effective treatment. According to historian Michael Bliss,
   "those who watched the first starved, sometimes comatose, diabetics receive insulin and return to
   life saw one of the genuine miracles of modern medicine." Michael Bliss, *The Discovery of Insulin*
   (Toronto: McClelland and Stewart, 1982), 11.

87

Kaiwaka Camp. March 2, 1913

Dear Miss Amelie:

[In English from hereon] At last, I had your second letter to Wellington (28.2). I thank you ever so much for it. It did give me such comfort that I do feel ever so much better now in my loneliness. I read it over many times. I see in every word your true friendship. It makes me happy to know that you are alright. I am sitting in the tent and writing these lines to you. I remember the old song *Du liebes Aug,' Du holder Stern, Du bist mir nah und doch so fern,* etc., etc.[1] Now let me tell you more. Your cards that had been posted almost one week later than the letter came first. I will send the date so that you can see it yourself. So you did enjoy your holiday. I had been thinking of you on that evening, just when you wrote the first line. I made myself a picture just as you did. *[In German from hereon]* Now, I will answer your letter. You received my letters from Port Said and Suez, but you don't write whether your dear mother received my letter. I wrote to your poor girlfriend's husband a letter of condolences after the loss of his wife. It is very kind of Mr. von Payer that he pleased you so much with the picture. If you have an opportunity, please pay him a visit sometime, since he often had invited you and your family. What do you think about the South Pole tragedy?[2] Here, all the newspapers are full with reports. I will send you some clippings. I also just see that a German scientific expedition is missing near Franz Josefs Land.[3] Since you are well informed about these things through Mr. v.P., it may interest you to consult a map. After my trapping adventures in Canada, I also have had an idea of what it means to travel by sleigh and to sleep in the snow. I am so sorry to hear that you had so much trouble because of the parcel to New Zealand. It is a

misunderstanding on the part of my family. I wrote to my mother that she should send the leather shirt (Indian shirt) to you, and the Indian moccasins to Mr. Pister. He collects such things. I will give the leather shirt to you as a keepsake. It is not a precious keepsake and would be of no value to somebody who does not know me. I wore the shirt on one of my most dangerous days. You know, it was the time when I fell into the water when it was -30 or -40 degrees. I nearly gave up any hope to see my mother and you again. Since everything went well, I told you about it. I wore these clothes when I saw certain death in front of me and thought of my mother, you, and my home with a heavy heart and crying eyes. So take this piece as a memento, unless you already delivered it to the post office. But I hope they will have discouraged you from sending it. It would cost more than it is worth. Anyway, I thank you for caring and going to so much trouble. I am happy that you received everything you wanted from Dr. L. On the last page of your letter, you write about "dangers." Yes, you are right, in such areas one is more or less <u>always</u> in danger. There are many bad people, trains collide, ships sink, and all cost many human lives; fever and contagious diseases, though, I do not fear. I hope that nothing of the kind will happen to me, and that I return in good health to "our beautiful Rax" and to my loved ones! Otherwise, I am healthy. Your letter made me feel so much better mentally. Thank you, dear doctor! Here it is summer, the days get shorter; there is much rain and wind, so we've lost working days. The people here are nice, but cannot be compared to the Canadians. They don't have such an open heart. I think that I will soon return to the Rockies, to the green forests, to the bears, etc., etc. When I travel from here to Canada, I will have almost gone around the world, don't you think? I learned and endured a lot, and more at thirty years of age than many people do by forty and even fifty. The clover leaf and snow rose pleased me and show that flowers bloom even in winter for the eye that loves nature and pays attention while passing through it. Here are some little flowers from New Zealand. Now I have to close. Hoping that the three of you are very healthy, I remain with hearty greetings, yours *Kon Kain.*

————————————— Addendum! Yesterday, I received a totally unexpected letter. The Alpine Club asks me to come back to the Rockies:

> *My Dear Con:*
> *I have received a letter from Mr. Hollister which gives us your address Wellington N.Z. —— So I am sending a line on the chance of catching you there. Are you coming back to Canada this summer? I can offer you a job on Photo-Survey work along the Continental Divide for the full summer, if you care to have it![4] At $3.00 per day. It will be a new territory. Mt. Assiniboine and south. I would need you by 1 June. We are holding two camps this summer, one at Lake O'Hara and one at Robson Pass. I should want you for Robson Camp. There will be several attempts to make the ascent of Robson from the East side. How does the prospect strike you, old boy? If you come back by 1 of May, we can get you work at the club house until we are ready to start in June. I expect you will know something about New Zealand Alps before you return. We miss you from the Rockies and we all hope you will come back. You know you are welcome any hour and we do our best for you. Auf Wiedersehen! Yours faithfully, A.O. Wheeler.*

> *Sidney, B.C. January 27, 1913*

Well, what do you say to that? It pleases me a little that one <u>misses</u> me there! I also know why!![5] So I have to go back to Canada. The wages are not bad, $3.00 and free room and board. And maybe I'll earn a little on the side. I will depart from here on April 25th or May 9th. Don't write anymore to New Zealand, but instead to the old address: Banff Alpine Club. I will write a few more times from here. Quite naturally, as I will still be here almost 2 months!

> *Con K.*

1. "You dear eye, you lovely star, you are near me and yet so far, etc., etc."

2. The British Antarctic Expedition of 1910–1912 was led by Robert Falcon Scott (1868–1912) with the objective of being the first to reach the South Pole. While Scott and four companions attained the pole on 17 January 1912, they did so only to discover that Roald Amundsen's Norwegian team had preceded them by 33 days. Disappointment soon led to tragedy: Scott and his party perished in unusually frigid conditions on their return from the pole. See Susan Solomon, *The Coldest March: Scott's Fatal Antarctic Expedition* (New Haven, CT: Yale University Press, 2001), 286–306. Their bodies and records were discovered by a search party eight months later. England was informed of the misfortune when the Terra Nova, the expedition's ship, reached New Zealand on 10 February 1913. The story made front-page headlines throughout the western world. Diana Preston, *A First-Rate Tragedy: Captain Scott's Antarctic Expeditions* (London: Constable, 1997), 229–30.

3. Franz Josef Land is an island archipelago located in the extreme north of the Eastern Hemisphere, in the northernmost province of Russia, 900 kilometres from the North Pole. In 1913, Jules de Payer, who was Julius von Payer's son and who had become naturalized as a French citizen, proposed "plans to complete his father's work by a scientific exploration of the north-east part of Franz Josef Land." "Julius von Payer," *The Geographic Journal*, 322. A preliminary trip was made in the summer of 1913, but the First World War prevented the main undertaking. Later, in the spring of 1926, the archipelago was annexed by the Soviet Union. It had been previously considered *Terra nullius* (No Man's Land).

4. In October, 1912, Wheeler was appointed the British Columbia commissioner of the three-member Interprovincial Boundary Commission, which was to survey and map the Alberta–British Columbia border, a sinuous line on a map, but marked by no monuments when it was defined in 1871. According to historian Judy Larmour, "the discovery of rich coal seams straddling the provincial boundary posed jurisdictional problems, more particularly after Alberta became a province in 1905. Forest reserves also straddled the boundary. Monuments on the ground would assist surveyors and others, including fire wardens, who needed to know in which jurisdiction their work lay. Industry, settlement, and transportation routes through the mountain passes demanded more accurate maps and appropriate registration of survey plans." Judy Larmour, *Laying Down the Lines: A History of Land Surveying in Alberta* (Victoria, BC: Brindle and Glass, 2005), 147. Specifically, Wheeler was charged with mapping the watershed line on the peaks adjacent to the main passes by means of photo-topographical survey. The work began in the summer of 1913 with the survey's first phase: from the summit of Kicking Horse Pass and south along the Great Divide toward Mt. Assiniboine and the international boundary beyond.

5. Kain's response is worth noting. The "why" was the ascent of Mt. Robson. Did Kain no longer believe what he himself wrote to Malek two years earlier from the Robson area (see Letter 55, written on July 30, 1911)—that the mountain had been successfully climbed by Kinney and Phillips in 1909? Or was Kain, here, now aware that Wheeler wanted to claim the first ascent for the Club? It is difficult to say with any certainty, but, as Scott noted, the ACC's executive may have privately withdrawn their support of the Kinney–Phillips claim made a year earlier: "Wheeler, Coleman, Mumm, and J.D. Patterson exchanged letters concerning some unknown 'Kinney matter.' Although he [Wheeler] did not reveal [in his diaries] what this matter was, it is clear that something was afoot.

The relevant entries are as follows: Thursday, January 18, 1912, 'Letter from Patterson re Kinney matter.' Wednesday, January 24, 1912, 'Letter from Coleman re Kinney.' Monday, January 29, 1912, 'Letter from Mumm.' Wednesday, January 31, 1912, 'Letter from Patterson re Kinney.'" Scott, *Pushing the Limits*, 80–81.

88

Camp Kaiwaka, March 16, 1913

Dear Miss Amelie:

Today was wash day again, but I did not have much to wash. Last week, I injured my leg with a hoe, just on a bad spot on my shin (right leg). I am working in awful pain. Here, the bad weather starts now with wind and rain. Next Sunday is Easter, when you will all be in Reichenau again. I am curious what kind of weather you will have. About my trip to Canada, I can tell you nothing definite yet, since I have no answer from the shipping company. But I hope to leave on May 9th. That would fit time-wise with June 1st. I look forward to seeing the Rockies again! I have news that might interest you. Whom do you think I share my tent with now?! —— It is marvellous what people you meet in a camp! Right now, he is sitting on his miserable bed three feet from me. Would like to know what thoughts he has, because he is used to a better life than this rough camp life in the bush. He is, or better, was, a minister of your Catholic Church of Ireland. 36 years of age and he has been in New Zealand only five months. He left the church. I asked him why. He said, "My dear friend, my heart is heavy when I think of it and perhaps thousands of souls would feel that way if they knew what nonsense takes place behind the secret walls." That is all I got out of him. He is a gentleman. I am sure that he won't last long in a bush camp. At least, it won't harm him to find out what "hard labour" means. I collect insects (and already have quite a lot) for my friend Hollister. I received a letter from him and his wife, whom I don't know personally. She wrote to me in very friendly words saying that she would like to meet me. Both invite me to spend a week with them, when I am back in America. It pleases me that Mr. Hollister thinks a lot of me and in a positive way. In Reichenau, I told you about him, didn't I? He is a gentleman, through and through. This week, I will expect your third letter to New Zealand. Now, Good Bye. *[In English from hereon]* I hope you are well. I have been well so far myself, not so terribly lonely any more, but still struggling along. With best regards to you and your dear mother and sister, and love to you, yours truly, *Con.*

Tell Miss Flora I will write her a long letter next week. —

89

[In German from hereon]

Kaiwaka Camp, March 30, 1913

Dear Miss Amelie:

Last week, I received your dear long letter as well as the newsletter of the German and Austrian Alpine Club. My best thanks for everything. It was so kind of you to send me something to read. You are always a kind, wise friend. Thank you for remembering me on top of the Rax. It is so nice when someone thinks of you thousands of miles away. I, too, thought of you during Easter week, and, in my mind, accompanied you on your walks. On Easter Sunday, I wrote a long letter to Miss Flora and wanted to write to you, as well, but preferred to rest a bit, so that you should not recognize my homesickness so much in my writing. So I went to the forest to be alone, sat down under a fir tree and let my thoughts wander through my mind. Many, many Easters so far away! Here, fall begins already. I hear the elks roaring, the leaves change colour, the days get shorter, it gets colder, so just the opposite to things at home. You will probably have just seen the first awakening of spring. In two months, you will be back in Reichenau and I will be in the Rockies! I can hardly wait to see the Pacific Islands, which are so much written and talked about.[1] I will send you some cards from my trip and, of course, a detailed travelogue. It is beautiful to see all that, but a pity to spend all that money! But no! I must not be envious and stingy! The trip is worth the money. Otherwise, one has nothing good in the world if one only works hard all the time. One has to treat oneself to some special distraction, don't you think, dear Miss? There will also be beautiful sunsets to see. I hope many passengers take that

trip, otherwise it might get boring. You know how I love the spectacle of nature. Often it makes me very melancholy. I gave the book
by Hermann Bahr, which you lent me, to a good friend to read while
I was in Nasswald.[2] Because of my quick departure, I did not see him
again. But don't worry: my friend will certainly send the book back
to you in good condition. Please don't be cross, it is not lost! Now
the package. It is too bad you had so much trouble with it because
of the misunderstandings of my people! With my next letter, I will
send notes again. I often write them, as you know, but it is hard: I
only have my knees as a table right now. I hope that you will have
most of the notes by perhaps the end of June. Then, from Canada, I
will send you some good maps, so that you can have a clear picture of
the names which I don't always write correctly. You have a hard time
with your pupil, don't you?! In a while, you will read a letter from
me in the *Schwarzataler Zeitung*, directed to all my friends who were
so kind to me in my home mountains. It will be a little travelogue.
Please send a copy of the newspaper to my mother, so that she too
can enjoy reading something in print by me, too. I think it will be a
little surprise for the local people who know me. My tent partner, the
minister, was fired. The poor man cried when he said Goodbye to me.
I accompanied him part of the way and gave him good advice for the
future. He promised to follow my advice. His heart was broken, but
nobody had pity. He only had 20 s when he left. His last words were
to me, "Dear Kain, you have been the kindest man I have met in this
country! I thank you ever so much for your kindness and good advice.
I will write to you and never forget you and, so, Goodbye!" ——— Yes,
he has to go through a lot until he knows what I went through. Once
he told me why he left his church. It must have been a sad case! He
had only one sister, who entered a convent. There, she was raped by
two priests in a cowardly fashion. They gave her a kind of a drug that
affected her body forever. I am sure that he is an honest man and told
me the truth. I gave him the advice that he should not be so honest
and tell everyone that he used to be a cleric, because there are people
everywhere who hate the clergy. I myself make no difference. I don't
think more of a cleric than of a stone breaker or a tree cutter, who

223

has a good character. It is not right to judge a person by their profession or religion. Even among the clergy, who teach THE WORD OF THE LORD, there are just as bad people as among other classes. It is an old story. You, the one with a big heart, will agree with me. Of course, one could not talk so openly about it with any other person, because there are many who believe a minister of the church can do no wrong. But he is also JUST A HUMAN BEING!! —— Before I leave here, I have to write to your dear mother, so that she too receives a few lines from the far South. You did not mention in your last letter whether your mother received my New Year's letter? I sent it together with the letters for you and Miss Flora with the card *Hands Across the Sea*. I will now have to close. Goodbye, and keep your nerves in good shape. May God keep you and yours in good health. My greetings to them. I am quite well. Now Goodbye, dear friend. With love and best regards, I am yours, *Con*.

224

CONRAD KAIN

1. During the late nineteenth and early twentieth centuries, several popular writers found new inspiration in the settings of Hawaii and the South Pacific islands. For instance, the famed author of *Treasure Island* (1883), Scottish writer Robert Louis Stevenson (1850–1894), wrote about the Pacific Islands in several of his later works, such as *The Wrecker* (1892), *Island Nights' Entertainment* (1893), *Ebb-Tide* (1894), and *In the South Sea* (1896). But it was Jack London (1876–1916), the American writer, who created perhaps the most vivid picture of the South Pacific, which seemed to him as exotic and untamed as the Arctic, in *South Sea Tales* (1911) and *A Son of the Sun* (1912). See Rebecca Stefoff, *Jack London: An American Original* (New York: Oxford University Press, 2002), 103–04.

2. A prolific Austrian dramatist and novelist, a producer of plays, and a literary critic, Hermann Bahr (1863–1934) was, perhaps, one of the most active and important Austrian intellectuals of his time. He was certainly one of the most prolific authors of his era. Taken together, his more than 100 books represent a cultural history of Vienna from the turn of the century until the advent of Hitler in 1933. See Dieter Wolfgang Adolphs, "Hermann Bahr (19 July 1863–15 January 1934)," in *Dictionary of Literary Biography: Twentieth-Century German Dramatists, 1889–1918*, ed. Wolfgang Elfe and James N. Hardin, vol. 118 (Detroit: Gale Research, 1992), 3–22.

90

Kaiwaka Camp, April 21, 1913

Dear Miss:

Here with the *[In English from hereon]* fourth letter from you to New
Zealand. My best thanks for it. I am ever so much obliged to you for
the parcel. It was very kind of you, that you made such a good needle-
work with the address. I had a card from the custom office that the
parcel is in Wellington. I cannot tell you more at present. *[In German
from hereon]* I am overjoyed to hear that you and yours are healthy
and happy. As I wrote you once before, I will sail on May 9th (Friday
before Pentecost) from Auckland, I am in Vancouver May 27th, and
May 29th in Banff. Four years ago, I said farewell to you on May 29th
before my trip to America. Do you remember? —— I thank you from
my heart for everything you sent to my poor brother David and to
Rosina. The two of them will perhaps not suffer anymore. ————
As far as the doctor goes, the one who told David that he should work
(seriously ill!!) —— all is clear to me. When a doctor sees that there
is no money available, then he is no doctor. That is the Christian love
for the human next to you: only MONEY, MONEY ———— I feel so
sorry for my poor mother, she will be so upset! Oh, if I had wings and
could be with her to console the poor woman in these sad hours! —
If she gets my letter, I will only open her wounds again! Perhaps you
visited her over Easter? That would have pleased her immensely. Yes,
my heart is heavy, when I think of my loved ones at home. It feels
as if my heart will break. You do know that I always thought a lot of
my mother and supported her since I left school. I also know that
my siblings now understand what it means to look after a mother
——— I cannot talk about my worries to anybody and have to keep
them to myself. I am at a loss, I know, that thinking about it and

reflecting upon it does not help, but what can I do? —— I hope the voyage to Canada will do me some good; if not, I have to see a doctor. *[In English from hereon]* If only I could speak to you for a short time and tell you how sorry I am for my mother, and all my sad thoughts about my poor brother and Rosina. —— It would help me, I am sure. —— Well, I shall write more next week. I want to make sure this letter catches the mail. This letter will go the shortest way over America. Once more, my best thanks for your kindness. *[In German from hereon]* Forgive my poor writing, I am so upset. Best greetings to your dear mother, to you and Miss Flora. Good bye, Good Night. I am yours thankfully, *Con.*

91

Kaiwaka Camp, May 1, 1913

Dear Miss Amelie:

I received your letter (Nr. 5) to Wellington. I was eagerly waiting for it.
So much bigger the joy! My best thanks. It is long and gives me lots
of pleasant things to think about. I wrote to you once before from
Canada, what a pleasant feeling it is, when one is so totally removed
from the world, to get good friendly news, and one can say to oneself:
no, you are not totally forgotten! I have been here for four months
now, and you will believe when I write that I would like to get out of
here! Life in the bush has its charm, there is no doubt about that, but
you realize all what you have to do without, and you begin to miss a
good bed, a warm bath, a little entertainment once in a while, etc.
However, soon comes the time when I will depart. I liked hearing
that you are all healthy and that you always have your rosy cheeks.
For myself, I could not give such a brilliant description. I am sorry, I
have to say that my face changed and very much at that. The sun has
tanned me, my cheeks are not round, and there are circles are under
my eyes—and I don't feel really well. But I hope all will be fine again.
The wound on my foot has healed. I had severe pain for a long time.
— It is pouring rain. ————

Continuing May 2, 1913

It is still raining buckets!! The creeks are unusually high. I hope it
will not hinder my trip out of the bush. Today, twenty-one years ago,
is the day we buried my father. — A long time ago, but I can still see
everything before me as if it had been yesterday. I am happy to hear
that my brother feels better (at the time when you wrote), and I am

touched when I think how lovingly you look after my family. ——
Perhaps one day I can do something for you in return. Your letter lies
in front of me, and I must answer it piece by piece. Don't fear, your
letters will not be lost in Canada. They are stored very well. I cannot
part with them. I am like you and keep everything!! When I get to
Canada, I will send you everything, but please <u>don't</u> burn anything!!
You saw Empress Katherina? I hope one did not act out her death.[1]
I recently read a book where this Empress is described. The title is
What Happens at the Royal Courts. It is amazing! Of course, many
things are exaggerated, but not everything can have been invented!
—— Yes, Emanuel Kain is quite a good man, and I am sorry to say
that he would have married my mother long ago and would have
been very good to her.[2] I know she wanted to be faithful to my father
until his death. And so Mother must be sorry now that she could
not overcome her feminine weaknesses. When I come back home, I
will really give a lecture in Reichenau. That would be a nice distraction, for you, too, don't you think? — With great interest, I followed
the newspapers because of the war. I read about new taxes, and I am
curious how long the people will put up with being suppressed? —
Do you remember I wrote to you about the minister who was here?
I recently read in the newspaper that a dead man was pulled out of
the harbour. He had no papers on him, and nobody knows who he is.
— The description of him and the things one found on him all point
to a clergyman. I wrote to the police, but have had no answer from
them yet. The poor priest probably went through bad times after he
left here. If he really sought death, then his clerical colleagues are
to be blamed. Now, I come to the end of the letter. I thank you very
much for all your good wishes. You will see that I get on in the world
alright. The school of my life is a hard one, yes it is, especially during
these hours. I have no friend to <u>talk</u> to about my opinion, so I have
to be grateful that I can <u>write</u>. I hope you live very well in Reichenau
and that you are all doing fine. These are always my wishes for you,
faithful Miss Amelie! My best greetings to your dear Mama and Miss
Flora. Now Good bye. I am yours, *CON KAIN*

It is raining heavier than ever. ——

1. A leading actress on the Vienna stage, Katharina Schratt (1853–1940) was the mistress and confidante of Franz Joseph I, Emperor of Austria; she was popularly known as the "uncrowned Empress of Austria." The actual Empress, Elisabeth of Bavaria (b. 1837)—who was also the Queen of Hungary and Bohemia—was murdered in Switzerland in 1898.

2. Emanuel Kain was no relation to Conrad's father, Eugen.

92

Kaiwaka Camp, May 16, 1913

Dear Miss Amelie:

I received your letter the other day. Thanks a lot. Now, let me tell you how miserable I feel. Today is Friday, pouring rain. This week, we could hardly work. It is raining incessantly, there's lots of wind, and it is very cold in the tent. I am now sitting by the fire, writing these lines on my knees. You will have been almost two weeks in Reichenau and perhaps are working hard. Yes, I know you are not lazy and do your housework well. Miss Amelie, I would love to hear the birds of my home country sing—their spring songs. I remember them so well. I hope the dear birds won't forget their songs before I return? When will that be? — When will I greet my mountains and you again? I know that in letters I cannot talk with anyone else like with you; I know you understand everything I write about. And so I say to you that never before did I have such yearning for my country and my home. If I were away from home for the first time, I would not be surprised. Of course, the reason is easy to explain: never before was I in such a sad situation. I thank you from my heart for your condolences at the death of my sister Rosina. I was expecting this sad news. Opening the letters made my heart ache. It is good that I got it through you. Your words are always consoling. I too think that it is better for poor Rosina to be released from her suffering, because there was no hope that she would be totally healthy again. The same I think about David. I have no hope that he can still live very long, even though he now feels better for a while. But if he gets worse again, it will even be harder. I pity my poor mother so much! I cannot describe my feelings, but you will understand. She will be so worried, and the worrying will affect her nerves. In case my mother would become ill, I would come home to be at her side during her last days. But you never can tell what fate will bring. If you write to her to console her and assure her of your sharing her worry, it will sure comfort her. I wrote to you already that I saw to it that she received money. I will always help out with money. — I am pleased that you are thinking in a generous way about my opinion about "saving," and you are right: it will not all be so easy! But I won't give up. After this trip, I will stay longer in one place again. I'll retreat to the forest next winter and live as a trapper. It is surely a hard life, but what choice do I have? I think it is still the best. I am thirty years old now. The beautiful time of youth is over. I don't care for dance or music or entertainment, and I look at life from a different angle now. I also think one must not be a coward, must not fear danger. I <u>never</u> was a coward and don't want to become one. If luck is on my side, I can perhaps make a few hundred dollars. Dear Miss, you say one has to take life as it comes, to take what life brings. You're right to say that one has to <u>plan ahead</u>. We white people are unhappy in this regard compared to black people or red people, who live from day to day.[1] Even the Bible says "don't worry about tomorrow etc. etc." Unfortunately, much has changed since that was written in the Bible. —————

——*(Continued)*———— Now, I can tell you that these are the last lines I am writing from here, and it is my last night in the tent. — The farmer came and paid us. He said the weather is too unstable and therefore he cannot continue to keep us working. It is no harm for me, since I would have to leave on Monday anyway in order to reach the boat on May 23rd. I am not satisfied with my pay, though: we had too much rain. Compared to Austria, it is a good wage, but, compared to Canada, it's a bad one. For today, I have to close. Many lines I wrote to you from this tent, and many dear beautiful lines from you I read in it. So Goodbye! I hope you are well in your dear little room in Reichenau. *Con.*

1. Kain's characterization of indigenous peoples as "happy" in their "primitivism"—and thus incapable of determining their own future—reflects the social Darwinist views popular in his day. Here, Kain is writing in accordance to his times, yet, at the same time, the context does reflect a sense of envy for the indigenous worldview.

93

Martinborough, Club Hotel, May 18, 1913, 8 P.M.

Now I will write something about my trip from Kaiwaka. We started yesterday at 8 A.M. To shorten the route, we crossed two small mountains, and then followed a swollen creek through which we waded about twenty times!! Two men were with me. I had a lot to carry. We reached a farm (Stonecreek) and were lucky to stay overnight there. The cook there was a Norwegian, who had already been through a lot himself, and so he gave us a good meal. The night was cold, the clothes damp, and I was very tired. I slept well. Today, May 18th, we left at 8 A.M. and arrived here at 5:30 P.M. Tomorrow, I will get the parcel you sent. I am too tired to continue writing. After four months, I am in a white bed again! I usually don't sleep too well in a bed after living in a camp for so long. — Well, Good Night! *K.*

May 19, 1913, 9 A.M.

Yes, it is really good to be a real HUMAN BEING again!! I slept like a dead horse!! At 7 A.M., I had a bath, got dressed in white shirt and collar —— I feel "fine"!!! I just returned from the post office. Finally, the parcel is in my hands and everything is in good condition. I did not have to pay anything. Your *sewn-on address* was a very fine, good precautionary idea. I will keep the address (your handy work). Everything was packed very well. I can <u>praise</u> the sender. Thanks from my heart. Especially for the oiling of the shoes —— that was more than dear of you! Take my very best thanks for now. When we climb the Dachstein and the Ortler, I will oil YOUR shoes in return!! You will see that I will remember. I <u>never</u> forget such thoughtfulness. — At 2 P.M., we travel to Featherstone and take the train to Wellington.

Wellington, May 19, 1913, in the evening

We arrived safely. I must wait here until the evening of May 25th. I am in a rooming house, have a whole room to myself, but it is not very nice. It is a windy spot. I wouldn't like to stay here forever. I will now go to a tea house, drink a few glasses of very hot tea. I don't feel very well. ——

Wellington, May 20, 1913 in a hotel

Well, I have just been up in the botanical garden, where I had been in January. The flowers are not so nice anymore, because it is fall or almost winter now. I don't feel too well. My heart is not quite right. I know you can feel with me, so I write this to you. But when you receive these lines, perhaps everything will be ok again. I was in the COOK OFFICE and brought my ticket up to date.[1] I also received several letters, but none from Europe: two from Australia and three from America. The old lady that I met on the *Orsova* wrote such a lovely, motherly letter. It is not right that I go to Canada. She had hoped to see me once more, and now it cannot be. Of course, she wishes me the best and also gives me good advice. She fears that I might not marry well, because of my wandering about, and thinks I should be careful that I don't get into a bad situation. I should make a good choice: she writes, "Young handsome men usually fall into deep water." She would be so sorry to hear that I am not happy. Her son made a mistake with his marriage. She says nothing can be more pitied than a good man who gets a bad wife. I can only agree with her. But I don't have to fret about such danger. I would like to know what the good woman would think of me, if she knew me better? —— From the Grand Trunk Railway, I also received a kind letter. I should keep my next summer free, because the hotel for tourist traffic won't be ready for this summer.[2] I also hope that one will permit me what I applied for, namely $4.50 per day and everything free. The Grand Trunk Railway did not mention in their letter that this was too much.

—— A letter arrived from Melbourne from my travel companion. They do well in Australia, they own a business there. ———

May 21, in the evening

Today I was in the zoo and in a museum. It was a windy day and very dusty. I met two colleagues who had been with me in Camp Kaiwaka. They took me to the boarding house, where they live when they are in town. Then we went to the theatre. I did not like the play. The music was nice, but I got so melancholy that I had to watch myself not to start crying. I did not feel being myself. *[In English from hereon]* I can't tell how I have been feeling. Just terrible! — Two nights more in New Zealand! I wonder what you will be doing now? Maybe you are at Neuberg, in Styria, with your friend? I wish you might be there and that you would have a good time. I had been once working there, when I was fifteen years old. That time I did not expect that I should become a wandering bird once. *[In German from hereon]* If I think about my young life, I often think that it was a pity that I did not have the chance to go to high school. Perhaps I would not have had to wander? Yes, it is a pity! I was poor, born very poor. Had my fate been different, I might have become a scientist. I often feel I should do something good and great for the world. I feel little sparks in my brain, but unfortunately I cannot bring these sparks to a flame all by myself. It also would be too late by now. —— So I have no choice but to take everything as it comes. But it is hard for a person, if one can see: here would be a better position for you, if you had been in high school! And if you did not go through one, one has to stand back. And how would it be if I had not met such good people and friends with whose help I could catch up in some ways? You know that you too are among these friends, don't you? Do you remember what I told you about it?

May 22, 1913, 10 A.M.

I spent a sleepless night. Now I am sleepy and tired. This afternoon, the steamer should arrive from Sidney. Her name is *Moana*.[3] The ocean is very stormy, perhaps she will be late. I will go for a walk with the two lads and will continue writing in the evening. ———

9 P.M. We were in New [?],[4] an hour from here by train, a nice outing. Then, I was down at the harbour and saw the boat, however could not go on board, since she was not anchored yet. The *Moana* is a small, old steamer that holds only 4,000 tons: that is just a quarter of the tonnage of the *Orsova*. Then, we went to see a movie which was quite nice. I am tired from walking on the cobblestones. —— My last night in New Zealand! Good Night! *Con*

May 23, 1913, in the morning,

I am going to the boat with my baggage now. We will depart at 5 P.M. Will continue writing later.

Afternoon. I am sitting under a big tree in a park. I was just on board the *Moana*. I don't like the boat. So, I have to say Goodbye to New Zealand. I don't think I will ever see it again. It is a wonderland, that is true, but for a <u>workingman</u>, who has to spend his life doing hard labour, it is not an especially good country, at least not as good as America. One is not so free. There is a similar class difference in Old England. But for people with money to start something, New Zealand is better than Canada. But Canada gives its poor people much more opportunities to get ahead than those which are available in New Zealand. I always believed that New Zealand is a free country, but now I know differently. The country is ruled only by capitalists. And, wherever that's the case, the labourer is only a free <u>slave</u>. He is free, but yet restricted. I don't regret having taken the trip to New Zealand. Nobody can take that experience away from me. I am very sorry to say that I don't feel quite well. I hope I won't get really ill. Perhaps the ocean air will be good for me. I have not gotten any mail from home lately, and I wonder how things are. ———— I hope I'll receive several letters in Banff from my family. I know there will be one from you, true Comrade! I now go on board and say Goodbye to you from the vast, far New Zealand. I travel CLOSER TO home. I know you will follow me on your atlas again. ——

On board the *Moana*, May 26, 1913

Dear Miss:

This is the second day on water. The weather is bad. Storm. And I am not feeling too well. I spend most of the time in bed. My heart is beating strongly. My thoughts are in the mountains of my home country. ——

On board the *Moana*, May 28, 1913

Yesterday, I saw the doctor. He said that once the weather is better, I will begin to feel better. Today is not so stormy anymore, and I feel a lot better. Am very tired since I cannot sleep. This morning, there was a funeral at high sea. A child died. I did not see the burial in the ocean. But one can imagine: the body is wrapped in sail cloth, then a piece of iron is attached, so that the body can sink. Just think: we have a crazy man on board! At night, he fired shots from a revolver, and there was a panic! The man was bound and will be taken into custody in Raratonga tomorrow. How are you all? I am looking forward with great joy to a letter from you.! ——

May 29, 1913

Four years ago today, I said good bye to you in Vienna. Do you remember the day? It had been a sad day, but not as bad as November 12, 1912. It is too bad that we human beings cannot do as we would really like to. Sometimes I think that life is not worth living. I am glad I am broadminded. —— At 2 or 3 P.M., we get to Raratonga.⁵ We can see land already. It is very beautiful. We see mountains too. The ocean is very calm. ——

May 30, 1913

Today, I feel much better. I slept well, too. Yesterday, the doctor gave me some drops I did not want to take, but he assured me that it is no poison. Now I will tell you about Raratonga. We were on land for four hours. It was wonderful! Unfortunately, it started to rain. I went on alone, walking for an hour. You can imagine how it is under palm trees!⁶ On the island, there are many kinds of fruit. The local population mainly lives off these. Most of the men are built very well. The women are all fat, and I did not like them. Most of them walk around almost naked. Outside the village, you can see some totally naked ones. The people are clean and are well washed. I collected some shells for you. It will bring you a little joy when you get a few objects from the far South, because it is not every week that a friend or acquaintance of you comes here and thinks of you!! — It was a joy to wander through the greenery and breathe the wonderful air in addition to the fruit smelling so good. The walk did me a lot of good, because the air on board was very bad. This old boat has no modern ventilation. Apparently, the ship is on her last trip. One gets very little for so much money one pays. Well, one is, after all, a poor fellow, if one has to travel third class! Up to now, I have not made any nice acquaintances on board. Most of the passengers were in America before and are going back there. One hears lots of complaints about New Zealand and Australia. I am not the only one who was disappointed by the South. There are two Germans on board. One of them has been around the whole world, and now he returns to America. He says that in one or two years a great revolution will take place in the cities of America, and he wants to take part in it!! One hears a lot about this matter. I can easily understand this. I fear that, in Europe, one will experience a very similar situation quite soon, because it cannot continue as it is now! The tax screw will reach its goal. You know that I am against war, bloodshed, and murder, but it won't be possible any other way. If it has to be, I too would offer my strength and my blood, but only if it was for the benefit of the poor. I would not want to die for the church, because the church does not die for me.

1. Widely regarded as the first "travel agent," Thomas Cook (1808–1892) began British tour operations and excursions in the early 1840s. By the late 1850s, the Englishman went continental. During the decades that followed, Cook became, according to historian Ovar Löfgren, "an institution, laying the foundation (together with his less famous competitors in the business) for mass travel south....It seemed as if Mr. Cook's helpful agents were everywhere and always ready to arrange hotel accommodation, guided tours, and rail tickets or solve conflicts whether in Naples or in Smyrna." Ovar Löfgren, *On Holiday: A History of Vacationing* (Berkeley: University of California Press, 2002), 161. After Cook's death, it was claimed that "Cook at present pervades the whole civilized world." John Pemble, *The Mediterranean Passion: Victorians and Edwardians in the South* (Oxford: Oxford University Press, 1987), 48.

2. Kain's employment with the GTPR never materialized. Like the CPR, the GTPR built several grand hotels, all stopping points on its rail line. Ottawa's Château Laurier (1912), Minaki Lodge (1914), and Edmonton's Hotel Macdonald (1915) all stood in their early years as monuments to the success of the railway company. In Jasper Park, the GTPR planned to build the "Château Miette," a hotel to rival its southern cousin, the Banff Springs Hotel. "This full-service resort," writes Gabrielle Zezulka-Mailloux, "was to have been built near the hot springs to serve as the pre-eminent tourist accommodation in the park, but, because of delays in the issuance of appropriate leases by the government, the death of the Grand Trunk Pacific Railway's main financial backer, Charles Melville Hays..., and the Great War and its attendant financial stresses, the hotel never came to be." Gabrielle Zezulka-Mailloux, "Laying Tracks for Tourism: Paradoxical Promotions and the Development of Jasper National Park," in MacLaren, *Culturing Wilderness*, 242.

3. The steamer *Moana* was built for the Union Steamship Company of New Zealand in Dunedin in 1879. The company was a "union" in that it was formed in 1875 by several New Zealand shipping companies to serve New Zealand ports and intercolonial trade with Australia and Tasmania. It soon expanded its service to Tahiti, Fiji, and the pacific coast of North America, and, thus, it required "a tremendous fleet of new ships." E. Mowbray Tate, *Transpacific Steam: The Story of Steam Navigation from the Pacific Coast of North America to the Far East and the Antipodes, 1867–1941* (London: Cornwall Books, 1986), 153. Classed as a Passenger Cargo steamship, the *Moana* had the capacity to accommodate 296 passengers.

4. The location was not legible on the original letter.

5. Rarotonga is the largest of the Cook Islands of the South Pacific. The island's central massif is the eroded remains of a volcanic pyramid that is, as in Kain's time, covered in dense jungle.

6. The romance of the South Pacific and the tropical beach in the early decades of the twentieth century was, perhaps, the first mass-media "paradise": it was a landscape not only experienced through letters, postcards, and illustrated magazines, but also through popular music. "As early as 1915," writes historian Ovar Löfgren, "the tune 'At the Beach at Waikiki' was a great hit at the Panama-Pacific Exposition in San Francisco." Löfgren, *On Holiday*, 216.

239

94

Tahiti, June 1, 1913, on shore

Dear Miss Amelie:

[In English from hereon] I am sure you cannot make yourself a picture where I am now! I am sitting on a hill under a cocoa tree in Tahiti. The sun is shining very fine, and the birds are singing. *[In German from hereon]* Last night, we arrived in good weather. We all went for a walk. I was up until 11:30 P.M. The sunset was beautiful! It made me melancholy. I felt very alone and lonely, and went for a walk with the German passenger. Tahiti is under the French government. There are not many white people here, but many Chinese and, of course, many natives. One sees that people in the South are lazy. I cannot write all what one can see in one evening—the German man said, "it is a shame that white men sink so low." It seems there are more women among the natives than men. Fruit is very cheap: for one franc you get a whole basket of oranges and bananas, as much as one can carry. We depart tomorrow at 5 P.M.

Tahiti, June 2, 1913

This morning, I got up very early and went to the fruit market. I then went for a walk along the ocean beach and collected some shells, which I am sending you as a greeting from the far South. Then I returned to the *Moana*. After breakfast, I went for another walk with the German man. It was very nice. We went through gardens and into a valley. It was ten o'clock when I returned. I bought this paper and sat down under the cocoa tree. I will stay here; I need no lunch. It is such a good feeling to stand on green grass again. Especially if you did not feel too well on water. At the moment, I am okay, but I don't know whether I can go up into the mountains right after getting to Banff. I will see my friend, Dr. Brett, there, and he will advise me. I feel that I have lost weight. How are you and yours? I hope you are all healthy and enjoy life in Reichenau. A few more weeks will pass until I will hear from you. I hope that they will keep my letters in Banff and won't send them on to New Zealand. In Banff, they know that I will arrive in two weeks. I will send a telegram from San Francisco. From New Zealand, it would have been too expensive. I don't regret having left New Zealand. The whole time there, I did not feel well. I am curious about what this year will have in stock for me? Up to now, it has been a bad luck year for me. I fear that I will get more bad news from home. Dear Miss, I like to wish that you will also come so far south sometime! One cannot describe the beauty as well as one should, at least I can't do it. It is wonderful here!! No tree or bush one sees at home, everything is <u>new</u> and <u>different</u> for the eyes. The birds too sing so beautifully and quite differently than at home. Today is actually the first day of spring for me, that is, I feel it that way. It was fall in New Zealand when I left. I will now lay down on the green ground and sleep. Good bye,

Yours, Con

95

On board the *Moana*, June 3, 1913

I wrote my last lines to you in Tahiti. I slept well under the cocoanut tree, and then climbed a higher hill from where I had a beautiful view in three directions. I sent good thoughts in all directions. ——— Now we have a storm again. One cannot see on deck. The ocean waves are coming with great force over the ship's railings. Never before did I see such high waves. One can do nothing but lie in bed. ———

June 5, 1913

The storm died down a bit. Yesterday, I saw the doctor again. He advised me to sleep on deck, once the weather gets nicer. He believes the air in the cabin is not good for me. That I understand myself. I am not alone on the sick list. There are many on it.

June 6, 1913

Last night, I slept on deck. It was the first night that I slept even a bit. Today, it is a beautiful day, but rather chilly. I heard that a passenger in 2nd class is very ill, and I am doubtful that he will recover. The doctor told me about it. He is a very old man. He asked me this morning where I come from. After that he spoke German with me quite well. I told him that I doubt whether I could go into the mountains in Canada right away, and he said, "Don't be scared, that is just what you should do." —— Did you go to Neuberg? I am sorry that I could not write much in my notebook. I had looked forward to it! Unfortunately, things did not work out. I cannot write in my cabin, and it does not work too well on deck either. You know how it is when one does not feel well while at sea. ———

June 7, 1913

Slept quite well on deck last night. The doctor saw me in the morning. The patient in the 2nd class is doing very poorly. The doctor predicts he won't see the morning. ———

June 9, 1913

Last night, the patient passed away. This morning, the body was put into the depth of the ocean. I watched from land. The captain acted as the minister. The deceased had no friends on board. He was an American, forty-seven-years old. It must be sad for his friends, who will wait for him—that is, if he has any friends. But who on earth has none? I feel better now already, and am on deck all the time. Up to now, we have had no particularly beautiful sunsets, none that could be compared to the ones in the Red Sea.

June 10, 1913

I am sitting on deck in the warm sun. Finally, the ocean is totally calm. In two days, we will be in San Francisco. In a month from today, it will be July 10th. Your precious name day! *[In English from hereon]* I wonder where I shall be on that day? I certainly will think of you. Two years ago, I wrote you a letter on a mountain peak of Moose Pass.[1] Last year I was in Mongolia and thought of you, and plucked some flowers for you. How quickly time passes by, doesn't it? — I wish I could spend the 10th of July in my home! Just once! I certainly would bring you some nice flowers with my best wishes. Well, I only can do it in thoughts, in spirit, I mean, but I think our thoughts will cross somewhere on this happy day. ——

[In German from hereon] June 11, 1913

A beautiful day and no wind. —— The sun is just setting. Tomorrow morning, we will see land when we awake. I am so glad that this is the last night on this boat! I feel a bit better today. But I am tired and weak. —— The sun disappeared; I would like to go to sleep. But since it is the last night, it will not be quiet for a long time. One will play the piano and that gets on my nerves! — It would be different, if <u>you</u> would play for me————!

1.   See Letter 55 (July 30, 1911).

96a[1]

San Francisco, June 12, 1913

American Hotel, Room 416, 9:30 P.M.

In the morning at 11 o' clock, we arrived in the harbour, and, after two hours of inspections, we finally went ashore. First, I went to the office and inquired about the trip to Vancouver. The ship *Watson* leaves on Saturday at 4 P.M. You know that after a cruise one likes to get ashore again. It was great to sit again in a quiet dining room and have a good dinner. I then went for a walk. Frisco is a beautiful city. In the evening, I went to a picture show, very cheap, only five cents. Some pictures were very good. It felt good to have a little distraction. I am glad the cruise is over. Tomorrow, I go to the Museum of Natural History and to the Zoo, which is said to be beautiful. And now I will go to bed. The bed, so wide and white, looks tempting after the cabin bunk. ——

Frisco, June 13, 1913, 6 A.M.

Good Morning! The bed was so soft that I slept very well for some hours, but have been up since for 4 o'clock. The rattling of the wagons on the cobblestoned street woke me up. It seems like it's turning into a beautiful day. After breakfast, I will walk along the ocean shore. Then to the Golden Gate Park. In 1915, there will be a world exhibition in San Francisco, and preparations for it are already made now.[2] One big building is almost finished. So, now my breakfast arrived. ———

In the evening. — Walked around a lot today. After breakfast, I went to the exhibition grounds, then I took the streetcar to the Golden

Gate Park (circumference 7 miles). I was alone, but later met an acquaintance from the *Moana*. I spent six hours in the Natural History Museum. The most beautiful one I ever saw! No comparison with the Natural History Museum in Vienna! The bones of the pre-historic animals, which were found in Alaska, are so interesting. One bone was much bigger than the entire circumference of my body. Then, I spent a long time in the picture gallery. It is impossible to see it all in one day. One needs weeks. I am looking forward to going to Washington sometime and to see in their museum the various animals that *I* caught in Siberia! After all the wonders I saw in the museum, a feeling of dissatisfaction grew over me again. I pity myself that I could not attend high school, and now it is too late. ——— Tomorrow, June 14th, the steamer *Watson* leaves for Vancouver. I am very much looking forward to seeing Canada! Now Good bye. I sent a card to you and one to Flora. This letter I will post in Canada.

Yours Con

1. Thorington (or Malek) mistakenly listed two letters—this one and the next—as "96."

2. The Panama-Pacific International Exposition was a world's fair held in San Francisco between 20 February and 4 December 1915. Its alleged purpose was to celebrate the 1914 completion of the Panama Canal, but it was widely seen as an opportunity for the city to showcase its recovery from the devastating 1906 earthquake and fire that left more than half the city's population displaced. Construction of the fairgrounds began in January 1913 and, within two years, the exposition turned 620 acres of landfill into "a beautifully landscaped wonderland with 11 enormous exposition palaces, dozens of state and foreign pavilions, and an amusement zone nearly a mile in length." William Lipsky, *San Francisco's Panama-Pacific International Exposition* (Charleston, SC: Arcadia, 2005), 7.

96b

Banff, Alta, June 20, 1913

My dear friend Amelie:

I just arrived in Banff. Yes, I have just been here for four-and-a-half
hours. I have found three letters from you (one from spring, 1912),
one from your sister, some from home, and many from my Canadian
friends. I was expected here on June 1st already. In the newspaper it
said that "the well-known mountain guide Conrad Kain returned!!"
Tomorrow, already, I shall leave for the camp, so I do not have much
time and will have to answer your letter, which I have not yet even
opened, once I reach the camp.[1] Now I go to my hotel, to see all my
friends. Good bye, Good Night! —

June 21, 1913

Yesterday, I saw many of my friends, and it was not until close to
around midnight that I read your letters. Yes, you are a faithful
soul, a true comrade. I was very surprised by the letter from your
dear mother. She wrote a really long, charming letter. After all those
many lines I rushed through, I fell asleep in tears. When I awoke this
morning, the lamp was still on. —— I can and must not write you
much about my health. Today, I feel fairly well, but I go to the camp
only tomorrow. I would have liked to rest here for one to two weeks,
but it is not possible. My friends say that I don't look too well. Yes, I
know that I left here long ago with a rosy face and in a happy mood.
I hope it will be like that again. I told Mr. Wheeler that, in the beginning, I won't endure too much work. He thought that if I go along
as cook only it would be easier to bear. Since being ashore, I feel
already much, much better. On board, I felt miserable all the time.

True friend Amelie, take my thanks for your letters and also my best wishes for your name day. May you live to enjoy many more and remain always in the best of health! God may protect and keep you. These are my wishes from my heart from far away. To all of you, my heartiest greetings and Good bye. In great haste, your grateful, *K.*

1. Kain refers not to an ACC camp, but to the camp of Wheeler's boundary survey party, which began its preliminary work at Kicking Horse Pass on 6 June 1913. The survey of the pass was completed on 17 July. R.W. Cautley, J.N. Wallace, and A.O. Wheeler, *Report of the Commission Appointed to Delimit the Boundary between the Provinces of Alberta and British Columbia, Part I, From 1913 to 1916* (Ottawa: Office of the Surveyor General, 1917), 26–32.

97

Department of the Interior
Topographical Surveys Branch

Great Divide, July 7, 1913

My dear friend Amelie:

Now I am in the mountains again. In the Rockies! It is spring in
the mountains! —— For the first days in the camp, I was the cook.
Now, I am working again on top of the mountains. I climb mountains again as a guide! I feel much better doing this, better than when
my I arrived in Banff, but not quite 100 per cent yet. I get tired more
easily than before, but I hope everything will be better again. The
topographical survey will be done in order to establish precisely and
correctly the border between Alberta and British Columbia. We all
know each other in the group, and I am convinced they all are happy
that I came back, because the people don't have the eye and the
experience to choose good routes to the tops of mountains. I wanted
to answer a lot of your questions in your letter in Banff, but, unfortunately, I see that the letters are in my pack at Castle...and I am on the
Great Divide between Laggan and Hector.[1] Since I have been here, I
received a card from you from the Rax, where you went on a school
outing. I know, you think of me when you are on the Rax. Thanks a
lot. You will write more about the tour, won't you? Each day, I wait for
news from home. It takes long until one gets the mail out here in the
mountains, because a letter must go through many hands before it
reaches its address. I have to write a very sad story. A good friend of
mine from Banff (John Wilson) was, four miles from here, stopped by
robbers and shot. Two shots in the chest and the neck halfway cut.
Just think: the poor guy is still <u>alive</u>! For thirty hours, he lay

unconscious, and now he is in the hospital in Banff. One bullet was removed, but he is too weak for another operation. He also worked for Mr. Wheeler and the Alpine Club. He is the son of an old Rocky Mountain guide, whom I mentioned in my notes, and who was on a bear hunt with a Spanish prince, the present king of Spain.[2] I wrote Miss Flora that the political situation is not very good in America. It seems the Balkan war affects business here, too. There will probably be a rebellion. Everywhere things slow down. I can only imagine how it will at home in Austria if peace does not come soon. — In two days, it will be your name day, and I will write you a few lines from a mountain top in the Rockies, just like two years ago when I was on the Divide between Alta and B.C. — I hope that, as always, many relatives and friends will think of you. I am one of the many but probably the farthest away. Please tell me the name day of your sister, I cannot find it in the calendar. During the time in Reichenau, if I did not address the priest with his title, please forgive me—as a semi-American. — You know that in America one does not use a person's title in a letter, except to a doctor. *[In English from hereon]* Now about your trip. Do you think your mother will let you go and see your friends at Veldes? You would enjoy it, would you not? Well, all I can do is wish you good luck to it! Life is so short, and I think one should make a good time of it, if one can. The only thing I enjoy now is nature, especially spring in the mountains. And if I do have some nice letters from good friends, I enjoy them too. Sometimes I think I have seen a little too much for a poor man. And there are many things that make a man unhappy, if he sees the wrongs and can't change them. I hope you understand me well. What are the flowers doing in your garden? They will look very fine around your balcony. I wish you may feel happy amongst the flowers and that you enjoy good health and that nothing wrong comes in your way. May all the people and nature too be kind and good to you. How is your dear mother? I hope and wish she is alright and enjoys her old days in perfect health in Reichenau. I often think of the nice letter your Mama wrote to me. It was a very kind deed of her, because I can understand that, when people are getting old, they do not like to write long letters. Now about the letter I thought to send to the *Schwarzataler-Zeitung*. I still have it. I shall send it to you, and, if you think it is good enough, give it to Mr. Prager for his paper, please! A week ago, I had a very kind letter again from Mr. Hollister. I tell you, I love this fellow!! He told me that he might go to South America next winter (collecting), and, if possible, he would take me along. But it is not sure yet, it is only a plan. He also sent me the report he wrote about the Siberia-Mongolia trip. He gives me a good credit. I will send it to you some day. We got thirteen new specimens. Mr. Hollister is very content and so is Mr. Lyman.

[In German from hereon] On July 15th, the Alpine Club camp near Hector will be opened for ten days. More than 150 tourists are supposed to take part. I don't go to that camp, but to the Mt. Robson Camp from July 28th to August 9th.[3] I think that we will have hard work there, and perhaps it will be dangerous, as well. Mt. Robson is a bad mountain. I know it well from having seen it. No, I have not climbed it yet. But I surely will get up there. In case the tour is very dangerous, I will only go with very good tourists and only for a high fee. A guide should be paid well for such a dangerous ascent, especially by people who have enough money and who often throw away a hundred dollars in one day for a few entertaining hours. From England, many acquaintances come to Robson Camp, such as Mr. Mumm, Cpt. Eaver, and many more whom I know. Some Swiss guides are also coming. *[In English from hereon]* Now I must say Good bye to you. I will soon post another letter. I am your wandering friend, *Con.*

My best love to your mother and sister.

---

1. "Castle" (Vermilion Pass), "Laggan" (Lake Louise), and "Hector" (Kicking Horse Pass) were all stations on the CPR line through the Bow Valley.

2. John Clark Wilson (1888–1932) was one of six children born to Tom Edmonds Wilson (1859–1933) and Minnie McDougall Wilson (1866–1936), who were guides, outfitters, and ranchers at Morley, Kootenay Plains, Banff, and Nordegg, Alberta. John's father, Tom Wilson, the so-called "Oracle of Banff," is widely credited as the first non-Native to lay eyes on Lake Louise, which he named "Emerald Lake," due to its colouring (caused by suspended glacial till) in 1882. Later, in 1884, the lake's name was changed to honour of Princess Louise Caroline Alberta (1848–1939), daughter

of Queen Victoria and wife of the Marquis of Lorne, John Campbell (1845–1914), the fourth Governor General of Canada. Hart, *Diamond Hitch*, 17.

3. The ACC held two summer mountaineering camps in 1913. The first was the official, eighth-annual mountaineering camp: "Cathedral Mt. Camp," as it was called, which was held from 15–25 July in the Lake O'Hara Valley near where the CPR line crosses the Continental Divide. See Arthur O. Wheeler, "Report of Cathedral Mt. Camp (1913)," CAJ 6 (1914–1915): 250–52. The second, special camp—the "Mount Robson Camp"—took advantage of the newly completed GTPR line and was held at Robson Pass, between Berg and Adolphus Lakes, from 28 July to 9 August. Of the latter, Wheeler felt it was "the most delightful camp the Club ever held." Arthur O. Wheeler, "Report of Mount Robson Camp (1913)," CAJ 6 (1914–1915): 253–55.

98

[No date]

My dear friend Amelie:

I wanted to write you a long letter from Robson Camp. But after what
you will hear, you will understand that I could not find the time. Well,
before all, I thank you ever so much for your dear long letters. Now I
can tell you that I do feel ever so much better, but still cannot say yet
that I feel like "the deer in the wood." *[In German from hereon]* But I
hope that I will regain my full health. My heart seems to be beating
in the right way and speed, but I don't know whether I will regain my
proper weight? That I don't know! — I changed a lot since last fall. I
look a few years older, and many people say that to me right into my
face! Well, one cannot do too much about that, don't you think? I will
try to be calm again. But now, I must begin to tell you things! — I was
one day in the camp near Lake O'Hara, then we went to Banff, from
where I wrote a card to you. Then we travelled to Edmonton, where I
saw my old Banff friend, Miss Maggee. Unfortunately sick in bed, she
has a serious ailment of the eyes. Already she has been in bed for
more than two months. I happened to see the doctor and asked him
what he thinks about the poor lady. "Not much good" was the answer.
The lady was very pleased about my visit. I promised to visit her again
on my way back. Unfortunately, I could not see her then, since the
doctor did not permit visitors. Poor girl, thousands of miles away
from her friends, and no real friends in this country! On July 27th, we
got to the Grand Fork at the foot of Mt. Robson and to the base camp,
stayed overnight, slept outside. On July 28th, we hiked in several
groups to Lake Kinney and over the cliffs past the great waterfall to
the Berg Lake. I don't have to mention that many thoughts went
through my mind, what I had experienced here two years ago. Here, I

met my old friend Phillips again and several other acquaintances. In the evening, we had a thunderstorm. I was busy nailing boots.[1] On July 29th, we had fresh snow! It was rather cold. Towards noon, the sun came out. In the afternoon, I went around Berg Lake with two ladies and a gentleman. We watched a slide or, more precisely, ice break off the glacier and plunge into the lake. On the way to the camp, we saw a mountain goat. In the evening, we had a camp fire. In all, we were sixty-five people. On July 30th, we started to climb Mt. Resplendent, two gentlemen and a lady. I took my blankets along, since in the evening at the tree line, I expected two gentlemen for July 31st. We were in clouds almost the entire way up Mt. Resplendent, but we reached the top at 1 P.M. It was the second ascent of this mountain, and the first ascent of the peak made by lady. So, I shook her hand with words of congratulation.[2] We took a new descent, a beautiful difficult hike along the crest, which we had to abandon because of a storm. At the glacier, I found my two gentlemen for the next morning. One was the minister of public works in the parliament of B.C., the other a rich New Yorker.[3] Near the last bushes we had supper, then we took along some wood and blankets and went even higher up. We slept on a moraine. The night was beautiful and not too cold. Early the next morning, I wanted to check the weather, but could not open my eyes for a long time. I wished for bad weather!!! My eyes were swollen and felt as if they were filled with sand —— similar to being in fog! Nevertheless, at 3:45 A.M., I made a fire and breakfast. We started at 4:30, and, after thirteen hours, sometime after 5:30 P.M., we reached the top of Mt. Robson (12,978 feet), "The King of the Rockies." I was half snow blind! I hacked 500 to 600 steps into the blue, shiny ice, and often I sank over my knees into the soft new snow. It was a hard day for me, but I reached my goal and did the real first ascent of Mt. Robson, because, as was established, Mr. Kinney and Phillips had not reached the true top.[4] The ascent was very dangerous and I did not want to use it for the descent. So, we descended on the southwest side. Even there, we had dangerous

> On the summit of Mount Resplendent, 1913. Photo by Byron Harmon. [WMCR, V263/936]

work to do. I knew we would have to camp, but I did not say a word about it. We went as long as we could see, and, after almost eighteen hours of hard labour, we bedded down on the ridge of a rock, 9,000 ft. above ocean level. We had not much to eat, and the night was too long for us. Our feet were wet, too, but in spite of it I slept a few hours. In the morning, the gentlemen had swollen eyes, just as I had had the previous morning. One of the gentlemen could hardly see. From this spot, the descent over the rocks was not easy. At 11 o'clock/noon, we reached Kinney Lake and at 5 P.M. Berg Lake, where we were received with Hurrahs. The tour had taken thirty hours.[5] On August 1st, I had a day of rest. One party returned to camp from Whitehorn and brought the record of my first ascent, which had at first been doubted!! (it is, however, so much better for me!) I made cold compresses for my eyes and they got much better. But I had pains over my whole face. August 2nd in the afternoon, we left the camp to do the Whitehorn (12,972 feet). We camped near the old camp, from where I had done the first ascent. On August 3rd at 4 A.M., I woke the people. We were eleven (in two parties) all together, including four ladies. I took two ladies and a gentleman. At 8 o'clock, a thunderstorm began, such that I thought I would have to abandon the ascent. But, in a short while, the weather cleared, so we continued. The ladies did very well, but I always had to wait for the other party. It was very late when we reached the top, and I saw that we would have another bivouac. So, we descended to the glacier to the northeast, down a very steep snowy slope. It was such hard work, and I had to go back to get the other people. At 11 P.M., we reached the rock where we would spend the night. I made a bed for the ladies as well as I could and told them how to protect themselves against the cold. I slept under a rock with the gentleman. Some hours I slept very well, but the gentleman, however, almost froze to death! A mouse had fun playing with my boots. Everybody was glad when the day began. After five hours over rocks and ice, we reached the camp. We had a good breakfast and a good rest. In the evening, we had a meeting in the

> *Conrad Kain, William Foster, and Albert MacCarthy after their ascent of Mount Robson, 1913. Photo by Byron Harmon. [WMCR, NA 71-932]*

camp. I gave a speech and talked about a few of my experiences. During the next days, I took a tour to Mt. Lynx (10,471 feet). On August 8th, we had to evacuate a sick Englishman, who had just a slight injury but got blood poisoning. On the 9th, the camp ended, and on August 10th, my 30th birthday, I made an attempt to get up to Mt. Robson from the southwest side. At 8 A.M., four of us left camp—the gentleman from New York, a gentleman from Vancouver, a Swiss guide and me (two days later, he made another attempt after our attempt on Mt. Robson, but he had bad luck).[6] —— We took blankets and wood along. At 8 P.M., we reached the campsite. Here, we had a little argument, which I ended, however, with good words. A terrible thunderstorm developed. The night was good, but the weather was bad. Nevertheless, we made an attempt at a new route. It began to snow and yet, at a height of 11,000 ft., it was still too nice to turn back. It began to storm, but since we already were so high up, we did not want to turn around, so we continued up to 12,500 ft. There, it really got rough and dangerous. (Later, I saw it was good that we abandoned the tour). Going downhill, we lost our way a bit in the fog. The storm was so strong and the fog so dense that often we could see only two to five steps ahead. Wet from top to bottom, we reached the things we had left behind, and, at around 9 P.M., we got to a hut at Lake Kinney, where we spent the night. The next day, we went to the station and took the train to Edmonton. The train ride was the worst. I was very sleepy and tired. The Mt. Robson camp was, on the whole, very successful. One more time, I made my name known forever in the Rockies! The people were also so nice and good to me! It made a difference that I had been away for a year. I also saw a high official from the Grand Trunk Railway. He could not promise me anything definite, but wants to do his best for me for next summer. Now I am back my work surveying. In a few days, we go to Mt. Assiniboine and just think —— August 24th–26th, my friend Dr. P. is coming to Banff. (I don't know whether I will see him?) Now, I like to speak to you about your dear letters. Yes, they are always nice to me. I wonder, who else could write such nice and kind letters to me? — From my poor brother, David, I got a letter and a card. He writes that he feels better. He also mentioned that you always write him such friendly letters. I hope he will perhaps get healthy yet. ———

As I read in the paper, I see the Balkan war will finally end. I feel the same about it as you: It is a shame! I did not hear anything from the Austrian South Pole expedition. I am not much for it, because who has <u>money</u> for <u>scientific</u> excursions in Austria?? The government, I think, will not help much with it!! — *[In English from hereon]* Now, do not think that I have been very lazy not to write more before. On July 10, I thought of you. I did not feel very well the first month and besides, I had lots of work to do. I knew you had been looking for some news, but at last you got my letter. *[In German from hereon]* I will send the shells in a few days. I also got a letter from the old dear lady from Australia. She writes to me like a mother. Of course, I also sent her a friendly letter. I can't help that I am dissatisfied with my schooling, although I know I would not even be so far had I not been so lucky to meet you in 1906. I also know that many people went through <u>high school</u> and are more stupid than I am. But that does not matter. They get positions with the government and in the city just like the <u>clever ones</u>! Hundreds of such cases you find in Austrian society. Real dumb and yet a <u>respected</u> man!! Now let's leave this alone. I will spend my life more in the forest and in nature anyway, and, for <u>that</u> life, I have enough education! —— The flowers I sent are from San Francisco. Yes, the poor priest is dead. I heard it from the police in Wellington. It is sad but unfortunately true. Somebody showed me the picture of his body. It was the one for sure. I sent you the *Canadian Alpine Journal* from 1912 and two small books, and, when I get to Banff now, I will send the journal of the year 1910.[7] With heartiest greetings, handshakes, and a Hail to the Mountains!

K. Kain

1. Nailed boots were the main type of mountaineering footwear until the 1930s–1940s—a necessity when climbing on ice of the most moderate slope—but were generally superseded by the end of the Second World War by the Vibram sole. There were two main types of nail: (1) soft iron nails,

which, secured to the sole of the boot, gripped as a result of the rock biting into them ("muggers" and "clinkers," they were commonly called), and thus needed to be replaced after extensive wear; and (2) hard steel nails (Tricounis) that, conversely, bit into the rock.

2. Kain and Byron Harmon were the first to climb Mt. Resplendent (3,425 m [11,241 ft.]) during the 1911 ACC–Smithsonian survey expedition to the Robson region. Wheeler, "The Alpine Club of Canada's Expedition to Jasper Park," 43. Also see Letter 56. Kain's second ascent was made from the club's camp at Robson Pass with three clients: Winthrop Ellsworth Stone (1862–1921), who was the president of Purdue University, and who would later perish in a climbing accident near Mt. Assiniboine; Herbert Otto Frind (1887–1961), who, later the same year, would travel to New Zealand to climb with Kain; and Miss D.A. Broadbent, whom Kain held in particularly high regard. See C.H. Mitchell, "Mount Resplendent and the Routes of Ascent (1913)," *CAJ* 6 (1914–1915): 65–73.

3. Hand selected by Wheeler, Kain's clients were William "Billy" Washborough Foster (1875–1954), the deputy minister of public works for BC, and Albert H, "Mack" MacCarthy (1876–1956), an ex–US Naval officer from Summit, New Jersey, who had, in 1910, purchased a ranch near Wilmer in the Columbia Valley. Of Foster and MacCarthy, Kain later wrote, "I could have wished for no better companions. Both Herren were good climbers and Nature lovers, and made me no difficulties on the way. Each had a friendly word of thanks for my guiding. In this country people are much more democratic than with us in Europe, and have less regard for titles and high officials; but still it was a great satisfaction to me to have the pleasure of climbing with a Canadian statesman." Conrad Kain, "The First Ascent of Mount Robson, The Highest Peak of the Rockies (1913)," trans. P.A.W. Wallace, *CAJ* 6 (1914–1915): 28.

4. While writer Chic Scott recently established that Kain may have been sympathetic to Kinney and Phillips's claim to a first ascent of Mount Robson in 1909 (see Scott, *Pushing the Limits*, 81), here, for Malek at least, Kain unequivocally asserts otherwise. By "established," Kain is likely referring to the purported omission made by Phillips, who, while outfitting the 1913 Mt. Robson Camp, confided to Foster one evening that he [Phillips] and Kinney "didn't get up the last dome." Elizabeth Parker, "A New Field for Mountaineering," *Scribner's Magazine* 55 (1914): 605. Writing in the 1914–1915 *CAJ*, Kain, as well, noted that "Donald Phillips himself said our ascent was really the first ascent of Mt. Robson. Phillips' words are as follows: 'We reached, on our ascent (in mist and storm), an ice-dome fifty or sixty feet high, which we took for the peak. The danger was to [*sic*] great to ascend the dome.'" Kain, "The First Ascent of Mount Robson," 27. Why Phillips never shared his "bomb-shell" omission earlier with Kain—remember, the two were very good friends; they spent the long and lonely winter of 1911–1912 trapping together (see Letter 60) on the upper Moose and Smokey Rivers within sight of Mt. Robson—seems odd, to say the least. Kinney, in contrast, maintained to his dying day that they had climbed to the very top.

5. While Kain and company were on Mt. Whitehorn, Swiss guide Walter Schauffelberger (d. 1914), in only 14 hours, led two amateurs—American Harley H. Prouty (1858–1916) and Vancouver-based climber Basil S. Darling (1885–1962)—to within 100 metres of Robson's summit via the West Ridge (now called the Wishbone Arête), by far the hardest route undertaken in the Rockies at the time. Had they succeeded in completing the route to the top, it would have easily equaled, if not

trumped, Kain's earlier achievement on the mountain's East Face (now called the Kain Face). See

Basil S. Darling, "First Attempt on Robson by the West Arête (1913)," CAJ 6 (1914–1915): 29–35.

Schauffelberger was killed a year later while ski touring in the Bernina Range of the Central-Eastern

Alps bordering Switzerland and Italy. See Arthur O. Wheeler, "Walter Schauffelberger," CAJ 6

(1914–1915): 237.

6. MacCarthy, Darling, Schauffelberger, and Kain climbed much of what's now called the South

Face Route, but turned back due to poor weather 150 metres below the summit. See Albert H.

MacCarthy and Basil S. Darling, "An Ascent of Mt. Robson from the Southwest (1913)," CAJ 6

(1914–1915): 37–48.

7. The 1912 CAJ contained Wheeler's detailed account of the 1911 Robson survey (an article that also

featured Kain's guides photo), and the 1910 CAJ contained various articles concerning activities at

the 1909 Lake O'Hara Camp where Kain, Wheeler wrote, first "proved himself to be a first class

man and became a great favorite." Wheeler, "Report of the 1909 Camp," CAJ 2, no. 2 (1910): 218.

99

Simpson Pass near Mt. Assiniboine in the Rockies[1]

August 23, 1913

Dear Miss Amelie:

From the Alpine Club, I sent two books to you, one magazine, the shells, and quite a long letter. We started travelling again and now are a few miles away from the post office. So it is possible that you won't hear from me for a longer time. It is beautiful here. Very many alpine meadows and a small lake. It is a new area for me. I wish that I could invite the three of you for a week in camp here. It would not even be too far away for your dear mother: twenty miles from Banff on a good horse trail.[2] We will stay here for about a month. Just as I left Banff, I received the newspaper with my story in it, along with a letter. Many thanks for your good editing. You really did a good job. I was overjoyed when I saw the lines in print. My very best thanks, dear good Amelie. I hope you are all well and have a beautiful fall in Reichenau. For this winter, I have a big tour coming up, not yet definitely planned. Perhaps I can soon write more about it. What do you say: I will perhaps take <u>my second trip around the world</u>, and, when everything works out, see my dear friend in the old home country again! Wouldn't that be beautiful? To come to Vienna in April and an outing in the "Vienna Woods" with you two in 1908. Did you hear how my poor brother is doing? I hope he will get well again. I wrote a long letter to him and some cards. So I have to finish now, since the packer rides off to take the letter to Banff. Now I say Good bye, dear good friends. My love to Flora and your mother. With warmest regards,

I am your friend in the Western woods, C.K.

1. Named to honour Sir George Simpson (1787–1860), governor of Hudson's Bay Company, Simpson Pass, situated about 30 kilometres by trail southwest of Banff, is at the headwaters of Healy Creek on the Alberta side and of a northerly branch of Simpson River on the British Columbia side. On 20 August, Wheeler and Kain returned to the survey at Simpson Pass, where two parties—under the direction Richard W. Cautley (1873–1953) and Alan J. Campbell (1882–1967)—were camped in the larch and spruce groves on the summit. Wheeler's crew worked from the pass for four weeks before heading southeast toward Mt. Assiniboine (3,618 m [11,871 ft.]), occupying survey stations along the way.

2. Prior to the appointment of fire and game guardians in Rocky Mountains Park, trails were either the work of hunters, timber cullers, or, in the case of recreational trails close to the railway line, CPR employees. In 1909, however, with the arrival of fire and game guardians, park officials began to establish a network of trails to aid in the enforcement of park regulations. Work began that summer (1909) with the cutting of a pony trail from Banff to the summit of Simpson Pass. Robert J. Burns, *Guardians of the Wild: A History of the Warden Service of Canada's National Parks* (Calgary: University of Calgary Press, 2000), 31. By 1913, the approach up Healy Creek to Simpson Pass was part of the most popular route from Banff to Mt. Assiniboine.

100

At the Alberta–British Columbia border. Southeast of Mt. Ball on a grassy hill.

August 30, 1913

My dearest friend Amelie:

It is totally impossible that you could image an image of the area where I am now. I saw so much of the world, of the mountains, as you know, but only a few pictures are in my memory that I could compare with the <u>images</u> I can see <u>now</u>: beautiful lake, mountains, glacier lakes, and on the ground, meadows, spruce and larch forests. All around us, the mountains. In the east and north, rocky mountains; and in the west and south, snow covered mountains. I am resting in the warm sun, writing these lines on my knees. Just read your letter of July 21st. Thank you so much for it. On the ascent, we saw <u>sixteen</u> mountain goats and some fresh bear tracks. The marmots give sharp whistles. —— Everything is full of life and I too feel so much better. Soon, I will be fresh and healthy again like the "stag in the forest!" — All this beauty of nature I observe with good and friendly thoughts. I think of you, too. — We are now in the "mobile camp." The camp lies at a lake between two tall rock cliffs: a wonder of nature! This valley and the lakes are the most beautiful scenery I have seen in Canada so far. Now Good bye, I will write more in camp.

———————————— Head of Red Earth Creek (South Fork) by the side of a beautiful lake.

August 30, 1913

My dear friend:

I am sitting here under a larch tree at the shore of a splendid, deep blue lake between two rocky mountains. At the end of the lake is a waterfall, which comes down from another lake located a few feet higher, and even higher is a third lake. In the background are mountains with snow and ice: an indescribably beautiful picture of nature, added to it the fine sound of the bell, which one of the horses carries around its neck. I see some mountain goats on the grassy slopes above the edge of the forest. It is one of the most beautiful spots I have ever seen with my own eyes. I know that our view of nature and its beauty is almost the same and so I think of you while observing with joy. Thousands of miles lie between here and Reichenau. So far and yet so near! I know how much pleasure the view of this wonder of nature would bring you if only you could sit under the nearest big larch tree next to me! I know you as a friend of nature and am convinced that you, just like me, would see this mountain world <u>as a paradise</u>. ——— Sorry, but I must interrupt and look after the horses. —— I don't hear the little bell anymore.[1] ——— Good bye.

———————————— August 31, 1913, 8 A.M.

Where was I one year ago today? What kind of day was August 31st, 1912? ——— It was a day full of joy! After my long travel, I saw my home country's mountains and my friends again and was in your beautiful house for the first time. What joy it was for me! Your dear mother, you, and Miss Flora were the first ones I saw and greeted at home, and you were the first ones to welcome me. I have a good memory and treasure good and friendly welcomes by other people. Today, it has been a year. Accept my most heartfelt thanks for the friendly welcome a year ago! I hope to experience once more such a joyful day! —— I have to go to the main camp now up to Simpson Pass in order to fetch a gun. It is raining and snowing, and we need fresh meat. ——

———————————— August 31, 1913. In the evening.

Was at the Simpson Pass and am back now, went hunting, but could not see because of fog and storm. It is pretty cold. I have to crawl under the blanket, because I am wet through. We have no tent. This is only a mobile camp. Good Night!

———————————— September 1, 1913, 10 A.M.

Here I am, sitting under the larch tree again with a fire at my feet, meat hanging in the tree. Early in the morning, I went hunting, and not far from the camp I shot a mountain goat. I have to bake bread and cook the meat. The others are on the mountain with the instruments. Don't know whether they can work in such fog? Excuse the interruption, I have to cook!! ——

In the evening: My friends came back to camp early and half frozen. I improved their lives with a very good goat soup. The bread also turned out quite well. Weather foggy and cold.

———————————— Simpson Pass, September 3, 1913

Yesterday, we were on a mountain, a cliff, and arrived here in the evening with the horses. Today, bad weather, therefore a day of rest. It's pouring rain and it's cold. I am busy with various little jobs in the camp. And now, I am writing an article for the magazine *Der Naturfreund* in Vienna. I beg you to polish the article a little and then send it to the magazine. Mr. T. is also a member of the Club, but I don't think you will need him for the acceptance of the article. I mean, you don't have to bother with it. I describe the life of a trapper.[2] I think it is a good article for the magazine *Der Naturfreund*. I don't know what you think about it? I would like the money you will get for it to go to my poor brother David. I don't really know whether *Der Naturfreund* pays for articles? The tourist club magazine pays well, but I would prefer my article to be in *Der Naturfreund* magazine. I think it would be a good idea if I could contribute some pictures. A very good one would be Nr. 1: tent in the snow, gun, skis, toboggan, and I sitting in front of the tent. Nr. 2: the loaded toboggan in front of the snowed-in hut, and Nr. 3: the wolverine in the iron. I leave it all to you, true comrade. I am convinced that you know better. I believe that I wrote pretty clearly; should something not be clear, then please decide according to your opinion—then it will be close to perfect! Choose the pictures yourself!

———————————— September 4, 1913

Rain and snow like yesterday. The article is done. I want to see it in print as soon as possible, since I want to write another article for the Austrian tourist magazine about the ascent of the highest mountain in Canada. As always, I can only do this with your friendly assistance. I know that you like to <u>help</u> me with this topic, don't you? By now, you will have received the books of the Alpine Club and read both with interest. I hope that you all are very well and that you have better weather than we do. On August 29th, Dr. P. was in Banff. He wrote a few lines to say that he had no time to visit me at the Simpson Pass. I am very sorry that I could not meet him! A year ago today, I was in the Habsburg House on the Rax. How fast time goes by! It's amazing what I've been through. Yes, more this year than during the other three years! But do not fear. I write you the truth. I now feel quite healthy and well. Only rarely am I not really well. If I cannot take the trip that I wrote you about earlier, I will return to the forest and nature during the winter. It pleases me when now and then I look in the mirror and notice that my cheeks are getting rounder again, and the bones in the face slowly disappear. ——

I haven't much time, the packer is riding to Banff, and I'm going to give him this letter to take along. Another thing I have to mention. Until you receive this letter, perhaps the time of the sad days of the year will return (I mean the day your good father passed away). I feel with you as with your family during these sad, dark days, and hope you don't take them too hard. And also my best thanks for your sympathy with my ill brother David. I hope to hear again from Miss Flora, too. With heartfelt greetings to you and yours. Good bye, true comrade! *Con.*

1. Horse bells were commonly used in the backcountry when stock was turned out to graze; they gave outfitters and wardens alike the security of knowing their animals were near camp and safe. And, if a horse did wander off, a bell made the animal easier to find.

2. This is perhaps an essay titled "A Trapper on the Athabasca," which was later supplied by Malek to Thorington and appeared in *Where the Clouds Can Go* (1935).

101

Simpson Pass (Rockies), September 8, 1913

My dear friend:

Late last night I received your dear long letter, which ended with the news of my brother's death. I have to thank fate that you are my true friend at home and <u>through you</u> I hear all good and all sad news. It would be quite different if I would hear this news first from my unhappy mother. I have been prepared for this sad news for a long time, but still had some hope for improvement. You can imagine how I feel knowing that my brother is dead. During the last three or four weeks, I often wrote to him. For David, it might be better this way. He could have never become totally healthy. What makes my heart ache is that I have a caring mother who loves all of us very much, and, now, within a short time, she has lost two of her grown-up children! It is not easy for a mother's heart to bear such pain. I myself know very well that I must not dwell too deeply on all this sadness <u>otherwise my mother's pain gets even more bitter</u>. <u>Don't worry about me</u>. I will keep myself together and be strong. Last spring, I was <u>very</u> miserable, and I doubt things would have ended well had I lost another seven or eight kilograms. I thank you for your sympathy and consolation and, again, for everything that you did in words and action for my poor brother. In a few days, I will write more. We are now starting a long four-day tour, so I have no more time to write today. Received a letter from Miss Flora and will answer it after my return. Greetings, please, to your dear mother and sister, and to all my best friends for their sympathy and condolences. Your grateful and sad, far away friend, *C.K.*

102

Simpson Pass (Rockies), Main Camp, September 15, 1913

My dear Friend:

Last night we returned from our mobile camp. My diary says:

September 8. Wrote letter to A. about my brother's death. Afternoon with pack train (Hilly Creek) Mobile Camp. Weather nice. Tired.

September 9. Day of remembrance 1907 (Ennstal, Haindlkar, Peterspfad, Planspitze). Climbed mountain alone, made stone man signal alone. Poor climbing <u>with pole</u>, snowstorm. Lightening on top.[1] Descent to the valley and to Assiniboine Trail. Saw two black bears and one deer.

September 10. Rain and snow. Wrote an article for the *Österreichische Touristen Zeitung*. The whole day in camp.

September 11, 1913. Climbed another mountain alone. The others climbed Mt. Bushow. Saw two goats. Weather good. Found two petrified shells in limestone. Received letter from my brother, Eugen. Sad mood. —— Mr. Wheeler slightly injured (rock slide).

September 12. Climbed Mt. Bushow. Very warm. Steep grassy uphill. Saw sixteen goats. View good. Bow Valley, Banff. Found petrified rocks. Descent alone, rushed to camp to cook. All tired. Hard work. —

September 13. Ascending top together. Campbell and Bruckmann. All the men in camp. Snowstorm on top. Had to leave because of electricity. Saw a spectre after the storm. Interesting! Descent to Simpson

Pass. Reached main camp tired and hungry at 6:30. (End of copy from my diary).

——————————— Today, September 14th is a Sunday, day of rest.

The night was very cold. Hoarfrost. Now, it is sunny and warm. There is a beautiful autumn picture in front of us. The larch trees change colour. It has been a long time that I wrote you a long letter, and I know that I owe you many answers to various questions in your letter. The opportunity to write is not always there, and often it is too cold in the tent. You will notice the dirty writing paper, which one cannot keep clean. One interrupts, puts wood in the stove, etc. Often you finish the letter in a great rush, because the packer is going to ride into the village, etc. My news is that, during the winter, you will be visited by three people from New York. A lady from New York writes to me: "We go to Europe in the winter, and when we get to Vienna we will, according to your wish, visit your friends." —— The name of the lady is Wilcox. She was with me on Mt. Whitehorn and had to sleep in the rocks for a night. Mr. and Mrs. MacCarthy were also in the camp. Mr. MacCarthy was on Mt. Robson with me. These people were very nice to me, and I thought it would interest you to meet mountain climbers from here. I asked them to pay you a visit, if they should come to Vienna, and that they could get some information about Vienna from you, about Austria, and winter sports. They promised to visit you and Dr. P. Further, I can tell you, that I now have a writer as a friend here. He writes a lot for newspapers and magazines. He is a private secretary for Mr. Wheeler.[2] He thinks a lot of me and believes that we can make money. We already wrote two stories. I mentioned it in my letter to Flora. He also speaks German very well. Now about the article that I sent to you: how do you like it? Do you think the article is written well enough for a Vienna newspaper and will fit in as description of nature and strenuous effort? — I am also finished the article for the *Touristen Zeitung*, but I have yet to write a copy of it. I will translate it into English so we can sell the article to a magazine. I am sending the article to you for corrections.

I can only send the pictures when I get to Banff. I will get them from Mr. Harmon. I am sure many people will be astonished to read the description of a tour by a mountain guide! Edit as you see fit! I leave it to you with a good conscience. I also have to write to Reverend G. about skiing in America. In general, as a man of nature and a socialist, I do <u>not</u> like the Catholic clergy, because it is definitely true that the clergy prevented (in many a country it still does) the labourer and the farmer from getting too much schooling. Look at the Tyrol in Austria, and Ireland in Great Britain. That shows it all! Of course, now they lose power because, today, the farmer and every common labourer <u>appreciate</u> school and what one learns there! So, now, I have to answer a few things from your letter: the old lady from the *Orsova* writes that she is ailing and is homesick for England. Her son added a few lines and asked me to please his mother from time to time by writing a few lines. She still likes to talk about "the kind gentleman!" I have met many of my friends here again. Young Wilson is already in the mountains. Again, a real miracle! As you know, one bullet was removed from his body, but the second one is still in there, and his throat was stitched together and ——— he feels fine!! Good Simpson also has to fight: unhappy love!! Last summer, Jim fell in love with an American lady, who had been on a three week tour with him. — Of course, there were several others with this party. As far as I could see, the girl loves him, too. I saw her picture in Jim's house; it hangs above the fireplace. I asked him who she is. He sighed deeply and said, "Con, that is the girl my heart is longing for. She is the right one." Her parents are against a marriage, which bothers him a lot. I feel sorry for Simpson, because I know that he is a sincere, nature-loving fellow and would sure be a gentleman for his wife.[3] In America, things are not any more as they used to be. People are increasingly evaluating others by the stupid money in their pocket, and for their social position and rank, rather than for their character as a man. Now about Mr. Hollister! That is a good idea of yours, but, unfortunately, I cannot do it. I do know that Mr. Hollister thinks well of me and I am convinced that he could provide work for me through the winter. But <u>now</u>, I cannot think of something like that, because city life might at present be too dangerous for my health. My good comrade, you of course don't know how I felt physically and mentally last spring! Now, I am almost healthy again, but not like I used to be. I think if I stay in the free nature, everything might turn out good again. And for my soul, it is best when I am where there are dangers. Yes, the three words "Love of Life" have a great meaning. If life turns dull and flat, one has to go where there are dangers. Then life is worth something for you! That is what I can write to you about that subject. I wish you from my heart that God and your guardian angel will <u>never</u> lead you into such situations. I wish that you never find out what dull and boring means in the truest sense of the words. I received a letter from my brother, Eugen, in which he writes about dear David's funeral, where you were present and comforted everybody. For this, I thank you many times from the bottom of my heart. Eugen writes that mother is very sad and she would have rather had the funeral in Nasswald. Poor David would then have had a dignified send-off. —— The people in Nasswald have a good tradition that <u>everybody</u> attends a funeral, young or old, poor or rich. Wiener Neustadt is too far from Nasswald, and to transfer the body would have cost too much money. It pains me to think of my good mother. The poor lady was born to misfortune. I promise you not to get too upset, because I know that one can do nothing against the law of nature. If I get to Banff now, I will send a larger sum of money to my unhappy mother. This year is an unhappy one for me, and I will be glad when it is over. Just now, a few minutes ago, the packer of the other group came and brought the mail for me. Again sad news from poor Miss Maggee's nurse. The unhappy girl asked me whether it would be possible for me to see her once more in her life? If so, then she asks I come <u>immediately</u>, because she won't suffer much longer. The nurse writes that there is not much hope that the patient will live much longer. The letter was written on September 10th. It is impossible for me to go to Edmonton. I am terribly sorry, since I know that the poor lady has nobody in this country. As I wrote you, I visited Miss Maggee during my trip to Edmonton, brought her flowers and consoled her as well as I could. She was overjoyed by my visit and I noticed from our talk that she thinks well of me and trusts me. — I wish she would soon be released from her suffering, since there is no hope for her. I will write to her, respectively to the nurse (for she herself cannot read), a letter of sympathy. So, one bit of sad news comes after another. Miss Maggee is a well-educated lady and has suffered much hardship. Her father was an engineer and drowned in a train accident. Her mother died a long time ago. Her only brother was not very courteous and brotherly to her concerning their inheritance; he died two years ago on a trip to India and was buried in the ocean. To have a better life, Miss Maggee came to Canada and was always homesick. So, I can sympathize how she feels now in the hospital. Yes, many are born to misfortune. ———— I am also sending you some notes and hope to have more time when I come back from the survey. Now I must say Good bye. Very likely, you will not hear from me for two weeks. — With love and warmest regards, I am yours, *C.K.*

1. Later, Kain claimed this mountain was dubbed "Mt. Electricity Storm" (see Letter 111), but, today at least, no mountain officially bears that title.

2. Kain is referring to Paul A.W. Wallace (1891–1967), Wheeler's camp secretary in 1912 and 1913, who later became a renowned historian, anthropologist, and folklorist, and the author of several books on colonial relations among Aboriginals and European settlers in the eighteenth century. In his short tenure with the ACC, Wallace penned several articles related to mountaineering, including several related to Kain's ascent of Mt. Robson. Kain's own account, which appeared in the 1914–1915 *CAJ*, for instance, was translated by Wallace. Kain, "The First Ascent of Mount Robson," 19–28. Also see Paul A.W. Wallace, "Climbing the Big Peaks: An Account of Alpine Climbing, 1913, by A.O. Wheeler's Camp Secretary, Paul A.W. Wallace," *Crag and Canyon* (Banff, AB), August 30, 1913, 3.

3. Originally from England, Jimmy Simpson (1877–1972) began working in the Rockies in 1898 as a cook, guide, and outfitter under the tutelage of Tom Wilson and Bill Peyto (1869–1943); Simpson described the latter as his "teenage hero." E.J. Hart, *Jimmy Simpson: Legend of the Rockies* (Banff: Altitude, 1999), 14. Like Wilson and Peyto, Simpson, too, became a legendary figure in the Rockies. In fact, Simpson's lodge, *Num-Ti-Jah*, which he built on the shores of Bow Lake during the 1930s, remains in operation to this day. As for the picture above his fireplace, it probably didn't hang for too long. In March, 1913, Simpson met Scotland-born Williamina "Billie" Ross Reid (1891–1968), who immigrated to Canada late in 1911. They sustained a relationship mostly through written correspondence until Reid moved to Calgary in 1915. A year later, they were married. Their union lasted 52 years. See Hart, *Jimmy Simpson*, 89–94.

103

Near Simpson Pass, September 18, 1913

Dear Amelie:

I am sure somewhere today our thoughts will cross: a year ago,
we went together to Knofeleben, Baumgartner-Haus (dear, old
Schneeberg!), Krummbachgraben–Kaiserbrunn. Hadn't we a lovely
walk together and a comfortable talk? These hours had been happy
ones, and I shall always remember the date and place. I wonder,
where you may be now? — I am sitting here under a big cliff on a
ledge of a rather fine mountain near Simpson Pass. I am hunting for
goats and I am quite alone by myself, nobody round me. Yet somebody is round me in my thoughts, with whom I am speaking now,
while I am writing these lines. I think it is nice that we have a brain
and can remember so many things in the past. This morning, I was
sent out hunting, and so I took the writing-map along with me.
I tried to write in English as nicely as I can. Let me tell you of my
surroundings: Here on the right is my rifle and pack. In front of me
across the valley these big Alps. Below there is a fine timber with
some larches in yellow colour amongst it. It gives a fine fall-picture.
The weather is not very good. — There is lots of new snow on the
higher mountains. Soon it will be snowing again. Till now I have not
seen any sign of game. I do not feel too bad but a little homesick. I
hope to get over it alright again. These days I have been thinking of
you so often and of your dear mother and Flora, as well as of my own
people. You will understand that. My heart is in good condition, and
I can walk as always and go on hunting-trips. I am often wondering if
I can have sometimes so happy hours again as I had in my old home?

Well, it is getting cold now, and I have to move on a little. —————
—————— Now I can tell you more: I shot a goat round the
mountains here!! Poor little thing! I do feel sorry for it, but we must
have the meat!! I light a fire here in the woods; by and by my little tea
kettle will be boiling and I shall have a cup of hot tea. I wish I could
say: "Miss Amelie, come on, have a cup of tea with me, won't you?"
Well, the tea is made, and I have a good lunch for when I go back to
the camp. A very bad storm is coming over the mountains from the
South! Good bye! —

In the camp, 3:30 P.M. It took me some hours to reach the camp with
my heavy load. Everybody had been pleased with my shooting! I got
into the bad storm, and now it is snowing like in winter! Very bad
weather for our work! If the weather keeps on like this, we shall soon
go back to Banff. I am looking forward to my mail and hope there
will be a letter from you waiting for me. I wonder where I shall be the
next 18th September? Wherever I might be, I will not forget to write
you again. You will see! There are some days that I will not forget as
long as I am alive. These are: the 6th September 1906, 9th September
1907, 31th August 1912, 18th September 1912, 12th November 1912, and
10th July of every year!![1]

[In German from hereon]

Now begins the copy from my notebook since September 14.

September 15, 1913. Did surveying at Bill Peyto's camp. —

September 16, 1913. The same. Bill is an old prospector, a trapper,
guide, a real western character! I have known him for three years! Bill
is full of memories and knows strenuous work.[2]

September 17, 1913. Moved camp five miles across the mountains.
Horse falls, wounded at one hind leg. A miracle it isn't dead. Arrival
at camp 5 P.M.

As described. It snows terribly now. Perhaps we have to quit. Then I will go with Mr. Wheeler to Crowsnest Pass for two weeks. I have not heard from the gentleman about the winter trip. Maybe it won't come about? Then I must return to the forest, as I wrote you already. Now you will soon receive my last letters. I am already curious how you will like the article about the life of a trapper. I have copied the article for the *Touristen Zeitung* correctly. The two days working near Peyto's camp near Simpson Pass were interesting. Bill is an old, honest man of the woods. He comes from Banff. Bill always has to tell something new. Luck has not always been with him all his life, but, in spite of it, he was happy. Eight years ago, he lost his wife. He said, "if she would still be alive, I would be 10 to 15 years further from the grave."[3] I know from other people, too, that he was not "the old Bill" anymore for a long time. He looks rough and rugged like a wildcat!! His eyes are unusually blue. If you look at him without talking to him you can easily understand that people are afraid of him. But this is only on the outside. I think I know him better. He is one of the Western characters: totally independent, doffs his cap to nobody, talks like he thinks, without any qualms. If somebody comes to him with problems, he will meet a soft hearted man. —— I hope you are all well. This letter will be in Banff in about a week. — Now Good bye, my dear friend at home. With my love to you and your people, I am yours, *C.K.*

1. With the exception of 10 July, which was Malek's name day, these were all dates that Kain spent with Malek in Austria: Amelie and her sister, Flora, spent 6 September 1906 with Kain on the Hochtor (2,369 m [7,772 ft.]), the highest mountain in the Ennstal Alps of Styria; on 9 September 1907, Kain led Amelie up the Petern Route on the Planspitze (see Kain, *Where the Clouds*, 154), also in the Enns Valley; 31 August 1912 was the occasion when Kain returned to Austria to be welcomed at the train station by the Malek family; a few weeks later, on 18 September 1912, he and Malek were on the Rax; and, lastly, 12 November 1912 was when he said his farewells and left Austria.

2. Englishman Ebenezer William "Bill" Peyto arrived in western Canada in 1887 and, still a teenager, found work as a railway labourer. In 1890, he briefly took up ranching and even settled northwest of

Cochrane, Alberta, but in 1893 he moved to the Rockies to work for Tom Wilson as a guide, packer, and outfitter out of Banff. Howard E. Sibbald (1865–1938), the first chief game guardian for Rocky Mountains Park, later hired Peyto as a deputy park warden in the spring of 1913. Built before Peyto joined the Warden Service, his cabin at Simpson Pass was regularly used as a warden patrol cabin thereafter. Burns, *Guardians*, 9, 15, 32.

3. Peyto married Emily Wood in Banff in 1902. Tragically, she died in 1906 of a brain hemorrhage. Not long after, Peyto gave up his outfitting business in Banff for a more solitary existence of mining and prospecting in the Simpson Pass area.

104

On top of Mt. Wonder (about 9,500 ft.), east of Mt. Assiniboine

September 26, 1913, 12:30

Dear Friend Amelie:

There are many days in life when life isn't worth much. But today is a day when one can see wonders of nature and has joy in life! — I am lying here on top of Mt. Wonder. Some yards away, Mr. Wheeler and Mr. Campbell are working with their instruments. I only try to describe the beauty to you, I know it is impossible, but I have the good will! Already the name Mount Wonder must tell you a lot. Three hours ago, the mountain was still nameless. We were right to christen it Mount Wonder. The top is on the Great Divide. The water on the eastern side has a long trip to make to the Atlantic, on the south-western side to the Pacific Ocean. On the Atlantic side are two lakes deep in the valley. One is one-and-a-half miles long, the other a half mile. We named both: the longer one Marvel Lake, the other Wonder Lake. The latter has an undescribably green-blue colour, hence the name. Marvel Lake is deep blue and has a few tiny isles. Around these, the water is not very deep, hence the varied colours. — Both lakes have thick forests of fir and spruce around them. 600 metres below the top, three wild goats are lying in the grass, enjoying a sunbath. As far as the eye can see, nothing but mountains from 7,000 ft. to 11,000 ft. high. Now, the Pacific side: first, I see mountain meadows and lower down I can count seven lakes; there is green forest and Mt. Assiniboine, which in its shape resembles the Matterhorn very much![1] In the West and South, I see high, snow-covered mountains. At the foot of Mt. Assiniboine, there is a lake, perhaps one-and-a-half miles long, and the glacier runs directly into it. Some little icebergs swim in it aimlessly. Our camp is at the shore of this lake in a forest of larch trees, which are all in the colourful fall foliage. Any man, any person, who can <u>see</u> such a picture would be truly <u>happy</u> about it. And I do feel happy in the peace and calmness of nature. — I think of you and many other friends of nature. I wish everybody an opportunity to see such a wonderful scene. I will take two stones from this peak: one I send to you, and one I will keep for myself. Once you have this rock in your hand and in your beautiful room, you will remember that your good friend far away had been thinking of you when he saw this miracle of nature, and that somebody travels in the big world who remembers you fondly at an area where the peace of the mountains reigns. I know that today and the following days of this month are sad days for you and yours. — I am thousands of miles away, but I feel with you all. ——— I have a few more minutes time, then I have to build a stone man. In the evening, I will continue writing. Tomorrow, Mr. Wheeler goes to Banff and takes the letter along. We are three days away from Banff. In one week, we too will leave the mountains. So now I finish my lines on top of Mt. Wonder. I look around once more and reread my lines.

———

At the camp, 7 P.M. We stopped on another hill and reached camp at 6:45 P.M., rather tired. My notes in my notebook (since September 18) are as follows:

September 19, 1913. Start 7:15 A.M., snow, cold. Climbed mountain. On top old stone man. Since 10:30, view beautiful. Deep down view to Brewster Creek, Bow Valley, two small lakes. On top very cold and windy. This season already <u>too late</u> for work on top. 4:30 in camp. Conversation about religion and socialism.

September 20, 1913. Move camp towards Mt. Assiniboine. Descent of 500 feet, trail very poor. Windfalls. Horses fall. At 3 P.M., stop for camp. Good meadow for horses, forest beautiful, green moss. Two small lakes, waterfall, fresh tracks of a moose. Good camp fire.

September 21, 1913, Sunday. At 10 A.M., ascent of mountain, first through windfall and across very pronounced moraines (soft limestone). Then strenuous climb over grassy slopes and scree to the top. I had a gun and went from the top to hunt for meat. At noon, we got a storm, fog and snow. Found nothing. Minor accident: broken rock fell four to five metres, minor injury to my hip. In my mind, I thought and talked with Amelie.

September 22, 1913. Snow in camp. Mended socks. The packer Warren was with me in the tent, we talked about our bachelor life: no home, nobody cares for you (unfortunately not a chance for a change at this time).[2] W. told me about India. The cook was hunting, one goat, was pleased.

September 23, 1913. Moved camp to the base of Mt. Assiniboine. Snow. Trail poor. Passed a lake, nice view. Camp at foot of alpine meadow next to the lake, weather warm.

September 24, 1913. Start 6:30 through forest. Snow on mountain north of the camp. Hard 3 ½ hour climb to mountain top. View marvellous! Sun warm (sunbath). On top of the mountain continued writing the article *The Lady-Climber*. 4:00 in the camp. Good fire. Talk about the war in Africa. Had disagreements. I and Brinkman were against the war.

September 26, 1913. At Noble Hill northwest of Mt. Assiniboine. View down to the lakes. A wonderful alpine picture! I could kiss nature! Thought of home and my dear mother. Saw a goat, built two stonemen and "castles in the air"!! — Would like to be a great writer!! 6:30 at the camp, roast goose, very good! (End of copy from my notebook)

I hope you are satisfied with the length of my letters. Another six days and I will get a letter from you. The last one I received September 7th. From now on, I will always copy my diary notes for you. I don't know why I did not think of that sooner? Now I must say Good bye. I hope you are all very well. Don't worry about me. I am alright now. When I get to Banff, I will have my picture taken and will send you one. Give my best love to your dear mother and Flora. With warmest regards, I am your true friend in the western woods, *C.K.*

1. At 3,618 metres (11,870 ft.), Mt. Assiniboine is the highest peak in the southern ranges of the Canadian Rockies. Due to its pyramidal shape, it was popularly called the "Matterhorn" of North America. The mountain was given its name, "Assiniboine," by surveyor George M. Dawson (1849–1901), in 1885, to honour the First Nations peoples in the eastern front ranges. From the nearby Mt. Copper, Dawson first saw Assiniboine with a distinctive plume of clouds trailing from its summit and, thus, likened it to smoke emanating from a Great Plains teepee. Mt. Assiniboine rises nearly 1,525 metres (5,003 ft.) above Lake Magog.

2. Born in Sussex, England, William "Billy" Warren (1880–1943) arrived in Banff in 1903 and found employment as a packer with Tom Wilson's outfit. Warren soon became a regular guide for Philadelphian Mary Schäffer, and with his assistant, fellow Englishman Sid Unwin (1881–1917), guided Schäffer's now-famous expedition in search of *Chaba Imne* (Maligne Lake) in 1907, as well as the successful trip to the lake and beyond the following year. During the 1908 expedition, Schäffer named Mt. Warren (3,300 m [10,824 ft.]) in honour of the guide. "There are older ones (guides)," Schäffer wrote, "there are better hunters, perhaps, with wider experience in forest lore, more knowledge of the country, but for kindness, good nature (such a necessary adjunct), good judgment under unexpected stress, he had no superior." Quoted from Jill Foran, *Mary Schäffer: An Adventurous Woman's Exploits in the Canadian Rockies* (Canmore, AB: Altitude, 2003), 44. Warren continued to guide Schäffer each summer until they were eventually married in 1915. In 1919, Warren gave up outfitting and became one of Banff's more prominent businessmen.

105

Banff, Alta, October 11, 1913, 12:25 P.M.

Dear Friend:

Yesterday, we returned from the forest and the mountains. Am
healthy and happy. I received so many letters and cards, also many
from home: a letter from Miss Flora and from you. I read it quickly,
have to study it later in the evening. Now I have no time, have to work
hard, but the clock shows 12:30 and the date October 11, *[In English
from hereon]* a day I will always remember. Tell me, had it also been
a happy day for you? Just now, a year ago, we had been by the Riss
on the Oberen Zimmersteig of our dear Rax! A year has gone by. It
had been a very bad one for me in most regards. But there is a small
paper in front of me on the table. The words I read on this paper tell
me that I shall have the great pleasure of seeing you and your dear
mother and Flora and your home. Yes, and my home, too, and my
mother and everyone. Yes, I shall be there in spring, dear friend of
nature, dear friend of flowers and my dear Kamerad! We shall look
at all beauties of the spring together; we shall listen together to the
call of the cuckoo! There will be SPRING FOR ME ONCE MORE!

—————

106

Crowsnest, Great Divide (B.C. and Alta),

October 19, 1913.

Dear Amelie:

[In German from hereon] Yesterday, I sent a card and two big letters to you. As you see, the second trip to New Zealand will materialize. Before I say more about it, I have to write what my diary says. It has been a while since I wrote my experiences from my diary, hasn't it? Now follows a copy from my diary:

September 27, Saturday. Climbed mountain northwest of Mt. Assiniboine, reached top at 3:40, cold, windy, half frozen. Built two stonemen. Descent to the lake across iced-up rock. Very dangerous. Everybody tired in camp. Brinkman totally exhausted.

September 28, Sunday. In camp resting and washday. We search for the horses. Saw a bull moose. Lake and north fork of Cross Creek made a marvellous autumn scene.

September 29. Rain and snow. Terribly cold. Too cold to write. Read a book, *The Class Struggle*, a book that opens your eyes.[1]———

September 30. Climbed mountain from Marvel Lake station. Ascent long and easy. Saw two goats and found a sheep's head with horns. View great. When I built a stone man, I had sad thoughts. Indescribably sad. Early in camp.

October 1. Station on mountain, named it *Mount Hill*. Built two stonemen. Weather fine, view fabulous. View deep down to Spray Valley. Early in camp. Dreamt of Hollister.

October 2. Warren came with mail. Had letter and card from Amelie, Flora, brother, from G.T.R., Frind, Miss H. and Broadbent sent pictures, mostly good news. —

October 3. 10 A.M. start. Said farewell to these mountains. Via Grand Creek to Spray Lakes, snow, path very poor, it snows like in winter, 6 P.M. camp at Spray Lake.

October 4. Gave a day of rest to the horses. Stayed in camp, snowing, re-wrote article about Mt. Robson. Afternoon, Sidney and Jack back from grizzly hunt with bearskin! Great!

October 5. Start 10 A.M. past large lake, one ft. of snow, very poor for walking. Winter scenery. Two hours. Camp at White Man Pass.

October 6. Start 9 A.M. Last day with pack train, path good, six miles on road (Spray Road). Two hours. In Banff, Club House. Had to cut wood right away. Got telegram from Frind: "Travel New Zealand, reserved seat on steamer." Found more letters in Banff. My friend Fred Chanter has gone crazy, wants to commit suicide. Poor faithful fellow! Evening in village. —

October 7. Headache, palpitations. Had to cut wood. Received news from Amelie, sad and cheerful ones.

October 8. Did not feel well. Perhaps the change of air? Stayed in bed.

October 9. Work around the house. Wheeler gave advice: I should settle down after winter travels, have a home, get married, make money. He means well, but unfortunately — Evening in the village. Fred had an attack, wanted to cut his throat. ——

October 10. Work in the house. Rain and snow. Had my picture taken.

October 11. Day of remembrance. (A year ago with Amelie on the Zimmersteig). Evening in the theatre. Got a suit for $29.00, fits very well! —

October 12. Day of remembrance. (With Flora on the Zimmersteig). Work at the house, rain. Mountains snowed in. Last day at the Club House. Dictated *The Ascent of Mount Robson* to Mr. Wallace for the English Alpine Club.[2]

October 13. 4 A.M. locked house, farewell from Mr. Mitchell and Miss Laboda. Saw Fred, got pictures from Harmon.

October 14. Took train to Calgary. Met Mr. Wheeler. Evening at the theatre, marvellous show! Pictures of nature in Africa and India. Stayed overnight at Queen's Hotel. It is great to sleep in a bed!! —

October 15. Saw friends, 6 P.M. departure. Arrival in McLeod 11 P.M. Fine hotel! (American).

October 16. 7:25 A.M. by train to Crowsnest, 11 hrs, camp half a mile from Pass next to Cautley's camp (Crowsnest–Divide).[3] Around us fine mountains, 9,000 to 10,000 ft.

October 17. Made comfortable camp, built table and shelves for cooking utensils.

October 18. In camp, I am the cook. Mr. Wallace with us. Wrote cards, posted letters.

——————— Today, October 19th, is a day of rest. First, many thanks for your dear letter. I received it just at a time when I needed encouragement. Day after tomorrow, the 21st, we will depart from here via Calgary to Banff. There, I will get a nice suit, perhaps stay a night, then I'll travel to Vancouver. On October 29th, I board a steamer for New Zealand. I am getting paid to travel this time, which I like very much. The gentleman with whom I travel is a very rich German-Canadian, perhaps as old as I am.[4] He wrote that we might stay in New Zealand until the middle of March. Once he mentioned Corsica, but did not say anymore in his last letter. But I hope that I can come home for a few months, since the trip from New Zealand to Europe does not cost more than to America. Now, something about my essay. How did it go with the article for the *Naturfreunde?* What did you say to the description of Mt. Robson? I am sending you the relevant pictures, have some here, but want those on glossy paper. I also will send you the 1910 book of the Alpine Club. In it, there is much about Mt. Robson. Then I am sending a magazine, *Canada,* in which the Alpine Club camp is described. As you will read, the author did not forget me! After reading this magazine, please send it as a loan to Mr. v.H. Perhaps it will please him or the Section. It contains good pictures. If he doesn't understand English, perhaps his daughter can read it to him. Now, how was it in the Tyrol? I was so pleased when I studied your letter. How happy you were, and how you admired and greeted all the mountains and peaks! I thank you ever so much for your prayer in Mariazell![5] That was very kind indeed. I hope I will receive your travelogue and card still in Canada, otherwise <u>much</u> time will pass until I will receive them! Please write to New Zealand to the old address again, c/o G.P.O. Wellington. Will you write me, too, about what I should bring you back from my trip around the world? Please give me an idea! — I know how I will please you, but that you will only see when we meet again! And what could I bring for your dear mother and Flora? Before I leave Canada, I will ask your dear mother for a special favour, her permission for an excursion for several days, and I am convinced that your mother will not say "No"! Flora wrote me a very dear letter, I owe her an answer, too. I wrote a few lines to the priest and included a few post cards. So now I have to cook!! — Will continue in the evening. —

Only a few days and the season will be over. This summer, I worked very hard and passed—as always—through many dangers and got out of them well and happy. You know how I lived with constant worry and great sorrow about my poor brother and little sister. Besides, I myself was not as healthy and strong as usual. However, I kept all these worries to myself, except what I revealed to you. So very often, I was tired in the morning and pretended to be cheerful and did not show anything. It is not easy to go around with a friendly face and a laugh, when the heart is sad. But what can you do? One cannot reveal one's worries to everybody, and, after all these happenings, I am a little beaten, what you call "run down" in English. I cannot say that I am really sick. In Banff, I was really unwell for several days. But now, I feel quite well. Yes, I can see that a man who has to work hard and strenuously must not begin to think too much about everything. Now, I will go on the ocean again, and this time I travel in a better class. I hope I can recover by resting a lot. If it is possible, I will write diligently on the entries in my diary. Last night, Mr. Wheeler asked what problems or sorrows I had this summer, and so I told him that I lost two siblings and that I was very concerned about my sad mother. This summer, Mr. Wheeler was a totally different person. Everybody says that. Never before had he been so good-humoured and agreeable. This summer, I did not hear a single cross word from him! You will see in the *Canadian Alpine Journal* (1912) that he thinks a lot of me. Mr. Wheeler always suggests that I should settle down, get married, and start a business, and that he would surely support me. He means well, but I cannot explain my feelings about marriage to a person who, in this case, has different views. I cannot think about these things, no, no, that would be too much for me. I now think about my winter journey around the world and that, if everything goes well, I can see my poor mother and my best friends again. I fear no dangers and will trust my luck in the future. In addition to the terrible loss of my brother and sister, I am burdened with the sadness about my good friend Fred Chanter, an Englishman in Banff. He is mentally ill, as I already wrote, and his case is hopeless. He was a very good friend of mine. Then, there is the sad story of Miss Maggee. She is still alive, but her condition is also hopeless. I got a letter from one of her lady friends whom I met two years ago. She writes that Miss Maggee often loses her mind for days. Of course, sad cases like that happen to everybody who has friends. Now I will close for today. I will write another letter before I leave Canada and will answer all the questions from your last letter. I hope that you and your family are well and wish you that you stay healthy for a long, long time.

[In English from hereon] Now Good bye in English! Fare well, dear friend Amelie. I am wishing you the best of luck in everything and I am thankful to you for all your kindness. With best love, I am yours, *C.K.*

1. *The Class Struggle* (1892) was written by Karl Kautsky (1854–1938), a Czech-German philosopher and politician, and a leading theoretician of Marxism. In fact, he became the leading promulgator of orthodox Marxism—he was even called "the pope of Marxism"—after the death of Friedrich Engels in 1895. Massimo Salvadori, *Karl Kautsky and the Socialist Revolution, 1880–1938* (London: Verso, 1990).

2. Kain, "The First Ascent of Mount Robson," 19–28.

3. While the work of the Topographical Division of the Boundary Survey officially concluded for 1913 in early October, a preliminary survey was made later the same month at Crowsnest Pass, where, according to the commission's report, "work was carried over about five miles of the distance but, owing to heavy frosts, no concrete monuments were at that time constructed. A certain amount of preliminary work was also done in a small pass a little more than a mile north of Crowsnest Pass. The Commissioners [Cautley and Wheeler] were here unable to come to an agreement for the proper location of the watershed, on account of certain peculiarities of the topographic formation." Cautley, Wallace, and Wheeler, *Report of the Commission Appointed to Delimit the Boundary between the Provinces of Alberta and British Columbia, Part I, From 1913 to 1916*, 56–57.

4. Kain was only four years older than Herbert Otto Frind, a Torontonian, who was schooled in Leipzig, Germany. Frind accompanied his grandmother on a visit to New Zealand in 1909 and remained there, delighted with the scenery and people, until 1911. He first visited the Rockies in 1912 and attended the ACC's Vermilion Pass Camp, after which he joined a club party on an exploratory mountaineering expedition to Vancouver Island. The latter experience instilled in him a passion for the out-of-doors that became a ruling interest in his life. See F.C.B., "Herbert Otto Frind," *CAJ* 45 (1962): 166–68.

5. Well-known for its winter sports, Mariazell is a town in the northern Styrian Alps. In the early twentieth century, however, it was best known as one of the most important Roman Catholic pilgrimage sites in Austria.

107

[In German from hereon]

Vancouver, B.C., Grandview Hotel

October 19, 1913

My dear Comrade:

I hope you received all my things, books, letters, and card. Your last card was from Riva at Lake Garda.[1] Since Saturday, I have been in Vancouver. We depart today at noon. I am sorry to say that it was no pleasure to be here. I was sick, had to stay in bed Sunday, and Monday was spent with a bad cold. Some friends came to visit. Yesterday, I was up and went to the theatre in the evening. I think the illness is nothing but a cold, but I have awful headaches and a somewhat nervous heartbeat. But I will go on board ship. I am sending you two pictures for the *Touristen-Zeitung* (Mt. Robson). I hope they don't arrive too late. I am sorry that I will not hear from you for so long. <u>When</u> will I receive your letter from October? And <u>where</u>? —— Please send a copy of my article to Miss Catherine B. Hollowes, Croften Schoolhouse, Vancouver, B.C. Well, I must go, the steamer blows the horn. Here you find three handkerchiefs, one for each of you. Perhaps that pleases you a little? The next letter will come from Honolulu. I hope I feel better in a few days. At the moment, I feel miserable. With heartiest greetings, your sincere friend *C.K.*

1. A popular tourist destination, Riva (or Riva del Garda) was a resort town in the northern Italian province of Trentino. Prior to 1918, it belonged to the Austro-Hungarian Empire. It is located on the northwestern shores of Lake Garda at the southern edge of the Italian Alps near the Dolomites.

108

On board *The Makura*, November 1, 1913.

My dear Friend:

The last three days have not been good. Today, however, I feel pretty
good. We have stormy weather and most ladies are seasick. I pity
them all. Now I have to tell you something about the ship. *The
Makura* has 8,000 tons.[1] I travel second class, my gentleman first
class. Of course, I travel much better than in third class. I think it is
inhuman to have a third class at all. I understand that one cannot
change anything now. The food is pretty good, in the evening there
are daily concerts. The steamer is occupied to the last berth, because
now is the time when many Australians and New Zealanders are
returning home for their summer. Up until now, I've only been
acquainted with an old doctor from Melbourne, a very nice and
educated gentleman, and a freethinker, too. He likes to talk about the
social-progressive movement. I can imagine what you are doing now.
You commemorate this very day. Perhaps you are standing with a sad
heart and tearful eyes at the grave of your dear papa. Or you are on
your way to the cemetery where I so often accompanied you. A year
ago today, I was in Kaiserbrunn at noon, and in the evening I was
invited to your house. I hope you will feel particularly well after your
beautiful trip. Oh, how will it be until I will hear from you! — The
storm gets worse, I must stop writing. ——

——————— November 2, 1913

Today, Sunday, the weather is beautiful. People are coming alive
again. The night was still somewhat stormy, but now the ocean is
calm like a lake in the woods. The sun shines and we are all on deck.

Just now, the bell rang for church service, but it seems nobody goes downstairs. I cannot blame people, because the sun does more good for you than a sermon in the poor air of the cabin. November 2nd is also a "remembrance day." Our last walk goes through nature is my memory. And where am I today? And where I have been during the last year! Well, Good bye.

——————— November 3, 1913.

Again a beautiful day! The sun is shining warmly, a sign that we go southwards. In the morning, I assisted a seasick lady on the promenade deck. Then, later, I had a discussion with the old doctor from Melbourne about people and their health in the north and in the south. Then I played a ring-toss game with a group and I lost. Now, I sit in the writing room and read a book that my gentleman brought over for me: *Pioneer's Work in the Alps of New Zealand*.[2] Last night, I had a dream about home, in which I also saw you and Flora. ——

——————— November 4, 1913.

Last night, we saw a sunset that brought back many memories. In the afternoon, I played bridge with three ladies (two English ladies and one from New Zealand). Of course, I always enjoy company. It was warm throughout the night, and I think that, from now on, I will sleep on deck. Today, it was <u>very</u> warm. I am sitting in the sun and write these lines. The ocean is calm. Now and then, a fish catches some fresh air!! What might you be doing now? Perhaps packing things for the return to Vienna? Or perhaps you are already in the old city of Vienna! Maybe you have received my books and pictures? I am already so curious how you will find the book *Camp-fires in the Canadian Rockies!*[3] I am convinced that you will often think about the life in camp. In Vienna, you will now be busy with cleaning your home. I just got a book to read from the old doctor on board and have already read a few pages. Its title is *The Freethinker*.[4] Will write you later how I like it. —— We always have all sorts of arguments in the smoking room. One often asks for my opinion. Of course, I don't play the silent one when I am asked. Tonight, we have a dance and lectures on deck. Tomorrow, we will be in Honolulu. ————— With heartiest greetings, your wandering friend, *C.K.*

1. The RMS *Makura* was built by the Union Steamship Company of New Zealand in 1908. Designed specifically for the Australian–Canadian trade, the steamer was the largest in the Union Company's fleet, being a vessel of 8,075 tons. The vessel worked the Pacific routes of the Union Company for twenty-eight years linking Auckland, Sydney, Suva, Honolulu, Vancouver or Wellington, Sydney, Rarotonga, Tahiti, and San Francisco.

2. *Pioneer Work in the Alps of New Zealand: A record of the first exploration of the chief glaciers and ranges of the Southern Alps* (London: T.F. Unwin, 1896) was one of the first mountaineering guide-books to the Southern Alps of New Zealand. Its author, Arthur Paul Harper (1865–1955)—known much of his life as AP or APH—made numerous holiday excursions to the Tasman district in the years 1889–1892 and, for the three following years, was employed by the New Zealand government to explore the valleys and glaciers of the west coast of the South Island. Along with Malcolm Ross and George Mannering (1862–1947), Harper helped form the NZAC in 1891 and was the club's president from 1914–1932. See Graham Langton, "Harper, Arthur Paul—Biography," *Dictionary of New Zealand Biography, Te Ara—the Encyclopedia of New Zealand*, available at http://www.TeAra.govt.nz/en/biographies/4h17/1

3. Published in 1906, *Camp-fires in the Canadian Rockies* was written by William Temple Hornaday (1854–1937), an American conservationist and sportsman, and chronicled his and John M. Phillips's 1905 hunting exploits in the Elk and Bull Rivers region of the East Kootenays. William T. Hornaday, *Camp-fires in the Canadian Rockies* (New York: Charles Scribner, 1906).

4. Founded in 1881, *The Freethinker* was a British secular humanist journal that took a hard anti-religion stance. In its first issue, its editor, the outspoken critic of religion George William Foote (1850–1915), wrote that "the Freethinker is an anti-Christian organ, and must therefore be chiefly aggressive. It will wage a relentless war against superstition in general, and against Christian superstition in particular. It will do its best to employ the resources of Science, Scholarship, Philosophy and Ethics against the claims of the bible as a Divine Revelation; and it will not scruple to employ for the same purpose any weapons of ridicule or sarcasm that may be borrowed from the armory of Common Sense." G.W. Foote, *The Freethinker* 1 (May, 1881): 1.

109

On board *The Makura*, November 6, 1913

My dear Comrade:

Yesterday, November 6th, we reached Honolulu at 2 P.M. I mailed a letter and a card for you. Honolulu is, of course, very beautiful, but not like I imagined. First, we strolled through the most beautiful streets, which were built after American patterns. Then, I went to the slums, where the Japanese and the Chinese are. It does not look very nice there. I was alone. Then, I took the streetcar out to the swimming pool, which was very good. I met some people from the boat there. On my way back, I stayed in a park for half an hour. It was nice among the flowering trees, the flowers, the many birds! Of course, I thought of you. —— It would be twice or three times as beautiful, if you could stroll through a tropical garden with Flora and me! I walked back into town, bought a shell for you and a magazine. At 10 P.M., we departed. Today, it is terribly hot. I perspired and am wet through and through. So I close for today. I hope you received the book already. Good bye.

——————— November 7, 1913

Good Morning, dear friend Amelie!

I just saw the sunrise at 5:30. You know that I think of you when I see something beautiful in nature. Last night, I barely slept at all. Too warm! And during the day it gets even warmer, so I would rather write a few lines now. I think I will stay on this ship and continue on to Australia and will visit the old lady (if she is still alive), then I would like to see the Blue Mountains of Australia. They are supposed to be

exceptionally beautiful! My gentleman also goes to Sidney. We shall
begin "our work" in New Zealand on December 20th. I will spend the
Christmas holidays in the mountains! I am in very good company
on the ship, but often I like to be alone. Yes, I am sending thoughts
and waving my arms to the mountains of home and to my friends.

———— I take a bath now and continue writing later, if it is not too
warm. Good bye. —

————————— November 8, 1913

Yesterday, I could not write anymore. It was too hot. I took two baths.
There is no wind so all the rooms on board are very stuffy. And on
deck, the burning sun! It is actually boring, when it is so warm.
Everybody is tired, one cannot read or write, and even eating is a
chore. In the evening, there was a rain storm, which was pleasant.
Many ladies fainted in the midday heat. It was 140 degrees Fahrenheit
(equals 60 degrees Celsius). Today it is great. I sit on deck. Most
passengers are still sleeping. It is 5:45. The sunrise was not spectacular, but that means it won't be so hot during the day. I am now
reading the book *Freethinker*. I like it. It is a book for friends of
nature and for people who think open and free. I would like to send
it to you, but I don't know whether you would read it because it is
written against the church, especially the Catholic Church. But the
Protestant Church is not left out either. You know that I don't think
highly of churches. I find my God in the stillness of nature. —

————————— November 9, 1913.

Sunday. There was a gorgeous sunrise. I slept on deck on a bench.
Breakfast is at 9 A.M. It will be another hot day. I am sitting on
deck, travelling is beautiful. I am glad that I travel second class. It is
supposed to be awful in third class.[1] I must say again, it is a shame
that on such a long journey people are treated like animals. I hope
that I will never again have to travel third class. I am against oppres-
sion. Each human being, each labourer, should be paid well enough

that he can travel like "a human being." It really opens your eyes when you look at life like that. Many people do not know how to spend the day and the time. Thousands of people don't know how and what they will live on tomorrow. Many millionaires spend more on women and wine in one evening than a common labourer earns in a year. Governments collect monies for new deadly weapons! Who pays all these taxes? Where does the money come from? Who wants more soldiers? Who says "soldiers" lives are governed by God, if God says in the Fifth Commandment "THOU SHALL NOT KILL!!" —
The world is big and rich, and yet there are thousands and thousands of people who don't know where to get work, housing, and food. And that is the same in every country. Perhaps it is good that people wander around hungry and without a roof over their head, because they <u>learn</u> through hunger and misery that they are ruined by exploitative laws. I am convinced there <u>has</u> to be change, and my wish would be that everything would happen without bloodshed. —— I have to end this topic. —— At 9:30 P.M., we will cross the Equator. For me, it is the third time. I wish you would have once the opportunity to take that long trip to the South. Of course, it would be great for me to take the same trip, at the same time, and on the same boat (!!), because I know that you and Flora would get seasick! I would nurse you, my dear friends; yes, I would look after you! Well, it is getting too warm for writing. Good bye! I hope that you are already in Vienna and that you are alright. ———

———————— November 12, 1913

A day of remembrance: today, a year ago, I said farewell to you and yours. I must not think of it too much, because I feel very emotional when I think of everything. In my mind, I go through all these thoughts. I am a sad and lonely boy. ——

———————— November 17, 1913

A few days, ago we were in Suva (capital of the Fiji Islands) on the Island of Viti Levu. I went ashore and walked in the gardens. I did not feel well, and I am also not really healthy right now. But don't worry, dear friend. In a few days, I will be alright again. It is very warm. In a few days we will get to Auckland, N.Z. Good bye. Yours, *C.K.*

———————— Sidney, Australia, December 17, 1913

True Comrade:

Don't get scared when I tell you that, for three weeks, I was in a sana-torium in Manly, near Sidney.[2] It had to be. I was, as one says, "totally exhausted." The stay in the sanatorium was good for me. Today, I will be discharged. I feel much better now, and, tomorrow, I return to *The Makura* to go to New Zealand. I once wrote to you that, as a true friend, I would not complain to you. I only wish to let you know that on the trip to Sidney, I felt awful. From now on, I will do my best to be quite nonchalant about everything. Please don't tell anybody except your family. I don't want my poor mother to hear about it. I will close for now, but will write more often from New Zealand. I thank you for everything you did for me and my family this past year. With the heartiest greetings, your grateful *Conrad*.

P.S. The dear old lady is dead.

1. The RMS *Makura* could accommodate 207 first-class passengers, 114 second-class, and 72 third-class, or steerage, passengers. Tate, *Transpacific Steam*, 154.

2. Manly was one of Australia's most famed "watering places" and pleasure grounds. Promoted by developers, civic boosters, some medical practitioners, and the ferry companies, the British-style seaside resort and sanatorium prominently featured in the emerging Australian beach culture of the early twentieth century. See Richard White, *On Holidays: A History of Getting Away in Australia* (North Melbourne: Pluto, 2005), 70–73.

110

Southern Alps of New Zealand

Government Hostel

Hermitage, December 29, 1913.[1]

My dear Comrade:

Finally, I am in the mountains again. In true faithful nature! Here, I feel better and more content. Today, I only write a few lines, because I'm about to leave on a three-day tour across mountain passes. After my return, I will write much more. Here, I am alone. My gentleman will come in five or six days. Yesterday, I got four cards from you (Tyrol trip), but no letter yet. Yes, these cards made a long journey: Europe—America—New Zealand—Australia, and back to New Zealand! I am already looking forward to a letter from you. Now, you will all be in Reichenau, perhaps you take a sleigh ride to Nasswald. —— I have to get ready for the tour now. Well, Good bye, dear friend!

Con

---

1. Near Aoraki/Mt. Cook, the highest and best-known mountain in the Southern Alps at 3,754 metres (12,316 ft.), the Hermitage—a tourist hostel set near and sheltered by the old terminal moraine of the Mueller Glacier—was built by Frank Huddleston in 1884–1885. A surveyor and watercolour painter from the nearby coastal port of Timaru, Huddleston constructed the small "cob" building and was appointed ranger of the area due to fears that grazing and burning would destroy local vegetation, especially the bush and the native lilies and daisies. While not designated as a national park until 1953, the first reserve was created in 1885 to protect the Mueller and Hooker Valleys as a "recreational reserve." In 1887, the Tasman Valley was similarly reserved, followed by the Murchison Valley in 1917 and the upper Godley glaciers in 1927. After the first ascent of Aoraki/Mt. Cook, which was made by Tom Fyfe (1870–1947), Jack Clarke (1875–1952), and George Graham on Christmas day in 1894, the government bought the Hermitage accommodation house and

engaged Clarke and Fyfe as mountain guides. Throughout the 1920s, the NZAC and other mountain clubs lobbied the government for a national parks system that unified the administration of the reserves. Their efforts were realized with the passing of the National Parks Act in 1952 and, subsequently, the four reserves became known as Mt. Cook National Park. See *Aoraki/Mount Cook National Park Management Plan 2004* (August, 2004), 26. Huddleston's "cob" house was the first of three hotels in the park—all called the Hermitage—and was abandoned in 1913 in favour of a sunny, nearby valley-side site from which the view of Mt. Cook and Mt. Sefton was unimpaired. Of the Hermitage, New Zealand climber-scholar W.P. Packard wrote that it "has served a much wider public than the mountaineer, and hundreds of thousands of visitors have relaxed, walked and skied in the alpine parklands, and on the great Tasman Glacier. The Southern Alps, their heart centred on the Heritage and Mt Cook region, became known to people all over the world. So also did the New Zealand guides—such as the Graham brothers, Vic Williams, Mick Bowie and Harry Ayres, who led generations of visitors on climbs and excursions." W.P. Packard, introduction to *Mount Cook National Park*, ed. H.E. Connor (1959; Christchurch, NZ: Pegasus, 1973), 10.

111

Hermitage, January 1, 1914

Cheers to the New Year!

Dear friend Amelie:

Finally, the unlucky year 1913 is gone. We will now see what the New Year will bring. I am sitting in my room in the Hermitage, all by myself. On my table are two pictures with flowers around them. You would recognize both pictures. Last night, I dreamt that I met you and Miss Flora on the Nasskamm,[1] but it was only a short dream. Unfortunately, I could not enjoy the tour. Now, I have to tell you about my "walk." On December 29th, I went with the group to the Ball Hut, fourteen miles from here on the Tasman Glacier. Here, we stayed for the night. On December 30th, we crossed the glacier and went further to the Malte Brun Hut.[2] It is in a beautiful location. The view to the glacier is particularly beautiful. We stayed overnight. On December 31st, we left early and went back to the Hermitage. Unfortunately, I could not enjoy the tour so much. I had new boots that were too tight and thus hurt a lot. We arrived very tired. I often thought of you because of the very beautiful flowers everywhere. On my return, I found a card from you in my room (from Anninger!). Thanks a lot! I am longing very much for a letter, because it has been a long time since I got the last one. I feel quite well at the moment, if I don't start thinking too much. I look for company wherever I can. On the excursion, we were five men and we had a good conversation. The people are all very friendly. The guides know my name from hearsay.[3] My gentleman is not here yet. You will now be in your beautiful home in Reichenau, and I hope you all feel very well. In a few days, I will write more. Tomorrow, I will go on an excursion again. Good bye in spirit! With heartfelt greetings, I am and remain your *C.K.*

Address: Wellington c/o GPO, New Zealand

———————————— The Hermitage. —

Today is a day of joy for me, a true indescribable day of joy: I got
your three letters and two cards! It is impossible to imagine my joy
that surrounds me. I am here in my room. The table where I write is
covered with letters. On my chest of drawers is your picture, a picture
of Flora, and one of my dear mother and my siblings. Next to them
stand flowers in a vase. I decorated the whole room. It is impossible
to describe my feelings. It is as if I had slept a long time, and all sad
parts of my fate were just a dream! Amelie, you are a faithful soul, a
beam of joy in my hard hours. I know that all your dear wishes come
from your heart. My heartfelt thanks, especially for your comforting
lines. I also have the letter from your dear, good mother here in front
of me. It is surely very kind of her that she writes such a long letter.
One can see from the handwriting that, for her age, your Mama is
still very fit. You know that I always feel joy when I receive a letter
from an older person. I am now in the mountains again, in free
nature, and I am healthy. My heart seems to be fine, and I feel strong,
and I will be quite content if there were no more bad blows of fate.
Nowadays, it is unfortunately almost impossible to live carefree and
contented. One thing I regret: I had to abandon my trip home. To
be sick in foreign countries is too expensive! But the sanatorium
did me a lot of good. I was quite run down. But perhaps all will be
fine again. My life is like a difficult school. I cannot say I am homesick, but I have had plans for years which I now have to abandon. It
is hard to abandon your dreams. I know it is useless to fret about it
and to take life too seriously. So, I am glad I found you as a comrade
and can tell you such thoughts. You understand me. I am a wanderer.
The wanderlust is in me. It is hard for me to stay in one place. And
if I yearn for a lovely home, THE WORLD WILL BE MY HOME. —
It is true, I meet good people everywhere, and I know that many
are thinking well of me too. —— Now, I want to answer the questions in your letter. It is clear to me that the reverend cannot agree
with the social democrats, because I also understand that it is hard

for a clergyman to see the <u>good</u> sides of the socialists. Although, there are many clergymen who understand that the present politics cannot continue forever. This is what the larger factions of the clergy fear: if the socialists get to sit in the saddle, the church will become powerless. Then, they will introduce laws in the schools that say that teachers should teach about matters of fact. With this, the church, which is considered by socialists to be a good servant of capitalism, will lose its reign over people. Everybody can see that. One must judge everybody by their character, not by their profession. ——
I can imagine vividly your stay in Bozen. Yes, this is the excursion I planned for my return. It is really very dear of you that you wrote to me from there. You know that I LOVE the beautiful Tyrol. At this time of the year, it must be wonderful at Lake Garda. Our thoughts are often crossing, yes they are. I am so glad you two were also in Trafoi. I could guess a few thoughts you had at the view of Mount Ortler. I almost have forgotten to say that I had received the *Arbeiter-Zeitung*. You good lady! I love to see my thoughts in print, and I always regret that I didn't have more schooling. There is no map yet from Mt. Assiniboine. Most mountains are still without names. We baptized the mountain I climbed alone on September 9th "Mt. Electricity Storm." I will try some time to write an article for the Alpine Club Paper —— with your help!!! About Mt. Robson, you probably know everything. I think I wrote everything clearly. It should be easy to understand. The first name of Mr. G. is "Albert." The picture of me, which I sent to you, shows that I don't look so well. What would you have said had you seen me when I left the sanatorium in Sidney? ————— Now, I answer your last letter, the one of November 15th to December 5th. You write about the book. Yes, I am pleased that you liked *Camp-fires in the Canadian Rockies* so much! On November 26th, I thought of you since I knew that you would remember me. Unfortunately, I was in a bad mood that day! It was a sad name day. I would not have minded if the ship had hit a rock. ——— I am very grateful if you correct the mistakes in my brother Eugen's letter. I wrote him so often about it, but it does not help at all! It is interesting that you saw a slide show about New Zealand at the Vienna

Urania.[4] But it is more beautiful to see it all with your own eyes. Soon, I will send you flowers from here. There are so many small and dear flowers. As I mentioned before, all the people here are very good to me, and I have found many friends. I even spent a few days with the Minister of Justice of New Zealand. He is a very nice man. He is a great friend of nature and so is his wife. They invited me to visit them when I get to Wellington.[5] It is very pleasant in these transatlantic countries that there is no such stupid difference between the classes like at home in Austria. We were on a tour for four days and did a first ascent. Unfortunately, the weather here is very changeable. I enclose a map and drew in the tour for you. It is possible that you will not hear from me for some time. I am leaving the Hermitage for a longer time. To travel home will not materialize. What a pity! It is possible that, on my return trip to Canada, I will stay in Honolulu for a few weeks. I would love to climb the mountains there. Otherwise, I have no particular plans. Often I think about a long trip to the cold North. But with an expedition, the honours are usually given to the leader, not the participants, who have to work just as hard, sometimes harder. You see this in life. What will Mr. Amundsen's people have gotten? Perhaps a small sum for the great effort. I have quite spontaneously a longing for wilderness and loneliness. Perhaps I will never have a beautiful and cozy home. Fortune has not smiled upon me in this regard. Now, I have a very big favour to ask of you! I have to ask you for something that will create a lot of work for you: would you please have my diary printed on loose sheets? Mr. Mumm, the Englishman, will gladly translate it into English, and will see what one could do with it. He thinks it would be quite interesting. Mr. Mumm's address is: A.L. Mumm, 4 Hyde Park Street, London, England. Now Good bye! With my heartiest greetings, yours *C.K.*

1.   A popular ridge hike on the Raxalpe, near Nasswald and Reichenau, Austria.

2.   Climbing huts were first built in the central Southern Alps by the government for guided climbers in the 1890s. Constructed in 1898, the Malte Brun Hut sat on a flat rock tussock some 150 metres above the Tasman Glacier at an altitude of 1,737 metres (5,697 ft.). Typically a five- to six-hour

walk up the glacier (northward) from the slightly older Ball Hut (built in 1891), the Malte Brun Hut afforded climbers access to the peaks of the Malte Brun Range and on the Main Divide, such as Aiguilles Rouges (2,966 m [9,728 ft.]), Malte Brun (3,176 m [10,417 ft.]), Elie de Beaumont (3,108 m [10,194 ft.]), and the Minarets (3,065 m [10,053 ft.]).

3. According to Thorington, until Kain's arrival in 1913–1914, "Zurbriggen was the only non-colonial guide who had stood on the summit of a Hermitage Alp." Kain, *Where the Clouds*, 375. Mattias Zurbriggen (1856–1917), of Switzerland, was one of the great alpinists of the nineteenth century. He climbed and guided throughout his native Alps, but also in South America, the Himalaya, and New Zealand. He made a considerable number of first ascents throughout the world, the most famous perhaps being Aconcagua, the highest mountain in South America at 6,962 metres (22,837 ft.). In New Zealand, he is remembered most for the stunning first ascent of what was subsequently called the "Zurbriggen Ridge" up Aoraki/Mount Cook in 1895. It was the second ascent of the mountain. Defying popular convention, Zurbriggen climbed it alone.

4. The Palace Urania was an educational institute and public observatory that opened in Vienna in 1910.

5. Kain is referring to Sir John George Findlay (1862–1929) and his wife Josephine Emily Arkle. A learned man with strong humanitarian principles, John Findlay was the minister of justice from 1909–1911 under Prime Minister Sir Joseph Ward (1856–1930). In 1911, Findlay accompanied Ward to the Imperial Conference in London, England, where he was appointed Knight Commander (of the Order) of St. Michael and St. George in the coronation honours of King George V. Whatever friendship was fostered between Kain and Findlay, it was later invaluable when the guide was persecuted in Wellington, New Zealand, as an "enemy alien" in 1916. See Letter 124.

112

Southern Alps of New Zealand

Ball Hut. January 29, 1914

Dear Amelie:

Since the day before yesterday, we have been here in this hut. We're waiting for good weather. The Ball Hut is fourteen miles from the Hermitage and lies on the left side of the Tasman Glacier on the NE slope of Mt. Cook (12, 349 ft.). The view from the hut is nothing spectacular, since it lies in a low terrain. But from the moraine, there is a beautiful view of the mountains at the end of the glacier (see map with names of the mountains). Yesterday, we tried to take out a group, but turned back because the rain was too cold and the wind blew too hard against us. That, and we had to carry a load of fifty to sixty lbs. In the afternoon, another group arrived at the Ball Hut: two ladies and two gentlemen with guides. A very nice group. Today, I got up at 3 A.M., made breakfast. Now it is 8 A.M. The group has started for the Hermitage. One of the ladies has travelled a lot in the Rockies and knows several people in Banff. So we chatted for quite a while about the mountains. She said, "you cannot find any better place than the Rockies with the camp fires in the evening!" —— Now heavy clouds are hanging in the sky. It does not rain here yet, but, on the higher mountains, there will surely be snow flurries. I don't think we will start to the Malta Brun Hut. The weather is really bad here. The mountains, by themselves, would not be so difficult. Today, I will collect a few flowers for you. I feel healthy now, so please don't worry about me! I have to build a whole new base for my future life, so that I can keep my inner peace. If things would continue as they are now, life would have no value for a person. It is the struggle I have

∧ Conrad Kain at the Malte Brun Hut, 1914. Photo by H.O. Frind.

[Hocken Collections, University of Otago Library, MS-1164-2/77/14]

to continue alone. You once asked me, what kind of struggle it is. I never wrote about it, *[In English from hereon]* but I can tell you, my dear friend: It is not easy to tell one's feeling, if it is so, that you don't find words for it. But I will tell it to you in short lines. These last five–six years I made plans about the future, and these plans seemed to me really possible, and so the plans worked out to be the only wishes I carried round with me. I had sometimes been the happiest man in the world, when I thought of my wishes and plans, but always by myself, I never told anybody about my happy feeling and I will never do so. It is true, I had been happy in many ways, I had many good friends and I know, some people think very good and kind of me. I also understand that I am a lucky fellow, seeing so much of the world and from so many sides, but what is all that, if one cannot have one's heart desire? I try hard to forget my mistakes and my misfortunes. I see I must not think too much of it, because it could ruin me, and I could get from bad to worse. But don't worry, my dear Kamerad. I will push it through. I might yet be happy someday, really happy, and so it is not good to think of the past, I know that. I shall be strong and brave, and I will not be a burden to anyone, no, I would rather go far, far back in the woods and wilderness to struggle for my life and to live a good, natural life. I can do many things in the mountains and wood, which not everybody can do. I know, you will be my dearest friend as long as you live, and that I can tell you many things, which I can't tell everybody. You know my life, the history of my life, better than anybody else. I believe and I am sure, I can write you my thoughts so far as I can express myself. — Well, dear Kamerad, now you know the "struggle" I have to fight out alone! — It is nobody's fault that my life is a hard one. No. You must feel happy and think that you have a friend far off in the world, a friend who is telling you his troubles, and his happy thoughts. I see many things you will never see yourself, I write you about many things which are new to you. I shall always remember, how much kindness you had for me and my people. I know I should not have learned English, and should not have seen so many beautiful and interesting things in the world, if I had not <u>known</u> you. I told you that before. I wish your dear mother might know what a good and kind-hearted daughter she has. I wish I could tell her all I think of you. I think she would understand it. Of course it is sometimes hard to put such things in the right light, so that one can see clearly through without being a big shadow in the negative. So, my dear friend, I must end. The weather is clearing up. I hope we go up Malta Brun Hut.

Good bye! Yours C.K.

113

[In German from hereon]

Southern Alps of New Zealand

Malta Brun Hut, January 30, 1914

Dear Friend:

We arrived here yesterday at 6:30 P.M. with a heavy load. Nobody is here, so we have the cottage to ourselves. This morning, there was such a storm, that we could not start. At 10 A.M., two guides came with a lady and a gentleman. I left the hut at 10:30, took supplies and went to the Tasman-Saddle, four hours from here. The snow was good, so I had hardly any difficulties. On the top, I got into a storm. I put my knapsack under a rock and started running back. Totally drenched, I returned. It is now 7 P.M. The others play cards, and I lie on my bed writing. How might you be? You will be back in Vienna. I am looking forward to hear how you spent the holidays. Perhaps you also saw my mother? How are your ailing friends? Is the poor lady still alive? —— I will go to bed now, since I am quite tired. It looks bad for tomorrow. —— Perhaps we will stay here a few days. The group goes down to the valley today (post office). I have to close. With heartiest greeting to all,

your Wanderer.

∧ *Mount Cook from the Hermitage, 1915. Photo by W. Crow.*

114

March 2, 1914

My faithful Comrade:

You will be surprised and may be worried about my long silence. First, I have to tell you that this week was very sad. I will tell you about it. On February 20th, in the afternoon, two parties left the Hermitage for Mt. Cook. Mr. Sidney King, an Englishman, with two guides heading for the Ball Hut, and I with Mr. Otto Frind and a guide from here (William Brass) to the Hooker Hut.[1] I took the guide along so that he could get to know the tour. In the Hooker Hut were the brothers Malcher, two fellows from Baden, near Vienna. We spent a nice evening together. On February 21st at 5 A.M., we started heavily loaded with tent, sleeping bag, etc. to get to the Bivouac. The Hooker Glacier is very broken. At one point, we had to climb across a rock wall, which was not easy. At 2 P.M., we got to the Bivouac site, which is located exactly across the Harper Saddle.[2] It was a very warm day. We made coffee and rested, then continued to the Bergschrund. I crossed the 'schrund alone and made steps across a steep, snowy wall. On my way back, I lost my old hat, the "Chamonix-Hat," which you know so well! It was still visible down the crevasse. On the way back to the Bivouac, there was a sunset with such a special light that makes you melancholy. We also saw the ocean ——— my heart almost stood still when I looked at all these wonderful, different colours. I think, there can be no human being who would not be delighted about such a miracle of sun and nature! —— I was very sorry about my Chamonix-hat. I had worn it for such a long time. ——— In camp, we cooked a very good soup and had quite diverse conversation. I did not feel very well—the cot was hard. However, we slept well, yes too well, because we overslept by a whole hour until

5 A.M.!! At that time, I wanted to be at the Bergschrund! — At 6:15, we started and followed yesterday's steps. We stopped at the crevasse where my hat was. I could not stand to lose my hat forever, because it had accompanied me on many a trip and tour. So I lowered myself down twenty metres into the hole and, with great effort, I got my old hat!!! —— At 8 A.M., we were on a long ridge, which was partly covered with snow. Wherever it was not difficult and dangerous, I let Brass take the lead. It was very warm, so we made slow progress. I soon saw that the tour would be a long one. We had to do much cutting, and the rock was brittle. At 12 noon, we stopped for a rest. The sun got warmer, and avalanches roared into the valley from left and right of the ridge. For 400 metres, it was very exciting. Some small avalanches went over our heads. We were lucky we had some rocks above that protected us. Yes, it was <u>dangerous!</u> If I would describe it in greater detail, it would be <u>hair-raising</u>! But, as always, I led the group through it <u>calmly</u> and without getting excited. Turning back would have brought the same dangers as the ascent did. So I continued. At 5:15 P.M., we reached the top of Mt. Cook (12,349 ft.), the highest point of New Zealand. We shook hands. —— We were now going to follow the tracks of Mr. King and his two guides, who were supposed to descend on our (that is the Hooker) side, but instead they descended the side they had climbed up. We left the top at 5:50, and followed the tracks of King via the crest to the Linda Glacier. I saw that we had to spend the night on the glacier. On the Linda Glacier, we came upon the debris of a huge avalanche that could have come down not more than five or six hours before. Here, the tracks of our friends disappeared. After strenuous hiking, we reached the end of the avalanche. Night overtook us, and we lost the tracks of the other group. Later, by the light of lanterns, we reached the tracks again. We still passed more avalanche debris and finally reached the Grand Plateau. Here, we rested and made tea. We almost froze in the process. We were glad to move on. We had two lanterns, so it was not difficult to follow the old foot path. Soon, we had to climb up 600 ft. to the Glacier Dome and saw fresh tracks, which led us to think that our friends were in the Bivouac. On the descent from

Glacier Dome, Bill Brass was a big help. He found the path to the Bivouac at night very well. I doubt I would have found it without him, since one had to cross broken rock where tracks were not visible. At 1:40, we came to the Bivouac at the Haast Ridge. Since we saw light inside the tent and heard voices, we were greatly relieved. Yes, it was no deception: there was light and there were voices! In a few minutes, we were greeted. "Hello, is it you, King?" —— That gave me a stab to my heart. ——— Our answer was "No, Frind's party!" — "Where is King?" —— "We did not see the party, only the tracks! They must long be in the valley!" ——————— The two gentlemen in the Bivouac were Mr. Dennistown, a friend of King, and Mr. Turner, a well-known New Zealand alpinist.[3] The two had left the Hermitage hoping to catch up with King's party, which, however, would have only been possible in bad weather. The gentlemen left the Bivouac at <u>Haast Ridge</u> at 3 A.M., and we lay down to sleep. We consoled ourselves that King's party had descended via a new path to the Ball Hut. At 9:15 A.M. (on February 23), we left the Bivouac and climbed down to the Ball Hut. There, we found the barometer of guide Thomson, but no entry by King in the hut book. I then knew for sure that our friends were buried in the avalanche. I mentioned my opinion, but Brass said that he did not remember that the guides the day before a climb ever made steps farther than the Glacier Dome. With differing thoughts, we descended to the Hermitage. For me, it was little consolation.

At 8 P.M., we reached the Hermitage. No trace of our friends. The chief guide, Peter Graham, was not there.[4] He was at the Hooker Hut with a group. At once, we sent a guide there with a letter. At 3 A.M., February 24th, Graham came to my room, dripping wet and agitated. I briefly told him everything and asked how far the guides usually cut steps on the day before an ascent. He said the steps would be cut to the point where the avalanche was reported to be. So it was clear that the tracks we found below the avalanche were those made during the <u>ascent</u> upwards on February 21st. At 5 A.M. in the morning, we five guides (Graham, Brass, Frank Milne,[5] and me) started our sad hike.

> *Conrad Kain and Herbert Otto Frind, Middle and Low Peaks of Mount Cook, 1914. Photo by W. Brass.* [Hocken Collections, University of Otago Library, MS-1164-2/34/9-S05-506a]

On the way to the Ball Hut, we met Mr. Dennistown and Mr. Turner, who had no further news of the missing group. Both turned around and went with us. After a short rest in the Ball Hut, we continued our way to the Haast Bivouac. We could not do any more that day. Graham and I made steps to the Glacier Dome. At 7:45, we were back. On the 25th, at 5 A.M., we left the Bivouac and went to the base of the huge avalanche. We searched around the site of the accident. No success, we continued the ascent. The avalanche was one km. long and one-and-a-half km. wide. Blocks of ice of all sizes were lying around, the biggest like a one story house.[6] On the 23rd, two more big avalanches came down from Mt. Cook. On our descent, Graham found the body of the guide Richmond. He was terribly disfigured. We cut the body out of the ice and searched for the bodies of King and Guide Thomson, but without success.[7] The three victims must have been killed instantly. The transport of Richmond's body to the valley caused many difficulties. The tragedy on Mount Cook was <u>the first</u> in the New Zealand Alps, and, as always, like everywhere, the daily newspapers wrote a lot of nonsense about it. I received a thank you letter from the Tourism Department for my assistance in the search for the accident victims. I was pleased about the recognition, which does not at all make me conceited, because I know that I did not do more than what <u>any</u> true mountain climber does or would do in such a situation. Mr. King was a member of the English Alpine Club and was often in Switzerland. Mt. Cook was his 101st summit. Several of these mountains he climbed two or three times. David Thomson was a New Zealander and one of the best guides. Richmond was also a local and had all the good attributes for becoming a first-class guide. It had been his first ascent of Mt. Cook. Here, I also want to mention that both were enthusiastic friends of nature and did their mountain guiding more or less as passionate friends of nature, because, here in New Zealand, there are many opportunities to achieve a better way of life than you can have as a guide. —

I wrote the story of the first major accident in the New Zealand Alps in a lot of detail. Perhaps the *Österreichische Tageszeitung* can use it.

Could you copy it and send it to them? You can imagine how hard
it is to search for dead people, especially if they are professional
colleagues and friends of the mountain with whom one was to meet
on the highest peak of the country. I will also send you some newspaper clippings about this accident. —— Now, everything is over. It
was an accident that can happen to anybody. For the local guides,
it was very hard, because they had never before seen death in the
mountains. Also, they were two guides who were popular among the
people. If the tour of Mt. Cook from the Hooker side had not been so
difficult and time consuming, we might have become victims of this
avalanche too. —— The guide Thomson and Mr. King probably have
the most beautiful site in New Zealand for eternal rest and peace, a
site surrounded by snow and ice with eternal peace around. I hope
that each mountain hiker who sees Mt. Cook will remember the
people buried there.[8] Later, I will describe this area in more detail.
Now we return to the mountains for several days. I have little time to
write. The *Touristen Zeitung* (Mt. Robson). I have received. It pleased
me very much! Your editing was very well done! Soon, I will write
more. I now feel very well and I hope that it stays that way. Don't
worry about me! I must answer your letter in more detail later on.
Please send a copy of the newspaper to Mr. L.A. Mumm, 4 Hyde Park
Street, London. Don't be angry if you don't hear from me for a long
time: I must pack because we are returning to the mountains for two
weeks. I hope you are well. With much love to you and yours,

The Wanderer.

1.   The two parties left to traverse Mt. Cook by directly opposite routes: Sidney L. King (d. 1914), a
     member of The Alpine Club, with local guides Darby (David) Thomson (d. 1914) and Jock (John)
     Richmond (1884–1914), intended to cross the mountain by way of the Linda Glacier, over the
     highest summit, and down the Hooker Glacier, while Frind, Kain, and William (Bill) Brass (1886–
     1915) desired to ascend the Hooker side and descend the Linda. The two parties planned to meet
     on the summit, taking each other's steps down. Kain, *Where the Clouds*, 380. Built in 1909–1910,
     the Hooker Hut sat at 1,127 metres (3,696 ft.) on the west side of the Hooker Valley and at the foot
     of Copland Pass, a little over nine kilometres from the Hermitage. The original structure was built

by the area's chief guide, Peter Graham (1878–1961), along with guides Jim Murphy and Darby Thomson, to serve as a transit hut for those wishing to cross Copland Pass to the West Coast or to explore the upper reaches of the Hooker Valley.

2. From the main summit of Mt. Cook, a buttress leads down to an isolated rock at its foot, known as "bivouac." It is from here, Kain later wrote, that "the real climb of Mt. Cook, from the Hooker side, begins…, the campsite (7,500 feet [2,286 m]), being the highest in the Southern Alps." Kain also added that it was "far from being a comfortable place" and that "some of the twinges of rheumatism that occasionally get into my bones may be traced to such bivouacs, and exposure in high altitudes." Kain, *Where the Clouds*, 389.

3. An enthusiastic mountaineer, James Robert Dennistoun (1883–1916), a New Zealander from Peel Forest, Canterbury, was a member of Robert Falcon Scott's 1910–1911 Antarctic Expedition for which he was awarded the King's Antarctic Medal and that of the Royal Geographical Society. Samuel Turner (1869–1929), a UK-born produce trader, settled in New Zealand in 1911. Already a prolific alpinist—see Samuel Turner, *My Climbing Adventures on Four Continents* (London: Unwin, 1911)—his most notable climbs were achieved in the Southern Alps: the first complete solo ascent of Aoraki/Mt. Cook, and the first ascents of Mounts Tutoko, Hooker, Hopkins, and McKerrow, and the second ascent of Mt. Aspiring. See Samuel Turner, *The Conquest of the New Zealand Alps* (London: Unwin, 1922). For the majority of his New Zealand ascents, Turner was accompanied by the leading guides of the period: Peter Graham, Frank Milne, and Kain.

4. New Zealand's Department of Tourist and Health Resorts first employed Peter Graham as a mountain guide at the Hermitage in 1903. He assumed the chief guide's position in 1906 and held it for the next 16 years. Over the course of his career, Graham made 13 ascents of the high peak of Aoraki/Mt. Cook, including six of the first eight ascents, the first traverse, a new route, and the first grand traverse of all three peaks. On this last climb, Graham guided Australian-born Freda Du Faur (1882–1935), who defied the popular gender constraints of the period and became the first woman to summit the mountain. See Freda Du Faur, *The Conquest of Mount Cook and Other Climbs: An Account of Four Seasons' Mountaineering on the Southern Alps of New Zealand* (London: Allen and Unwin, 1915), 99–111, 238–46. Known for an impeccable safety record, Graham built and maintained many of the huts in the park. His autobiography was published posthumously. See Peter Graham, *Peter Graham, Mountain Guide: An Autobiography*, ed. H.B. Hewitt (Wellington, NZ: A.H. & A.W. Reed, 1965).

5. Francis Middleton Milne (1891–1933), known as Frank, began his job as porter and mountain guide at the Hermitage in 1913. Apprentice to Peter Graham, Milne quickly developed into an outstanding guide and mountaineer. For example, in 1916, he and assistant guide Jack Lippe led Sam Turner on the successful "Grand Traverse" of Aoraki/Mt. Cook—the third time the feat had been accomplished. Although he was a quiet and reserved man, Milne assumed the position of chief guide at the Hermitage upon Peter Graham's retirement in 1922.

6. According to Dennistoun, "Peter Graham and Conrad agreed that in all their long Alpine experience they had never seen such a huge avalanche before. They had seen nothing which approached it in size either in New Zealand, Switzerland, or Canada." James R. Dennistoun, "The Accident on

CONRAD KAIN

Mt. Cook. Death of Mr. S.L. King and his Guides Thomson and Richmond," *The Alpine Journal* (hereafter *AJ*) 28 (1914): 225.

7. According to Phil Dowling, "The bodies of King and Thomson were not recovered until fourteen years later. Their badly mutilated remains appeared at the toe of the glacier in 1928." Phil Dowling, *The Mountaineers: Famous Climbers in Canada* (Edmonton: Hurtig, 1979), 95.

8. Thomson, who was about 30 years old when he died, was from the West Coast of New Zealand; he was Peter Graham's second in seniority at the Hermitage and "his right hand man." Five years younger, Richmond, who had only been added the Hermitage's guiding staff two seasons earlier, "was looked upon as the most promising of the younger guides. Peter Graham, who had a partic-ular affection for him, believed him to have the makings of one of the best guides he had ever had in his hands to train." Dennistoun, "The Accident on Mt. Cook," 229. First used during the 1917–1918 season, the high King Memorial Hut was built on the site of the Haast Ridge bivouac to honour those who perished—Thomson, Richmond, and King—on the Linda Glacier in 1914.

115

The Hermitage, March 18, 1914

Dear Friend:

In my last letter, in which I wrote about the accident on Mt. Cook, I mentioned the *Touristen Zeitung*. I was in a hurry when I wrote. Now, we will talk about it in more detail. First, I have to say that I feel very healthy. Yes, AS HEALTHY AS THE ELK IN THE FOREST, Amelie! You can hardly imagine with what feelings I write these words: I FEEL HEALTHY! I wish you could see me now! Look into my eyes! There is a different spark in them than on the picture which I sent to Flora with the words, "Don't get scared!" I know what you good friends must have thought of me when I wrote that I was in a sanatorium in Australia. I don't remember anymore what I wrote in the long letter—the last one on the *Makura*—? Perhaps the letter revealed something about my "studying" and worrying. — Yes, I was "finished," the world meant nothing and if I were not of such good nature, things could perhaps have been awful. Life taught me hard things and perhaps will remain hard. Because of my travels and reading of different books, I learned to think a bit. Something tore the net I was in and if one knot of the net opens, then more do the same! And I, a good honest breaker of stones, could not grasp the new picture of the world. It was too much for me. But now I see everything with calm eyes and strong nerves. I don't get too excited. I live from one day to the next, enjoy nature, and think of my good friends. It is no use to make plans for a further life as a labourer, because we now live in a very critical time. This time needs rest to mature. When the fruit falls off the tree by itself, the fruit will rot, but the seed of the fruit will plant itself according to the laws of nature. And those who live long enough will then enjoy this fruit. What we hope for is

freedom and justice. — I enjoy nature and its wonders, and I will
remain like that. To establish a good home—those plans and wishes
I had to abandon, the noble and honest wishes of my heart I had to
banish. Yes, all this had to go, as I realized that these plans could not
be fulfilled by a simple labourer. The world and people do not allow
it for a labourer! You know the saying by Schiller about the good and
the bad souls, don't you?[1] Amelie, can you imagine the struggle I had
to go through, can you grasp what I felt in my heart? Are you
surprised that I was not content? And that I became ill? I think I
know you will not be surprised. You have an open and healthy way to
look at life and about the unfairness of the world and the struggle of
survival! — But now, you will hear something different that I can tell
you with great joy. In the newspaper clipping you read, that people
here think very highly of me.[2] But that is not everything. — I gained
great confidence in myself with everybody's praise here. The government even asked the Department of Tourism to invite me back to
New Zealand as a guide for the next season and asked that I train and
teach the local guides according to my own experiences.[3] One would
also give me work for the whole year. But I cannot accept that, since
in summer I can make more money in Canada. I think—if I may say
so just to you—I can be proud of it! All the guides are encouraging
me to stay. The manager of the Hermitage and his wife are very
friendly to me, and all the doors are open for me in the house.[4] We
were gone for thirteen days, two days longer than we had planned. So
they were all worried about us! My gentleman is also highly respected
here. Now, I have to tell you about our hard work here. We were, as
mentioned before, gone for thirteen days, and made six first ascents,
crossed two new passes (Murchison Glacier), and made one first
ascent at the Tasman Glacier.[5] It was all hard work, no trails. We had
a small tent and two sleeping bags, no wood, and had to cook with
kerosene. Our knapsacks were heavy. The first days, I carried much
more than 50 kilos! The trail we used was a long one. Some ascents
were very dangerous, particularly the last one, which was very
exciting because of rock slides. Aside from the hard work, we had
splendid nights of moonlight and wonderful sunsets. — In the West,

there were grandiose oceans of fog, which one <u>only</u> sees in alpine mountains. Pure miracles of nature that move your soul. Not just once did I think of you: hundreds of times you stood in these beautiful mountains next to me! I think with great delight of you when I see such wonders, because I know you would enjoy such arrays of colour with me. Yes, you would do your best and happily <u>help</u> me with the description of a sunset and correct everything very well, that is, if I would manage to write an article about it. But I cannot find the proper words. ——— I know, you don't like it when I complain about my schooling, but I cannot get it out of my mind, and it makes me dissatisfied. I get a feeling that there are great injustices that rule the world, so that it is impossible for a simple labourer to bring up his children properly. Unfortunately, the working class has much larger families than the rich. Barely fourteen years old, the child of a labourer has to go out into the world, has to work ten-to-twelve hours a day so that he can barely make a living. Of course, I understand, too, that for the children of the rich, on the other hand, it is not so good to have to study and to cram seven to eight hours a day. Later in life, it often hasn't much value for many of them: to know, for instance, the "dead languages." Most people in the world still live in darkness. But I feel sorry for every innocent human being, born into a family who knows and can see that a child cannot be properly educated and is therefore more-or-less destined to be a slave to the exploiters. This is especially true in the European countries. How long will it take until people become aware of it? How much time will be needed for the classes of labourers and farmers to begin to <u>think</u> and claim their rights as human beings? To be <u>acknowledged</u>? What do you think? Already for two thousand years, people have preached the gospel with good words and beautiful examples. What is the success? I don't see any. I see theft and murder. The best example is the army. One has to swear in the name of the Almighty to do one's best in times of war—that one will aim carefully to shoot one's neighbour or beat him to death! Yes, and the best is that if one refuses the oath because one's religion is dear to oneself and tells "Thou shall not kill," then one is declared a coward and will be shot or hung by the neck according to the law! ——— When I look at religion from this point of view, I see nothing good. Of course, the Gospel is good, but it is often used to do bad things. As long as the churches teach and preach the Gospel to the people in <u>this</u> way, one will not really be successful! If one could use all of the huge sums of money given to armies and war expenditures and give them instead to schools and the welfare of all classes, it would be a better world ——— Now, we have to change the topic!! —— I wrote an article about the traversing of Mt. Cook and the big avalanche accident. I have to copy the article once more, and then I will send it to you with pictures. Of course, again, there will be a lot of editing for you to do! — I don't care whom you will give the article to, Friends of Nature, the Touristen Club, the Alpine Society, or to the Austrian Alpine Magazine. The president of the Mountain Club is Imperial Counsellor Doménig. He knows me very well and would assist you very gladly. I leave it totally up to you. I believe that I described everything well and perhaps in an interesting way, too. Since Mt. Cook is the highest mountain of New Zealand, and that next to nothing has actually been written in the German language about it, the essay should be of value without question. Actually, the tour was very dangerous. Add to this the sad fate of our friends. —— One joyful piece of news I can add: The English *Alpine Journal* has accepted my story about Mt. Robson and was kind enough to add a picture of myself.[6] That also makes me better known among the English people. I have a good reputation in the Alpine Club anyway. Now Good bye.

——————— Hermitage, March 20, 1914

Continuation. Yesterday and today, I was on short excursions with the employees of the hut. The manager also came along. We had a beautiful time. Tomorrow, March 21st, we will start another tour for one week. I think on April 10 I will board a ship in Auckland. Please don't write to New Zealand anymore, but to Banff again. On April 10th, the *Niagara*, a new, modern boat will depart.[7] Perhaps I will stay a week or so in Vancouver, that is, in the area, or I will go bear hunting to the area where I was three years ago and dreamt of you, do you remember? In case I do go somewhere, I must write a lot. I hope that on board ship, I will write many pages, if it is not too stormy. I feel very well now, also in my soul. Nothing could upset me now, I think. At Easter time, you will be—as always—in your house in Reichenau. I hope you will have a nice time there. The little spring flowers and the songs of the birds will please you, and I will look out at the restless ocean and think of you often. Maybe our thoughts will meet sometime! — It is such a pity that you don't know where I will be at Easter. Faithful comrade, now I have to say something quite serious, and I hope you will not be angry about it. Here we go. Since the accident on Mt. Cook, a new rule was instated here: Each climber who undertakes dangerous tours has to leave his address or that of his next of kin in the hotel. That is a good idea. I did not know which address I should leave, Banff or Nasswald. If I were to have an accident, I would not want somebody to write or telegraph directly to my mother. So, I left your address as my best friend (but also because of the language). I always hope for the best. But should something happen to me, then you will be the first person in Europe to hear about it. I will add a few lines to my will, when I get back to Canada. It is not pleasant to have to make such arrangements!! For my own person, it does not matter, where and how and at which place my life comes to an end. But I have to think of my family and therefore have to leave something in writing. I already confronted death in various situations, and I am sure I can now stand it more often without trembling in fear. —— I enclose a map on which I will mark our tour. The map is not very good. Later, I will get a better one and send it to you. Now, I have to close. With heartiest greetings and my wish that you and your beloved Mama and your sister Flora may be well,

The Wanderer

> *Conrad Kain on the third ascent of Mount Darby (N.E. Arête), 1914. Photo by H.O. Frind.*
[Hocken Collections, University of Otago Library, MS-1164-2/34/11-S05-506e]

1. Friedrich Schiller—the German philosopher, whom Kain had read while aboard the *Orsova* in 1912, upon recommendation from Malek (see Letter 69)—published several papers elaborating Christoph Martin Wieland's concept of *Schöne Seele* (beautiful soul): the idea that a person's emotions are educated by reason, so that *Pflicht und Neigung* (duty and inclination) are not in conflict with one another. Beauty, then, for Schiller, was more than simply aesthetics—it was also moral; thus, the Good is Beauty. For Kain, a romantic "friend of Nature" who found beauty there, the equation of goodness with beauty no doubt firmed his uneasy conviction that his wandering life in the "wilds" of the world was indeed a moral and righteous one.

2. What follows is an extract from the *Christchurch Press* for 28 February, printed in the days following the avalanche incident: "Fortunately for them, in Conrad Kain, a man well used to such accidents in Europe and other parts of the world...his experience was of the greatest value. This plucky man had, with Brass, who also joined the search party, crossed the mountain from the Hooker side, and immediately on being informed of the probability of an accident, started out to help in the rescue work. Peter Graham, who is a past master in alpine work, says he could not find words to express what he thought of Conrad." Quoted in Kain, *Where the Clouds*, 382.

3. An official notice of Kain's appointment was printed in the 1915 *Alpine Journal*: "The Guide Konrad Kain. — It will be remembered that Kain made a journey to New Zealand in 1914....He has now been appointed, by the New Zealand Department of the Interior, one of the official guides for the Mount Cook district. He is certain to find many willing pupils among the keen mountaineers of the Island." *AJ* 29 (1915): 84.

4. The second Hermitage opened in 1914 and was operated by the Department of Tourist and Health Resorts. The Mount Cook Motor Company had been running service cars to the Hermitage beginning in 1906 and was thus keen to have the hotel open year round. Eventually, the motor company applied to lease the property and took it over in 1921. The Hermitage was then renovated and expanded, camping facilities were developed, and package tours were offered—perhaps for the first time in New Zealand. Further expansions came in 1924. In 1944, the lease expired and the Mount Cook and Southern Lakes Tourist Company, as the motor company became known, returned the Hermitage to the Government. As for Huddleston's original "cob" building—which, for years, was increasingly unable to accommodate the tourist demand—it was severely damaged by a flood as work began on the second hotel; months later, it was destroyed by another flood.

5. Kain's specific accomplishments are noted by Thorington in Kain, *Where the Clouds*, 376–79, as well as in Dennistoun, "The Accident on Mt. Cook," 345–46.

6. Conrad Kain, "The Ascent of Mount Robson," *AJ* 28 (1914): 35–38. The caption under Kain's photo reads as follows: "Conrad Kain, of Nasswald, Raxalpe, now in the Employ of the Alpine Club of Canada." Kain, "The Ascent of Mount Robson," 35.

7. Owned by the Union Steamship Company, the RMS *Niagara* was launched in August 1912. Nicknamed the "Queen of the Pacific," the ocean liner sailed the Sydney-Auckland-Fiji-Honolulu-Canada route until it was sunk in 1940, in Hauraki Gulf, New Zealand, by mines laid by the German merchant raider *Orion*. Carrying eight tons of gold bullion to aid in the war effort, the ship famously became the object of several salvage operations. See Keith Gordon, *Deep Water Gold: The Story of the RMS* Niagara—*The Quest for New Zealand's Greatest Shipwrecked Treasure* (Whangarei, NZ: SeaROV, 2005).

116

Banff, Alta, June 5, 1914

Dear Amelie:

I wrote a card to you to say that I had safely returned to Banff. That was in the morning. In the afternoon of the same day, I sprained my hand at the woodpile. I wanted to roll over a log, slipped, and sprained it. During the night, the hand got swollen up to the elbow. I saw the doctor who gave me some ointment as a rub. In a few days, I got better, but I could not even think of working. When I let my hand hang, I had awful pains. Since I could not work, I walked around in the forest, watched the awakening of spring, listened to the songs of the birds, picked some flowers—it was wonderful! Various thoughts crossed my mind. Often, I was with you and your family in Reichenau and in Nasswald, and on my beautiful Zikafahnler Alm, without being homesick. I am feeling quite well now, quite healthy. Unfortunately, I have to say that, at the moment, the conditions in Canada are not the best. Thousands of workers are out of work. Even in Banff, there are several hundred of them. For that reason, wages are low. You will be surprised to hear that my salary, too, was cut, lowered by 25 dollars per month. It is very annoying that the price of food is still as high as before. The market for labourers is over-crowded and so the capitalists have good choices. I don't get excited about it, but you will see that my prediction regarding a revolution in a few years may come true!! I can only say that in CANADA one must be glad to have work.[1] ———— On May 29th, I remembered my fare-well from you in Vienna at your home. Five years! Yes, time goes by and so I am not surprised when in the morning while combing my hair I saw white. It's getting whiter all the time. In the end, I might be grey before you!! —— Otherwise, I found Banff as always, no change.

But my good friend Chanter is dead. He was found on the railroad tracks out towards Calgary without feet and hands. Two months later, he died in the hospital. Miss Maggee is in an asylum, that is if she is still alive. In Vancouver, I saw Miss Hollowes (she is a teacher). I had supper with her and then we went to the theatre. A play by Shakespeare was performed (very good). Miss H. has my article about Mt. Cook and will translate it for me into English. I hope she will finish by the end of this month. Then, I will send it to you right away. It seems to me that my description is the best I have written up to now, but, of course, your red pen is still needed very much. I know you will polish the article very well, just as you did with the others. Lady, what must you think of me (because of the English essay)? It is for sure that you are the first to whom I am sending such things. *The Innthaler* did not receive that from me, because I only have had this little copy since May 21st. I think that Cpt. Farrer, the editor of the *Alpine Club Journal*, sent a copy to *The Innthaler*.[2] But, dear friend, I don't mind if you call me "a bad boy!" You can say to me whatever you like, because I know you mean well. You are too kind-hearted to say something nasty. I know you. Now, I have to answer your question from your last letter. I received the letter #6 to Wellington here. As I see, you spent the winter in Vienna quite well and in the best of health. Sometimes it feels as if you were only a few miles away. It is interesting that each day you add a few lines to the letter. Piece by piece, a few pages get filled. Yes, I already have a pile of letters from you (and you also from me). Don't worry, I won't lose any of them while travelling. Burning them, as you say, is ok, but I cannot bring myself to do it. I often re-read your letters. — I like your letters. I know that you know me, but there is something to my love for your letters, that you <u>do not understand</u>. ———— How dear of you to send me a leaf from a lemon tree from the Imperial Court Garden. I read part of Amundsen's work.[3] Surely, his trip was better organized than Scott's. I heard from some Englishmen that one makes too much fuss about Scott. I myself believe that Scott's disappointment at the Pole contributed much to the catastrophe. —— In your letter, you gave me a long sermon!! Yes, on those cases you are right, and I accept your word well and am grateful, but unfortunately —— to be contented is not so easy. And it isn't quite right when you write that otherwise my world trips had no meaning. — The flowers I sent I picked on my way to the Tasman Glacier. I will write to Mr. Polster once more and ask very nicely about the pictures. I don't think he has forgotten it, but he is very occupied in his business and does not take the time to do it. The Canadians are like that, too. Last summer, about fifty people promised me pictures, and only three kept their word! You will understand why one gets quite distrustful. And next summer, as people make promises again, I will indicate that I will *remind* them of their promise without hesitation, if they won't keep it! Mr. Frind had very beautiful pictures. He had extraordinary success with them. When I asked him for two pictures for my article on Mt. Cook, he wanted to give me the two *poorest* of all the many pictures. I did not accept them and gave him a piece of my mind. Afterwards, one of the guides gave me some. A few days ago, I received a letter from Mr. Frind, in which he gives me a lot of praise regarding the pictures and that I could choose according to my taste and preference what I want. Such little things hurt you as a guide. One connects one's life to the gentleman on the rope, goes first in all dangerous situations, is ready to risk one's life for the gentleman, and the thank you is to deny you some little favour! There is no doubt that the old mountain climbers of, let's say, twenty-five to thirty years ago, were much more accommodating towards their guides. Mr. Frind was otherwise always very good to me. ——— On March 22nd, we took our last tour together. I enclose a newspaper article. We were out for thirty-five hours. I took a young New Zealand lad along who had never been on such a tour before. He was a nice lad and very grateful that I took him along. Mr. Frind was very proud of the tour, and he was totally different towards me![4] — Mr. Cook, the manager of the Hermitage, had noticed it and said the following to me: *[In English from hereon]* "Well, Con, you are through now, aren't you." — "Yes, I think so." — "Con, do you remember, what I told you about that other Australian lady and her guide?" — "Yes, I do." — "Well, and that is just the same with you and your Master. Now, you can go to Hongkong! — I would not care to be a guide, and I am sure I would not allow my boy to be one! A guide's life is a hard one, and after you have done some good work, all the credit, you get your <u>pass</u>!" — *[In German from hereon]* Mr. Cook is someone who talks exactly like he thinks. He was really very good to me. He once told me of a lady who had climbed many mountains with guides. She also talked nicely and with praise about her guides, and when she was finished with her program, she did not want to hear one word any more from her guides!! I inquired a little more and found out that it really was true. I myself had such experiences, too. But yet, I am not narrow minded: not <u>all</u> of them are <u>that</u> stingy, and they all don't want all the praise for themselves. I am convinced that Frind will later think that I was a true companion for him in the mountains. — Yesterday, I received a letter from the Department of Tourism in Wellington. The letter was not very enjoyable for me. They consider what I charge for my wage is too high. I will answer very friendlily that it is impossible for me to work for any less, since the work is hard and dangerous, and that the tremendous responsibility has to be paid, too. I had sent you the letter that I received from the Department of Tourism after the accident on Mt. Cook. You see how people are! They have good words to thank you if you do something for them for <u>free</u>. It is quite certain that I would not ask to be paid for such services. It is very nice when people are grateful, but, on the other hand, we see how quiet and reluctant people are when they hear about money! The sad fact is that the director and the employees in the government have no idea what "danger in the mountains" means since they are not mountaineers themselves. — I will not reduce my wage even by even a cent. — When they take <u>what</u> I ask for, then that is fine; if not, I will be able to live my life just the same. In a few days, we go into the mountains. This summer, we get to the Elk River, to the area where Hornaday (*Camp-fires*) was.[5] From July 21st to August 25th, the Alpine Club camp takes place in Yoho Valley. I will be there.[6] More news that will interest you: on the new map, which is not quite finished yet, one mountain is listed as "Nasswald Peak." It is over 9,000 ft. high. I climbed this mountain alone on September 21, 1913. Do you remember? I wrote you about it.[7] I went hunting and tumbled downhill some feet, because one hook broke off. I think one day I will send a little description FIRST ASCENT OF *MT. NASSWALD* IN THE ROCKIES. For today, I have to close, but soon I will write more. I hope that the three of you are healthy, and have a good time in your beautiful home. With best greetings,

The Wanderer

1. The long years of prosperity that accompanied the Laurier years were over. In Canada, as early as 1912, a worldwide depression was taking hold. Immigrants, who were arriving in greater numbers to escape economic hardship at home, joined growing armies of unemployed in Canadian cities. In 1913 and 1914, the prairies suffered their first widespread crop failures, and the new transcontinental railways found themselves in a credit squeeze. Railway bankruptcy destroyed Canadian credit with foreign investors. Later, in August of 1914, when the crisis that bubbled out of the Balkans escalated to Britain's declaration of war with Germany, it was hunger, in fact, as much as patriotism, that drove thousands of young men into the Canadian Expeditionary Force. See Desmond Morton, *A Short History of Canada* (1983; Toronto: McClelland and Stewart, 1994), 163, 166.

2. John Percy Farrar (1857–1929) was the assistant editor of *The Alpine Journal* from 1909–1926 under George Yeld (1845–1938), who, chosen as editor in 1896, held the position for 30 years, the longest in the journal's history. "It is an open secret," T.S. Blakeney wrote, in a history of the journal and its editors, "that Farrar was the real Editor for much of this time…Farrar's hand is to be detected in some of the massive volumes of the *AJ* prior to 1914, but even more so in the volumes (29–32) that covered the years of World War I." T.S. Blakeney, "The Alpine Journal and its Editors II. 1896–1923," *AJ* 80 (1975): 120–21.

3. Roald Amundsen (1872–1928), the Norwegian leader of the first Antarctic expedition to successfully reach the South Pole, published his two-volume Antarctic account in 1912. It was translated and printed a year later as *The South Pole: An Account of the Norwegian Antarctic Expedition in the "Fram," 1910–1912,* trans. A.G. Chater (New York: Lee Keedick, 1913).

4. Kain refers to the ascent of Mt. Sefton (3,151 m [10,338 ft.]), which he climbed with Frind and a young aspirant New Zealand guide named R. Young. Not only was it the fifth ascent of the mountain, theirs was a new route, described as follows: "New route, from Green Rock by route for Mt. Thomson as far as icefalls off E. face of latter, thence traversing to Brunner névé, Douglas Glacier and Karangua Saddle. Up W. snow face to summit." Kain, *Where the Clouds,* 379.

5. During the summer of 1914 Kain was again engaged on the Interprovincial Boundary Survey, under surveyor Alan (A.J.) Campbell (1882–1967). Campbell led a reconnaissance of the portion of the watershed at the summit of the pass dividing the waters of Elk River from those of the Kananaskis River, where several mineral lots were affected by the boundary. Cautley, Wallace, and Wheeler,

Report of the Commission: Part I, 58. Bound for Morley, Alberta, Kain left Banff with Campbell's party on 10 June. Work with the survey parties concluded for 1914 on 17 July.

6.   Kain worked at the ACC's ninth annual mountaineering camp held 29 kilometres from the railway at Field, BC, in the meadows at the head of the Upper Yoho Valley from 21 July to 11 August 1914. In all, 206 people were "placed under canvas," which was, then, the largest ACC camp to date. An account of the camp was supplied in the 1914–1915 CAJ: see J. MacCartney Wilson, "The Camp in the Upper Yoho Valley (1914)," CAJ 6 (1914–1915): 217–28.

7.   See Letter 104. Named by the Interprovincial Boundary Survey in 1913, Nasswald Peak (2,995 m [9,827 ft.]) rises from the headwaters of Fatigue Creek, in the Valley of the Rocks, on the border of Banff National Park and Assiniboine Provincial Park.

117

Morley (C.P.R.), June 14, 1914

Dear Amelie:

Today is my last day in civilization. Tomorrow, we will leave with
our pack train. We are six men and ten horses. Morley is an Indian
village.[1] There is only a storage house and a station. We were here
for several days. I waited in vain for your next mail. Now I have to
wait until July 20th, until we get to the Crowsnest Pass. I hope to find
news from you there. First of all, I must say that I am healthy, only my
hand is not yet totally as it should be. I still have to be very careful.
— I read in the newspaper that there are big floods in Carynthia. I
also read about the avalanche accident on the Ortler. I am sure it was
very bad. A big joy was to hear about "the book," and I understand
quite well that you will have to omit some things from it. I leave all
that to you alone. I only beg you <u>not</u> to omit yourself, you who did
so many good things for me!! If it is possible for me, I will finish
writing my experiences in 1910.[2] I talked with Mr. Harmon about the
pictures from here and will also write to my old friends, but it is very
difficult to get anything from tourists. When I return in July, I will
send you money for your expenses for the book up to now. I don't
think I have to mention more about your great sacrifice for me and
about your love for my book. You know that, for as long as I live, I
will be grateful to you for it. One part in your last letter is particularly
touching, where you write about friendship. I thank you especially
for these dear words! I would love to write my thoughts about them,
but I don't find the right words, but remember what I told you about
it on the trail on September 9th, 1912. How are your dear mother and
Flora? Are they both well? Sometime, I have to write to your sister
again. There are many friends that I did not write to for a long time.

The Wanderer, 1912–1916

On June 10th, I thought about it, that your precious name day will be in a month. Another year has gone by! I ordered two little books for you, which I want to give you with my best and sincerest wishes for this year's special day. However, I have not yet received them. I will write to my friend Unwin, who has a bookstore, that he should send you the books right away. These are two short stories from the North, *The Call of the Wild* and *The White Fang*. I am convinced that you will enjoy them. *The Call of the Wild* is especially good. I love the book because I know myself that there is "a call of nature." I feel it in me. I am drawn to nature again and again![3] — On July 10th, I will be thinking of you, wherever I might be, on top of a mountain or in a valley. You know that I do that every year, don't you?[4] — Don't worry about me: I am healthy and in good company. The mountains we will climb seem not to be dangerous. Between August 3rd and 6th, you will receive my next letter. I will now and then write a few lines while in the camp, just like last year. My best greetings to you, and to your Mama and your sister.

Your Conrad

1. In 1877, under the terms of Treaty Number Seven, the three bands of the Stoney First Nation— the Bearspaw, Chiniki, and Wesley groups—were specifically limited to settling on reserve lands at Morley (or Morleyville, as it was sometimes called), in the eastern foothills along the Bow River, where a Methodist mission had been built in 1873. The mission included a church, an orphanage school, agricultural crops, a sawmill, and a trading post. See Ian A.L. Getty and Eric D. Gooding, "Stoney," *Handbook of the North American Indians—Plains* 13, 1 (2001), 599. Being on the CPR line, after 1883, Morley was often the last staging point for pack trains heading south toward the Crowsnest Pass area.

2. "The book," likely Kain's diary, was supplied to Thorington by Malek after Kain's death (see Don Bourdon's epilogue in this volume). It appears in print as the first half of *Where the Clouds Can Go* (1935). Edited by Malek, as well as Thorington, the journal ends in the spring of 1910. Whatever Kain hoped to write beyond 1910 was not completed. Malek later wrote to Thorington to say that Kain "always promised to continue to write, but he never did. Maybe he had no leisure for it, because he had to work hard and earn money even in the winter by trapping." See Kain, *Where the Clouds*, 510.

3. Jack London is best remembered as the author of *The Call of the Wild* (1903) and its companion novel *White Fang* (1906), both of which were set in the Yukon during the famed Klondike Gold

Rush of the late nineteenth century. Kain's attraction to these texts is hardly surprising: both were highly romantic tales that celebrated and perpetuated the very popular ideas of nature and civilization to which Kain so dearly subscribed. Evidenced in his books, London, like Kain, exhibited a "lifelong curiosity about far-flung peoples and places, his class consciousness, and his self-definition as an author and adventurer...." London's daughter and biographer, Joan London, noted that "The dominant theme in all his writings was struggle—the struggle of an individual to survive in a hostile environment or to be successful against all odds." Quoted in Jeanne Campbell Reesman, *Jack London's Radical Lives: A Critical Biography* (Athens: University of Georgia Press, 2009), 6.

4. Malek's name day.

118

On an unnamed mountain near *Elk Pass*.

June 25, 1914

Dear Amelie:

I am sitting here on an unclimbed mountain top! It is not very high, but offers gorgeous views. The top is on the Great Divide. In the East and South, there are bare mountains like the Dolomites, only not so steep. On the scree below, I see wildlife tracks, but no goats or sheep. East of the top, the Elbow Pass can be seen. A week ago, there must have been snow on the Pass. Now it is spring green. In the South, the mountains turn into hills. North of here, the two Kananaskis Lakes can be seen. The upper one is especially beautiful. The colour changes very distinctly. If the sun is shining the lake is light green, but in the shade it is deep blue. On the lake are four little isles and one tiny one with only three or four trees on it. Northwest, one sees the Elk Valley, at the end of which are two larger lakes and, in between them, a small one. In the background, there are high mountains, without names, with hanging glaciers. North-north-west, one can see a bit of Mt. Assiniboine, that is to say we <u>believe</u> this beautiful mountain to be Mt. Assiniboine. The forest consists of fir, spruce, and larch trees. The bottom of the valley is mossy and, thus, many bad flies inhabit it! What can I tell you about the flowers? I cannot find the words! I wish only you could <u>see</u> this garden of flowers! You would be happy like a child, and I would be the happiest man to see you in such happy moments! The flowers are mostly in yellow or white colours. But there are also some red ones. This morning, I found the first forget-me-not in a blue colour for which I have no words. — Yesterday, we were in the forest all day. I thought of you almost all day, because I saw so many flowers, which brought such fond memories. I put some of the flowers in a book to press them for you. What a pity that the life of the flowers is so short! How beautiful it would be if the flowers could reach you fresh, like just picked! ——— There is a cold wind. I have to stop writing and put on gloves. At this windy elevation, I say Good bye for today! ——

————————————— In the camp, June 26, 1914

Today, we have snow and all the mountains are in fog. It is rather cold. We are going into the forest and hack out a baseline.

————————————— In the camp, June 28, 1914

Yesterday, we went up on a little mountain. It was terribly cold. We stayed on top for five hours! On the way back, Mr. West shot a wild goat, so we will have a good goat soup today. Tomorrow, we will move on to Crowsnest Pass. Perhaps for five to six days. Good bye.

————————————— Crowsnest Pass, July 7, 1914

We arrived yesterday and what joy, Amelie! What joy! I received the *Naturfreund*, the *Arbeiterzeitung*, the letter of March 27th, which came via New Zealand, and then your dear letter of June 16st!! How can I thank you for all this, my true friend. I was quite touched by joy! Today, I cannot answer all the questions, because we are very busy. But I have to chat with you about several things. You will be very surprised. ——— The *Naturfreund* ("Love of Life") pleased me much more than the article about Mt. Robson. How well you corrected all the mistakes and polished up the whole thing. I thank you so much and hope that you remain my good comrade and editor forever, that means I hope and wish that you remain in the best of health and that the work you do for me in such an accommodating way means <u>no burden</u> for you. Now let's continue! I am well, only my hand is still weak. I worked very hard with the axe for a few days, and the hand became swollen again. But everything will be okay now. You know that a sprain often lasts longer than a fracture. The trip is beautiful; much of it has been through beautiful forest. And what wonderful flowers! I picked some for you with friendly thoughts. Hundreds of hundreds of miles away and yet so near! I wrote a short article for the *Schwarzataler Zeitung* and would like you to send it. Please also send it to the *Arbeiterzeitung* with the comment that they do not have to pay for it, since I copied the article from my diary. The title is to be "A Cold Day." After the article goes through your hands, it will be quite an interesting and amusing read. It would be my wish to have it printed in the month of August! It should be possible. I don't think the *Schwarzataler Zeitung* is overloaded with material. And now comes the unexpected news: Yes, you will be <u>very</u> surprised to hear that, in the month of August, I will be on the high seas again! A real wanderer, a globetrotter, that is your far away friend!!

—— Early in August, I start a trip from Vancouver or San Francisco to New Zealand.[1] What do you say?!! And I will have to stay eight months! I am sending you a copy of the letter I received, and then you'll know everything. And now I have to ask a favour, if it is not too much! Oh no! Not too much! I know you! You <u>like</u> to do it. Please write a few lines for me for the *Österreichische Touristen Zeitung* with the announcement that: I will be employed by the government of New Zealand until next spring, then I will teach a two-month course for the mountain guides, just like the German and Austrian Alpine Clubs are doing, and, for the remaining time, I will be working as "a special guide" for the high mountain touring. Please give my address: Hermitage Mt. Cook, New Zealand. You understand, you can also take a few lines from my letter. The trip to New Zealand comes as quite a surprise! I had already planned to go back to the forest for the winter time and had other plans as well: Greenland—The North! — The North! — You don't like to hear that, but I have to tell you the truth and write about my longing for the North. It is right what you think about it, but—unfortunately——I cannot help it. But no more of it for now, for as you see: I go <u>South</u>!! Yes, to the far, far South! I do not know yet when the departure will be. My friend, Miss Hollowes, still keeps me waiting for the article about Mt. Cook! I would have liked to have sent it to you by now! It is good and will surely be interesting for the people at home. —— I hope that all three of you are very well and wish that your planned trip to Veldes materializes, since I know it would please you very much. You will see the mountains there again and dear old friends. If you really can go, I wish you beautiful weather and nice company, and may you experience only good memories. Now I must say Good bye, dear friend. I hope you are well and I wish you the best of luck. Kind regards to your dear ones. With much love, I am,

The Wanderer

1. With his steamer delayed for a few days, Kain offered his services via telegram to Albert and Elizabeth (Bess) MacCarthy (1877–1944) following the ACC Upper Yoho Valley Camp. The MacCarthys had interests in the unclimbed Mt. Farnham and Farnham Tower, which, located in the Purcell Mountains, were not far from their "Karmax" ranch near Wilmer, BC. The tower had been deemed "absolutely unclimbable" by a party of climbers only a year earlier. They happily accepted Kain's services, and, on August 10, the three completed the first ascent of both the mountain and its tower. Before reaching the main summit, Kain dropped to the rear and invited Bess MacCarthy to lead to the top. In just two seasons, Kain led the first ascents of the highest mountains in two Canadian ranges. Albert MacCarthy had joined him for both. See A.H. MacCarthy, "First Ascents of Mt. Farnham and Mt. Farnham Tower," CAJ 6 (1914–1915): 112–24.

119

Hermitage, Mt. Cook, November 4, 1914

Dear Amelie:

A few days ago, I received your card of August 25th, and today a card of August 5th. I got a letter from Mr. Hollister, in which he wrote that he received a letter from you, which he sends to the Alpine Club. I have not received it yet. From my trip, I wrote a long letter to you and mailed it in Wellington. Afterwards, I saw in the papers that no mail was forwarded to Austria. So, I wrote the next letter from the Hermitage and sent it to my friend Seaver in New York.[1] Before I continue, I must thank you from my heart for your true, faithful friendship. My heart is aching! How I feel, I can and must not write, since it is clear to me that you are overburdened with sorrow. No half-day passes, when I do not think of you and yours. Your picture stands here on my table and to honour you, I put fresh flowers in the vase that stands in front of your picture. It would be absolutely impossible that at the present you could have an idea of my inner feelings. It is a matter of fact that right now I would like to be at home, although I am AGAINST the war with all my heart and soul. The bad and sad times, however, are yet to come! You see, it is totally impossible for me: I am not permitted to write about the war, no, I must not.[2] ——— One thing I am glad to say, and it is the pure truth, that I am healthy like the "elk in the forest," and you have not heard that from me in a long time, have you? The people are all very friendly, and there are many who sympathize with Austria, because our old Emperor is very popular here in New Zealand. You know that he shipped some chamois over here for the New Zealand Alps that are doing very well and multiplying. A week ago, I saw three of them![3] I have money and would like to send 100 Kronen to my mother. I will write to Hollister about it, perhaps he can do it from America. Now, in these sad times, I have to surprise you with something joyful. Yes, I know, nobody in the world will have more joy than you if I am successful with my endeavour. AND IT HAS TO BE A SUCCESS! I wanted to surprise you with my novel directly: Yes, a novel that you will understand very well! In this novel, you will hear a lot of new things about me. I only fear that tears of laughter will roll down your cheeks. The title of the novel is *The Zillertaler Sepp*. Contents in short: Sepp, born in Mayerhofen (Zillertal), son of poor mountain people, had hardly any schooling, but was by nature a clever boy.[4] He had a keen eye and love for nature. From his twelfth to sixteenth year, he was employed in the hotel in Mayerhofen. His employers were exceptionally good, open minded people. In his second summer, Sepp served the guests and tourists in the garden. Here, many a thing happened. The awakening of love! Sepp met the girl, who plays a big role, if not the biggest in his life. She was the daughter of a merchant from Innsbruck. Because of her, Sepp got his first "slap in the face." In the times that followed, he had a great need for school and science. Also "wander-lust." Became a waiter in Jonbach, then an apprentice at the brewery. But after bad things happen there, he runs away. Later, he becomes a chimney sweep. Returns to his home valley. Becomes a porter at the Berlin Hut. Here, again, he meets the girl, now already a Miss. Both recognize each other. — Sepp later has many more sad experiences, until he gets to Vienna to study. I will tell you later what Sepp does and experiences. For the time being, this gives you an idea of the person, doesn't it? I already wrote more than fifty pages, and, in a few weeks, I will get a typewriter. I'll type it out and send you part of it.[5] In a week, I will write again. Now I'm off to bed. I think and feel with you in these bad times, and I wish I could see you and your people. Remember me kindly to your Mama and to Flora, and please give my love and respect to them. Don't worry too much about the war, and take care of your nerves. It would be a terrible worry for me to hear that you are ill. With many greetings, I am,

your C.K.

1. A member of the ACC since 1907, Benjamin Frank Seaver (1858–1929) was an early member of the American Alpine Club and, for 11 years, served as its treasurer, as well as the vice-president and chairman of its New York Section. His participation with the ACC was limited to its summer camps, where he made Kain's acquaintance. See "Benjamin Frank Seaver, 1858–1929," CAJ 17 (1928): 74–75.

2. By midsummer, Serbia, Russia, and France had allied against the Austro-Hungarian and German empires. At midnight on 4 August, the British ultimatum to Berlin expired and another empire entered the fray. Canada, like New Zealand and Australia, immediately pledged its expected loyal support. Public enthusiasm was resounding. In the Prairie provinces, the war ended the depression in agriculture. But the global turmoil was nevertheless worrisome for any Canadians of Germanic origin. Public mail service at home was necessarily reduced owing to the extensive mobilization, and service to Europe was disrupted. Across the country, as well, peoples of Germanic origin faced prosecution. Germans and Austrians were dismissed from public employment, and the teaching of German in schools and universities was banned. The city of Berlin in southwestern Ontario was pressured by patriots to change its name to Kitchener. By the following spring, public clamour was such that the government interned several thousand largely harmless people. See Morton, *A Short History of Canada*, 164–65.

3. A goat-antelope species native to Europe, chamois arrived in New Zealand in 1907 as a gift from the Austrian Emperor, Franz Joseph. The original release of eight animals (two male, six female) was made in the Aoraki/Mt. Cook region. While only two additional animals were released in 1913, the chamois populations quickly grew and spread throughout the Southern Alps.

4. Mayerhofen was a mountain village in the *Zillertal* (the Ziller River Valley) of Tyrol, approximately 70 kilometres east of Innsbruck, Austria.

5. The manuscript of Kain's seemingly autobiographical romance novel has disappeared. It appears to be his first attempt at writing fiction.

120

Hermitage [no date]

Dear Friend:

Thousands of miles lie between us, and now the whole mail service
has stopped. The long, long letter I mailed in Wellington you will
only receive when this inhuman, terrible, voracious, and murdering
war is over. I must not start to write down my thoughts or I will go
too far, because it will go on, oh, how long. I will not hear from you
and my people! Can you imagine how I feel? There is no travelling
home. It is quite impossible! I inquired about it. If it is possible, I
even think more about all of you now than ever before! Miss Flora
will probably be in the war with the Red Cross, and you will live with
worry from day to day! Believe me, I feel with you and your dear
Mama. In my mind, I am in my home country protecting you from
all dangers! There is no sense in writing much, if one does not know
whether you will receive the letter. I am trying to send it via America,
so perhaps it will reach you. I will send it to Mr. MacCarthy in New
York. If that works, then you can write me too, and you send it to my
friend Seaver. He will be so kind and send the letter to New Zealand
with American stamps, just as he will do it with this letter. I write the
address, seal the letter, and put it in an extra envelope. Then it will be
sent with a five-cent stamp. That is the only way I can see it working.[1]
I am healthy and feeling quite well. I hope and wish that this war will
be over soon! I would like to send my mother a few hundred Kronen,
but cannot risk it. Now I will close. Dear Amelie, if you experience
much sadness at this time where one cannot hope for anything
good, then know that your wandering friend feels everything with

you. Greetings to your mother and Flora (if possible!). Farewell, dear friend, farewell, sweet home, I am with you in spirit.

Yours C.K.

Address: Benj. F. Seaver Esq., 338 Piersepont Street, Brooklyn, N.Y.

---

1. The United States initially pursued a policy of non-intervention and maintained diplomatic relations in hopes of brokering peace. However, after several US merchant ships were sunk by German U-boats in an unrestricted military campaign at sea, and following the publication of the "Zimmerman Telegram" (which exposed Germany's invitation to Mexico to join as an ally and, with German investment, invade the US from the south), the US declared war with Germany on 6 April 1917.

121

Hermitage (Mount Cook), January 25, 1915

Dear Amelie:

Yesterday, I received your dear letter of September 29, 1914. It was
such a joy for me! My best thanks for it! It is a great comfort for me
to hear that you and yours, and my family, are all well. There are
already many tourists here, and we are all busy. Don't worry about
me, but please comfort my mother if she worries. Next summer, I
am supposed to travel to Switzerland with two ladies from New York.
Unfortunately, there will be no peace yet in Europe. People here are
all very good and friendly to me. In one way, I feel at home in the
Hermitage, but not quite happy. I shall travel North again to a cold
climate in the wilderness, but have to stay here until the end of April.
You have no idea what joy my novel *The Zillertaler Sepp* brings me!
You too will read it with joy. Of course, you have to work hard and
well at the manuscript. Once I finished *Sepp*, I will write a short story
for the *Arbeiterzeitung*. The title is *"Der Alm-Wastl."*[1] I cannot imagine
what is the matter with my Vancouver lady friend. Up to now, no
answer about the article about Mt. Robson. In the *Canadian Alpine
Journal* (1914–15), an article of mine (Mount Robson) appeared. I
wrote to Mr. Mitchell and asked him to send you this magazine. Two
weeks ago, I was on the West Coast. It was a marvellous tour: beautiful forests, flowers, and so many birds! It was a pleasure for the soul
to wander through the forest. I collected flowers for you. I am so
sorry to think you cannot see for yourself once in your life this beauty
of nature in the Far South! Again and again, I have to say that I don't
find the right words to describe such beauty. Amelie, don't get too
upset about these cruel times! Together, we must see some more of

the beautiful mountains and nature and for that we need, above all, <u>our health</u>. With the heartiest greeting to all,

your Conrad

1.   "The Waste Land."

344

122

Hermitage, Mount Cook, March 30, 1915

Dear Amelie:

[In English from hereon] Time is passing very fast. The season here is
coming to its end, and I am very glad too. I have been working very
hard these four months. By now, I climbed over <u>forty</u> peaks in New
Zealand, and I feel rather overworked now.[1] Let me tell you some
news. I am sailing on the 17th of May from Auckland to Vancouver.
Next summer, I shall be again in the Rockies with Mr. Frind for three
months, and next winter I shall go trapping far North again.[2] It seems
to me the best time a man can have is, when one is far away in the
woods. Of course, I am thinking many times of you and my people
and all my friends at home. Let us hope too that this terrible War is
over before the next winter sets in. Then we shall again be able to
hear regularly from each other. Now it is very difficult. *[In German
from hereon]* You will understand, but you don't know what postal
regulations exist here. I am healthy and saved a small sum of money.
Unfortunately, I cannot send any money home to my mother. I thank
you so much for caring like that for my mother. Please comfort her
regarding me. I am among good people, and it is not likely that
something bad should happen to me. I hope you are healthy, so
that you can write to my mother from time to time. I know what joy
it is for her when she receives a letter from you. Now farewell, dear
Amelie, greetings from my heart to your dear mother and to Flora. I
am and remain your sincere *C.K.*

P.S. Didn't have much time to continue writing my novel (Sepp)!!

1. The list of Kain's 1914–1915 climbs in New Zealand was compiled by Peter Graham and published in Kain, *Where the Clouds*, 399–401. Many of these ascents were made with local aspirant guides, whom Kain was hired to instruct (a role for which Kain would later receive official recognition); other guides were with new and repeat tourists and clients. Kain made first ascents of Mt. Jean (2,519 m [8,264 ft.]), Eagle Peak (2,548 m [8,360 ft.]), Mt. Low (2,942 m [9,652 ft.]), Mt. Jellicoe (2,827 m [9,275 ft.]), Mt. Sturdee (2,708 m [8,884 ft.]), Mt. Jeanette (2,485 m [8,153 ft.]), Mt. Meeson (2,716 m [8,911 ft.]), Spence Peak (2,458 m [8,064 ft.]), and Mt. McKerrow (2,316 m [7,598 ft.]). During this season, Kain continued to dabble in literary fiction and wrote "The Millionaire Guide," perhaps his best-remembered story, and was recounted by him in the Altai, in New Zealand, and at many Canadian campfires. The story was pure fiction: Kain never ascended the Grossglockner (3,798 m [12,460 ft.]), Austria's highest mountain. The short story was published in 1915 in the *Christchurch Press* and was later reprinted in P.A.W. Wallace's *The Twist; and Other Stories* (1923). Most recently, "The Millionaire Guide" was reprinted in Bruce Fairley, ed., *Canadian Mountaineering Anthology: Stories from 100 Years at the Edge* (Vancouver: Lone Pine, 1994), 338–49.

2. In the spring of 1915, upon returning to Canada, Kain went to work for Albert and Bess MacCarthy at their Karmax ranch in the Columbia Valley. He guided at the 1915 ACC Ptarmigan Valley Camp later that summer, but not as an employee of the club; rather, he attended as the private guide of H.O. Frind. After the camp, Kain again joined the MacCarthys in the Purcells and, with Frind and Winthrop and Margaret Stone, explored the Big Salmon and Horsethief Valleys. A considerable number of first ascents were made, among them Mt. Jumbo (3,437 m [11,276 ft.]) and a smaller unnamed peak, which Albert MacCarthy, having scaled it with Kain on 10 August, named "Birthday Peak" to honour the guide's thirty-second birthday. Of their adventures in the Purcells, Winthrop Stone, whom Kain had first guided on Mt. Resplendent in 1913 (see Letter 98), wrote a detailed account in the 1916 *CAJ*. See W.E. Stone, "Climbs and Explorations in the Purcell Range in 1915," *CAJ* 7 (1916): 12–32. After the Canadian summer of 1915, despite his plans to spend the winter trapping, Kain voyaged to New Zealand for a third climbing season, this time as a private guide.

123

Honolulu, November 2, 1915

Dear Friend:

I don't know what you will think about my long silence. Yes, I was
back in the Rockies during the summer. At present, I am on my way
back to New Zealand. I hope you were, or are, not worried about me.
The bloody war is still raging in Europe, which even here you feel in
many ways. As a foreigner, I often face difficulties. To avoid all this I
wrote to <u>nobody</u>. I personally cannot complain, since I manage everywhere quite well, but, still, it is good to be cautious. However, I have
a few hours in a "neutral country" and can mail the letter myself,
so I use the opportunity to write. First of all, I have to tell you that
I am in the best of health. I feel stress only when I think of you, my
home country, and of my family. But I must not begin to <u>dwell</u> on
it. You know why! — The last summer in the Rockies was not the
best. First, there was bad weather, but, in spite of it, we did some
first ascents. The last two months, I worked on Cpt. MacCarthy's
ranch in the Columbia Valley. The Cpt. and his wife will also come
to New Zealand for six weeks. I hope I will have no trouble landing
there. In spring, I hope to go back to Canada. For the future, I don't
have many plans yet. It is possible that I still might travel, finally to
the cold North (North Pole). I know you don't like this idea of mine,
but what shall I do? You know that the course of my life was and is
a hard one. From year to year, I lived with the hope to reach a goal,
and in the end I see my plans would be good, but for the injustice of
the world with its money-hungry people makes so much impossible
to achieve for most of us poor people. I realize that more from day
to day. So I came to the decision that I would lose nothing were I to
lose my life on a North Pole expedition. Don't get scared because of

my plans. I will not forget my poor, good mother and will look after her. I will leave life insurance in order. Wherever I will be, I will never forget you and your family. You know how fond I am of you. If only I could write everything that is in my heart, then I would be happier. Now I will write about other matters. With this letter, I am sending you the *Canadian Alpine Journal* (1914–1915).[1] I hope you receive it, even though probably much later than the letter. Since the book is in English, it will of course be carefully censored. Here, I can say that this evil, bloody, capitalistic war, which destroys the lives of young people, should make no distinctions among people and nations, and then there would be no war. — You will be pleased when I tell you that last summer that I wrote several articles about mountains and climbing that are already in print. One day, you will read them. At the moment, I am writing about trapping experiences. I did not write much of my novel, *The Zillertaler Sepp*, but I don't give up this work. It is possible that I will use the whole month of April for writing. I can write now more fluently than before. *[In English from hereon]* I have developed my thinking power and sometimes I really cannot believe that my life should be a failure! You see, I have not lost all my hopes and should I be able to keep on thinking and developing my brain, I might still be of some use in the world, for my class, the working-class, down trodden by the capitalism. I know I shall have luck with my trapper-stories. I found out a better way of writing. First, I write down notes, and then I dictate them to a stenographer and have it copied. Then I work it out, ready for print. I found out that I save time through this system. — *[In German from hereon]* I would like to know, how many colleagues and acquaintances in Europe I have lost because of this war. Already, there are many on the English side. I rarely read the war reports in the newspapers. I get too upset about them. I must say that, for a long time, I lived in doubt whether there is a higher being. Now I see that clearer in many ways. I often wrote to you about my thoughts and ideas, and so I will also tell you now about my conclusions after long and deep thinking: it is impossible for me to believe in a God the way he is explained to us. No, that is totally impossible. But it is possible that there is a power in nature, as yet not researched, and perhaps remaining unexplainable for us average human beings. I am convinced that, because of this war, the various branches of the Christian religion will <u>lose</u> many members and followers. I hope this will only be for the best of mankind. In my opinion, the Christian religions are by now nothing but <u>servants of capitalism,</u> dedicated to their own well-being. ———— In case America remains neutral, do write to Mr. Seaver in New York sometime. Do write how many of my colleagues are already lost. I must close now. I hope you and yours are all well. Please give my greetings to all acquaintances you are in touch with. I remain your grateful friend

C.K.

1. The volume, CAJ 6 (1914–1915), contained Kain's account of his ascents up Mounts Robson and Whitehorn, as well as several other articles written about Kain's exploits in 1913 and 1914: Kain, "The First Ascent of Mount Robson (1913)," 19–28; Kain, "First Ascent of Mt. Whitehorn (August 12th, 1911)," 49–51; W.W. Foster, "Mount Robson (1913)," 11–18; Albert H. MacCarthy and Basil S. Darling, "An Ascent of Mount Robson from the Southwest (1913)," 37–48; W.E. Stone, "A Day and a Night on Whitehorn (1913)," 55–64; C.H. Mitchell, "Mount Resplendent and the Routes of Ascent (1913)," 65–73; MacCarthy, "First Ascent of Mt. Farnham and Mt. Farnham Tower (1914)," 112–24; Arthur O. Wheeler, "Robson Glacier," 139–42; K.B. Hallows, "Mount Robson Camp (1913)," 212–25; J. MacCartney Wilson, "The Camp in the Upper Yoho Valley (1914)," 217–28. The sheer number of articles that featured Kain and his exploits in just this single volume of the CAJ is striking evidence of his importance to the ACC in 1914–1915. For Kain, it was one of a half-dozen extraordinary climbing seasons.

124

RMS *Niagara*, Easter Sunday, 1916

Dear Amelie:

I know that you think of me often. Hardly a day goes by that I don't think of you and my home country. Unfortunately, I could not write, since that would have had difficult consequences for me. In a few days, we get to Honolulu, an American port, so I am in a place to mail the letter myself. You will be surprised to hear that I was <u>imprisoned</u> for three weeks (in Wellington, N.Z.) because of my nationality, and it happened to me in a very strange way. Last year, I worked for the government. This year, I went there on my own account. This caused terrible jealousy among the local guides! In one way, I cannot hold it against the dummies because I did more <u>first ascents</u> than all of the guides did between themselves!![1] Of course, they could not find any mistakes I made. So they sent letters to the Department of War and to the police, and when I got to Wellington and asked for a passport for Canada, I was detained! — Since all my papers were in order, they could not send me to the island, where all the German and Austrian prisoners of war are held.[2] An investigation was started, and one found out that I am an honest man and that the reason for this "blackmailing" was only envy and business jealousy. I have many good friends in New Zealand who came to my help with advice and action. Two members of parliament took care of me. I also had friends who wrote to the Minister of War to say that they always found me to be an honest and decent man. They also said that I am an "Anti-War-Man." So, finally, I was let go and received my passport for Canada! There, I am quite a different man again and I am among quite different people! Here you saw an example what jealousy can do! I talked with the Minister of War in person. He said, "I am

convinced that you are a good man, otherwise Sir John Fyndly, M.P.,
Mr. Field, M.P., Mr. Lee, M.P., and so many of your friends would not
have vouched for you <u>so</u> convincingly. When the war is over and you
come back to New Zealand, then I will climb Mt. Cook with you!"[3]

——— During the past months, I wrote several articles which I will
send to you when the war has ended, that is, if there will be an end
at all! — As for my novel, *The Zillertaler Sepp*, I don't write anything
more. You will understand that, at present, it is hard to write in
German. I write everything in English and make progress with it
more and more. The last story I wrote was "My Recollections as a
Tramp."[4] Yesterday, I began a new story. The title is "What She Did for
Her Husband's Sake." I write most of the time. Up to now, we always
have had good weather. Today is Easter Sunday. Most people attend
church service, and that gives me the best opportunity to write in
German. I don't know whether the letters from America are censored
in Austria, therefore I rather write German to not create any problems for you. How I would like to tell you a lot more, dear Amelie.
What joy it will be once there is no more war. I can then write to you
as often and as much as in former times! — And just now, I am in a
situation where I need your advice. I went through a lot since I was at
home the last time. I am tired of so much travelling. I want to settle
down and have my own home, etc., but I wait until that awful capitalistic war is over. I hope the revolutions after the war will not last
as long as the war itself. You will for sure realize, dear Amelie, that
revolutions <u>have</u> to take place when the war ends. It is sad, but true!
Please write to me sometime, again via Mr. Seaver. I hope that you
are healthy, my dear friend. Greetings to all my acquaintances. How
are your mother and Flora? I hope you all are enjoying good health.
Don't worry about me, my good comrade. I'll get through anything.
Today I will write to my mother. Now I say Addio. Stay well in these
hard times. With best greetings and wishes, I remain your wandering
friend,

C.K.

1. Kain's presence at the Hermitage in 1915–1916 undoubtedly took business away from the government guides. He was now well known in the area and well liked. By the end of his third season in the range, Kain had climbed 59 mountains, of which 29 were first ascents. It was a record matched by few. What created the greatest controversy, though, was his successful repeat of the Aoraki/Mt. Cook "Grand Traverse" on 31 January 1916 with Jane Thomson (1858–1944) of Wellington. The route—a marathon, which connected all three summits of the massif—had only been climbed once before—just three years earlier, by Freda Du Faur, Peter Graham, and Darby Thomson. Du Faur and her guides prophesized that "the greatest climb in New Zealand" "would not be done again for twenty years, if ever." Du Faur, *The Conquest of Mount Cook* (1915), 206–07. Thus, it was presumably with great shock that those assembled at the Hermitage received Kain and his client back from their ascent. Not only did Kain guide the route alone, he completed the traverse considerably faster than did the first ascentionists—and with a client who was 59 years of age. Arthur Harper (1865–1955), the president of NZAC, was vocal about his concern: "I always think his most daring bit of work and, if I may say so, a climb he should not have done, was when he took Mrs. Thomson over the three peaks of Cook. She was an oldish lady of 59, who had gone through a long course of lower peaks and was very keen, but personally I do not think Conrad was quite right to do this alone with her." Kain, *Where the Clouds*, 405. Add to all of this the fact that it was the height of the First World War—arguably the most traumatic event in New Zealand's experience—and Kain, despite being naturalized, was seen by many as an enemy. He was soon after notified that the government would no longer permit private guiding in the Southern Alps. No explanation was given. Kain, *Where the Clouds*, 416. Kain would never guide in New Zealand again.

2. During the First World War, "enemy aliens" in New Zealand were interned in camps on Motuihe and Matiu/Somes Islands. Kain is likely referring to the latter (Matiu/Somes Island), which was the largest of three small islands in Wellington Harbour and held 300 prisoners during the war. See David McGill, *Islands of Secrets: Matiu/Somes Island in Wellington Harbour* (Wellington, NZ: Steele Roberts, 2001).

3. New Zealand's minister of defense during the First World War, James Allen (1855–1942), was no doubt impressed by Kain's ministerial connections. Indicative of the class dimensions of mountaineering's early patronage in New Zealand (as elsewhere), it was an impressive list of people that vouched for Kain's character: Findlay, "a great friend of nature," was the ex-minister of justice (see Letter 111); William Hughes ("Willie") Field (1861–1944) was the Reform MP for Otaki; and Ernest Page Lee (1862–1932), the MP for Oamaru, and later the minister of foreign affairs, had accompanied Kain on several guided ascents from the Hermitage during the 1914–1915 season. See Kain, *Where the Clouds*, 399.

4. These adventure tales form the opening chapters of Thorington's *Where the Clouds Can Go* (1935). Jane Thomson, Kain's client on the Grand Traverse that January, recalled that "when stormbound in a hut he was fond of writing stories for publication. One I remember was called 'The Adventures of a Hobo,' but I do not know if it ever appeared in print." Kain, *Where the Clouds*, 424.

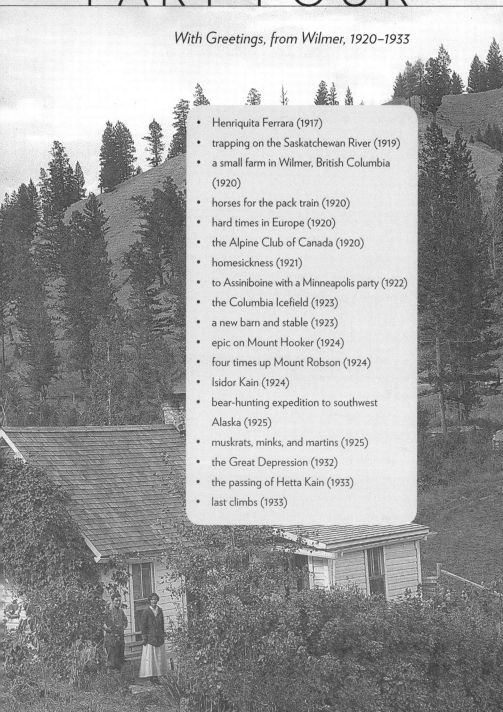

PART FOUR

With Greetings, from Wilmer, 1920–1933

- Henriquita Ferrara (1917)
- trapping on the Saskatchewan River (1919)
- a small farm in Wilmer, British Columbia (1920)
- horses for the pack train (1920)
- hard times in Europe (1920)
- the Alpine Club of Canada (1920)
- homesickness (1921)
- to Assiniboine with a Minneapolis party (1922)
- the Columbia Icefield (1923)
- a new barn and stable (1923)
- epic on Mount Hooker (1924)
- four times up Mount Robson (1924)
- Isidor Kain (1924)
- bear-hunting expedition to southwest Alaska (1925)
- muskrats, minks, and martins (1925)
- the Great Depression (1932)
- the passing of Hetta Kain (1933)
- last climbs (1933)

125

[In English from hereon]

On train from Golden to Laggan, January 13, 1920

My dear friend Amelie:

At New Year I came home from the woods and to my joy I found a letter from Mr. Mitchell and the one you wrote to him. Two days ago I got your kind letter ——— well, Amelie, I always knew that you are a real friend to me, yes, I felt it since I met you in the Ennstal. And now after I had been in the wide world and had met all kinds of people, I appreciate your friendship more than ever. I know you must have wondered, why I did not write anymore since Easter 1916, when I posted my last letter at Honolulu. During wartime it was a dangerous affaire to correspond with anyone outside Canada, and when Peace was proclaimed, I was far away. Now first of all let me tell you, that I am very sorry to say that I have nearly forgotten my German!! But I shall soon catch it up again. I shall have to read in German!! It is more than three years that I had not had any chance to speak my mother-language. *[In German from hereon]* Now, I will tell you in short what I experienced during the last four years. After my return from New Zealand to Canada in 1916, the summer was spent with mountain guiding.[1] In the fall, I travelled back to the old forest. Oh, it was nice to live in peace in the wilderness. Never before in my life had I felt the mysterious calmness so much as in the winter of 1916. For five months, I was completely alone there.[2] I did not see a soul and thought a lot about life. I was homesick, and often my heart nearly broke with pain. Although I was and am an

> Hetta Kain in a wheat field at the Kains' farm in Wilmer, 1923. Photo by Byron Harmon. [WMCR, V263/4236]

opponent of militarism, I felt I should have been <u>there</u> in wartime! About this feeling I will write in detail in my next letter. That letter which I will write to you in my cabin will be a long one, maybe the longest you ever received. When I returned from the jungle to Wilmer[3] in the spring of 1917, I found my best lady friend here was very ill. The doctor did not know what to do, so I took the patient to the hospital in Cranbrook, the nearest town. The doctor there said that the only help would be a dangerous operation, otherwise there would be no possibility to save my friend Hetta's life. That was in the morning. On that same morning, I gave Hetta my hand and we got married. It was a sad wedding. The next day, my wife was operated upon, which took six hours to complete. After five weeks, Hetta returned to Wilmer and, after the operation had been paid, we both possessed a wealth of only a few cents!! Her money and my money was gone![4] Canada is a good country as long as one is healthy and strong. For the sick people and the poor, Canada is nothing. It is heartless! At the present, there is only one single free hospital in the country. Afterwards, we lived on a ranch and got back on our feet. In summer 1918, I worked in a mine in the mountains and was always away from home.[5] The winter 1918/19, I spent again with trapping, and, in the summer 1919, I worked with A.O. Wheeler.[6] I am now on a trapping tour again. So, I am still a wanderer and perhaps I will have to put up with this hard life for a few more winter seasons. The consequences of this hard life become visible on me: wrinkles and a weather beaten face have set in to stay. I will come home for a visit once there will be peace in all countries. I want to see my mother once more, and it is my wish to spend several years at home, yes, and if possible, I will spend my last years AT THE FOOT OF THE RAX.
—— But peace is not yet at the right place. USA and Canada have also had to bear the bad consequences of the war, and it would be no surprise to hear that the revolution erupts here. Here, too, the prices are high. It is unbelievable—but it will even get worse, I'm afraid.[7] I shall convey my experiences and opinions about these matters to you. Yes, there would be so much to tell each other, if we could meet now! My observations might be quite different from yours, having

been in three countries during the war. My brother Eugen wrote two letters to me, but he did not give me extensive news about the conditions in Austria. I hope and wish that everything gets better, and that you and yours get through the crisis well. I want to find you all alive and spend some days with you and yours. In the paper, I read about the hardships in Austria, but one cannot always believe such views. I wish that there will be _real_ peace. I believe many changes will have to be made, before it is possible that peace comes and remains. I cannot see yet, how this is possible. ———— Tomorrow, at 4 A.M., I will leave civilization and, since the train is already in Laggan, I have to close for now, hoping and wishing that you, your dear mother and Flora are healthy. I forgot the married name of your sister.[8] With heartiest greetings, your wandering friend *C.K.*

1. It was a remarkable guiding season, perhaps Kain's greatest. Upon his return to Banff in mid-July, Kain immediately went to work for Albert and Bess MacCarthy. After a brief visit to the ACC summer camp, held in 1916 in the Healy Creek Valley, not far from Simpson Pass (see "Report of Healy Creek Camp," CAJ 8 (1917): 145–48), the MacCarthys and Kain, along with Winthrop and Margaret Stone, made a day excursion on 19 July to the Forty Mile Creek area, behind Mt. Edith, just northwest of Banff. What was to be a "day's picnic," "to view the scenery," resulted in Albert MacCarthy and Kain making the first ascent of Mt. Louis. A.H. MacCarthy, "The First Ascent of Mount Louis," CAJ 8 (1917): 79–86. Their good luck continued throughout the summer. The group, reunited with H.O. Frind, returned to the Purcells for a 23-day trip with Madeline Turnor, who helped with the cooking, and Bill Williams, from the Shuswap Reserve, as packer. See W.E. Stone, "Climbs and Explorations in the Purcell Range in 1915," CAJ 7 (1916): 43–70. Massive spires to the northwest beckoned them from every high peak they had climbed, and, so, late in the summer, Kain, the MacCarthys, Frind, and Mrs. George E. Vincent and her son, John, along with two packers, travelled to the headwaters of Bugaboo Creek. A.H. MacCarthy, "The Howser and Bugaboo Spires, Purcell Range," CAJ 8 (1917): 17. Thorington summarized the trip well: "here were peaks to be compared with Conrad's best efforts in the Alps. It was pioneer work, and the loftiest mountains were the attraction; but these, unlike highest summits of many groups, were needles to test one's mettle. Howser Spire and Bugaboo Spire were conquered. Ever afterward Conrad would think of Bugaboo Spire as his most difficult Canadian ascent." Kain, *Where the Clouds*, 426.

2. From October to May, Kain spent the long winter alone in a cabin near the headwaters of the Simpson River, on the western slope of the Divide, northwest of Mt. Assiniboine.

3. Wilmer, BC, was a small hamlet, just north of Invermere, in the Columbia Valley. After leaving his trap line in the spring of 1917, Kain went to work for Albert and Bess MacCarthy, at their Karmax Ranch, which sat on the bench lands above the hamlet.

4. Kain married Henriquita ("Hetta") Ferrara (née Granito, 1884–1933) in June 1917. She was then in the employ of the MacCarthys and had lived in Wilmer since 1913. Originally from Georgetown, Guyana, she was educated in a Roman Catholic convent, where she learned to speak English, and, at graduation, married J. Ferrara. They had one daughter, Beatrice. After her husband died, Henriquita followed her brothers, John and Anthony Granito, to Canada. She travelled with her mother, her sister, Ursula, and her daughter. Henriquita and Kain continued to live at the MacCarthys' ranch for three years after their marriage. Prior to marrying Kain, Henriquita's last name was often spelled as "Ferreira," which, according to her grandniece, Barb Neraasen, is incorrect.

5. Little is known about Kain's activities or whereabouts in 1918, although most commentators believe he remained near Wilmer. See Kain, *Where the Clouds*, 436. Transcriptions from the Conrad Kain file at the Windermere Valley Museum claim that it was in this year that "he promised Hetta that he'd give up his mountaineering. He bought a few horses and broke them in with the help of Mrs. Bill Palmer and Rosie Kinbasket. Hetta always prepared a special dinner on the days that the Indian women came to help Conrad." In a letter to his New Zealand client Jane Thomson, written in the spring of 1917, Kain admitted that "I sometimes think that I must have been mad that I did follow up mountain guiding as long as I did. I do not say that mountain guiding is foolishness, no, by no means. I think it one of the finest healthy sports. I love mountains, the climbing, and the view from a summit, but I think it is first class folly to try to make a living off it...Nobody but my friends in the old country know about it, but as I now have decided to give up mountain guiding I will tell you." Kain, *Where the Clouds*, 434–35. Kain made a brief appearance at the ACC's 1917 Cataract Valley Camp, where he guided Albert and Bess MacCarthy up Mt. Hungabee (3,492 m [11,457 ft.]), but that remains, it seems, his last guiding work for some time. It was the first climb of Mt. Hungabee made by a woman. See "Report of the Cataract Valley Camp," *CAJ* 9 (1918): 169.

6. In March of 1919, Kain climbed Jumbo Mountain (3,437 m [11,276 ft.]) alone and in snowshoes. It was the first high winter ascent of a peak in the Purcells and perhaps the first winter ascent of a mountain that exceeded 3,353 metres [11,000 ft.] in the Canadian ranges. Later that spring, in May, Kain wrote to Wheeler seeking summer work. As in previous years, Wheeler employed Kain with the Boundary Survey, which, in 1919, surveyed the major passes along the divide from Thompson Pass (Castleguard Meadows) north to Fortress Lake. See R.W. Cautley and A.O. Wheeler, *Report of the Commission Appointed to Delimit the Boundary between the Provinces of Alberta and British Columbia, Part II, 1917 to 1921, From Kicking Horse Pass to Yellowhead Pass* (Ottawa: Office of the Surveyor General, 1924), 55–81. According to Thorington, "during the wet and cloudy days, when the surveyors could not photograph, Conrad had used the time building cabins and shelters along the lines of his trapping." Kain, *Where the Clouds*, 438. Later in the year, Kain returned and spent the winter (until February) trapping around Castleguard and Alexandra Rivers, just south of the Columbia Icefield.

7. The years immediately following the First World War were lean ones for most Canadians. Once the war ended in November 1918, so too did the heightened demand for goods and services, triggering a rise in unemployment in manufacturing sectors. Those with jobs had increased difficulty maintaining their standard of living as prices rose rapidly. By 1919, a wave of industrial unrest swept to country; according to historian John Thompson, "3.4 million workdays were lost through strikes." John Herd Thompson with Allen Seager, *Canada, 1922–1939: Decades of Discord* (Toronto: McClelland and Stewart, 1985), 17. In the West, by the early 1920s, inflation, a prairie drought, and the continued Eastern insistence on protectionism all conspired against farmers, who hadn't forgotten how, in 1917, Borden's Unionist government stripped their labour force by failing to exempt their sons from military service. Loyalties to the old-time political parties were swept aside, as evidenced by the phenomenal rise of the National Progressive Party, the first of several western-based political reform movements in the twentieth century that signaled the region's dissatisfaction with the Ontario-Quebec political bloc. See Thompson and Seager, *Canada, 1922–1939*, 16.

8. Amelie Malek's younger sister, Flora, married Karl Rotter of Reichenau.

126

Wilmer, B.C., May 16, 1920

Dear Friend:

Last winter in February, I was sick and alone in my cabin at the west fork of the Saskatchewan River and thus had time to write. I wrote as long as I had paper. Through this, I lightened the load on my heart. But after reading it all, I found that my long letter painted too sad a picture of me and would for sure not please you to read. I have to clarify this matter. — In my last letter, I mentioned that I spent as many as five months alone in the wilderness. I observed within myself, as well as in other men, that if you live in nature, which by now has not yet been damaged or destroyed, these surroundings make an unbelievable impression on you. One becomes simple and natural like nature itself. And when you are like that, one talks and writes as one thinks. And I wrote exactly as I thought about every-thing, what concerns you, my people, and my home country. I want to tell you everything so that you perhaps can imagine. All the years when there was war, I was far from happy. Oh, Amelie, it is indescrib-able how my heart was heavy much of the time. Often I was so home-sick that I did not know what to do. I did not burden anybody by talking about my pain and worry, but I am not ashamed to tell you that, in the wild forest, I often cried. Tears shed from the eyes of a grown, tough man are the most painful. You know that I was never was a friend of militarism and had no positive views about it. But, anyway, Austria is MY HOME COUNTRY and I LOVE my moun-tains! It is MY WISH FROM MY HEART that I will find my final resting place in MY HOME COUNTRY. ——— Like so many others I also anticipated that a war like this war would be unavoidable. Unfortunately, things turned out worse and the time brought

more misery and hardship than one could have anticipated. I spent many a sleepless night because of it and felt that I SHOULD BE AT HOME WITH MY FAMILY AND WITH MY FRIENDS! But could I have helped somehow? I think, hardly. Deep down in my heart, I had an urge to help in this time of need in Austria! I think that I mentioned in my last letter that I marvelled at the strength and power of the press and religion during the years of war. I must repeat that it is quite unbelievable the influence a newspaper can have on people. I am very sorry that the churches (Catholic and Protestant) did not do anything good for humanity. On the contrary, the religions and their teachers permitted nationalistic propaganda. You would be astonished if I could describe everything I read and heard with my own eyes and ears! Perhaps you heard or read that during the peace negotiations the word "GOD" was never mentioned. The League of Nations does not impress me very favourably.[1] What do you think about it, dear Amelie? I consider the whole movement as a veiled monument. The veil is humanity. But what is beneath the veil?
——— I am convinced that many representatives of the League of Nations are honest thinking men, but today there is more money in the world than ever before, and it is a sad truth that God and money can only lead honest men to bad decisions. With this sentence, I want to end my thoughts about this subject. ——— On April 13th, I returned home from the "jungle" (to Wilmer, B.C.) and found letters from my mother, my brother, and Emanuel Kain. My wife let me read the letter you wrote to her. I wish I could write English as well as you. My good mother asked me for help, and I am gladly willing to help her. I went to the bank right away and asked about current exchange rates. Then, I went to the post office and could not get an exact answer to my question. In the end, I got the wrong information. I wrote to a friend in New York for information and received an answer yesterday. So now I can breathe easier. I will remit the money right away. I also found out with great joy that one can send shoes, cloth, and linen to Austria. If you write on the parcel "gift of love," the recipient does not have to pay duty.[2] My dear friend, now I have to ask a great favour of you. You have done so much good for my mother and

myself. You did so much for <u>me</u> that I can never repay you. That is impossible. My favour I am asking is: Amelie, permit me to send you a new pair of shoes from here. And I beg from my heart: write me, whether I can do anything for you. I am not a rich man, but I gladly would help you, if I can. My brother wrote about the dollar parcels, but it was not very clear to me. I have the solution. Here it is: *[In English from hereon]* "The Canadian Bank of Commerce carries Red Cross drafts for 10 Dollars and 50 Dollars each, on which food for that amount is given out in Vienna." So now I will go to the bank and see what can be done. What I would like to know is this: how much food-stuff will the Red Cross in Vienna hand out for 10 Dollars? *[In German from hereon]* I also learned that for 60 Dollars you now get 10,000 Kronen. I don't know what to do. Of course, I want my mother to benefit from this. I could send money. How much could my mother buy for 1,000 Kronen? Can she get things she needs? This is what I'm trying to figure out. —— Hetta will write and answer your dear letter. She will tell you that, the day before yesterday, we returned from a short excursion. These were our first holidays since we got married.[3] Yesterday, I received your dear letter and was full of joy about it. Then, I thought about the misery in Austria, and I became quite melancholy and thought about it all night. Now I decided the following: first, I will send a draft to the Red Cross in Vienna so that my mother gets groceries for it and also send her some dollars via a bank in Chicago. Now, dear Amelie, listen to me. My heart is also aching to know whether you and your dear mother, who was always so good to me, have enough to eat. Earlier, I begged you to accept a pair of new shoes from me as a gift. My heart tells me: "Please don't ask! But you owe Mrs. and Miss M. a lot, and it is your duty to help!" That is what a voice in my heart tells me. Yes, the voice is right. I DO OWE both of you a lot. Don't be angry, dear friend, I MUST follow this voice. I will send a 10 Dollar draft from the Bank of Commerce from which you will get food, and, I hope, good and nutritious things. Please write, what kind of food they distribute. ——

Continued May 17

This morning, I went to the bank. The matter will soon be settled. The bank here is a very small one, and I could not get a draft here. But the bank manager will fix things for us. He asks for a draft from the Bank of Commerce in Calgary. I am sorry, it will take a few days, but I am sure it will be in your hands in about a week. The banker believes that you will have no difficulty to buy food in Vienna with this draft. One draft for 10 Dollars is for you and your mother, and one is for my mother. I shall also send her some money. I believe she will receive about 2,000 Kronen for 10 Dollars, or food from the Red Cross. Please help my mother in the event that she has trouble with the exchange. I hope there will be no difficulties. The official could not give me much information, since the Imperial Bank here has no Red Cross drafts for Austria. Amelie, you cannot imagine how I feel to know that you and your mother are suffering! I don't at all want to flatter you. You were and you still are my best and truest friend, for as long as you live. I often speak of "my dear friend Amelie." Yes, I know how to appreciate friendship. I experienced many a thing on my wanderings concerning friends and friendship. Sometime, I have to write you about my experiences with friends in this country. It will interest you very much. For today, I have to close my writing, since we only have two mail days per week and the post office will be closed in one hour. But I will soon write again and will have a long letter ready for the next mail which will leave Friday. And once more, Amelie, accept my gift! It is not much, but it comes from my heart! I know that never in my whole life will I be able to match all your good deeds and the kindness you have given me and my family. Greetings from my heart to your dear Mama and your sister. Next week, I'll write to both of them. Excuse my mistakes and the poor writing. In my next letter I will do better!! With heartiest greetings, your *Conrad.*

1. Established at the Paris Peace Conference of 1919, the League of Nations was an international organization founded on the principles of collective security and the preservation of peace. Although its efforts to achieve collective security were ultimately unsuccessful, the league lasted until the founding of its successor, the United Nations, in 1945. See Margaret MacMillan, *Paris 1919: Six Months that Changed the World* (2001; New York: Random House, 2003), 83–97.

2. After the First World War, Austria was but a fragment of what its new prime minister, Karl Renner (1870–1950), called a "vanquished and fallen Empire." Of the months following the armistice, historian Margaret MacMillan recently painted the following grim picture: "Alarming reports reached Paris about conditions in Austria: the countryside picked bare of its livestock; the empty shelves in the shops; the spread of tuberculosis; the men in ragged uniforms; the thousands of unemployed—125,000 in Vienna alone. Factories stood still and the trains and trams ran sporadically. The former commander-in-chief of the imperial armies ran a small tobacconist's shop, and lesser officers shined shoes. Starving children begged in the streets and there were long queues outside the soup kitchens. Girls from good middle-class families sold themselves for food and clothing. When several police horses were killed in one of the frequent demonstrations, the flesh was stripped from their bones within minutes." Without immediate relief, complete social collapse was likely. Not wanting Austria to go the way of communist Russia or Hungary, the Allies lifted their blockades. Austria became the fourth largest beneficiary of aid, after Germany, Poland, and Belgium. MacMillan, *Paris 1919*, 246, 248–49.

3. Hetta only once joined Kain on the trail. Kain, *Where the Clouds*, 436.

127

Wilmer, B.C., October 6, 1920

Dear Amelie:

It is ever so long ago that I received your kind letter and, no doubt, you will be angry with me for not answering. But if you knew how my time is spent, you would understand. Your last letter I received when I returned from a mountain excursion. I went with an old acquaintance (Mr. Harmon of Banff) to the mountains to take "living pictures." Above all, I have to thank you from the bottom of my heart for the big help you gave my mother. My sincere thanks, too, for the good, wise advice you gave her that she should deposit the money in the bank. Yes, Amelie, that was exceptionally good advice. It brings me great joy that my mother does not have to live in fear and hardship any more. Now, I have to tell you the biggest news: I now have <u>my own home</u>![1] A small farm. It consists of a house, stables, eight acres of land, four old horses and two young ones, twenty chickens, one pig, one dog, one cat, and four rabbits. Next week, I will bring home a cow and a calf, which I sort of bought. In the garden, we have twenty-seven fruit trees, cabbage and beets, peas, beans, potatoes, onions, etc. Also grain. Red currents, raspberries, gooseberries. In front of the house are various beautiful flowers. I am sorry I have to say that all summer I had hardly three hours' time to enjoy the flowers. Yes, Amelie, it is lovely to have your own home, but all beginnings are hard, and so it is also hard with a home and a small farm. When I was at home, I often worked fourteen to sixteen hours a day, and often I was so tired that I could hardly sleep. But I hope it will be better next year, since I stay at home this coming winter to put everything in order. I bought the property from an old German, who was here for several years.[2] He lived alone, and the house was simple and small. I have to make

∧ *Conrad and Hetta Kain in front of their home in Wilmer, 1923. Photo by Byron Harmon.*
[WMCR, V263/4235]

quite a few improvements to have a really comfortable home. I
bought six more acres of land. First, I have to prepare the ground.
Trees and bushes have to be cut, stumps and roots have to be pulled
out, and then comes the ploughing! I hope that by next spring I have
two of the six acres ploughed. Once everything is in order, I want <u>one
thing</u>, and that is <u>a wish of the heart</u>. But I don't know whether I will
be so lucky. —— Here is the wish of my heart: All my life, besides my
<u>Hetta</u>, I only deeply and honestly loved two persons. One is my
mother, the other person is you, Miss Amelie. It would be my greatest
joy to spend a year with my mother and you. Do you think it is <u>totally
out of the question</u> that you could visit us in Canada? I told Hetta my
wish, and she supports me fully. I know when the time comes you
will receive a warm invitation from Hetta. If there weren't such difficulties at present, I would try to get my mother to come over here

right now. I don't know whether she would come, but I will try. I am convinced that, for my mother, they would be the <u>best days</u> of her life. For you, Amelie, it would, of course, be quite different. In your young years, you had good times and a happy life at home. — We live simply, but well. Surely, after the war years and the difficult times, a stay here would be a big help for your nerves, in other words, for your health. Yes, I know, you would travel through Canada with wide eyes. What I don't know is whether you would love the winter in Canada. There is also hardly any spring and <u>no cuckoo</u>!! In spring, I have a yearning for the call of the cuckoo. *[In English from hereon]* Well, Amelie, it would be nice, if my wish would come true, and I know you would enjoy a good rest after all those hard troubles you must put up in the old land. I read once and for a while in the newspapers about home, but I have not much time to read in these days. I am always hard at work, but we shall soon have winter, and as I shall stay at home, I trust I shall find more time for reading and writing. Yes, Amelie, I will try to write soon about my life in Canada, and I also will finish *The Zillertaler Sepp*. I know you will like *Sepp*, and I also know that no one will understand that novel better than you. I must mention once more your coming to us some day. You see, I owe you so much that I can't see how I shall be able to return to you some kindness. I know you don't expect it, but, all the same, I would like to do something for you, by which you could benefit. —— In winter 1917, I had been trapping on the Simpson River, near Mount Nasswald (about 9,900 ft.), and I wrote a novel which I have yet at home. I wrote in English, and as you know and see, my English is very bad, I ought to have someone to go over it. I believe, it would really make an interesting reading.[3] I would beg Hetta to do it for me, but she has always so much work to do. Besides, she always says that she can't write. But this is not so. She just believes she can't. *[In German from hereon]* Now a little more in German, otherwise my German will become as bad as my English!! I speak English quite well, and many ask whether I am a Frenchman. Very seldom am I asked whether I am German. But to <u>write</u> in English is still an effort. In New Zealand, I wrote articles for the newspaper, and an elderly lady helped me with this and corrected my English. I will send you some samples. Now I have a little farm and animals that have to be looked after, and, consequently, I will not have so much time left for writing. Yet, I am still hopeful that I will write just one good book before I die. During the early war years, I had collected material in New Zealand, Australia, USA, and Canada. I had an idea to write a book titled *Religion and War*. But the topic is so disgusting that I gave up this idea. The truth is that it <u>would not be of benefit to anybody</u>. It would be best if one could forget the whole bloody war once and for all. Unfortunately, that cannot happen, because the aftermath is also horribly long-lasting. I pity the old people (like your dear mother) in Austria! Yes, it is sad when one thinks how many of the old people, who worked and saved for the last years of their life, lost <u>everything</u>. The saddest part of all is that in all countries many people became millionaires because of the war and will remain rich! It also bothers me to hear that the Austrian government is now more than ever before so <u>one-sided</u>. I can understand quite well that now <u>the Jews</u> will not too easily relinquish the leadership![4] And it is just like in former times in Austria. As you will probably read in the papers, peace in Great Britain is not so solid either. There are also dissatisfied people there like everywhere else. A few months ago, the prospects in Canada were also not quite so favourable, but it seems the worst is over here. Canada is a large and prosperous country, and once the population grows and more land comes under the plough, it would be one of the best countries in the world, in spite of the long and cold winter. But, as everywhere, politics in Canada isn't doing what it could and should. The leaders work more FOR THEMSELVES than for the people. Of course, it is the <u>responsibility of the people</u>, because they let things happen without being concerned. When elections are held, people vote as they did before.[5] In the next election, women will also have the right to vote. If I am not mistaken, that is the case in Austria, too. As far as the votes of the women are concerned, I must say that, from my observations in New Zealand and Australia, where women already have the vote, I did not notice any difference. Women, just like men, very often do not <u>know</u> what they do when they use their ballot. Many women vote with their husbands and fathers, and so everything remains as before.[6] — Now I told you just about everything. I am ashamed that I write such poor German, but it is hard for me, since I do not write or read much German anymore. Maybe you could send me some German magazines of the Alpine Club, good Amelie? It would be very helpful. Perhaps Herr von Haid has some which he does not need anymore. If you see him, give him my greetings and tell him that I now have a home in Canada. Please give my love and greetings to Reverend G., if he is still in Reichenau. I don't know whether you know that Hetta is Catholic. I am still like before: I attend no church and need no priest. However, I do have a religion deep in my heart and my thoughts. I am probably just as good as most people who pretend to be "religious." A few days ago, a Catholic priest was visiting here. I did not see him myself and have nothing against him coming again. But if he comes too often and tries to stick his nose into my business, then, of course, I will show him the door. As far as religion goes, everything goes well between Hetta and me. I have nothing against her religion, and she lets me have my own views. What I don't like about the clergy is that they become bold and curious when they visit too often. They want to know all about the affairs of the family!! The Protestant pastors are just as curious as the Catholic priests! — These are my views of the clergy here. A few years ago in Banff, I met a Catholic priest who made a good impression upon me, just like Rev. G. in Reichenau. Besides these two, I never met one whom I would want to have as an acquaintance or friend. Hetta is sitting next to me and is writing a few lines to you and my mother. She is sending you some pictures of our house. We received them today. I hope you will get them. I am so sorry to have no pictures of our horses! I love my horses and my dog. They are my good friends. In a few years, I will have more, as I have two mares. Then there is a young horse (six months) named Nellie. That dear animal comes to me and begs for dear words. I hang on her neck and whisper into her ear that she is my darling, etc!! The youngest horse, a four-month-old stallion called Mayor, is almost twice as big as Nellie, but I have not tamed him yet. As soon as I will have time, I will also whisper into his ear what I think of him!! — All the horses have already earned what they had cost me.[7] Next spring, they will fetch me something. One horse I have is a female, the mother of Nellie, and is named is May. This animal does not like Hetta and always shows her teeth when my wife comes near her! My riding horse is Bill. He can run like a hunting dog, but has a few naughty habits! — But we manage to get along! Belle, the mother of Mayor, is my working horse. She has no faults, is calm and obedient, pulls well, and eats for two!! Of course! Mayor, her son, needs lots of milk! That is why he is so big! — It is already late, and if I don't finish the letter I will miss the mail. I hope you are satisfied with the length of the letter!! I must write more often or else I will forget everything what I learned from you, dearest Amelie! In a little while, I will send 10 Dollars to you for my mother. Please deposit the money for her in the bank. When my mother needs money, please send her a money order. I thank you again for your great help and the good advice you gave to my mother. Please also write to my mother that she should not tell everybody that she gets money from me again. I think it is much better for her, if, except for you, nobody knows how much money she has. I hope with all my heart that soon better times may come for Austria, so that also your dear old Mama can enjoy some sunny days yet. I should really write to your sister again, but, as I wrote to you already, I have to work hard now, more than ever before. But soon, soon it will be winter, and then I will have more time. Today, I worked fourteen long hours on the new fence. It is like that every day, and I am tired. But Hetta told me, "Con, you HAVE TO finish the letter to Amelie, since it is mail day tomorrow." —— I believe you and Hetta will be good friends when you meet and get to know each other. — Don't forget that I have an urgent wish from my heart, and if it is fulfilled then you and Hetta will meet! Hetta knows that you are my best friend back home who has done so much good for me and my mother. Thus, it is quite natural that, as a matter of fact, we often talk about you. In fact, no day goes by that we do not talk about you! Your picture is hanging in my bedroom above my head. Next to it stands a flowerpot. The first thing I see in the morning is your picture and the flowers, *[In English from hereon]* and there are times when I feel that you are near me. And I wish I could really be near you, even if I could do nothing else for you and your dear mama, I could at least bring firewood and help you in the garden! Well, let us live in hope. Someday I shall shake your hands, and the joy will be so great, my dear, true friend, that I shall take you in my arms and kiss you!! Why shouldn't I? You are the best of all my friends! Now really I must end up or I will miss the mail. Give my love and best wishes to your mother and sister. With the best wishes for you, too, and with kind thoughts, I remain your grateful *Conrad*.

1. During the summer of 1920, the Kains purchased a small two-room white clapboard house on 8.3 acres of sloping land above the village of Wilmer, a quaint setting overlooking the Columbia Valley. Not long after, their friend from Banff, Byron Harmon, purchased a neighbouring property.

2. The property's original owner was Bill Colmert.

3. The novel's manuscript has never been found.

4. Circa 1918, the Jewish population in Austria was approximately 300,000, spread across some 33 different settlements; however, the majority of Jews (about 200,000) lived in Vienna. There, many leading figures of the Social Democratic Party, which formed the government of the First Republic (1918–1934) under the leadership of Karl Renner, were Jewish. In fact, it was the only political party in Austria that permitted Jews as members. In 1934, when the Austrian Civil War (also known as the February Uprising) broke out, leading members of the party were arrested or forced to flee from a new, conservative-fascist regime. Any period of prosperity for Jews, however, abruptly ended four years later with the annexation of Austria to Nazi Germany (the *Anschluss*). Most Austrians, if they were not Jewish or communist, greeted the Anschluss with relief. See MacMillan, *Paris 1919*, 256.

5. If the 1921 Canadian federal election result was any indication, Kain's discontent was shared by many Canadians in 1920. Three years earlier, the 1917 federal election—a particularly bitter affair fought over the issue of conscription—resulted in a large majority for Sir Robert Borden's Union government, while the Laurier Liberals took what few seats remained, mostly in Quebec. While the conscription crisis had divided the Liberal Party, and the Conservative Party had expanded its base in the newly-named Unionist Party, the political landscape in Canada was still generally dominated by the same old parties. In the years leading up to the 1921 election, with the Union government plagued by internal divisions, and the Liberals still in the process of rebuilding, a new populist movement in the West—the National Progressive Party—emerged as powerful force. When it came, the 1921 election thus resulted in Canada's first minority government and a dramatic shift in Canada's political landscape. See Brown and Cook, *Canada, 1896–1921*, 315–20, 336–38.

6. The federal election of 1921 was the first in which all women 21 years old and older (excluding status Indians) were eligible voters. While the war helped turn the tide of public opinion in favour of this important, long-sought reform, not everyone—as displayed here by Kain—viewed it as a true sign of progress. See Brown and Cook, *Canada, 1896–1921*, 296; and Thompson and Seager, *Canada, 1922–1939*, 70–71.

7. With his pack train of horses, some of which he broke himself, Kain began guiding and outfitting hunting trips throughout the nearby Purcell Mountains in fall and spring. Outfitting supplemented much of his income for the remainder of his life.

128

Wilmer, B.C., December 29, 1920

Dear Amelie:

[In German from hereon] My best thanks for your dear long letter of
November 27, which I received more than one week ago. I wanted to
answer it right away, but unfortunately there was too much work to
do. Compared to other years, we have had an unusually warm winter
here. I wish that Austria too would have a mild winter. *[In English from
hereon]* Amelie, you can't imagine how I felt, when I read in your dear
letter with how little coal you have to do your cooking and keep a
room warm if possible. It is a shame! I wish I could hand you over the
amount of wood I burnt unnecessarily in this country, then you need
not freeze any more for the rest of your life!! I know it must be
terribly hard for your dear mother to suffer in a cold house. I see of
your handwriting that you must feel better than you did a year ago,
and I wish from all my heart that you might get back your strong
nerves once more and that fortune should be very kind to you. I wish
there should yet be for you some fine sunny days in your future life.
This is what I wish you first of all. And I also wish happy times for the
whole land of Austria, which I still love very deeply. There will always
be a warm spot for my country in my heart. Believe me, I feel so sorry
that Austria has not a good government, one that is just to all classes!
Well, I was always a little afraid that the Jews will get the <u>lead</u> in
Austria if the <u>Social-Democrats</u> came to power.[1] I really was thinking
of this. <u>And so it happens</u>. Well, it will take a long time until everything is adjusted. But it is now up to the people themselves <u>to vote</u> for
a good government, which is no easy matter. It is a matter of fact that
"free countries," or better said "the so-called free countries," are
always up against governments. I made a study of all the different

governments of those so-called "free countries." I am sure we shall talk about it personally, you and I. It will interest you. I am sorry to say that the Republic of Austria will get the same "weak points" in the politics: craft and party-favouritism. Those weak points are nearly in every so-called "free country." There is only one republic which has so far come out safe from those weak and selfish points, and this is little Switzerland. But all the rest of the free countries have "party politics." Do you know what I mean by "party-politics"? —— *[In German from hereon]* In other words, we see and have proof that the governments in the free countries, i.e. in republics, have more expenses and costs than in monarchies. The difference is that in a monarchy, the reigning monarch with his relatives and followers has to be kept by the taxes of all classes. It would not be so bad to keep an emperor or king and his family and followers with the taxes of all classes of his subjects, but when there are more and more followers and the taxes are too high, then dissatisfaction and hatred overcome the country. So many have to suffer because of the number of people who don't produce and work, but consume so much of all the good things. In republics, where party politics are the basis, the good results reach far greater numbers of the people—that means the followers of the party in power. These have the benefit indirectly. The other people in such a state who do not belong to the ruling party pay, of course, taxes too, but receive only the bare necessities. And so we see that, in the end, it is almost the same: Monarchy or free state. If Austria had not been so much under the power of militarism, it would have been better for the country to live under a monarch. I cannot explain it any other way but that in Austria militarism predominated too much. Progress, contentment, and honesty cannot thrive under militarism. Well, let's leave politics alone. It was a big surprise for me that a parcel arrived with the newsletter of the German-Austrian Alpine Club and the *Touristen Zeitungen*. I will keep everything safe, don't worry about it. Already in the first magazine, I read about the death of three men I knew. I am convinced that it will be good for me to read German. I already read two magazines from the beginning to the end. As you see, I am totally out of practice with my German! There is only <u>one</u> German living here in Wilmer. It is the man from whom I bought my house. Colmert is his name. I visit him sometimes. His situation with the German is just like mine. We try to speak German, but always get caught up in the English language. C. has some German newspapers that he gave me to read. Unfortunately, these papers are written in very poor German. But one gets some news that way, which you don't find in the English papers. I will send you some of them, so that you can see what poor German is spoken and written in Canada. There is also a lady here in Wilmer, who was born in Vienna, but I have not yet had the opportunity to meet her. And now about the *Canadian Alpine Journal*. I will write to Mr. Mitchell. Perhaps he can help me. Since 1913, I have only received one volume, which contained nothing special. The Canadian Alpine Club did not make much progress since 1910. I often told the officials that the direction of the club is too narrow-minded. For this reason, it will never reach a high number of members. I often made it clear to Mr. Wheeler that the society of an OUT-OF-DOOR-Club should not make distinctions between classes, certainly not in a democratic country. I pointed out these mistakes.[2] But, since I do not work anymore for the Club, I now hear very little about their activities. Mr. Mitchell is a gentleman. He writes to me once a year (at New Year), and from the others I hear next to nothing. That is how friendship looks in these democratic countries. As soon as a person has no more use for a friend, the friendship is valueless. Oh, Amelie, how much could I tell you! My eyes were opened! I was blind during the first years. I believed everything I was told and took it to be the truth! After <u>being hurt</u>, I <u>knew better</u>! Experience is the best teacher for everything.

——— Hetta is sending you a book and hopes it will interest you. And I have copied *The Zillertaler Sepp* so that I can send you the novel. As you know, years ago, I wrote the *Sepp*, but only in pencil. Many pages are barely legible. I am convinced that the *Sepp* will interest you, and nobody will understand the story better than you! *Sepp* had many traits and plans for the future, just like a good friend of yours when he was young!! ——— I cannot send the English novel, as it would claim too much of your never tiring friendliness *[In English from hereon]* and it would not be right to do so. But, if I get it type-written, I shall certainly send it to you to read. Now, my dear friend, a few words in English about your visit to Canada in the future!! Well, I knew you could not think of coming <u>now</u>. I quite understand that you couldn't and wouldn't leave your dear mother behind for such a long trip, especially in her old days. But surely you don't consider yourself old?! Do you? Never mind your years! You are still young! And the end of your life is not yet in sight. It does not matter <u>when</u> I shall have the pleasure of seeing you and my mother because <u>I have learned TO WAIT</u> for things till it is their time to come. And I feel sure our time will come, when I shall see you and when I am in a position to make you happy for hours at a time! <u>HOURS</u>, if we speak of <u>life-times</u>. Well, dear Amelie, I was so glad to hear you say that "postponement is not abandonment!" Of course, you will come to Canada someday, I am sure you will, and I feel sure you will never be sorry to have come! Now I want to tell you something. You know I am no more the little boy from Nasswald!! I am a full-grown man, and life has not been a picnic for me all the way along. You know more of my happy and unhappy times better than anyone knows in my old home. But there were many things I never told you, because they would have worried you. But I'll cut the story short and come to the point. As I told you, my life so far was <u>not</u> a happy, lovely, joyful way all along. There were some trails I had to travel that were really hard ones, full of disap-pointments and cruelty. And these hard trails have <u>hardened</u> my heart for many sorrowful events. I tell you, dear friend, sometimes I was even ashamed of myself for being <u>so</u> hardened up! For it had never been my wish to be hard-hearted to anybody or anything in this world. Many a time I wish I could weep, <u>but I could not</u>. Fortune has not always been kind towards me, and you know that I have seen more of the world and of life with its different sides than the average man. And so it came that I have not lost a tear for so many years, yes, Amelie, for <u>many years</u>. But your last dear letter was too much for me. Amelie, my dearest of dear friends, I know that I have to thank you forever for so many kind deeds and millions of kind words that I received from you! —— And now, after all that, I have to thank you

for having softened my heart, and having shed those tears when I
read your lines. You wrote: "In the course of my life, I have made
many a sacrifice for my parents. I will remain true to my mother as
long as she lives and will never leave her.—" These lines are the most
beautiful lines and the best and kindest words I have ever read in a
letter. These words made me cry like a little child. I will never tell
anybody about it except you. Afterwards, I had a most beautiful
dream of you and your mother and sister. In this dream I saw you all
so plain and real! —— Well, I thought to have more time for writing
and reading in winter, but, up to now, I have not done anything. I
don't know why? Times goes by so fast! Of course, there is one
reason: at day-time, I am always more or less working outside, and,
when I get into the warm room, I feel lazy and sleepy! Amelie, when
we meet again, I shall tell you many of my ideas with regard to
writing novels, and I feel sure some of my plans would make a good
hit. Of Katie (my friend, the school-teacher), I have lost all track. She
went to Alaska, and I have never heard from her since. So it goes:
some of my girl-friends from the first few years in Canada got
married, and now have their hands full of work! You know yourself,
how things go in a household, don't you? Yes, my dear friend, there is
really a mountain named Mount Nasswald, and it is on the map and
likely will be there forever. Mount Nasswald is near Mount
Assiniboine. I made the first ascent, and I don't think it has been
climbed since then. — I was under the impression to have written
you about it in 1914? — I shall try to get a map for you. I wonder
whether the *Österreichische Touristen Zeitung* would care to print an
article about Mount Nasswald in the Canadian Rockies? Do you
think? By the way, I have an article with pictures of Mt. Cook written
in English. I think the *Österreichische Touristen Zeitung* would be glad
to get such an article published within. I shall write and ask them. In
your last letter, you wrote that I did not say anything about the death
of Mr. Polster. I must have forgotten. I was sorry to hear that he met
with an accident while climbing in the Rax. He was a good friend of
mine, and he was surely "a true Viennese." I shall write a few lines to
Mrs. P.—I would also like to write some lines to Herrn Pfarrer G., but

the trouble with me is that it takes so long to write a letter, and I can't write a short one! — What you write about priests in general is alright. I know there are many gentlemen among them. But if you would be in Canada or in the USA, you would not find a few gentleman amongst all the priests of the 120 different churches!! You know there are so many sects in America. *[In German from hereon]* I was in about twenty different churches—just, of course, for sheer interest—since I don't go to church to pray. My thoughts about higher things are always in the outdoors, in the forest, or on top of a mountain. I have no hatred against church or religion, but, since the Great War, I've lost my sympathy for the "hypocrites." In reality, they were there to preach the word of God, which they did not do in wartime. Ninety-nine per cent of the so-called servants of God were used as tools to preach nationalistic hatred. And, as far as I know, they all were quite willing to be used. Don't forget, what I am talking about here is only what I saw in the places and countries I travelled in during wartime. —— I believe that a higher being has influence over us, and I have many good thoughts and feelings for this HIGHER BEING. But I think that this being cannot have much joy about modern Christianity! And, with this, we will end the subject of Religion. I hope my opinions don't make you sad. I will now end my long silence and will, very soon, write a long letter to you again. Hetta also wrote you a long letter, so you will hear quite a bit about the goings on around here. I hope that both letters will bring you a little distraction. And I wish you, your dear mother, and Flora all the best for 1921! May you all remain healthy and have a better year than the last one was. With my best wishes and love to you and your people, I am your *Conrad*.

1. Austria's first experience with independence was not a happy one. Throughout the 1920s its economy limped from one crisis to another and was barely kept afloat by parsimonious loans from the winners of the war. Discontent was widespread.

2. The European alpine clubs were very different from the British original, which the Canadian club was modelled upon. While the European organizations were large and wholly inclusive to members across a wide social and economic stratum, the Canadian club, despite permitting women in its

membership (something the British club did not do until 1974), was small, almost exclusively white, and drew largely from middle-class factions. Of the British club, historian Walt Unsworth claimed that "it was not until after the Second World War that The Alpine Club began to shed its blinkers and enter the world of modern climbing." Unsworth, *Hold the Heights*, 69. The same could apply to the Canadian organization in the postwar period, although, to this day, neither the club's presidency nor executive directorship has ever been assumed by a woman.

129

Wilmer, BC, Canada August 21, 1921

Dear Amelie:

I am really ashamed that I have not written for so long. The truth is that this spring, I worked too hard and then we had such a hot summer, almost no rain at all, that much of the work and toil was for nothing. This is so bothersome that you lose all your drive to work. Yes, building your home and farming is hard labour and here, too, not everything that sparkles is pure gold! But, soon, we will have winter again, and that is my consolation. —— During September and October, I will go hunting with a group, and, in November, I will return to the wild forest again. I earn so little that I only taste the money, but, without dollars and cents, you can do nothing at all. I think Hetta wrote you most of the news already. It is a pity that the other letter, which also contained a few pages from me, got lost. I will claim it because I also included a five-dollar bill for my mother. I am sure you will do me the favour to exchange the money for her in the bank. I have no idea how much one Krone is worth at the moment, but I hope that the five dollars is a little help for my mother. I wrote mother a long letter, also to Rev. G.—I have planned to write him a long letter for years, but unfortunately I have just never got around to it. I don't know how time can pass so quickly!! —— I never reach my goals! Here is an example: last Sunday, I visited my horses that are an hour away from here and left Bill there. To my astonishment, Bill came home the day before yesterday!! He had jumped three fences and had his front feet hobbled!! Now I have to feed him and drive another horse up there. That takes up another evening. — I have a two-month-old little horse and want to name the little animal "Amelie," but since it has yet to show anything beautiful in its appearance, I've postponed the baptism!! I don't know whether I wrote to you that I bought two horses at very reasonable prices: a female named Baldy and a yearling, Peter. —— Now, how is everybody in Reichenau? There the trees will soon wear the autumn colours. Oh, Amelie, I wish I could once more in fall go with you through the Gesäuse and along the Peternpfad! — Yes, these were beautiful days, don't you think? I often think of them, and, on September 9th (the 14th anniversary), I will have especially good thoughts! I feel I was happier then, compared to now ——— yes, the time of youth is just the most beautiful time in life! —— I often say to my wife, how glad I am that I was not born in this country, because such a happy married life, like in the old home country, you don't see here among young people. I am often homesick and have only one consolation: where I was born I wish to die. For the end of your life, where you were born is the most beautiful place! I know, Amelie, that for you, poor dear, the world is not as beautiful anymore as it was ten or twelve years ago. Yes, the horrible war made many a young life sad and lonely. But nature will always be nature, and its beauty is still there as it was before and will remain as it has been. There exist just our inner worries and pain, which will not reveal to us a beautiful picture of nature. We don't see it, because we are sad. For myself, I am sure I will again be able to enjoy all the beauty. I will again live alone in the heart of nature. So, I hope that you too can again find much beauty in nature. — I know that now, poor dear lady, you don't have the same opportunities to wander in the forest like before. A few days ago, I said to Hetta, "Amelie is tied down at home. Perhaps she would enjoy some beautiful flowers from our sweet peas. I will send some sweet pea seeds to my Amelie. I believe these flowers will do well at Reichenau." —— You must not mind me calling you "My Amelie."

I always say so when speaking to Hetta about you. I feel that you somehow belong to me. The great kindness you have always shown me makes me feel so. It also gives me a bad feeling when I don't write to you for such a long time! But you will forgive me. —— I will also send you some newspapers from here. I was in the mountains when an accident occurred. It involved a friend of mine, Dr. Stone.[1] You will also see that here, too, the war has had tragic results. I hope you and your loved ones are as well as possible and that, soon, better times will come for Austria. My greetings to the old dear Rax. With my heartiest greetings to you, your mother and sister, your *Conrad*.

1. Winthrop E. Stone, the president of Purdue University, who had joined Kain on Mt. Whitehorn in 1913 (see Letter 98), as well as on several trips to the Purcells in 1915 and 1916 (see Letters 122 and 125), fell to his death while making the first ascent of Mt. Eon (3,310 m [10,860 ft.]), a prominent peak that sits beside Mt. Assiniboine. In the years since climbing with Kain, Stone had become an experienced guideless climber and even published on the joys of amateur climbing in the CAJ. See W.E. Stone, "Amateur Climbing," CAJ 11 (1920): 1–8. Margaret Stone, who was with her husband when he fell, spent eight days alone on a high ledge before being rescued by a party led by the Swiss guide Rudolph Aemmer (1883–1973). A second party that included Aemmer, Edward Feuz Jr., Kain, Albert MacCarthy, and Lennox Lindsay was quickly assembled to recover Winthrop's body. See A.H. MacCarthy, "The First Ascent of Mt. Eon and its Fatality," CAJ 12 (1921–1922): 14–25.

130

Wilmer, B.C., Canada, December 6, 1921

Dear Amelie:

[In English from hereon] It must be fully two weeks since we received your dear letter. I already began to worry about you, but then I thought you had gone back to Vienna and had not much time for writing the first few weeks. *[In German from hereon]* Anyway, you are still alive, even if life is not anymore what it used to be. But one lives and hopes for the best. We, too, hope for better times. At the moment, there are elections and in such times there is always deep dissatisfaction in a free country. Since Austria is a republic, one will hear many different opinions during election time. I am tired of politics and have little interest left for it. I will go to the elections and vote for a better government. Whether it gets better, I do not know. Hetta is writing a long letter to you and will surely tell you the news from here, and I use the opportunity to talk with you about nature and the home country. A few days ago, I returned from a short trip. I was searching for a good trapping area. Unfortunately, the prospects are not the best. But it was a nice time for me. I spent the week in a cabin with my dog. My horses came to the door, and I gave them salt and kind words. I love my animals. Then, there was the cooking that gave me joy. I had a real yearning for Nasswald home cooking: Sterz, spätzle, potato soup, etc. Yes, I lived like the Nasswald lumberjack!! And, in the evening, even until morning, I read in GERMAN! The one German I bought the house from is a very well-read man and always gets many newspapers and books. He gave me a lot to read, and, to my greatest joy, I found two stories by Ganghofer: "The Kaser-Mandl" and "The Devil's Mill on Funtensee." Have you read anything by Ganghofer yet? If the name Ganghofer had not been there in black

and white, I would have said, "That is by Peter Rosegger!"[1] —— Oh,
Amelie, can you imagine what I felt when quite unexpectedly I came
across the Nasswald dialect? Oh, it was beautiful! I lived the whole
story, so to speak. I shot the chamois, I kissed the dairymaid, and
I drank the wine, and I played the Zither!!! And when I reached the
end of the book, I began to read it all over again! After finishing it, I
talked to my dog in the Nasswald dialect. ——— And then I started
thinking again of my youth, my happy and sad hours, and became
homesick like never before. A longing for being at home came over
me, for my mountains, for the alpine meadows. —— In my imagination, I saw the alpine roses, violets, gentian, and the lilies of the
valley. I heard the bells of the cows on the Alm, saw the girls in their
dress and the boys in Lederhosen, bare-kneed, Tyrolean hats with
cockfeathers. ——— Yes, for a while, it felt as if I was back home.
——— I am afraid you might now think that it looks bad in my
mind, when you read these lines about my dreams! But don't worry,
Amelie! My senses are in good condition! — I can calm my homesickness myself without complaining to anybody. You know that I am
my own philosopher! ——— Yes, I also can imagine that, at present,
things in the old home country are not what they used to be in my
youth. I also know that I might not have survived the war had I not
left my country. What do you think? —— But one thing I know for
sure: nature, mountains, and everything beautiful in nature will
still be there as it has always been. I also know that I will see everything that was dear to me again. And, for all of this, I look forward
in joy! — I did not write yet that last summer I almost could have
come home!! Mr. MacCarthy wanted to take me along to Switzerland.
Unfortunately, at the last moment, something crossed his plans.
What joy it would have been for me to walk from the Payerbacher
station to the Villa Malek and enter your house as a stranger! —
Could you have trusted your eyes and ears, if I had greeted you
with the words "Hallo, Miss Amelie, hallo Mrs. Malek." Yes, I know,
with these words I would not have been a stranger to you anymore!
You can imagine how I felt when the plan to visit Switzerland
was abandoned! Yes, I would have come home without any prior

announcement! But one day, I will come back! The wish of my heart is that I find my mother, my Amelie and her family all still alive and well. I had already planned <u>how</u> I would spend my long four days at home. Here goes: I would bring along a light tent so that I could <u>camp</u> wherever I wished in mountains and forests. The shelter huts and alpine houses are nice and pretty, but a camp is like <u>your own home</u>. Amelie, just imagine, I might camp on the Knofeleben and send invitations to you and Flora. A "No" will NOT BE ACCEPTED!!! —— What would you do, Amelie? Imagine: —— an absolutely free life in beautiful nature! I am the cook, and a <u>good</u> camp-cook at that! If not too tired, you two ladies can help me do the dishes!! In the evening, we all sit around the campfire. Flora would have her husband and the children from his first wife along. We sit around the fire and tell stories; maybe we would also sing a song or yodel. Then, we sleep on spruce branches that smell so good, and in the morning, when the sun rises and the birds are singing, we would rise too and enjoy life. Often, I think what joy camp life would be for friends of nature and for children. Here in this country, camping has become second nature to people. If my mother is not too old yet, I will hike with her to the Zikafahnler Alm. — Should I be rich one day (which I can hardly hope for), do you know what I would do then? I would create camps for poor kids—if money permits, for rich ones, too—in the mountains! Oh, this would be an indescribable joy for me, to see kids in the healthy alpine air, running around happy and cheerful! —— Dear Amelie, it gave me great pleasure to read in your letter that you were on the beautiful Knofeleben and on the Rax. I know that you went through bad times and that the last years did not bring you much joy, that you did not have any time to be outdoors and wander about free of sorrow and worry. I hope, however, that you remain in good health, and that for many more years you will be able to climb up to the height where the air is pure and good. I believe that up on the mountains there is something good and beautiful for everyone to find. —— I don't know whether these lines will still reach you in this year, but, in any case, it won't be too late to wish you and your dear mother all the best for the coming year. Let us hope that 1922 will be better in many ways than the last years have been. I will also write to Mrs. Rotter. Please say hello to the gentlemen I know in Reichenau and give greetings also to the old dear Rax! With my best wishes and hearty greetings,

your Con.

---

1. It is perhaps not surprising that Kain nearly mistakes works by Ludwig Ganghofer (1855–1920) for those of Peter Rosegger (1843–1918). Ganghofer, a German writer and journalist, set many of his short stories and novellas in the Bavarian mountains of southern Germany, settings not unlike those famously employed by Rosegger. Rosegger, a prolific Austrian poet and author, hailed from the small, mountain village of Alpl, near Krieglach, approximately 60 kilometres south of Nasswald in the neighbouring province of Styria. Often written in a Styrian dialect, Rosegger's descriptions of alpine scenery and the life of its inhabitants made him one of the most popular authors in Austria and Germany. He nearly won a Nobel Prize in 1913 and, to this day, is considered something of a national hero in Styria.

131

Wilmer, B.C., Canada, January 30, 1923

Dear Amelie,

[In English from hereon] No doubt, you will have received by now
Hetta's letter. I am glad that she writes and answers your letters more
promptly than I do! Hetta read her last letter for you to me, and I
agree with everything she told you. I am sure you will come some
day and live with us for some time. It will do you good. I really can't
think how to explain my long silence. I admit it is not nice of me
to write so little but somehow there seems to be always something
to keep me from writing. Besides, we have so many newspapers to
read, and whenever I find a good story I simply can't stop reading!
Sometimes, when I have been outside all day, I fall asleep in the chair
as soon as I sit down in the warm room!! I believe that sometimes I
am anything but good company to Hetta. ——— Last summer, I was
away from home most of the time. I did fairly well, but I had to work
hard: cooking for four to five people and looking after ten horses
keeps one busy from morning to night.[1] I have been at home since
November and done much work around the place, but now I will go
for a little trapping trip. I'll enjoy myself. — After all, it seems to me
that the life in the wood, in the open air, is the best. — Of course, I
know that every one can't spend such a life as a trapper leads. ——
I was very glad that you had good day's outing on the Rax. I wonder
whether we shall ever visit the dear old mountains together again?
Well, Amelie, I will tell you once more, I am glad (and that is the
truth) that I was born in the Austrian mountains, and that I spent
my young years where I did. If nothing else, at least I have nice and
pleasant memories of it. This country is alright to make a living, but
one has to work hard, and, apart from that work, there is not much

pleasure. Hetta sometimes gets very tired of the lonely life here. This is one reason why I would like you to come and live with us. I am sure you would be good company to Hetta, and she would be the same to you. You know, for my part, I can spend weeks and weeks all by myself in the woods without getting lonesome, though not every man or woman has such a disposition to stand a lonely life. I hate to ask you: what do you think of the world politics now? For the winter months, we are getting the New York Times, one of the best papers in America, and thus we get a great deal of European news, far more than in the Canadian papers. At present, the European situation does not look bright. Well, I sincerely hope that no nation will fly down on poor Austria! What do you think of the League of Nations and of "Humanity" that is so much spoken of? As for me, I think very little of both. Nor do I think very highly of the so-called "Christianity." I believe the only way we can improve the bad way of the world is to do a little more thinking for ourselves and to try hard to overcome the bad disease, which we know as SELFISHNESS. The motto of all nations and individuals should be: "Live and let live!" —— But the world sticks to its present motto: "Life for life." We surely will not make much headway. It seems to me that there is altogether too much selfishness in this world for the present, and because everyone knows that there is too much selfishness amongst us all, nobody cares to admit it and to suggest a cure for it, simply because everyone thinks: "What is the use? The other fellow would not admit it!" ——— It is true that we could help each other more, if we would cast away selfishness and distrust. The diseases have taken such a strong hold on all nations, that it would require years and years of hard work and good will from all sides to stamp them out and put something better and more beautiful in its place. —— But — WHO WILL MAKE THE START?!!! ——— Now I will write in German. *[In German from hereon]* It has been a while since I spoke my own language, and at the moment I'm not receiving any German newspapers. If that continues, I fear I will neglect my original language. Last fall, a visitor from Switzerland was here, and I had a hard time to speak German rapidly and fluently. The Swiss man told me about the Swiss mountains and also about the war. The Rockies made a good impression on him, but he did not seem to like the lifestyle and working ways of the people here very much. I could not help laughing when I showed him my horses, and he remarked that I probably must be very rich!! He was not satisfied with the progress that his Swiss contemporaries made here in Canada. He said, "They don't even have a single horse!" ——— I wrote you recently that I named a young horse "Amelie." Unfortunately, I did not have the pleasure to love my little Amelie very long. The little animal drowned in the swollen waters of a mountain creek. I don't expect young ones this year, but I will have another opportunity to call a young horse Amelie. The names of my last horses are: Frank, Buster, Pedro, and one has yet to be named. — I hope that next summer that I can go to the mountains again. For now, I have no definite plans. In a few weeks, I will distribute my announcements. I will also send one to you, even though I know that, at present, you will not be able to come. But it will give you an idea how one has to go about "business" here. Since I have horses, I had to learn quite a few new things. I also learned that you cannot depend on anybody. Yes, Amelie, that is life! I could tell you a lot about the country and the people and—friendship!! I have experienced quite a few disappointments, now I am much more cautious and expect NOTHING from anybody else. I'll tell you about one experience, and you can imagine how I felt. Last summer, I had a group of six people from Minneapolis here. The program was that I would meet the group at Mt. Assiniboine and lead them up this mountain and several other mountains. — Mr. A.O. Wheeler now has horses, too, and, for the last two years, he ran a camp for tourists near Mt. Assiniboine.[2] *[In English from hereon]* When Mr. Wheeler heard that I had a party for Mt. Assiniboine, and that I was using my own horses, he tried all he could to take the party away from me.[3] He even said bad things about me to the people. He told them that they would do better to send me a wire not to come and that they would save money by staying in his camp. Now what do you think about such a man?? —— I have twice saved Mr. Wheeler's life in the mountains and have long done work for him that no one else would do, but he has forgotten all that! — You see, as long as I was working for him and the Alpine Club, I was always "a fine fellow," but, as soon as I became my own master, I was no good to him! —— I had a few more disappointments in such "friendships," but nothing will stop me! I will go ahead in spite of all. Of all the men I have met in the mountains here, I like Mr. Harmon best. He has PROOF that he is a real man and a true friend of mine. ——— What kind of Xmas and New Year did you have? Were you at Reichenau? We spent a most miserable holiday, Hetta and me. We were both sick with a bad cold in the head. How is your dear mother keeping? Is she well? I often think of you all. I can understand how sad you all must feel, if you think of the past and look at the present conditions all around. Well, it is hell to think upon it, and worrying does not help, but it is hard not to worry! I have not heard from my people for a long time. In their last letter, I heard that my mother was well and that I must not worry about her. I have tried to get permission for the immigration of my nephew, Isidor Kain, who is shoemaker at St. Leonhard N.Ö., but it was not granted. But I shall get the permit some time, I imagine. The boy wants to come to Canada, and I would like to help him, but there is still a little of this race-hatred in the air. I will end for today, and will again write when I come back from the woods. With kindest regards and best wishes to you all, I am yours, *Conrad Kain.*

1. Upon the commencement of the ACC's Palliser Pass Camp in 1922, Kain led a party of six (from Minneapolis) to Mt. Assiniboine in early August. Afterwards, and for much of September, Kain took two members of the Minneapolis party, Cora May Johnstone Best (1878–1930) and Audrey "Belle" Forfar Shippam (1883–1975), along with Byron Harmon and a "camp boy" named Tom, on a pack train trip to the Lake of the Hanging Glaciers in the Purcells. Motion picture cameras were packed in from Windermere, as well as 36 sticks of dynamite, to capture Nature in a final act that was to be called "The Birth of an Iceberg." Best's amusing trip account in the 1923 CAJ is as much about the antics of amateur filmmakers as it is about the antics of Kain's horse "Old Bill." See Cora Johnstone Best, "Horse Thief Creek and the Lake of the Hanging Glaciers," CAJ 13 (1923): 229–41.

2. Beginning in the summer of 1920, Wheeler initiated his circular "Banff to Mount Assiniboine Walking and Riding Tour" along a 120-kilometre route, by way of the Spray Lakes, Wonder Pass, Healy Creek, and Bow River, with permanent camps strategically situated along the way. The

venture ran each year until 1926 and was made possible through his connections with the ACC, Canada's national park service, and the government of British Columbia.

3.   Kain is referring to the Cora Best and Audrey Shippam party, which attended the ACC's summer camp at Palliser Pass with Wheeler prior to meeting Kain. Cora Best was the Chair of the ACC's Minneapolis Section.

132

[In German from hereon]

Wilmer, B.C., October 22, 1923

Dear Amelie:

I really neglected you for a long time! I don't know how long it has been since I last wrote you. I now depend too much on Hetta! — But now I want to write!! When you have lived in this country for many years, you become, without noticing it, jealous and careless. And one deteriorates in the midst of culture! All this results from nature or, better said, from the climate. In summer, it is very hot here, and if you have cattle you have to be prepared to have enough fodder for the long winter, which is very cold and long. If you are outdoors all day and then come into the warm house, sleep overcomes you ——— and time goes by and you get old. —— I often say to Hetta (as I also already wrote to you several times) that I am glad I was not born here, or else I would have to become old without <u>knowing</u> that once I was <u>young</u>!! —— And something else: up to now I have been so used to work that I am not happy when I have nothing to do. Did I write to you that last spring I worked for a film company (moving pictures)? While doing this I had the opportunity to fly in an airship! It was quite beautiful to fly across the mountains! One day, I was airborne for almost three hours.[1] — In the month of June, I was on a bear hunt. In spite of the poor weather, we killed five bears. In July, I took a mountain trip with Dr. Ladd of New York, and Dr. Thorington.[2] We did several first ascents and the second ascent of Mt. Columbia. On July 10th, we did the first ascent of the North Twin. We were on that tour for twenty-three hours. That was on your dear name day. I thought of you and when we were on top I sent my greetings and wishes to you with the wind. At this height, beautiful thoughts and dear memories of you went through my mind. I won't say more or you would perhaps shake your head with the word "sentimental!" — But to me, sentimentality often has a great value, indeed it often helps one to enjoy life. In the book *In the Heart of the Canadian Rockies* you can find the Twins north of Mt. Columbia.[3] Altogether, we climbed eight mountains: Mt. Castleguard, Mt. Columbia, the Twins, Mt. Saskatchewan (first ascent), Mt. Athabasca, Mt. Gordon, Terrace Peak (first ascent), Mt. Louis (third ascent). Mt. Louis is the most difficult one in the Rockies. I made a first ascent in 1916 with MacCarthy. It is pure climbing. One chimney is similar to the Schmitt-Kamin on the Fünffingerspitze.[4] On the rocks, I am still as good as fifteen years ago, but if I am not paid well I don't want to do these extraordinarily difficult tours any more. You are only rarely paid very well for difficult climbs in this country. I find my pleasure in the forest and on the alpine meadows. I like bear hunting in the spring. Yes, there is life and singing in the spring! And if one lies on a Schneid waiting for bears, one has time to absorb everything, the beauty and the joy! I hope that I can go hunting again with the same man next spring. I still remember very well my home mountains and all the various paths and climbs, and when you write about your excursions I can imagine everything even better. In the mountains not much will have changed drastically. Of course, the way of life has changed a lot in the old home country. If I think about it, I often get sad and downtrodden. So I don't read the newspaper articles anymore about this terrible suffering of the Germans. *[In English from hereon]* I agree with you that the socialists have not done anything good for Austria and no doubt <u>never</u> will do much good. I believe that the doctrine would be all right, but that the trouble in human nature is deceit. I am sorry that the Jews got such a stronghold in Austria, and it will no doubt take some time before you get a good government. Let us hope that all will come out right in the long run. *[In German from hereon]* I am very sorry to hear that the old Innthaler still has to do such heavy work in his old age! By now, he has to be already over seventy years old? It is a sad situation, and I think that of the many friends he used to have, not too many are still alive. And many of those are probably also in a poor situation. The old proverb says a lot about it: "When poverty grows, friendship is wilting!" A few years ago, I thought about my old age and also about Hetta, in case I would die in an accident. I took out life insurance. When the payments are due, it is often hard for me to come up with the money; however, it is for a good purpose. Often, I think I made a big mistake buying more land, because there is no end to the expenses. This summer, I built a new barn for the hay and a new stable, which, however, is not quite finished yet. The lumber cost loads of money! The work I did all by myself. If I ever sell my little "estate," I will hardly get all my money back.[5] For this winter, I have no definite plans yet. Perhaps I will be at home most of the time. I still keep on hoping that one day you will come over here to see us! Hetta, too, likes you and speaks of it often. I know, it cannot be right away, but it is good if you hope for something beautiful in your life. A few days ago, I wrote, again, asking for information about whether I can bring my nephew to Canada. If it is possible, I will let him come. Often, I have an urgent wish to have somebody from back home near me. I hope that everything works out well. The lad would like to leave Austria. I wrote to him and his mother, and, in a short while, I will write to your sister; yes, I should have done so a long time ago already! — I am sure I will remember your mother's 8oth birthday on September 3, 1924, and write to her, too. For today, I will finish now, hoping that you are all healthy and remain that way. With best wishes and heartiest greetings to all, your *Conrad*.

1. During March and April, Kain was employed by Cosmopolitan Pictures, an American film company based in Hollywood, as a stunt double and location scout for the shooting of a silent, black-and-white film, *Unseeing Eyes* (1923). Partly shot in Paradise Basin, west of Invermere, BC,

the 90-minute adventure/drama featured Seena Owen as the sister of a silver-mine owner, who hires a renegade pilot (played by Lionel Barrymore) to fly her to her brother's rescue.

2. William Sargent Ladd (1887–1950), a physician from New York City, and later the president of the American Alpine Club (1929–1932), had climbed Mt. Fay with Kain and Stanley Mitchell from the ACC's Consolation Valley Camp in 1910. He engaged Kain, along with Jimmy Simpson as outfitter, to guide him and Thorington for much of July. Kain knew the Columbia Icefield well. He was in the area for much of the summer of 1919 with Wheeler's survey parties, and he remained there alone the following winter to trap. For Thorington, it was the beginning of a relationship with Kain that would last for what remained of the Austrian's life. Of his first trip with the guide, Thorington remembered it as follows: "Those were good days. Conrad was continually pointing out the features of the country, helping with the packing, keeping us in an uproar with his stories and making himself generally useful. Here, he had cached his traps; there he had spent a cold night in the snow, dreaming of warm fire. For those who took part, this journey stands out in memory as one of the happiest and most successful ever made in the Canadian mountains." Kain, *Where the Clouds*, 444. Also see William S. Ladd and J. Monroe Thorington, "A Mountaineering Journey to the Columbia Icefield," CAJ 14 (1924): 34–47; and J. Monroe Thorington, *The Glittering Mountains of Canada: A Record of Exploration and Pioneer Ascents in the Canadian Rockies, 1914–1924* (Philadelphia: John W. Lea, 1925), 51–103.

3. *In the Heart of the Canadian Rockies* (1905) was written by Sir James Outram (1868–1925), the famous English vicar, who cured his so-called "mental breakdown" in 1900 by travelling to Canada and making first ascents along the Continental Divide. In fact, during the summers of 1901 and 1902, Outram, always in the company of Swiss guides, made the first ascents of Mounts Assiniboine, Bryce, Forbes, Alexandra, and Columbia. And while he chose to call Canada home after his two impressive climbing seasons, he quit serious mountaineering almost as abruptly as he began it. An engaging travelogue and history, Outram's book documents his two seasons of climbing and includes a sketch map of the Rockies from Canmore north to the Columbia Icefield. James Outram, *In the Heart of the Canadian Rockies* (London: Macmillan, 1905). For a compelling analysis of Outram's life, see Paul R. Deslandes, "Curing Mind and Body in the Heart of the Canadian Rockies: Empire, Sexual Scandal and Reclamation of Masculinity, 1880s–1920s," *Gender & History* 21, no. 2 (2009): 358–79.

4. Nestled in the famous Langkofel group, near Sella Pass, the Fünffingerspitze (2,997 m [9,833 ft.]) was one of Kain's favourite peaks in the Italian Alps. See Kain, *Where the Clouds*, 428. The Schmittkamin (or Schmitt Chimney Route) is considered demanding by today's standards and is likely similar to chimneys high on what's now called the Kain Route on Mt. Louis. The third ascent of Mt. Louis was achieved by Kain and W.S. Ladd near the end of July, from Banff. According to Thorington, "so much damage was done to the seats of the trousers," presumably from wedging their way up and down the upper sharp, limestone chimney, "that they waited until dark before daring to reappear in the village." Kain, *Where the Clouds*, 446.

5. Hetta's niece, Vera Wikman (née Hurst, 1918–2011), remembered the Kain's home as follows: "They had a wonderful garden. They had a root cellar, like you could go down through the kitchen door,

they had a trap door there, and you'd go down the stairs. Those were dirt floors...and there were bins; that's where they kept their vegetables, so that they would never freeze there. And then they had another room, which was still pretty well under the house, and she kept her canning and jars and stuff there. And then he had built an extension there just like a part, with dirt on top, and there they kept storage things, like garden tools....That's where he made his [currant] wine. He had a special recipe that he brought from the old country." "Interview with Vera Wikman," Brian Patton and Rhonda Allen, 10 March 2005. Archives, Whyte Museum of the Canadian Rockies, Banff, AB.

133

Wilmer, B.C. December 7, 1925

Dear Amelie:

It is really a pity that we have not written for so long. I just cannot
grasp that so much time has passed. It is almost unbelievable how
fast a year flies by, and how short life is! —— The best about it is that
we all live with hope and always expect better things to come. This
way, we don't realize how fast time goes by and —— that we get old!
And should hope and love for life ever leave us, then not much of life
can remain. I believe you will agree with me in this case. With writing,
I have problems: I have to search for the word when I write in German
which you will notice by the many mistakes I make. In spite of it, I
will continue to write, since I know that you can read it anyhow. Now
I will write the news that might interest you. In the summer of 1924,
I was on mountain tours for three months in Jasper Park and in the
area around Mt. Robson. First, I was together with two doctors from
Philadelphia and one student for a month.[1] We did a tour to the
Athabasca Pass, where Mt. Hooker and Mt. Brown stand. These
mountains were two of the first peaks in the Rockies that became
known. And for a long time, in fact, almost for one hundred years,
most believed that these peaks were the highest in the Canadian
Rocky Mountains. Even today, you find Mt. Hooker on old maps as
16,000 feet and Mt. Brown with 14,000 feet.[2] In reality, however, Mt.
Hooker is about 11,000 ft. high, and Mt. Brown a little over 9,000 ft.
high. Since this group of mountains is, or rather was, a far distance
from the railway, it happened that hardly any climbers got there.
Even now, it takes two to three days to get there from Jasper. *[In
English from hereon]* The Whirlpool River is a bad river to ford, and
the trail is far from good. Our first climb from Athabasca Pass was

Mt. Kane (10,000 ft.). It was a first ascent, not very hard, but a very long snow tramp. And as this tour was our first climb in the season, and our first march on a glacier, we must have been a sad looking bunch: our faces were swollen and scorched. Next, we climbed Mt. Brown (which was easy). Then we went back to the Scott Glacier and climbed Mt. Oates (about 10,000 ft., first ascent). On this climb, we decided that we would attempt a traverse of Mt. Hooker next. We left camp at 4 h. A.M. and reached the summit at 9 h. P.M. We had a bad rockfall, and, because we changed our way, we were delayed. When we reached the summit, one of the fellows got cramps in his stomach, and, for a while, the situation looked very bad. But finally we could move on. The descent was easy as long as we could see. We found a good bivouac about 10 P.M., and we all hoped to reach camp early next day. At about 3 A.M., though, there was thunder in the distance, and heavy clouds rolled up from all corners. It started to snow, a sharp wind rose, and we soon were chilled to the bone. We thought that the best we could do was to move to a lower level, but it got so foggy that we could see very little. Finally, we found shelter and waited there in misery. The weather got worse. I built a wall around the overhanging rocks and plastered it up with snow. It kept out the wind but not the cold, and soon we knew that we had to spend another night on the mountain. As for me, I was alright, though I was cold and a little hungry, but not worrying about the future. But the two doctors had lost all hope that we would get off this mountain alive. Dr. Strumia, an Italian from Turin, got so cold that he was hardly able to speak. I massaged him and did all I could for him. At about 4 P.M., it got a little warmer, and, as soon as Dr. St. was warm enough to write, he wrote his last will and testament. He gave me a copy in case I would reach the valley alive and that later on perhaps his body could not be found. I told Dr. St. that all of us would get out of this hell alive, but he did not believe me. He was ready to go to "the happy hunting grounds"—(the heaven or hereafter in the religion of the Indians). Well, I had to do some talking to cheer them up and keep them alive. At midnight, Dr. Thorington got very ill. We had no food or medicine with us, so all I could do was to talk and to hand Dr.

Thorington a snow-ball to suck. I can't write you all the details. ——
It was a very long, long and cold night! At five in the morning, there
was a little break in the fog, so I left our bivouac at once to locate the
pass, which we had to find to get back to camp. I told the others to
follow as soon as possible, which they did. I found the pass and made
marks on the snowfields, then I ran back to take charge of the party
and told them that all was well. I nearly spoke too soon!! Just as we
reached the pass a terrific storm broke loose, *[In German from hereon]*
in which we almost suffocated! —— Finally, we reached a better place
and could see the valley for a few seconds. I don't know how it
happened, whether we did not pay enough attention or did not watch
our steps, or were too excited about the sunshine in the valley ———
but all of the sudden the two fell into a glacier crevasse——! I still
had the strength to pull them out. We unroped at the moraine and,
from there, it was easy travelling to camp. It was 9 A.M. Since we had
been out for two nights, our cook and our packer believed that we
had been in an accident. The packer, in fact, had gone out to Jasper
to get help. Since I was totally exhausted, I begged the cook to ride as
fast as possible and try to catch the packer so that the rescue expedition would not have to come so far into the mountains for nothing. I
knew there would be a long and stupid story in the newspaper. And
so there was. A long story! Hetta, of course, read it, but thank goodness she did not get too upset. These are the experiences we had on
Mt. Hooker![3] After Hooker, we went north to the Ramparts and did
the first ascent of Mt. Simon (11,000 ft.), the highest peak. Then, we
went into the Mt. Robson group, and, in two weeks, I climbed Mt.
Robson four times: first tour, twenty-six hours; second tour, twenty-
three hours; third tour, seventeen hours; and the fourth tour, fifteen
hours.[4] On the second tour, I almost had an accident because of the
carelessness of another climber. —— On August 8th, I went with
another group into the Columbia group (Athabasca River).[5] On this
side of Mt. Columbia, there are almost no glaciers. We did the first
ascent of Mt. King Edward, which rises next to Mt. Columbia. Then
we wanted to climb Mt. Columbia from that side, but we had such
difficulties with a small ice fall that we gave up the tour. Then it

rained for three weeks. —— On September 12th, I came back home and found my nephew <u>Isidor</u> here. At present, he is on the farm with Hetta's sister. He is learning English easily, and he really likes the trapping life here. He thinks he will spend many years here. I cannot write much about my house yet. I have done a lot of work on it, but that won't interest you very much. This past spring, I went to Western Alaska on a bear hunt.[6] It was a long tour of seventy-two days, and twenty days were spent at the ocean. Otherwise, I did not see any new geography. One thing is clear to me that I would not want to live there for a longer time, because I love the forest. In western Alaska, there are no trees, only bushes and even they only grow to about 1,000 ft. above sea level. Nevertheless, I did benefit from the trip —— my little home looked <u>good to me</u> on my return!! Two years ago, I began to raise Muskrats, but this project did not turn out too well. Next spring, we will try our luck with minks and martens. During the last few months, I trapped coyotes, but you cannot do much with these shy animals.[7] —— I don't know what I will do the next season yet. I have made no plans. Next September, I will go to the mountains again, for a longer time, I think, and will set up my "headquarters" on the western branch of the Saskatchewan River. I am sorry that I stayed home this winter. I think you will be satisfied with the length of this letter. I will write again in a few months. You must not think that I have forgotten you. I think of you very often and of your good deeds. I must not write more now or you might call me a dreamer!! I hope you are all well, and may better times come for you. I wish it with all my heart. With best greetings to you, your dear mother and sister, your *Conrad Kain*.

1. With 14 horses furnished by Donald "Curly" Phillips, Kain, Drs. Thorington and Max M. Strumia (1896–1972), and a 16-year-old Alfred J. Ostheimer (1908–1983) made what was perhaps the third expedition to Athabasca Pass for purely mountaineering purposes. The group climbed in the Athabasca Pass and Tonquin Valley areas for most of June and early July. See Thorington, *The Glittering Mountains*, 172–201.

2. The peaks were given their exaggerated heights by the Scottish botanical collector David Douglas (1799–1834), who, in the spring of 1827, crossed Athabasca Pass with an eastbound Hudson's Bay

Company brigade. There, Douglas claimed to have climbed Mt. Brown, which, like the nearby Mt. Hooker, he named in honour of his scientific betters. Moreover, he claimed the two peaks were "the highest yet known on the Northern Continent of America." *Journal kept by David Douglas during his travels in North America, 1823–1927* (1914; New York: Antiquarian Press, 1959), 72. They remained the highest points on any map of British North America for almost three-quarters of a century, and so became the siren call for Canadian mountaineering exploration. See Zac Robinson and Stephen Slemon, "Deception in High Places: Revisiting Brown and Hooker," CAJ 94 (2011): 12–17.

3. The epic first ascent of Mt. Hooker is also related by Thorington in both *The Glittering Mountains*, 185–98, and in J. Monroe Thorington, "A Mountaineering Journey through Jasper Park," CAJ 16 (1926–1927): 86–107.

4. Kain and company were based in the ACC's 1924 Mt. Robson Camp, held from 22 July to 4 August. During the camp, according to its official report, Kain, incredibly, led 15 people to the summit of Mt. Robson in little over a week, with only occasional assistance of the other guides, namely the Oberland guides Alfred Streich and Hans Kohler, who were on loan to the ACC camp from the CNR. See "Mt. Robson Camp, 1924," CAJ 14 (1924): 148–53. From a high camp situated near treeline in a gully above Kinney Lake, all four ascents were made on what's now referred to as the South Face Route, Kain's second new route on the mountain. Today, three days are typically taken to climb the route, but, according to the region's guidebook "a fit team could do it in two." Sean Dougherty, *Selected Alpine Climbs in the Canadian Rockies* (Calgary: Rocky Mountain Books, 1999), 302.

5. Kain travelled up the Athabasca Valley with Howard Palmer (1883–1944), author of the classic *Mountaineering and Exploration in the Selkirks* (1914) and co-author of *A Climber's Guide to the Rocky Mountains of Canada* (1921), and Joseph Hickson (1873–1956), the president of the ACC. See H. Palmer, "The First Ascent of Mt. King Edward, Canadian Rockies, with a Note on Mount Alberta," AJ 37 (1925): 306. While bad weather and forest fires in the area ultimately prevented an attempt of the unclimbed Mt. Alberta (3,619 m [11,873 ft.]), Kain and Hickson would, in addition to ascending Little Alberta (2,956 m [9,698 ft.]) and Mt. King Edward (3,490 m [11,450 ft.]) with Palmer, make the first ascent of Mt. Edith Cavell's East Ridge at the trip's commencement.

6. Although it seems that Kain did little to no mountaineering during the three summers that followed his busy 1924 season, he continued to guide and outfit hunting parties in the spring and fall. Much of his hunting—at least five trips between 1926 and 1930—was done with Randall W. Everett, whom he met in southwestern Alaska while working as a special guide to the former proprietor of the *Glasgow Herald*, Scottish-born James Cameron Dun-Waters (1864–1939), of Fintry, Okanagan Lake. Written in an essay titled "Conrad, Hunter of Bear," Dun-Waters's recollections of Kain were printed by Thorington in *Where the Clouds Can Go* (1935), 475–83.

7. For as long as the fur market was profitable, Kain and Hetta, who both had a talent for handling animals, raised mink, marten, and chinchillas at their small farm.

134

Wilmer, B.C, May 7, 1932

Dear Amelie:

A short while ago, we received the sad message and we convey our sympathy to you. We can only imagine how lonely life will be for you. I said to Hetta repeatedly that one will rarely find a daughter as good as you were to your mother, "true until death."[1] May God and the angels bless you with health and wellbeing, as long as you are on this earth. — It has been a long time since we have last written, so I will now write a long and beautiful letter. Unfortunately, times and conditions are such that one can hardly write something beautiful.[2] Sad news does not help someone in mouring. So, I will not bother you with our conditions. I have not felt too well for the last two years, and I have come to the conclusion that something is wrong with my health. I had my teeth pulled and am feeling ever so much better now. Hetta was been very sick for three months, but is a little better now. She is still far from well, though. For years, I have not heard any German spoken and am out of practice with writing it. You will read in the papers that we have bad times here in Canada, just like in America, but the picture seems different for Europe. In the USA, millions are out of work and thousands starve. And in the banks are billions of dollars. They are not dead, but SLEEP—SLEEP.——. And how the human condition is so linked now to the dollar: when it is sleeping, it does not produce. — The interesting thing in this world economy is that nobody knows what to do. No one even knows how long the Depression will drag on! Here in Wilmer, we have enough to eat. But there is no opportunity to sell our products. We would not get good prices for them even if we could. But we do not suffer. Tomorrow, May 9th, I will go on a bear hunt in the mountains. Since

I will be alone most of the time, I will have the opportunity to write a long letter. Writing is much easier when one is in nature. I still find joy in the forest and in the mountains and in everything that belongs to wilderness. Very often, I dream of my mountains at home, of my youth, and my old friends. The next letter will be a long one. Both of us are sending hearty greetings and hope that you will recover from your sorrow and all your efforts and exertion. Your friends, *Conrad and Hetta*

[In English from hereon, to the end of correspondence]   403

1. Amelie Malek's mother, Amalie, passed away in March, and her sister, Flora, had died a year earlier.
2. Kain is writing at the height of the Great Depression.

135

Wilmer, B.C., February 17, 1933

Dear Amelie:

I have been waiting for an answer to my extremely long letter I wrote you from Toby Creek last May.[1] Sometime ago, I received a letter from my brother Eugen, and as he did not mention you, I hope you are alive. — I have lost Hetta.[2] She was a good and loving wife to me. I miss her. I am very glad to know that I have done all I could for her while she was with me. We are having a terrible time here. Everybody is feeling the Depression. If you receive this letter, and are able to write, I would appreciate very much if you would write me a few lines. With the kindest regards and best wishes, yours sincerely, *Conrad.*

1. This "extremely long letter" is missing from this edition. Malek claimed to have never received it. See Letter 138.

2. Suffering from a bowel obstruction, Henriquita Kain was taken to Saint Eugene's Hospital in nearby Cranbrook, BC, for an operation in late January. Infection later set in, and she died on 7 February. Henriquita was 48 years of age. She was buried in the Roman Catholic section of the Cranbrook Cemetery. Kain included a newspaper clipping with this particular letter that read as follows: "Wife of well-known B.C. guide dies suddenly. Invermere, February 14. The death occurred suddenly of Mrs. Kain of Wilmer, wife of Conrad Kain, the well-known guide, who was the first of the Swiss guides to be brought to Canada by the Alpine Club. He will be remembered as the guide who found and helped to bring out Mrs. Stone and the body of the late Professor Stone who were lost in climbing in the Selkirk Range. During the last few years, Mr. and Mrs. Kain ran a fur farm at Wilmer, near here. Besides her husband, Mrs. Kain leaves her mother, Mrs. Ferara, a married daughter at Port Angeles, US, and two brothers John and Toni Granito who both served overseas in the war. Mrs. Kain was born near Georgetown, British Guiana and came to this district in 1913."

136

Wilmer, B.C., March 8, 1933

Dear Amelie:

About a month ago, I hurt my shin-bone and have neglected the
wound. Now, I suffer for it. I can't work outside, so, to kill the loneliness, I have retyped an account that appeared in *The American Alpine
Journal* (1932) on my experiences on Mt. Cook in New Zealand, which
I mailed to you.[1] If you think it worthwhile to translate it and have it
published in some alpine paper or the *Arbeiter-Zeitung* and that you
can get some money for your work, please, do so; but you must keep
for yourself whatever you get for it. If you are able to get money for
the Mt. Cook story, you probably can make use of another article,
"Reminiscences of Seven Summers in Canada," which was printed
in the *Alpine Journal* 1931.[2] You are the only one in this world that I
owe obligations. The debt is large, I know, but I will try to pay off in
full. I miss Hetta very much. I am lonely. I long to hear from you and
my mother. I wonder whether you have received that very long letter
I wrote you from Toby Creek last May? I am under the impression
that Hetta put a short note in the same letter. Then again, I wonder
if I hurt your feelings in some way and caused you not to reply? I
am far of being an expert with the typewriter, but I hope to improve
a little. It is easier for the eye than my bad hand-writing, don't you
think? I am looking forward to getting a letter from you. I shall feel
better knowing that you are still on this earth. I wrote my mother and
brother and expect to hear from them next month. I received an invitation to spend some time for a change with a friend who has been
bear hunting with me several times. But I cannot leave my home. I
still have chickens, rabbits, and there are also five horses to take care

of. Trusting that you received this letter and that you are well, I am with the kindest regards and best wishes, yours sincerely, *Conrad.*

1.   Conrad Kain, "Long Ago on Mount Cook," *American Alpine Journal* (hereafter *AAJ*) 1, no. 4 (1932): 490–96. Thorington reprinted the article as "Long Ago on Aorangi" in *Where the Clouds Can Go* (1935), 417–23.

2.   Conrad Kain, "Reminiscences of Seven Summers in Canada," *AAJ* 1, no. 3 (1931): 290–95. The essay was reprinted by Thorington in *Where the Clouds Can Go* (1935), 427–32.

137

Wilmer, B.C., March 20, 1933

Dear Amelie:

On March 9th, I mailed some papers and a letter for you. I hoped you received it. In the letter, I mention that I was suffering with a sore foot. I am glad to say that it is much better now. The weather is also better. We get a little more sunshine now. But I am still lonesome and cannot make up my mind what to do to keep from getting the blues. The enclosed paper that I typed might be of some use or interest to you. I should have thought of it before, because it is the best of the two articles I wrote on New Zealand. In my spare time, I will write a story in which Daniel Innthaler appears as a character. The plot is laid in America, but one of the leading characters had to make a trip to Vienna and, on a trip to the Rax, meets Innthaler. Just half an hour ago, my sister-in-law was here, and I read the first chapter to her.[1] She enjoyed it. I wonder how you are? And I hope you will drop me a line. As soon as I hear from you, and know that you care to have more news from me, I shall be happy to be of some use to you. With the kindest regards and best wishes, I am sincerely yours, *Conrad*.

1. Ursula Hurst (née Granito) arrived in Wilmer with Henriquita and their mother in 1913. The three had followed Henriquita and Ursula's brothers, John and Anthony Granito. Ursula settled, married a rancher who lived near Wilmer, and raised two girls, Enid and Vera. The former, Enid Hansen (née Hurst), Conrad's niece, often visited him and helped with chores around the house.

138

Wilmer, B.C., April 5th, 1933

My dear Amelie:

I received your letter by last night's mail. It would be impossible for you to imagine how glad I am that you have written to me so promptly. Many, many thanks for your sympathy and the kind words you wrote about Hetta. I miss her very much. In one of my philosophical views, I take consolation in the thought that, after all, seventeen years of living with Hetta is something, and happiness for that length of time is something not everybody gets. We loved each other as man and wife, too. We had the same views on Life and Death. For the last three months, Hetta was prepared to die. She was exceptionally affectionate to me. That was, of course, very hard for me, but she told me many times: "Con, we all have to go someday, and, for us, it is best that I go before you. For me, it would be a hard world to get along without you!" — So, you see, Hetta was a very brave and sensible girl! She was not afraid of death, nor am I. To me, it matters little when and how the end comes. But I confess that I wish to see my mother and you once more, my dear friend. If all goes well, I expect to be with you both next Christmas, but please, don't mention this to my mother. I wrote her that I will come to see her at the first chance I have. To avoid disappointment, I will not set a date. We have mail day only twice a week now, and, because I want to get this letter away with the outgoing mail, I shall not be able to write you all that I wished to say. But I will write you again soon. Before I go further on, I beg you not to consider me a "sentimentalist" if I should lose control of my feelings. I also beg you to forgive me, if I hurt your feelings when I addressed you per "Du" in my last letter. (I am so sorry you did not receive my long letter from last spring! I am still under the impression that Hetta also put a note in). You will naturally understand that I seldom think in German now, and, when I do, I give you that title, because I have done so in my thoughts so often since we met on the sixth of September, 1906, when I went up to Hochter with you and Flora. —— I wrote my mother and asked her not to worry about me regarding the loss of my Hetta. I told her that I am quite capable of taking care of myself. In case she should write you or pay a visit, please explain to her that worrying is useless. (I mean, if you see that she _is_ worrying about me). Now I will tell you one reason why I am so glad that you are yet alive and have written to me. I have a Life Insurance Policy with the Great West Life-Insurance Comp, (Head Office) Winnipeg, Manitoba, Canada. The policy is for $2,000 (dollars), to which is attached double indemnity for accidents. If I should meet death through accident, the amount payable is 4,000 dollars. Hetta is mentioned in the policy as sole beneficiary. Now she is gone. I am alone and probably will be for a long time, if not for the rest of my life. I do not owe anybody. I have no debts. To my knowledge, there are only two persons that I owe obligations: that is _you_ and _my mother_. Therefore, I named you as the beneficiary in the policy. In case I die a natural death, you will receive 2,000 dollars. If I get killed by accident or die within ninety days resulting from accident, the indemnity will be 4,000 dollars. Whatever it is, please give my mother half, and _I beg you_ from my heart that you keep the other half to yourself. Similar provisions are made in my Last Will and Testament. I will end for today to catch the outgoing mail. With the best wishes and kind regards, and thanking you again for your nice letter, sincerely yours, _Conrad._

P.S. —— Kindly remember me to Mr. T. I would like to write him a letter. Do you know if he reads English? — I am writing my story in my spare time, the one in which Innthaler appears. If you don't feel well, please don't work on any of the articles I mailed to you. And I beg you again, if you do translate anything, and get something for the article, keep the money for yourself. And if you know any way that I could be of service to you, let me know. Remember that: whatever I will do, it will be little in comparison to what you have done for me. _C.K._

139

Wilmer, B.C., Easter Sunday 1933

My dear Amelie:

Several days ago, I had a letter from my brother Eugen in which he painted in words the situation in Austria. The picture is not very pleasant to look at, but he probably could not paint otherwise. Having before me his letter and yours, I came to the conclusion that, after all, we here do not know bad times. Although there is very little money in circulation, and times are far from being normal, we still have plenty to eat, and certainly those who are living in the country don't suffer with starvation. I have more vegetables in the cellar than I could use up before the fresh crop comes on. Besides holding vegetables, the shelves are loaded with jars containing fruits and meat (wild goat, deer, chicken, and rabbit). Hetta was very good in the canning business, and I am very glad that I always helped her with putting up things. By helping her, I have <u>learned</u> how to take care of all perishable goods and provide for the long winter. Yesterday, I was at Invermere and had all my papers fixed up. Knowing that you are still on this earth and that you will benefit through my death, in case anything should happen to me, is A GREAT CONSOLATION to me. Not to alarm you in any way, I had better explain to you that one meets here—like anywhere else in the mountains—with dangers. Two years ago, I had a very narrow escape by breaking through a bridge. I was on horseback and alone with ten horses. Last year, I got tangled up with a large grizzly bear. I wrote you all about it in that long letter <u>you did not get</u>. Several years back, I was nearly shot by a careless hunter. In the book enclosed, on page thirty-six, you will note another close call that I had. If I wrote an account of the "First Ascent of Mt. Hooker," it would read quite differently. I am still strong and enjoy all that belongs to the mountains, but I have made up my mind that I will leave to others now the more dangerous climbs. Now a few words about myself. I miss my Hetta. There are times when I feel very lonely, and then Hetta's last words come to me: "<u>Don't worry</u>." These were <u>her last words</u> to me. I don't find it so hard when I can work outside. It is in the house that I miss her most. Up to date, it was not much like spring, but I hope we soon shall be able to work the ground. I made the hotbed ready and will seed it in a few days. If I could sell my home for about half of what we put into it, with what little I have, I believe I could return home and stay there <u>for good</u>. But it is out of the question to find a buyer while the Depression continues. So, I can't do anything but wait and see. My mother-in-law and friends are of the opinion that I shall not be able to run the place by myself. I know that I shall have to neglect my home if I go in the hills. And I am not ignorant of the fact that there are many women who look for a mate and would be glad to find a home and a husband. No doubt, some of them would be good. But I can cook and can keep myself and the house clean. Several weeks before Hetta died, she had given me sound advice regarding marriage. Hetta loved me, and she said her only regret was that she had not known me longer. She was very unhappy with her first husband. I know that there are more unhappy marriages than happy ones. I know a great deal more about women and marriages than my friends. — I'll tell you the truth: I don't know why so many unhappily married women confide in me? I realize that it was to my good that they have taken me in their confidence, because I learned from them how to treat them and what they expect from a man. —— Now about yourself. I hope that you are well and that you have received my letters, and that it means something for you to hear from someone who is far away and who remembers your kind deeds. There might be a letter from you on the way? I hope there is, and that you are telling me things about yourself. I told you in my last letter that if there is something I can do for you, please, let me know. You have been good and kind to me. I remember one Easter—I believe it was 1908—you gave me 10 Kronen. You went with your people to Semmering that year. How times have changed since then! I wonder how many more changes will take place in our time? Well, my dear friend, write me, tell me how you are. Do not hesitate to let me know if I can help you, and, please, bear in mind that you do not put yourself under any obligation. You have been good and kind to me. Now is my turn to <u>repay</u>. If you see or expect that times in Austria will get worse, and if you wish for a change, and if your health is good so that you can stand a sea-journey, I would certainly be pleased to have you here <u>as my guest</u> for a time. My home is far from being a palace, but it is a home of plenty. If my mother would be ten years younger, I would send for her at once. This is a fairly long letter, and you will find many mistakes. I will also write to my mother, and so I have to close for today. You will hear from me again before very long. Trusting that you are well, with the best wishes and kind regard, I am sincerely yours, *Conrad*.

140

Wilmer, B.C., June 8, 1933

My dear Amelie:

I received your card from Vienna and the long letter from Reichenau.
Many thanks for both. I was very much relieved to learn that you are
feeling much better again, and it gives me great pleasure that you
are not in such a poor situation as I thought you were. Now, don't
blush, my dear friend, when I tell you now that I loved you deeply
from the day I first met you. I still think the world of you, and, in my
estimation, I think you are one of the very best human beings that I
have had the good fortune to meet. So you will understand why I ask
you if I can be of any help to you. Further, I believe it is best to offer
one's friend a few flowers, while he is still alive, than to put loads of
them on his grave. — Yes, Hetta did love you. I know she would have
invited you to come and spend a time with us. Your picture is still on
the same place on the dresser, where she put it. — I wanted to send
a few dollars to my mother, but can't get a money-order through the
post office. I will try the bank. To avoid these troubles in the future,
I shall send a sum to you. You will be kind-hearted all your life, and I
shall take advantage of your kindness and ask you to send so much to
my mother every month, so that she gets a few happy days in her old
age. I am in a great hurry today: we are having some trouble with the
water, so I will write in a few days. Hoping this letter finds you in the
best of spirits and good health, yours sincerely, *Conrad*.

141

Wilmer, B.C., June 13, 1933

My dear Amelie:

In my last letter, I mentioned that I wanted to send some money to my mother, and that I could not get a Post Office Order. Several days ago, I went to the Bank and made arrangements to have the sum of $50 forwarded to you. This order has to go through the Head Office, so it might be a few days longer. When you receive the money, please send 45 Schillings to my brother Eugen. He should buy a goat for the money. And I beg you to send to my mother 25 Schilling each month. The Austrian money is at present not quoted in the paper, so I don't know how much a Schilling is? — In my last letter, I told you that I was in a hurry, as we had trouble with the water. Well, I am in trouble again: my very best horses broke through the fence and went in all directions!! I got up at 3 A.M., walked about 20 miles —— all for nothing! So, I have to go again now. I might catch some when they come for a drink at a certain place. We have mail only twice a week, and, as I wanted you to get this letter before the money arrives, I hurried back. But as soon as I have time, I shall try to answer all your questions. I hope you will not mind my sending the money to you? If I could get a money-order at any time, I would not bother you, but, as it is, I have to take advantage of your generosity! Hoping that you are well again, and that you enjoy good health for many years to come, I am with the best wishes and kind regards, yours truly *Conrad*.

P.S. My garden is looking very good now! I take special care of Hetta's flower-corner. I think you would like my place.

142

Spillimacheen, B.C., August 31, 1933

Dear Amelie:

No doubt you will wonder what became of me because you have
not heard from me for such a long time! Well, here's the explanation: quite unexpectedly, I got work for myself and my horses.
My last letter to you was regarding the money I forwarded to you
through the bank. Shortly after, I had a letter from my old friend
Thorington. He wanted me to meet him on June 21st at this place.
I just managed to get my horses, but I delayed a day because of a
terrible flooding. We went up the Bugaboo-Valley and stayed there
twelve days.[1] It took me two days to get back to Wilmer. I had to
start at once, too, so I could get my home in order. I worked hard for
several days to get the garden in shape, and then we drove the horses
back to their summer pasture. This meant another two days. I then
cut my hay: I had a fair crop, but not as good as usual on account
of my being absent for so long. Then, I had hardly finished the hay,
when I received a wire from Lake Louise, Alberta, that I should be
there on the 14th of July.[2] After being there only a day, we left Lake
Louise for Bow Lake. We crossed Bow-Pass the next day and made
camp at the foot of the Peyto Glacier, and then began to climb. We
made four first ascents and several new routes on mountains that
had been climbed before. We finished the expedition by crossing
the Yoho snowfields to Field, B.C.—twenty-four miles, more than
half of the distance was <u>on snow</u>!![3] With one of the members of the
party, I then continued on to the Alpine Club camp, which was held
in the Paradise Valley near Lake Louise. I have not been with the club
for many years. While there, I met many of the old-time climbers.
Then we climbed a few peaks around Lake Louise. I celebrated my

fiftieth birthday by climbing Mount Louis near Banff. Mt. Louis is looked upon as one of the best climbs in the Rockies. The climber who was with me, Mr. Kingman of Minneapolis, enjoyed the climb and was much impressed with what ease I overcame the difficulties of the climb. On our return, we had some drinks and a good supper in the Mt. Royal Hotel. Many of my friends of long ago came to see me.[4] For one reason or the other, I had you in my mind that day. Oh, Amelie, what would not I have given, if I could have seen you to press your hand! I know you call that sentimental, but, never mind, there is no harm done! After I was through with Mr. Kingman, I was engaged for a week by a lady who came from Boston. She was no spring chicken, but was very gay for her age. We climbed in the Yoho Valley. On my return home, I found your two cards. Many thanks for them and many thanks, too, for paying a visit to my mother! I am very glad to hear that you are feeling better, and that you are strong enough to take some walks. I hope your strength will come back to you and that you will yet get some joy out of your life. I hope that it will be granted to me to spend a few happy days with you. Had I known before that I would get so much work this summer, I could have made arrangements to go home in the coming winter, but, as it is, I have no plans. I quite agree with you that I would get more joy out of a visit to my home if the times were better. I note in the papers that Austria must get more help from the rest of the nations that had a hand in destroying this country. On my arriving home, I was welcomed by my mother-in-law. She had a large birthday cake ready for me and was very disappointed that I was not at home for the occasion. She told me that Hetta had taken her in confidence regarding her plan in celebrating my fiftieth birthday. I don't know if I told you once that none of Hetta's people had any use for me. Well, it is quite different now. They are all very nice to me. I had a letter from Hetta's daughter.[5] She wrote that she will come and stay with me for a time next month. I just got through with my work at home, and looked forward to a long chat with you, when along came a wire from

< *Conrad Kain and J. Monroe Thorington on the summit of Trapper Peak, 1933. Photo by H.S. Kingman. [WMCR, V622-NA66-1778]*

a party (English people).[6] I had to go for my horses and start out at once. I arrived here in time and then came along or rather I brought along—the rain! I took the opportunity to write you. We shall be out for ten to twelve days, and then it will take us another two days to get home to Wilmer. The chances are that I shall not have much time to write then, as I expect that I shall have to go hunting for two weeks. But if I have time, I will then answer all your questions! After the hunt, I would like to go trapping for several weeks. The money I shall make (that is, if I have any luck), I will ear-mark for my visit home! Sometimes I try to imagine how you look now, and what you will say when you will open the door. ——— It has now been twenty-one years since I have last seen you! How quickly the time went by! I too (of course!) look a bit older, but I feel very good. The trip in the mountains this summer has done me good after my troubles. When I am at home, I am apt to get lonely. Of course, everything around me reminds me of my Hetta———. I hope that this letter finds you in best of health and that you keep well for many years to come.

With the kindest regards and good wishes,
I am yours sincerely,
Conrad

1. On 22 June 1933, Kain took Thorington and his wife, Christine Rehn, along with Kain's nephew, Isidor, and a pack train of horses laden with supplies into the Bugaboo Group. The party made several ascents, including the first ascent of Crescent Spire (2,842 m [9,324 ft.]). See J. Monroe Thorington, "The Bugaboo-Howser Watershed, Purcell Range," *AAJ* 2 (1934): 182–91. Of Kain, Thorington wrote that "he had aged (he was only 49), but was by way of regaining his old spirits and regaled us with many a fine tale." Kain, *Where the Clouds*, 505.
2. In Lake Louise, Kain met Thorington and Henry S. Kingman (1894–1968), a leading banker from Minneapolis, and the party travelled north with outfitter Jimmy Simpson to Peyto Lake. See H.S. Kingman and J.M. Thorington, "Climbs in the Northern Waputiks (Canadian Rocky Mountains)," *AAJ* 2 (1934): 205–09.
3. The group made first ascents of Peyto Peak, Mt. Trapper, Mt. Mistaya, and Barbette Mountain. They completed their tour with the long glacier traverse across the watershed from Peyto Lake to the Yoho Valley.
4. Kain had not been away from the Columbia Valley since 1925.

∧ *Conrad Kain, 1933.* [Windermere District Historical Society, C2089]

5. Beatrice Ferrara, Henriquita's daughter, came to Canada from South America with her mother in 1913, but left Wilmer soon after to pursue nursing studies in Victoria, BC. She later married an American and moved to the United States.

6. This was Kain's last climbing trip. Fittingly, it was to the Bugaboos, a place Kain knew better than any other mountain guide. His clients were Ivor Armstrong Richards (1893–1979), a famous professor of literature from Cambridge University, and his wife, Dorothy Pilley Richards (1894–1986), a prominent mountaineer and the author of the well-regarded memoir, *Climbing Days* (1935). The party made what was perhaps the second ascent of Pigeon Spire and the long first ascent of the highest peak in the Bobbie Burns group—"No. 7," as Kain called it by its survey designation. It is now officially known as "Mount Conrad" (3,252 m [10,669 ft.]). Conrad Kain died in the hospital of Cranbrook, BC, on 2 February 1934.

EPILOGUE

The Kain–Malek Correspondence: Provenance, 1934–2005

DON BOURDON

In an archivist's career, there are many unbelievable stories about the circuitous paths that records take before they come to a repository to be preserved and appreciated by the public. This is one of my favourites.

On 4 August 2000, Gerhard Pistor, a semi-retired writer on vacation from his home in Vienna, Austria, came into the Archives and Library at the Whyte Museum of the Canadian Rockies in Banff, where I served as the head archivist. It was a beautiful day. His family was off enjoying the town. But he saw a photograph on a Canadian Ski Museum interpretive panel at the local shopping mall that stopped him in his tracks. The name of the young mountain guide in the photograph, Conrad Kain, sparked memories of conversations the man had with his father, Dr. Erich Pistor, more than 46 years before. The credit line on the photograph prompted the son to seek out the Archives, which was where the image came from.

Gerhard Pistor wanted to know if we had information about Kain and the role Dr. Erich Pistor played in Kain's journey to Canada. He had come to the right place. Together, we searched catalogues and finding aids, locating a number of references to Pistor senior and a wealth of information about Kain. Dr. Pistor and his first wife, Sara, figure prominently as Dr. and Mrs. "P" in *Where the Clouds Can Go* (1935), Kain's autobiography assembled by J. Monroe Thorington, the American mountaineer and alpine historian. This was a revelation to Gerhard Pistor.

The doctor's son became engrossed in the Kain autobiography and spent a quiet afternoon in the Eleanor Luxton Reading Room at the Archives. Meanwhile, I directed him to two key letters his father had written in 1909, one addressed to the Canadian Pacific Railway "Tourist Department" and another written several months later to A.O. Wheeler, president of the Alpine Club of Canada.[1] Both were in the extensive records of the Alpine Club of Canada. These are not simple letters of introduction, but sincere testimonials to a remarkable young mountain guide written by his older client and friend. Dr. Pistor felt Kain deserved a chance to pursue a promising mountain career beyond the confines of Austria and solicited employment in Canada on his friend's behalf.

After examining articles in journals of both the Alpine Club of Canada and the American Alpine Club, Gerhard Pistor asked where he might obtain a copy of *Where the Clouds Can Go*. Though the book was then out of print, I directed him to the local bookstore. It often carried good reader's copies in its mountaineering section and occasionally a first edition—the book had inspired several generations of climbers. Mr. Pistor returned with a copy of his own. He then told me he owned a number of Conrad Kain's papers and photographs that his father had kept, including a substantial collection of personal letters. I was astounded that Kain's records should come to light at this late date. We discussed the idea of future donation of the records, and he agreed to contact me when he returned home. I wrote the particulars in my "lead book" for follow-up.

A routine survey of that notebook four years later prompted me to write Gerhard Pistor on 15 August 2004. He replied in November and agreed to donate the Kain–Pistor papers. Originally planning to use the papers for a book, Pistor had become engrossed in a different writing project and now felt that the Whyte Museum Archives would be the best permanent home for the Kain records. He promised to deal with the matter upon his return from a Christmas vacation. I was elated, obviously, but kept the matter quiet to avoid jinxing our good fortune.

On 26 December 2004, the world reeled in horror at the enormous devastation caused by the Indian Ocean Tsunami. Unbelievably, 200,000 people perished, with many swept out to sea. As I watched eyewitness images of the tragedy on television, it dawned on me that the Pistors were vacationing in Sri Lanka. I wrote a tentative email, hoping for the best. To my great relief, I received a brief reply stating that the Pistors had narrowly escaped.

In early January, shipping arrangements for the papers were concluded and Gerhard Pistor obliged me with background notes about his father, the Renaissance man, who had apparently planned to write a German-language version of Kain's autobiography.

January 13, 2005

Dear Mr. Bourdon,

The FedEx man has just left and I send you a few points on my father's life. I learned most [more] about my father in the book "Where the Clouds Can Go." My father, Dr. Erich Pistor, was born on August 24th in 1873 in Graz. He studied Law 1898.

He started working at the Chamber of Commerce in Graz (Styria) and attended [in] 1899 the International Commercial Congress in Philadelphia (he earned the money for the journey by giving private lessons). His reviews about the Congress earned him a call to the Chamber of Commerce in Vienna, the most important one in the Austrian-Hungarian Empire. The title of his first book: "Der Exportförderungsdienst des Handelsmuseums in Philadelphia" (1900). 1901 and 1902 he travelled through Siberia, Japan to Australia and New Zealand by order of the Chamber of Commerce and wrote a book "Durch Sibirien in die Südsee" (1903). He organized for the Chamber of Commerce many exhibitions not only in Europe, but also Buenos Aires and Toronto. Just before the First World War, he travelled again around the world—Canada, Japan, Peking, Siberia.

He became director of the Chamber of Commerce, was Vice President of the Austrian-British Committee and President of the Austrian-Greek Society. (And now I am married with a Greek—the love for the country and the people must be in the genes). Other books: *"Die Volkswirtschaft in Österrich," "Griechenland und de Nahe Osten." My father spoke twelve languages. He had a lot of decorations. His first wife, Sara, was a British citizen and they had three children, two of them died in Stalingrad during the Second World War. She died in 1930.*

My father loved the mountain Rax (about eighty kilometres from Vienna) very much; there he met Conrad Kain, who was born in a very small village near the mountain. What a daring mountaineer my father was, I only learned in Kain's book "Where the Clouds Can Go," that I bought after we met (our house in Vienna with all the books has been vandalized first by Russian soldiers, then by Americans). How he recommended Kain to the Canadian Railway you know better than I do. 1932 my father married a second time, I am the only son of that marriage, born 1938. 1944 we escaped the bombs and lived first in Prein/Rax and then in Reichenau, that is also at the foot of Rax. Dr. Erich Pistor died September 1st 1954 and is buried in Prein/Rax. His grave is viewing the mountain.

Gerhard Pistor

The carefully wrapped package of records arrived in perfect order with a note from Gerhard Pistor saying that "I think it would have also been the wish of my father to donate [the records] to your museum." As I reverently examined the contents, I realized that materials accumulated and augmented by Dr. Pistor consisted of a draft manuscript by Pistor (in German) of the Kain autobiography, with related correspondence and notes, drafts and published articles by Kain, and, of course, the typewritten transcripts of the Kain–Malek correspondence.

Also included were letters between Pistor and Conrad Kain, J. Monroe Thorington, Amelie Malek, and others. Twenty-seven photographs, many entirely new to me, included portraits of Kain, his climbing and trapping views, and the Kains' farm at Wilmer, BC. There were also images of a ceremony, perhaps the dedication of the monument to Kain sponsored by Pistor and other friends erected following Kain's death.

So many questions came to mind. Who was Amelie Malek and what was her connection with Kain? What became of her? Did the letters form part of the autobiography and, if so, how much? Or, perhaps, they were a parallel account? Those questions would have to be left for historians to answer. But I needed to determine the basic nature of all the records in order to document and describe them. Who typed the letters and why? What had become of the originals? What were they about? What had become of Malek's letters to Kain?

I discovered that the typescript letters by Malek to Thorington, written in 1934 and 1935 in connection with the autobiography, were identical in typeface and editing marks to the Kain–Malek correspondence. That the transcripts had been in the possession of Dr. Pistor initially caused me to speculate that his wife, Sara, had transcribed the letters—she had taught Kain some of his early English. But, no, the letters had been carefully typewritten and painstakingly proofed for Thorington by Malek herself in the immediate years following Kain's death. Thorington, after publishing *Clouds* in 1935, then sent the typescript letters back to Europe to Dr. Pistor, who had embarked on an ill-timed German version, which Pistor was still trying to publish in 1939.[2]

The origins of the typescript, as well as the nature of the friendship between Conrad and Amelie, became clear in the beautifully written, and sometimes anxious, letters Amelie Malek wrote to Thorington. These letters, too, alternate between English and German, but a key passage confirmed my belief (Malek to Thorington, September 28, 1934):

> As soon *as I can,* I shall send letters from Con (pre-war time) to meet your request. I am more willing to offer any help whatever for your biography of Kain. His letters to me were really letters to a friend, and so were mine addressed to him. You may use them *at will,* they do not contain any secrets or private affairs, and I am going to copy as many letters as possible (most of them are interesting for the description of his excursions or adventures, I used to read them to my people at home). Please let me know *by what term*

you must have them, dear Mr. Thorington. Of course I shall send
these copies registered.[3]

Another letter to Thorington, written on 5 January 1935, confirms Malek's role in creating the typescript letters that she sent to America, only to turn up 60 years later in Vienna. More importantly, Malek understood the true essence of Kain's letters to her, his dear friend:

Today I posted the second series of letters from Con. (page 43 till page 92). Another series will follow next month. Though these letters are of no use for your book they will be welcomed by you, I am sure, giving a complete character-portrait of our late friend in his younger years. I tell you again that they are your property, dear Dr. Thorington. I know you will keep them and treasure them all, because you liked and loved and appreciated the man who has written all these letters. They are no master pieces of elegant style and learnedness, but they are full of [the] glow and enthusiasm of youth, they show the fire of Con's roving nature and above all, they show his love of nature, and his kind-hearted, grateful and just feeling in everything. I am eagerly looking forward to your next letter to hear your opinion. The first series of letters I sent a month ago, are already in your possession by now. It contained many letters I copied on simple letter-paper about twenty years ago. Now I want you to have this series quite properly and neat and I am going to copy these letters again with my typewriter, so that the pages are all the same size. You could put...all the letters in a kind of book–map, so that the leaves are like bound.[4]

I came to realize how many perils had threatened the precious Kain–Malek–Pistor papers. There were many times when they could so easily have been destroyed. And they might never have found their way to Banff. Again, the gracious donor provided background information:

February 8, 2005

Dear Mr. Bourdon,

It is a story like many others of this time: My parents left the house in Vienna [in] 1944 when the bombing of the capital increased. We lived with friends at the village of Prein, half way up the mountain Rax, that my father loved so much. We took nearly nothing with us. At the end of the war we could not live again in our house, because as I wrote to you, it was first occupied by Russians, then by Americans. Thousands of my father's books were just thrown out of the window and landed on our garden.

My mother was allowed to collect things and she stored boxes in cellars of friends' around the town. Two boxes survived. About six years ago, I got a call by a lady that she found the forgotten boxes: one with the Conrad Kain manuscripts, the other with a manuscript for another book by my father with poems.

In the year 2000, travelling with my wife and boy in Canada, I saw in a food stall in Banff a picture of Kain. I remembered my father telling me about him and about a book he wrote. (My father died when I was 15 years old.) So, I went to your museum and met you! The book by Kain was lost but I could order it at the "Mountain Book Store" (something like that is the name) [Banff Book and Art Den] at Banff. As I read "Where the Clouds Can Go," I learned more about the daring side of my father than at the time he was still alive (with my mother he made the Grossglockner for honeymoon).

The tsunami: We were really born a second time. It was a very cheap occasion to go to Sri Lanka. 1000 Euros: fourteen days including all meals and sightseeing tours through the island and nine days at the beach it was well worth it. We stayed at Koggala beach, less than ten miles south of Galle, the worst hit place. Our room was on the ground floor just fifty metres from the seashore. Nothing is left. We came back the night of December 24th. Two days

earlier, we rode the train to Galle, the same train where more than
a thousand people were killed. It just was not our time to get killed.

Greetings from Vienna
Gerhard Pistor

I showed the letters to Chic Scott and Zac Robinson to further my analysis and hoped there would be interest in sharing the letters with a larger audience. The Kain to Malek letters are part of a much larger story. I am so pleased that Zac Robinson has undertaken the work of placing Kain's letters, which stand perfectly well on their own, into a larger context. I am also gratified that Maria and John Koch undertook the hard translation work, as I had assisted them at the Archives while they worked on projects concerning Martin Nordegg, the founder of the town that bears his name in the eastern slopes of the Alberta Rockies. I found them to be deeply committed to their work. Above all, we should be grateful to Gerhard Pistor for following his journalistic instinct, finding the ideal home for the records, and for his generosity.

Amelie Malek's love for her friend and her faithfulness to his memory have come full circle. The letters, "a complete character portrait," are contained in a book for all to enjoy. Love letters in so many senses, they are labours of love and brimming with love for life.

1. Erich Pistor, February 8 and April 9, 1909, Alpine Club of Canada fonds, (M200/AC0M/52), Archives, Whyte Museum of the Canadian Rockies, Banff, AB.

2. Erich Pistor to J. Monroe Thorington, October 6, 1936 and July 8, 1939, J. Monroe Thorington fonds, (M106/142), Archives, Whyte Museum of the Canadian Rockies, Banff, AB.

3. Amelie Malek to J. Monroe Thorington, September 28, 1934, J. Monroe Thorington fonds, (M106/file 192, photocopies), Archives, Whyte Museum of the Canadian Rockies, Banff, AB.

4. Amelie Malek to J. Monroe Thorington, January 5, 1935, J. Monroe Thorington fonds, (M106/file 193, photocopies), Archives, Whyte Museum of the Canadian Rockies, Banff, AB.

BIBLIOGRAPHY

Adolphs, Dieter Wolfgang. "Hermann Bahr (19 July 1863–15 January 1934)."   429
In *Dictionary of Literary Biography: Twentieth-Century German Dramatists,*
1889–1918. Vol. 118, 3–22. Edited by Wolfgang Elfe and James N. Hardin.
Detroit: Gale Research, 1992.

Allen, E. John B. *The Culture and Sport of Skiing: From Antiquity to World War II.*
Amherst: University of Massachusetts Press, 2007.

"Alpine Club Notes," *Canadian Alpine Journal* 1, no.1 (1907): 160–63.

Amundsen, Roald. *The South Pole: An Account of the Norwegian Antarctic*
Expedition in the "Fram," 1910–1912. Translated by A.G. Chater. New York:
Lee Keedick, 1913.

Aoraki/Mount Cook National Park Management Plan. Christchurch, NZ:
Department of Conservation, 2004.

"Arthur Oliver Wheeler," *Canadian Alpine Journal* 29 (1944-1945): 140–46.

Barcott, Bruce. "Cliffhangers," *Harper's Magazine,* August 1996.

Bella, Leslie. *Parks for Profit.* Montreal: Harvest House, 1987.

Beller, Steven. *A Concise History of Austria.* Cambridge: Cambridge University
Press, 2006.

"Benjamin Frank Seaver, 1858–1929," *Canadian Alpine Journal* 17 (1928): 74–75.

Best, Cora Johnstone. "Horse Thief Creek and the Lake of the Hanging
Glaciers," *Canadian Alpine Journal* 13 (1923): 229–41.

Binnema, Theodore (Ted), and Melanie Niemi, "'Let the Line Be Drawn Now':
Wilderness, Conservation, and the Exclusion of Aboriginal People from
Banff National Park in Canada," *Environmental History* 11, no. 4 (2006):
724–50.

Birney, Earle. "Conrad Kain," *Canadian Alpine Journal* 34 (1951): 97–100.

Bishop, Ted. *Riding with Rilke: Reflections on Motorcycles and Books.* Toronto:
Penguin, 2005.

Blakeney, T.S. "The Alpine Journal and its Editors II. 1896–1923," *The Alpine Journal* 80 (1975): 120–27.

Bliss, Michael. *The Discovery of Insulin*. Toronto: McClelland and Stewart, 1982.

Boles, Glen W., Roger W. Laurilla, and William L. Putnam. *Canadian Mountain Place Names: The Rockies and Columbia Mountains*. Calgary: Rocky Mountain Books, 2006.

Bothwell, Robert, Ian Drummond, and John English. *Canada, 1900–1945*. Toronto: University of Toronto Press, 1998.

Brewster, F.O. (Pat). *Weathered Wood: Anecdotes and History of the Banff-Sunshine Area*. Banff, AB: Crag and Canyon, 1977.

Bridgman, P.W. *Theodor Lyman, 1874–1954: A Biographical Memoir*. Washington, DC: The National Academy of Science, 1957.

Brown, Robert Craig, and Ramsay Cook. *Canada, 1896–1921: A Nation Transformed*. Toronto: McClelland and Stewart, 1974.

Burns, Robert J. *Guardians of the Wild: A History of the Warden Service of Canada's National Parks*. Calgary: University of Calgary Press, 2000.

Cautley, R.W., J.N. Wallace, and A.O. Wheeler. *Report of the Commission Appointed to Delimit the Boundary between the Provinces of Alberta and British Columbia, Part I, From 1913 to 1916*. Ottawa: Office of the Surveyor General, 1917.

Cautley, R.W., and A.O. Wheeler, *Report of the Commission Appointed to Delimit the Boundary between the Provinces of Alberta and British Columbia, Part II, 1917 to 1921, From Kicking Horse Pass to Yellowhead Pass*. Ottawa: Office of the Surveyor General, 1924.

Clark, Ronald W. *Men, Myths and Mountains*. London: Weidenfeld and Nicolson, 1976.

Clarke, Frank G. *The History of Australia*. London: Greenwood, 2002.

Coleman, A.P. *The Canadian Rockies, New and Old Trails*. Toronto: Henry Frowde, 1911.

"Constitution," *Canadian Alpine Journal* 1, no.1 (1907): 178–81.

Cronon, William, ed. *Uncommon Ground: Toward Reinventing Nature*. New York: W.W. Norton, 1995.

Daem, M., and E.E. Dickey. *A Short History of Rogers Pass and Glacier Park*. Revelstoke, BC: Vernon News, 1968, 33–34.

Dahlie, Jorgen. "Skiing for Identity and Tradition: Scandinavian Venture and Adventures in the Pacific Northwest, 1900–1960," in *Winter Sports in the West*, edited by E.A. Corbet and A.W. Rasporich, 99–111. Calgary: The Historical Society of Alberta, 1990.

Bibliography

Darling, Basil S. "First Attempt on Robson by the West Arête (1913)," *Canadian Alpine Journal* 6 (1914–1915): 29–35.

———. "Up and Down the Yoho," *Canadian Alpine Journal* 3 (1911): 157–71.

Demars, Stanford E. *The Tourist in Yosemite, 1855–1985.* Salt Lake City: University of Utah Press, 1991.

Dennistoun, James R. "The Accident on Mt. Cook. Death of Mr. S.L. King and his Guides Thomson and Richmond," *The Alpine Journal* 28 (1914): 222–30.

Deslandes, Paul R. "Curing Mind and Body in the Heart of the Canadian Rockies: Empire, Sexual Scandal and Reclamation of Masculinity, 1880s–1920s," *Gender & History* 21, no. 2 (2009): 358–79.

Dewdney, Edgar. "Report of the Indian Commissioner." *Annual Report of the Department of Indian Affairs* (ARDIA), 1880.

Douglas, David. *Journal kept by David Douglas during his travels in North America, 1823–1927.* 1914; New York: Antiquarian Press, 1959.

Dougherty, Sean. *Selected Alpine Climbs in the Canadian Rockies.* Calgary: Rocky Mountain Books, 1999.

Dowling, Phil. *The Mountaineers: Famous Climbers in Canada.* Edmonton: Hurtig, 1979.

Du Faur, Freda. *The Conquest of Mount Cook and Other Climbs: An Account of Four Seasons' Mountaineering on the Southern Alps of New Zealand.* London: Allen and Unwin, 1915.

Duiker, William J., and Jackson J. Spielvogel. *World History: From 1500.* Belmont, CA: Thomson Wadsworth, 2007.

Ellis, Reuben. *Vertical Margins: Mountaineering and the Landscapes of Neoimperialism.* Madison: University of Wisconsin Press, 2001.

F.C.B. "Herbert Otto Frind," *Canadian Alpine Journal* 45 (1962): 166–68.

Fairley, Bruce, ed. *Canadian Mountaineering Anthology: Stories from 100 Years at the Edge.* Vancouver: Lone Pine, 1994.

Fleming, Fergus. *Killing Dragons: The Conquest of the Alps.* New York: Grove Press, 2002.

Foote, G.W. *The Freethinker*, May 1, 1881, 1.

Foran, Jill. *Mary Schäffer: An Adventurous Woman's Exploits in the Canadian Rockies.* Canmore, AB: Altitude, 2003.

Foster, W.W. "Mount Robson (1913)," *Canadian Alpine Journal* 6 (1914–1915): 11–18.

Fraser, Esther. *The Canadian Rockies: Early Travels and Explorations.* Edmonton: Hurtig, 1969.

———. *Wheeler.* Banff, AB: Summerthought, 1978.

Friesen, Gerald. *The Canadian Prairies: A History*. Toronto: University of Toronto Press, 1998.

Galt, A.C. "Consolation Valley (Rocky Mts.), Annual Camp, 1910," *Canadian Alpine Journal* 3 (1911): 137–46.

Gerngross, Albert. "Auf Korsika's höchsten Gipfeln," *Österreichische Touristen-Zeitung* 39, nos. 20, 21.

Getty, Ian A.L., and Erik D. Gooding. "Stoney." In *Handbook of the North American Indians—Plains* 13, 1 (2001): 596–603.

Gordon, Keith. *Deep Water Gold: The Story of the RMS Niagara—The Quest for New Zealand's Greatest Shipwrecked Treasure*. Whangarei, NZ: SeaROV, 2005.

Graham, Peter. *Peter Graham, Mountain Guide: An Autobiography*. Edited by H.B. Hewitt. Wellington, NZ: A.H. & A.W. Reed, 1965.

"The Guide Konrad Kain," *Alpine Journal* 29 (1915): 84.

Hall, Richard C. *The Balkan Wars, 1912–1913: Prelude to the First World War*. London: Routledge, 2000.

Hallows, K.B. "Mount Robson Camp (1913)," *Canadian Alpine Journal* 6 (1914–1915): 212–25.

Hart, E.J. *Diamond Hitch: The Pioneer Guides and Outfitters of Banff and Jasper*. 1979; Banff, AB: EJH Literary Enterprises, 2001.

———. *Jimmy Simpson: Legend of the Rockies*. Banff, AB: Altitude, 1999.

Hollister, N. "Camp in the Alti," *Canadian Alpine Journal* 5 (1913): 73–81.

Hornaday, William T. *Camp-fires in the Canadian Rockies*. New York: Charles Scribner, 1906.

"Ich bin ein Cowboy," *The Economist* 26 (May 2001): 84. Available at http://www.economist.com/node/630986

"Julius von Payer," *The Geographical Journal* 46, no. 4 (1915): 322.

Kain, Conrad. "The Ascent of Mount Robson," *The Alpine Journal* 28 (1914): 35–38.

———. "First Ascent of Mt. Whitehorn (August 12th, 1911)," *Canadian Alpine Journal* 6 (1914–1915): 49–51.

———. "Long Ago on Mount Cook," *American Alpine Journal* 1, no. 4 (1932): 490–96.

———. "Reminiscences of Seven Summers in Canada," *American Alpine Journal* 1, no. 3 (1931): 290–95.

———. *Where the Clouds Can Go,* ed. J. Monroe Thorington. 1935; Calgary: Rocky Mountain Books, 2009.

Kain, Conrad. "The First Ascent of Mount Robson, The Highest Peak of the Rockies (1913)." Translated by P.A.W. Wallace. *Canadian Alpine Journal* 6 (1914–1915): 19–28.

Kauffman, Andrew J., and William L. Putnam. *The Guiding Spirit*. Revelstoke, BC: Footprint, 1986.

Kelley, Ninette, and M.J. Trebilcock. *The Making of a Mosaic: A History of Canadian Immigration Policy*. Toronto: University of Toronto Press, 2000.

Kingman, H.S., and J.M. Thorington, "Climbs in the Northern Waputiks (Canadian Rocky Mountains)," *American Alpine Journal* 2 (1934): 205–09.

Kinney, George, and Donald Phillips. "To the Top of Mount Robson, Told by Kinney and Phillips," *Canadian Alpine Journal* 2, no. 2 (1910): 21–44.

Klucker, Christian. *Adventures of an Alpine Guide*. London: John Murray, 1932.

La Force, Gina L. "The Alpine Club of Canada, 1906 to 1929: Modernization, Canadian Nationalism, and Anglo-Saxon Mountaineering," *Canadian Alpine Journal* 62 (1979): 39–47.

Ladd, William S., and J. Monroe Thorington, "A Mountaineering Journey to the Columbia Icefield," *Canadian Alpine Journal* 14 (1924): 34–47.

Lang, Michale. *An Adventurous Woman Abroad: The Lantern Slides of Mary T.S. Schäffer*. Vancouver: Rocky Mountain Books, 2011.

Langton, Graham. "Harper, Arthur Paul—Biography," *Dictionary of New Zealand Biography*. *Te Ara—The Encyclopedia of New Zealand*. Available at http://www.TeAra.govt.nz/en/biographies/4h17/1

Larmour, Judy. *Laying Down the Lines: A History of Land Surveying in Alberta*. Victoria, BC: Brindle and Glass, 2005.

Lipsky, William. *San Francisco's Panama-Pacific International Exposition*. Charleston, SC: Arcadia, 2005.

Löfgren, Ovar. *On Holiday: A History of Vacationing*. Berkeley: University of California Press, 2002.

Longstaff, T.G. "Across the Purcell Range of British Columbia," *Canadian Alpine Journal* 3 (1911): 26–39.

Luxton, Eleanor G. *Banff: Canada's First National Park*. Banff, AB: Summerthought, 1975.

Lyman, William Dennison. *The Columbia River: Its History, Its Myths, Its Scenary, Its Commerce*. New York: G.P. Putnam, 1909.

MacCarthy, A.H. "First Ascents of Mt. Farnham and Mt. Farnham Tower," *Canadian Alpine Journal* 6 (1914–1915): 112–24.

———. "The First Ascent of Mt. Eon and its Fatality," *Canadian Alpine Journal* 12 (1921–1922): 14–25.

433

———. "The First Ascent of Mount Louis," *Canadian Alpine Journal* 8 (1917): 79–86.

———. "The Howser and Bugaboo Spires, Purcell Range," *Canadian Alpine Journal* 8 (1917): 17–29.

MacCarthy, Albert H., and Basil S. Darling. "An Ascent of Mt. Robson from the Southwest (1913)," *Canadian Alpine Journal* 6 (1914–1915): 37–48.

Macintyre, Stuart. *A Concise History of Australia*. Cambridge: Cambridge University Press, 1999.

MacLaren, I.S., ed. *Culturing Wilderness in Jasper National Park: Studies in Two Centuries of Human History in the Upper Athabasca River Watershed*. Edmonton: University of Alberta Press, 2007.

MacLaren, I.S., with Eric Higgs and Gabrielle Zezulka-Mailloux. *Mapper of Mountains: M.P. Bridgland in the Canadian Rockies, 1902–1930*. Edmonton: University of Alberta Press, 2005.

MacMillan, Margaret. *Paris 1919: Six Months that Changed the World*. 2001; New York: Random House, 2003.

McGill, David. *Islands of Secrets: Matiu/Somes Island in Wellington Harbour*. Wellington, NZ: Steele Roberts, 2001.

Mitchell, C.H. "Mount Resplendent and the Routes of Ascent (1913)," *Canadian Alpine Journal* 6 (1914–1915): 65–73.

"Mt. Robson Camp, 1924," *Canadian Alpine Journal* 14 (1924): 148–53.

Morton, Desmond. *A Short History of Canada*. Toronto: McClelland and Stewart, 1994. First published 1983.

Munro, J. Forbes. *Maritime Enterprise and Empire: Sir William Mackinnon and his Business Network, 1829–1893*. Suffolk, England: Boydell, 2003.

Murphy, Peter J. "Following the Base of the Foothills: Tracing the Boundaries of Jasper Park and its Adjacent Rocky Mountains Forest Reserve." In MacLaren, *Culturing Wilderness*, 87–88.

Mush, George. *Canadian Pacific: The Story of the Famous Shipping Line*. London: David and Charles, 1981.

Outram, James. *In the Heart of the Canadian Rockies*. New York: Macmillan, 1905.

Palmer, H. "The First Ascent of Mt. King Edward, Canadian Rockies, with a Note on Mount Alberta," *The Alpine Journal* 37 (1925): 306.

Packard, W.P. Introduction to *Mount Cook National Park*. Edited by H.E. Connor. Christchurch, NZ: Pegasus, 1973. First published 1959.

Parker, Elizabeth. "The Alpine Club of Canada," *Canadian Alpine Journal* 1, no. 1 (1907): 2–8.

———. "Clara Wheeler: An Appreciation," *Canadian Alpine Journal* 13 (1923): 181.

———. "A New Field for Mountaineering," *Scribner's Magazine* 55 (1914): 605.

Patton, Brian, and Rhonda Allen. "Interview with Vera Wikman." March 10, 2005. Archives, Whyte Museum of the Canadian Rockies, Banff, AB.

Pemble, John. *The Mediterranean Passion: Victorians and Edwardians in the South*. Oxford: Oxford University Press, 1987.

Preston, Diana. *A First-Rate Tragedy: Captain Scott's Antarctic Expeditions*. London: Constable, 1997.

Reesman, Jeanne Campbell. *Jack London's Radical Lives: A Critical Biography*. Athens: University of Georgia Press, 2009.

"Report of the Cataract Valley Camp," *Canadian Alpine Journal* 9 (1918): 169.

"Report of Healy Creek Camp," *Canadian Alpine Journal* 8 (1917): 145–48.

Robinson, Bart. *Banff Springs: The Story of a Hotel*. Banff, AB: Summerthought, 1988.

Robinson, Zac. "Off the Beaten Path? Ski Mountaineering and the Weight of Tradition in the Canadian Rockies, 1909–1940," *The International Journal of the History of Sport* 24, no. 10 (2007): 1320–43.

Robinson, Zac, and Stephen Slemon. "Deception in High Places: Revisiting Brown and Hooker," *Canadian Alpine Journal* 94 (2011): 12–17.

Salvadori, Massimo. *Karl Kautsky and the Socialist Revolution, 1880–1938*. London: Verso, 1990.

Sandford, R.W. *Emerald Lake Lodge: A History and a Celebration*. Calgary: Canadian Rocky Mountain Resorts, 2002.

———. *High Ideals: Canadian Pacific's Swiss Guides, 1899–1999*. Canmore, AB: Alpine Club of Canada, 1999.

Scott, Chic. "Mountain Mysteries," *Canadian Alpine Journal* 84 (2001): 100–01.

———. *Powder Pioneers*. Calgary: Rocky Mountain Books, 2005.

———. *Pushing the Limits: The Story of Canadian Mountaineering*. Calgary: Rocky Mountain Books, 2000.

Schäffer, Mary T.S. *Old Indian Trails of the Canadian Rockies*. Vancouver: Rocky Mountain Books, 2007. First published 1911 by G.P. Putnam's Son.

Skidmore, Colleen, ed. *This Wild Spirit: Women in the Rocky Mountains of Canada*. Edmonton: University of Alberta Press, 2006.

Solomon, Susan. *The Coldest March: Scott's Fatal Antarctic Expedition*. New Haven, CT: Yale University Press, 2001.

Spry, Irene M. *The Palliser Expedition: The Dramatic Story of Western Canadian Exploration, 1857–1860*. Calgary: Fifth House, 1995. First published 1963.

"Stanley Hamilton Mitchell, 1863–1940," *Canadian Alpine Journal* 27, no. 1, (1939–1940): 101–06.

Star, Paul. "Humans and the Environment in New Zealand, c. 1800 to 2000." In *The New Oxford History of New Zealand*, 47–70. Edited by Giselle Byrnes. Melbourne, Australia: Oxford University Press, 2009.

Stefoff, Rebecca. *Jack London: An American Original*. New York: Oxford University Press, 2002.

Stone, W.E. "Amateur Climbing," *Canadian Alpine Journal* 11 (1920): 1–8.

———. "A Day and a Night on Whitehorn (1913)," *Canadian Alpine Journal* 6 (1914–1915): 55–64.

———. "Climbs and Explorations in the Purcell Range in 1915," *Canadian Alpine Journal* 7 (1916): 12–32.

Stutfield, Hugh, and J. Norman Collie. *Climbs and Explorations in the Canadian Rockies*. London: Longmans, Greene, 1903.

Tate, E. Mowbray. *Transpacific Steam: The Story of Steam Navigation from the Pacific Coast of North America to the Far East and the Antipodes, 1867–1941*. London: Cornwall Books, 1986.

Taylor, C.J. "The Changing Habitat of Jasper Tourism." In MacLaren, *Culturing Wilderness*, 199–232.

Thompson, Charles Sproull. "Mt. Lefroy, August 3, 1896," *Appalachia* 2, no. 1 (1897).

Thompson, John Herd, with Allen Seager. *Canada, 1922–1939: Decades of Discord*. Toronto: McClelland and Stewart, 1985.

Thorington, J. Monroe. "The Bugaboo-Howser Watershed, Purcell Range," *American Alpine Journal* 2 (1934): 182–91.

———. *The Glittering Mountains of Canada: A Record of Exploration and Pioneer Ascents in the Canadian Rockies, 1914–1924*. Philadelphia: John W. Lea, 1925.

———. "A Mountaineering Journey through Jasper Park," *Canadian Alpine Journal* 16 (1926–1927): 86–107.

Turner, Samuel. *The Conquest of the New Zealand Alps*. London: Unwin, 1922.

———. *My Climbing Adventures on Four Continents*. London: Unwin, 1911.

Unsworth, Walt. *Hold the Heights: The Foundations of Mountaineering*. Seattle: The Mountaineers, 1994.

von Payer, Julius. *Second German North Polar Voyage*. Leipzig: Brockhaus, 1874.

———. *New Lands within the Arctic Circle: Narrative of the Discoveries of the Austrian Ship "Tegetthoff" in the Years 1872–1874*. New York: Appleton, 1877.

Wallace, Paul A.W. "Climbing the Big Peaks: An Account of Alpine Climbing, 1913, by A.O. Wheeler's Camp Secretary, Paul A.W. Wallace," *Crag and Canyon* (Banff, AB), August 30, 1913, 3.

Wedin, Neil. Foreword to *The Rockies of Canada*, by Walter Wilcox. Surrey, BC: Rocky Mountain Books, 2008. First published 1900 by G.P. Putnam's Sons.

Wheeler, Arthur O. "The Alpine Club of Canada's Expedition to Jasper Park, Yellowhead Pass and Mount Robson Region, 1911," *Canadian Alpine Journal* 4 (1912): 1–83.

———. "Report of Cathedral Mt. Camp (1913)," *Canadian Alpine Journal* 6 (1914–1915): 250–52.

———. "Report of Mount Robson Camp (1913)," *Canadian Alpine Journal* 6 (1914–1915): 253–55.

———. "Report of the 1909 Camp," *Canadian Alpine Journal* 2, no. 2 (1910): 147–63.

———. "Robson Glacier," *Canadian Alpine Journal* 6 (1914–1915): 139–42.

———. "Walter Schauffelberger," *Canadian Alpine Journal* 6 (1914–1915): 237.

Wheeler, E.O. "Mount Babel and Chimney Peak," *Canadian Alpine Journal* 3 (1911): 73–79.

White, Richard. *On Holidays: A History of Getting Away in Australia*. North Melbourne: Pluto, 2005.

Whymper, Edward. *A Guide to Zermatt and the Matterhorn*. London: John Murray, 1897.

Wilson, J. MacCartney. "The Camp in the Upper Yoho Valley (1914)," *Canadian Alpine Journal* 6 (1914–1915): 217–28.

Wilson, L.C. ("Jimmie"). "The Club House, 1909–1959," *Canadian Alpine Journal* 42 (1959): 112–15.

Wilcox, Walter D. *The Rockies of Canada*. New York: G.P. Putnam's Sons, 1900.

Willmott, H.P. *First World War*. New York: Dorling Kindersley, 2003.

"Work on the N.T.R., Progress Made on the Big Road is Encouraging," *Globe and Mail*, March 8, 1910, 2.

Yeo, William B. "Making Banff a Year-Round Park," in *Winter Sports in the West*. Edited by E.A. Corbet and A.W. Rasporich, 87–98. Calgary: The Historical Society of Alberta / University of Calgary Press, 1990.

Zezulka-Mailloux, Gabrielle. "Laying Tracks for Tourism: Paradoxical Promotions and the Development of Jasper National Park." In MacLaren, *Culturing Wilderness*, 302–39.

Zurbriggen, Mattias. *From the Alps to the Andes: Being the Autobiography of a Mountain Guide*. London: T. Fisher Unwin, 1899.

Amelie Malek to J. Monroe Thorington, September 28, 1934, J. Monroe
Thorington fonds, (M106/file 192, photocopies), Archives, Whyte Museum
of the Canadian Rockies, Banff, AB.

Amelie Malek to J. Monroe Thorington, January 5, 1935, J. Monroe Thorington
fonds, (M106/file 193, photocopies), Archives, Whyte Museum of the
Canadian Rockies, Banff, AB.

Erich Pistor, February 8 and April 9, 1909, Alpine Club of Canada fonds, (M200/
ACoM/52), Archives, Whyte Museum of the Canadian Rockies, Banff, AB.

Erich Pistor to Arthur O. Wheeler, ACC President, April 9, 1909, Alpine Club of
Canada fonds, (M200/ACoM/52), Archives, Whyte Museum of the Canadian
Rockies, Banff, AB.

Erich Pistor to J. Monroe Thorington, October 6, 1936 and July 8, 1939,
J. Monroe Thorington fonds, (M106/142), Archives, Whyte Museum of the
Canadian Rockies, Banff, AB.

Interview with Vera Wikman by Brian Patton and Rhonda Allen, March 10,
2005. Archives, Whyte Museum of the Canadian Rockies, Banff, AB.

Bibliography

INDEX

Index